THE
IRISH
SKETCHBOOK
1842

A CAR TO KILLARNEY.

W.M. THACKERAY

THE
IRISH
SKETCHBOOK
1842

WITH NUMEROUS ENGRAVINGS
ON WOOD
DRAWN BY THE AUTHOR

ALAN SUTTON

Alan Sutton Publishing Limited
Brunswick Road · Gloucester

First published 1843

British Library Cataloguing in Publication Data

Thackeray, W.M. (William Makepeace), *1811–1863*
    The Irish Sketchbook.
    1. Ireland. Description & travel, 1800–1899
    I. Title
    914.15'0481

    ISBN 0-86299-754-2

Cover picture: detail from Sackville Street, Dublin (*now O'Connell Street*)
by Michael Angelo Hayes. (Photograph: The National Gallery of Ireland)

Typeset in 9/10 Bembo.
Typesetting and origination by
Alan Sutton Publishing Limited.
Printed in Great Britain by
The Guernsey Press Company Limited,
Guernsey, Channel Islands.

TO

CHARLES LEVER, ESQ.,

OF TEMPLEOGUE HOUSE, NEAR DUBLIN

My dear Lever,

Harry Lorrequer needs no complimenting in a dedication; and I would not venture to inscribe this volume to the Editor of the Dublin University Magazine, who, I fear, must disapprove of a great deal which it contains.

But allow me to dedicate my little book to a good Irishman (the hearty charity of whose visionary red-coats, some substantial personages in black might imitate to advantage), and to a friend from whom I have received a hundred acts of kindness and cordial hospitality.

Laying aside for a moment the travelling-title of Mr Titmarsh, let me acknowledge these favours in my own name, and subscribe myself, my dear Lever,

Most sincerely and gratefully yours,

W. M. THACKERAY

London, April 27, 1843

CONTENTS

BIOGRAPHICAL NOTE

WILLIAM MAKEPEACE THACKERAY (1811–63). A photograph of Thackeray taken a few years before his death at fifty-two shows him to be a well-dressed hefty man (he was six foot three inches, and fifteen stone in his forties), with white hair, clean-shaven, with a well-defined mouth, broad-nosed and bespectacled. Behind the spectacles, even in a photograph, the sparkle and depth of his eyes show humour, sadness and insight.

Although Thackeray achieved his ambition of becoming a famous writer, his personal life was one of almost unremitting sadness, relieved only by his loving relationship with his two daughters. His personal experiences and the characters he knew were to be the substance of most of his fictional writing.

He was born in Calcutta, India, on 18 July 1811, the only child of Anne and Richmond Thackeray. The Thackeray family were a well-established Yorkshire family, with branches at Cambridge, as well as in India. When William was four, his father died, and his mother married a previous lover, Captain Henry Carmichael-Smyth. Thackeray, meanwhile, was sent to England, to be looked after by his paternal aunt and his maternal grandmother. He went to school at Chiswick Mall, with a disastrous interlude at an inhumane school in Southampton, until his adored mother and respected step-father returned from India in 1820. Then he transferred to Charterhouse, one of the better public schools, but Thackeray was no scholar, and although he was intelligent and ambitious, with a love of reading and the theatre, he showed little persistence in his studies.

This lack of application continued when, after a long break in Devon at his parents' home, he finally went up to Trinity College, Cambridge. He stayed there for only sixteen months, his good intentions to study being continually shattered by his attraction to lascivious indulgences, including the gambling

table, and his unfortunate liaisons with disreputable characters. However, he made his literary debut in *The Snob* and
continued writing for it and its successor, *The Gownsman*, as
well as meeting literary men who were to be his friends and
acquaintances in the future, among them: Edward Fitzgerald,
Tennyson, and William Brookfield. For the next few years,
after leaving Cambridge, he lived extravagantly: he spent
some months in Weimar, where he met Goethe, fell in love,
gambled and learnt German. He then returned to London, and
after spending a year deciding not to study law, and then
running a literary newspaper at a loss, he retreated to Paris to
study art as a poverty-stricken student (since his father's
fortune had been mismanaged). Here he met and fell in love
with Isabella Shawe. He resolved to marry her in spite of her
mother's disapproval, and was pleased to accept the post of
French correspondent for *The Constitutional*, a radical newspaper launched with financial assistance from his stepfather.
He also produced his first book: *Flore et Zéphyr*, a satire, in
1836, and continued to endeavour to establish himself as an
artist.

By July 1837 Thackeray was married to Isabella, a father to
baby Annie and unemployed, as *The Constitutional* had folded,
and so he was forced to become a freelance journalist, to
escape debtor's prison (a situation he explores in *Samuel
Titmarsh and the Great Hoggarty Diamond*). He worked as a
book reviewer, art critic, poet and serial writer for *The Times*,
Fraser's Magazine, Dickens' journal *Bentley's Miscellany* and the
New Monthly Magazine. In 1838 the Thackeray's second
daughter died shortly after her birth (another experience
relived in *The Great Hoggarty Diamond*), but one year later
another girl, Minnie, was born, and Thackeray saw the
successful publication of *The Paris Sketch Book*, which received
good reviews and interested the important publishing houses
of Chapman and Hall, and Longmans. So Thackeray was now
an established writer, able to support, if modestly, his young
family. However, a happy family life was not to be his, since
very soon after the birth of Minnie, Isabella showed the first
signs of madness which was to change her personality, and
force Thackeray finally to realise that she would never be
cured, and to accept a permanent separation. During these

unhappy years he wrote *The History of Samuel Titmarsh and the Great Hoggarty Diamond* (first published in *Bentley's Miscellany*) and then made his first claim to fame as a full length novelist with *Barry Lyndon* (1844). However, the latter was unfavourably received as morally outrageous. In the meantime, he had started to write for *Punch*, and in 1846 he made his first significant impact on Victorian society with his study of English society in *The Snobs of England*. This was followed in 1847 by the first episode of *Vanity Fair*, which was to put Thackeray into the same literary class as the great Dickens, then publishing *Dombey and Son*, and to reintroduce him to the aristocratic circles of London society.

Thackeray had installed his family in a house in Young Street, and was comforted by the memory of the early days of his marriage, his present fame and the company of his daughters. But his heart was lonely for the love of a woman. Consequently he was unable to resist a developing passion for Jane, the young and attractive wife of his old Cambridge friend, William Brookfield. She was Thackeray's 'perfect woman'. He loved her whole-heartedly, and it is this love which pervades *Pendennis*, an autobiographical novel, written 1848–50. But the relationship was doomed since the Brookfields were determined to stay together in spite of their incompatability and finally Thackeray was compelled to break away from both William and Jane. In *The History of Henry Esmond*, completed in 1852 after his separation from the Brookfields, he further explores the commotions of an unhappy marriage, like that of the Brookfields, the frustrated lover and the dominant mother figure. (As an only child, Thackeray was adored and to some extent dominated by his possessive strong-willed mother throughout his whole life.) *Henry Esmond*, set in the early eighteenth century, was his most carefully prepared work: 'Here is the very best I can do . . .', and did not suffer from the fact that Thackeray was seldom at home when he wrote. He had decided, after the publication of *Pendennis* to find another more reliable source of income than writing and had taken up lecturing, a comparatively easy way of making money, and positively lucrative when taken across the Atlantic.

After successful tours in England, he lectured in the States for six months, returning in May 1853, having once again fallen in love, and once again futilely. He knew that Sally Baxter was too young for him. Nevertheless, he was upset by her marriage two years later, and kept in touch with her until her lonely death from tuberculosis in 1862. Sally provided the inspiration for Ethel, the heroine of Thackeray's next novel, *The Newcomes* (1853–5), which again tackled problems of marriage and mothers, and was to be set partly in Rome. To this end, Thackeray took his two daughters to Italy, where he contracted malaria, which was to trouble him for the rest of his life, along with occasional outbreaks of a longstanding and painful bowel condition. It was during the illness in Italy that Thackeray wrote *The Rose and the Ring*, with the close collaboration of a little girl called Edith Story.

When the Thackerays returned to England in 1854 it was to a new house in Onslow Square, with Amy Crowe as companion to Annie and Minnie. Very soon Thackeray was planning a return visit to the States, to lay by some capital for his daughters by giving another lecture tour, this time on the four English King Georges. The expedition was financially successful, but Thackeray was upset by some negative press criticism. However, he came home to deliver the same lectures in England and Scotland. In 1857, with the offer of £6000 for a new serial outstanding, and his name made both as novelist and lecturer, Thackeray made his only stand for Parliament, for the City of Oxford, and was defeated by sixty-five votes. Unsurprised by the result, Thackeray returned to London to concentrate on his next novel, *The Virginians* (1859), which contained English and American characters, and was well received in England and the States.

Thackeray, by now a wealthy man, was able, at the age of forty-nine to achieve his last ambition: to edit his own literary paper. This was the *Cornhill Magazine*, which first appeared in 1860. Contributions included George Eliot, Anthony Trollope, Tennyson and Thackeray himself. He published *The Roundabout Papers*, a notable collection of essays, and his final completed novel: *The Adventures of Philip on his Way Through the World*. His final extravagant gesture was to rebuild a house, No. 2, Palace Green, Kensington, where he lived for only two years in increasingly poor health, until his death in 1863 from a brain haemorrhage. He was buried in Kensal Green.

SHEILA MICHELL

INTRODUCTION

'We encountered a foreign friend some years since, who was making the tour of Britain,' wrote William Makepeace Thackeray in a review of a book of travel literature for the *Morning Chronicle*:

He had seen the sights of England and Scotland – London, of course; Oxford, Birmingham, and our manufacturing towns; the Lakes of Cumberland, too. He had been to Loch Catherine, and the scenes of Walter Scott. He was going to Ireland. What to do? To see the grand misére. He went, and came back not in the least disappointed. He visited Scotland for its romantic recollections and beauty – England for the wonders of its wealth – Ireland for the wonders of its poverty. For poverty and misery have, it seems, their sublime, and that sublime is to be found in Ireland. What a flattering homage to England's constitutional rule over a sister country.[1]

When William Thackeray himself made his tour of Ireland in the summer and autumn of 1842, the Ireland he visited was one of the poorest nations in Europe, teetering on the brink of famine. When that famine did come in 1845 it was to bring about the deaths of over a million people, and cause another two million to flee the country.

The Thackeray who toured this poverty haunted world of pre-Famine Ireland was a 31-year-old, with a good education, the beginning of a good career, and an empty wallet. He had begun to write in 1837, with the series of satiric sketches

---

[1] 'William Makepeace Thackeray, rev. of *Ireland*, by J. Venedy, *Morning Chronicle* (London) 16 March, 1844; in Gordon N. Ray, ed. *William Makepeace Thackeray: Contributions to the Morning Chronicle* (Urbana: University of Illinois Press, 1955): 1.

known as *The Yellowplush Papers*, which appeared serially until 1840. This was followed by his first novel, *Catherine*, published in parts in *Fraser's* magazine during the winter of 1839–40, which was followed in turn by his *Paris Sketch Book* of 1840. However, Thackeray had written none of these works under his own name; indeed, the first book to appear under the name of 'William Makepeace Thackeray' was *The Irish Sketchbook* – and even then his name only appeared in the dedication. *The Irish Sketchbook* was thus written at a difficult and important juncture in Thackeray's career. In the decade that followed its publication, with the appearance of *Vanity Fair* (1847–8), *Pendennis* (1848–50) and *Esmond* (1852), he was to leap from relative anonymity to a level of popular fame matched only by Dickens.

Thackeray had originally signed the contract to write *The Irish Sketchbook* for Chapman & Hall in 1840; but his domestic life was to prevent him from making his Irish tour until 1842. In 1836 he had married an Irishwoman, Isabella Creagh Shawe, of Doneraile, Co. Cork, whose father, Colonel Matthew Shawe, had been Secretary to the Marquess of Wellesley in India. The couple had three daughters: Anne, born in 1837 (who was later to edit the collected edition of her father's works); Jane, who died in infancy in 1838; and Harriet, who was born as Thackeray was negotiating the terms of *The Irish Sketchbook* in 1840. After Harriet's birth, however, Isabella Thackeray began to suffer from severe depression; and while the family were sailing from London to Cork in September of 1840 to begin Thackeray's Irish tour, she threw herself into the Irish Sea. The crew of the ship rescued her, only to have her make another suicide attempt the following evening. By 1842, after having spent several years in and out of clinics in France and Germany, her psychological state had worsened to the point at which her marriage to Thackeray had all but collapsed. It is against this background that we can read Thackeray's interest in the 'lunatic asylums' he finds throughout Ireland. 'When,' he asks on finding a particularly 'neat and comfortable' institution in Derry, 'will the middle classes be allowed to send their own afflicted relatives to public institutions of this excellent kind, where violence is never practised.'

When Thackeray finally managed to settle his affairs enough to begin his Irish tour, he had already spent the publisher's advance, and he was two years behind his deadline. If this were not enough, as soon as Thackeray began to write he was to find that the territory had already been thoroughly covered before he arrived. Thomas Crofton Croker had published his *Fairy Legends and Traditions of the South of Ireland* in 1828; W.H. Maxwell's *Sports of the West of Ireland* had achieved great success in 1832; John Barrow's *Tour Round Ireland* had come out in 1836; Gustave de Beaumont's *Ireland: Social, Political and Religious* had been translated into English in 1839; the American Nathaniel Parker Willis's *The Scenery and Antiquities of Ireland* had appeared just before Thackeray left London; moreover, both Samuel Lover's *Ireland: Its Scenery and Character* and the phenomenally popular *Hall's Ireland* were appearing at the same time as Thackeray was writing in 1842. Little wonder that Thackeray should exclaim, on finding these earlier accounts anthologised in a guidebook:

> The Guide's remarks concerning the works of these gentlemen inspired me, I must confess, with considerable disgust and jealousy. A plague take them! what remains for me to discover after the gallant adventurers in the service of Paternoster Row [a London publishing district] have examined every rock, lake, and ruin of the district, exhausted it of all its legends, and 'invented new,' most likely, as their daring genius prompted?

Unlike Dickens – who was writing his *American Notes* at the same time as Thackeray was in Ireland – Thackeray could not rely on his name alone to interest readers. He was thus forced to write a type of Irish travel literature completely different to any that had been written before – and the result was *The Irish Sketchbook*.

Thackeray makes use of this 'anxiety of influence' in *The Irish Sketchbook* to shift the work into the realm of the satiric and the parodic. Often, he simply incorporates passages from previous guide books into his own text, and then undercuts them with his own remarks. For instance, when the guide book advises him to see an 'aboriginal forest' outside Limerick, he sets off 'with visions of gigantic oaks, Druids, Norma, wilderness and awful gloom, which would fill the soul with horror.' On arriving in the forest, however, he finds that the forest had been regularly cut by landowners short of funds, 'and the monarchs of the woods which I saw round about would scarcely have afforded timber for a bedpost.'

Nor is Thackeray's own descriptive language immune from such satiric treatment when he finds himself lapsing into 'guide bookese'. When describing the Giant's Causeway, for instance, he writes: 'It looks like the beginning of the world, somehow . . . when the world was moulded and fashioned out of formless chaos, this must have been the bit over – a remnant of chaos!' Thackeray quickly undermines any suggestion of majesty, however, by focusing the reader's attention on his metaphorical use of the word 'remnant': 'Think of that! – it is a tailor's simile. Well. I am a Cockney: I wish I were in Pall Mall!' At another point, arriving in Wicklow, guide book in hand, he writes: 'As that romantic and beautiful country has been described many times in familiar terms, our only chance is to speak thereof in romantic and beautiful language, such as no other writer can possibly have employed.' He then proceeds to describe the landscape in a mock-romantic passage, replete with 'purple mountains' and a waterfall 'roaring' with a sound 'like to the respiration of the great sea, as he lies basking on the sands in the sunshine.'

Like all great satirists, however, Thackeray is not without his moral purpose; and behind his mocking of the Victorian fashion for wild, uncultivated and picturesque landscapes lies an understanding of the social conditions which such landscapes mask. Where the conventions of Victorian travel literature decreed that the traveller should wonder at the height of mountains and the immensity of ravines, Thackeray wonders at the almost unimaginable depths of poverty. While passing early one day through County Mayo, he meets a starving glass-blower in a small shebeen, or pub, and the man tells him how he has walked 150 miles in a fruitless search for a job. 'Heaven help us!' exclaims Thackeray. 'On this very day, throughout the three kingdoms, there are a million such stories to be told!' Later that same day, Thackeray finds himself indulging in a rare piece of landscape description, as he writes of 'the most beautiful view I ever saw in the world, I think':

> The sun was just about to set, and the country around about and to the east was almost in twilight. The mountains were tumbled about in a thousand fantastic ways . . . the bay, and the Reek, which sweeps down to the sea, and a hundred islands in it, were dressed up in gold and purple, and crimson, with the whole cloudy west in a flame. Wonderful, wonderful!

However, in the midst of this rapturous description, he turns back to his encounter with the glass-blower earlier in the day: 'I suppose there is not a soul to be seen . . . by the shores of the ghastly lakes, where the poor glass-blower from the whisky-shop is faintly travelling now.'

The figure of the starving man is always present in Thackeray's Irish landscapes, 'that livid ghastly face interposing between you and it'. While in Cork he writes:

> The traveller is haunted by the face of the popular starvation . . . . The epicurean, and traveller for pleasure, had better travel anywhere than here; where there are miseries that one does not dare to think of; where one is always feeling how helpless pity is; and how hopeless relief, and is perpetually made ashamed of being happy.

By juxtaposing the 'diseased and hideous' face of poverty against the majesty of a mountain or a sunset, Thackeray is reacting against a set of aesthetic values known as 'the sublime', a sudden, overwhelming flash of religious awe and terror in the face of the magnificence of nature. With the translation of Longinus's *On the Sublime* in the seventeenth century, and Edmund Burke's *The Sublime and the Beautiful* of 1757, English travellers went all over Europe in search of wild gorges and mountain crags in whose presence they might experience the sublime. Consequently, the world as mapped by much of the English travel literature of the eighteenth and nineteenth centuries was a place of wild, uncultivated splendour and florid prose. Indeed, the sublime was a concept well suited to the transitory experience of the traveller, for, by definition, the sublime itself was a momentary, inspirational experience. One did not need to know a country to experience its sublimity; one did, however, need to know a country to understand why it was poverty stricken.

Thackeray's *Irish Sketchbook* provides a corrective to this yearning after the sublime. 'I declare,' writes Thackeray of the Giant's Causeway, 'upon my conscience, the barge moored at Hungerford Market is a more majestic object, and seems to occupy as much space.' He believed that it took more than an emotional response to the scenery to be able to provide that other staple of 'the Irish tour book' – a solution to 'the Irish Question'. In a letter to his mother written while he was in Ireland, Thackeray wrote: 'A man ought to be forty years in the country instead of 3 months, and then he wouldn't be able to write about it.'[2] In *The Irish Sketchbook*, Thackeray notes that there are 'some nine shades of politico-religious differences, [and] an observer pretending to impartiality must necessarily displease eight parties, and almost certainly the whole nine.' In another passage, the numbers become even greater:

> It is awful to think that there are eight millions of stories to be told in this island. Seven million nine hundred and ninety-nine thousand nine hundred and ninety-eight more lives that I, and all brother Cockneys know nothing about.

Thackeray's recognition of the complexity of pre-Famine Irish society was not welcome in the early 1840s. On 15 October 1842, while Thackeray was still in Ireland, a group of romantic nationalists, including Thomas Davis, founded the *Nation* newspaper. The influential version of 'the Irish Question' which these young nationalists were to popularise was one which strove to simplify the 'Irish Question', making it a straight-forward opposition between England and Ireland. As a consequence, Thackeray fulfilled his own prediction, and

[2] William Makepeace Thackeray to Mrs. Carmichael-Smyth, 25–30 September, 1842; in Gordon N. Ray, ed. *The Letters and Private Papers of William Makepeace Thackeray* (1945–1946; New York: Octagon, 1980): II, 78.

managed to offend all 'nine shades of politico-religious differences' in Ireland when *The Irish Sketchbook* was published in 1843. Perhaps it is only now, as new ways of writing Irish history have alerted us to the complexities and contradictions of the pre-Famine period, that we can read Thackeray properly; perhaps it is only now that we can empathise with a man who insisted on the impossibility of telling the eight million stories of Ireland, even as he was in the act of telling a few of them in one of the most entertaining prose styles of his time.

CHRISTOPHER MORASH
Trinity College, Dublin

FURTHER READING

The only full length study of Irish travel literature is still Constantia Maxwell's *The Stranger in Ireland from the Reign of Elizabeth to the Great Famine* (1954; rpt. Dublin: Gill and Macmillan, 1979), which provides a useful, but selective, survey of the field.

In the area of Thackeray studies, most of the basic research has been done by Gordon N. Ray. The second volume of *The Letters and Private Papers of William Makepeace Thackeray*, ed. Gordon N. Ray (1945–6; rpt. New York: Octagon, 1980) contains the letters written by Thackeray while he was in Ireland in 1842. Also of interest are several articles on Irish matters in *William Makepeace Thackeray: contributions to the Morning Chronicle*, ed. Gordon N. Ray (Urbana: University of Illinois Press, 1955). The standard biography of Thackeray is Ray's two volume work: *Thackeray: The Uses of Adversity* (London: Oxford University Press, 1955), and *Thackeray: The Age of Wisdom* (London: Oxford University Press, 1958). More recent biographical work can be found in Catherine Peters' eminently readable *Thackeray's Universe: Shifting Worlds of Imagination and Reality* (London: Faber & Faber, 1987). Also of use to anyone interested in Thackeray's ideas about Ireland are his sketches of 'Irish snobs' in his 1848 *The Book of Snobs* (rpt. Gloucester: Alan Sutton, 1989).

The literature on pre-Famine Irish society is vast. However, the sections on the first half of the nineteenth century in Roy Foster's *Modern Ireland: 1600–1972* (London: Viking, 1900) manage successfully to incorporate the quantitative research of Joel Mokyr's *Why Ireland Starved* (London: George Allen & Unwin, 1985) and the more qualitative work of Gerrard O. Tuathaigh's *Ireland Before the Famine 1798–1848* (Dublin: Gill and Macmillan, 1972).

Finally, *The Irish Journals of Elizabeth Smith: 1840–1850*, ed. David Thompson and Moyra McGusty (Oxford: Clarendon,

1980), are as entertaining in their own way as Thackeray's *Irish Sketchbook*; the *Journals* provide a fascinating glimpse of the world through which Thackeray was passing from the perspective of one who lived there.

THE
IRISH
SKETCHBOOK
1842

CHAPTER I

A SUMMER DAY IN DUBLIN, OR THERE AND THEREABOUTS

The coach that brings the passenger by wood and mountain, by brawling waterfall and gloomy plain, by the lonely lake of Festiniog, and across the swinging world's wonder of a Menai-bridge, through dismal Anglesea to dismal Holyhead – the Birmingham mail, – manages matters so cleverly, that after ten hours' ride the traveller is thrust incontinently on board the packet, and the steward says there's no use in providing dinner on board because the passage is so short.

That is true; but why not give us half an hour on shore? Ten hours spent on a coach-box render the dinner question one of extreme importance; and as the packet reaches Kingstown at midnight, when all the world is asleep, the inn-larders locked up, and the cook in bed; and as the mail is not landed until five in the morning (at which hour the passengers are considerately awakened by a great stamping and shouting overhead) might not Lord Lowther give us one little half hour? Even the steward agreed that it was a useless and atrocious tyranny; and, indeed, after a little demur, produced a half-dozen of fried eggs, a feeble make-shift for a dinner.

Our passage across from the Head was made in a rain so pouring and steady, that sea and coast were entirely hidden from us, and one could see very little beyond the glowing tip of the cigar which remained alight nobly in spite of the weather. When the gallant exertions of that fiery spirit were over for ever, and burning bravely to the end, it had breathed its last in doing its master service, all became black and cheerless around; the passengers had dropped off one by one, preferring to be dry and ill below rather than wet and squeamish above; even the mate, with his gold-laced cap (who is astonishingly like Mr Charles Dickens, that he might pass

1

for that gentleman) – even the mate said he would go to his cabin and turn in. So there remained nothing for it but to do as all the world had done.

Hence it was impossible to institute the comparison between the Bay of Naples and that of Dublin (the Bee of Neeples the former is sometimes called in this country) where I have heard the likeness asserted in a great number of societies and conversations. But how could one see the Bay of Dublin in the dark? and how, supposing one could see it, should a person behave who has never seen the Bay of Naples? It is but to take the similarity for granted, and remain in bed till morning.

When everybody was awakened at five o'clock, by the noise made upon the removal of the mail-bags, there was heard a cheerless dribbling and pattering overhead, which led one to wait still further until the rain should cease; at length, the steward said the last boat was going ashore, and receiving half-a-crown for his own services (the regular tariff) intimated likewise that it was the custom for gentlemen to compliment the stewardess with a shilling, which ceremony was also complied with. No doubt she is an amiable woman, and deserves any sum of money. As for inquiring whether she merited it or not in this instance, that surely is quite unfair. A traveller who stops to inquire the deserts of every individual claimant of a shilling on his road, had best stay quiet at home. If we only got what we *deserved*, – Heaven save us! – many of us might whistle for a dinner.

A long pier, with a steamer or two at hand, and a few small vessels lying on either side of the jetty; a town irregularly built, with many handsome terraces, some churches and showy-looking hotels; a few people straggling on the beach, two or three cars at the railroad station, which runs along the shore as far as Dublin; the sea stretching interminably eastward; to the north the hill of Howth, lying gray behind the mist; and, directly under his feet, upon the wet, black, shining, slippery deck, an agreeable reflection of his own legs, disappearing seemingly in the direction of the cabin from which he issues; are the sights which a traveller may remark, on coming on deck at Kingstown pier on a wet morning – let us say on an *average* morning; for according to the statement of well-informed natives, the Irish day is more often rainy than otherwise. A hideous obelisk, stuck upon four fat balls, and surmounted with a crown on a cushion (the latter were no bad emblems perhaps of the monarch in whose honour they were raised), commemorates the sacred spot at which George IV *quitted* Ireland; you are landed here from the steamer; and a carman, who is dawdling in the neighbourhood, with a straw in his mouth, comes leisurely up to ask whether you'll go to Dublin? Is it natural indolence, or the effect of despair because of the neighbouring railroad, which renders him so indifferent? – He does not even take the straw out of his mouth as he proposes the question, he seems quite careless as to the answer.

He said he would take me to Dublin 'in three quarthers,' as soon as we began a parley; as to the fare, he would not hear of it – he said, he would leave it to my honour, he would take me for nothing. Was it possible to refuse such a genteel offer? The times are very much changed since those described by the facetious Jack Hinton, when the carmen tossed up for the passenger, and those who won him took him; for the remaining cars on the stand did not seem to take the least interest in the bargain, or to offer to over-drive or under-bid their comrade in any way.

Before that day, so memorable for joy and sorrow, for rapture at receiving its monarch and tearful grief at losing him, when George IV came and left the maritime resort of the citizens of Dublin, it bore a less genteel name than that which it owns at present, and was called Dunleary. After that glorious event Dunleary disdained to be Dunleary any longer, and became Kingstown henceforward and for ever. Numerous terraces and pleasure-houses have been built in the place – they stretch row after row along the banks of the sea, and rise one above another on the hill. The rents of these houses are said to be very high; the Dublin citizens crowd into them in summer; and a great source of pleasure and comfort must it be to them to have the fresh sea-breezes and prospects so near to the metropolis.

The better sort of houses are handsome and spacious; but the fashionable quarter is yet in an unfinished state; for enterprising architects are always beginning new roads, rows and terraces; nor are those already built by any means complete. Besides the aristocratic part of the town is a commercial one, and nearer to Dublin stretch lines of low cottages which have not a Kingstown look at all, but are evidently of the Dunleary period. It is quite curious to see in the streets where the shops are, how often the painter of the sign-boards begins with big letters, and ends, for want of space, with small; and the Englishman accustomed to the thriving neatness and regularity which characterise towns, great and small, in his own country, can't fail to notice the difference here. The houses have a battered rakish look, and seem going to ruin before their time. As seamen of all nations come hither who have made no vow of temperance, there are plenty of liquor-shops still, and shabby cigar-shops, and shabby milliners' and tailors' with fly-blown prints of old fashions. The bakers and apothecaries make a great brag of their calling, and you see MEDICAL HALL, or PUBLIC BAKERY, BALLYRAGGET FLOUR-STORE, (or whatever the name may be,) pompously inscribed over very humble tenements; some comfortable grocers' and butchers' shops, and numbers of shabby sauntering people, the younger part of whom are barelegged and bareheaded, make up the rest of the picture, which the stranger sees as his car goes jingling through the street.

After the town come the suburbs of pleasure-houses; low, one-storied cottages for the most part; some neat and fresh, some that have passed away from the genteel state altogether, and exhibiting downright poverty; some in a state of transition, with broken windows and pretty romantic names upon tumbledown gates. Who lives in them? One fancies that the chairs and tables inside are broken, and the tea-pot on the breakfast-table has no spout, and the table-cloth is ragged and sloppy, and the lady of the house is in dubious curl-papers, and the gentleman with an imperial to his chin, and a flaring dressing-gown all ragged at the elbows.

To be sure, a traveller who in ten minutes can see not only the outsides of houses but the interiors of the same, must have remarkably keen sight; and it is early yet to speculate. It is clear, however, that these are pleasure-houses for a certain class; and looking at the houses, one can't but fancy the inhabitants resemble them somewhat. The car, on its road to Dublin, passes by numbers of these – by more shabbiness than a Londoner will see in the course of his home peregrinations for a year.

The capabilities of the country, however, are very very great, and in many instances have been taken advantage of; for you see, besides the misery, numerous handsome houses and parks along the road, having fine lawns and woods, and the sea in our view, at a quarter of an hour's ride from Dublin. It is the continual appearance of this sort of wealth which makes the poverty more striking, and thus between the two (for there is no vacant space of fields between Kingstown and Dublin) the car reaches the city. There is but little commerce on this road, which was also in extremely bad repair. It is neglected for the sake of its thriving neighbour, the railroad, on which a dozen pretty little stations accommodate the inhabitants of the various villages through which we pass.

The entrance to the capital is very handsome. There is no bustle and throng of carriages, as in London; but you pass by numerous rows of neat houses, fronted with gardens, and adorned with all sorts of gay-looking creepers. Pretty market gardens, with trim beds of plants, and shining glass-houses, give the suburbs a *riante* and cheerful look; and, passing under the arch of the railway, we are in the city itself. Hence you come upon several old-fashioned, well-built, airy, stately streets, and through Fitzwilliam square, a noble place, the garden of which is full of flowers and foliage. The leaves are green, and not black as in similar places in London; the red-brick houses tall and handsome. Presently the car stops before an extremely big red house, in that extremely large Square, Stephen's Green, where Mr O'Connell says there is one day or other to be a Parliament. There is room enough for that, or for any other edifice which fancy or patriotism may have a mind to erect, for part of one of the sides of the square is not yet built, but you see the fields and the country beyond.

This then is the chief city of the aliens. – The hotel to which I had been directed is a respectable old edifice, much frequented by families from the country, and where the solitary traveller may likewise find society. For he may either use the

Shelburne as an hotel or a boarding-house, in which latter case he is comfortably accommodated at the very moderate daily charge of six-and-eightpence. For this charge a copious breakfast is provided for him in the coffee-room, a perpetual luncheon is likewise there spread, a plentiful dinner is ready at six o'clock; after which, there is a drawing-room and a rubber of whist, with *tay* and coffee and cakes in plenty to satisfy the largest appetite. The hotel is majestically conducted by clerks and other officers; the landlord himself does not appear after the honest comfortable English fashion, but lives in a private mansion hard by, where his name may be read inscribed on a brass plate, like that of any other private gentleman.

A woman melodiously crying 'Dublin Bay herrings,' passed just as we came up to the door, and as that fish is famous throughout Europe, I seized the earliest opportunity and ordered a broiled one for breakfast. It merits all its reputation: and in this respect I should think the Bay of Dublin is far superior to its rival of Naples – are there any herrings in Naples Bay? Dolphins there may be, and Mount Vesuvius to be sure is bigger than even the hill of Howth, but a Dolphin is better in a sonnet than at a breakfast, and what poet is there that, at certain periods of the day, would hesitate in his choice between the two?

With this famous broiled herring the morning papers are served up, and a great part of these, too, gives opportunity of reflection to the new-comer, and shows him how different this country is from his own. Some hundred years hence, when students want to inform themselves of the history of the present day, and refer to files of *Times* and *Chronicle* for the purpose, I think it is possible that they will consult not so much those luminous and philosphical leading articles which call our attention at present both by the majesty of their eloquence and the largeness of their type, but that they will turn to those parts of the journals into which information is squeezed into the smallest possible print, to the advertisements, namely, the law and police reports, and to the instructive narratives supplied by that ill-used body of men who transcribe knowledge at the rate of a penny a line.

The papers before me (*The Morning Register*, Liberal and Roman Catholic, *Saunders's News-Letter*, neutral and Conservative) give a lively picture of the movement of city and country on this present fourth day of July, and the Englishman can scarcely fail, as he reads them, to note many small points of difference existing between his own country and this. How do the Irish amuse themselves in the capital? The love for theatrical exhibitions is evidently not very great. Theatre Royal – Miss Kemble and the Sonnambula, and Anglo-Irish importation. Theatre Royal, Abbey-street, – the Temple of Magic and the Wizard, last week. Adelphi Theatre, Great Brunswick-street – the Original Seven Lancashire Bell-ringers, a delicious excitement indeed! Portobello Gardens – THE LAST ERUPTION BUT SIX, says the advertisement in capitals. And, finally, 'Miss Hayes will give her first and farewell concert at the Rotunda, previous to leaving her native country.' Only one instance of Irish talent do we read of, and that, in a desponding tone, announces its intention of quitting its native country. All the rest of the pleasures of the evening are importations from cockney-land. The Sonnambula from Covent Garden, the Wizard from the Strand, the Seven Lancashire Bell-ringers from Islington, or the City-road, no doubt; and as for The last Eruption but Six, it has *erumped* near the Elephant and Castle any time these two years, until the cockneys would wonder at it no longer.

The commercial advertisements are but few – a few horses and cars for sale; some flaming announcements of insurance companies; some 'emporiums' of Scotch tweeds and English broad cloths; an auction for damaged sugar; and an estate or two for sale. They lie in the columns languidly, and at their ease as it were: how different from the throng, and squeeze, and bustle of the commercial part of a London paper, where every man (except Mr George Robins) states his case as briefly as possible, because thousands more are to be heard besides himself, and as if he had no time for talking!

The most active advertisers are the schoolmasters. It is now the happy time of the Midsummer holidays; and the pedago-gues make wonderful attempts to encourage parents, and to attract fresh pupils for the ensuing half-year. Of all these announcements that of MADAME SHANAHAN (a delightful name) is perhaps the most brilliant. 'To Parents and Guard-ians. – Paris. – Such parents and guardians as may wish to

entrust their children for education *in its fullest extent* to
MADAME SHANAHAN, *can have the advantage of being conducted
to Paris* by her brother, the Rev. J.P. O'Reilly, of Church-
street Chapel,' which admirable arrangement carries the
parents to Paris and leaves the children in Dublin. Ah,
Madame, you may take a French title; but your heart is still in
your country, and you are to the *fullest extent* an Irishwoman
still!

Fond legends are to be found in Irish books regarding places
where you may see a round tower and a little old chapel,
twelve feet square, where famous universities are once said to
have stood, and which have accommodated myriads of
students. Mrs Hall mentions Glendalough, in Wicklow, as one
of these places of learning; nor can the fact be questioned, as
the universities existed hundreds of years since, and no sort of
records are left regarding them. A century hence some
antiquary may light upon a Dublin paper, and form marvellous calculations regarding the state of education in the
country. For instance, at Bective-house Seminary, conducted
by Dr J.L. Burke, Ex-Scholar T.C.D., no less than *two
hundred and three* young gentlemen took prizes at the Midsummer examination: nay, some of the most meritorious
carried off a dozen premiums a-piece. A Dr Delamere,
Ex-Scholar T.C.D., distributed three hundred and twenty
rewards to his young friends; and if we allow that one lad in
twenty is a prizeman, it is clear that there must be six thousand
four hundred and forty youths under the Doctor's care.

Other schools are advertised in the same journals, each with
its hundred of prize-bearers; and if other schools are advertised, how many more must there be in the country which are
not advertised! There must be hundreds of thousands of
prizemen, millions of scholars; besides national schools, hedge
schools, infant schools, and the like. The English reader will
see the accuracy of the calculation.

In the *Morning Register*, the Englishman will find something
to the full as curious and startling to him – you read gravely in
the English language how the Bishop of Aureliopolis has just
been consecrated; and that the distinction has been conferred
upon him by – the Holy Pontiff! – the Pope of Rome, by all
that is holy! Such an announcement sounds quite strange *in*

English, and in your own country, as it were; or isn't it your own country? Suppose the Archbishop of Canterbury were to send over a clergyman to Rome, and consecrate him Bishop of the Palatine or the Suburra, I wonder how his Holiness would like *that?*

There is a report of Dr Miley's sermon upon the occasion of the new bishop's consecration; and the 'Register' happily lauds the discourse for its 'refined and fervent eloquence.' The doctor salutes the Lord Bishop of Aureliopolis on his admission among the 'Princes of the Sanctuary,' gives a blow *en passant* at the established church, whereof the revenues, he elegantly says, 'might excite the zeal of Dives or Epicurus to become a bishop,' and having vented his sly wrath upon the 'courtly artifice and intrigue' of the Bench, proceeds to make the most outrageous comparisons with regard to my Lord of Aureliopolis; his virtues, his sincerity, and the severe privations and prosecutions which acceptance of the episcopal office entails upon him.

'That very evening,' says the 'Register,' 'the new bishop entertained at dinner, in the Chapel-house, a select number of friends; amongst whom were the officiating prelates and clergymen who assisted in the ceremonies of the day. The repast was provided by Mr Jude, of Grafton Street, and was served up in a style of elegance and comfort that did great honour to that gentleman's character as a *restaurateur. The wines were of the richest and rarest quality.* It may be truly said to have been an entertainment where the feast of reason and the flow of soul predominated. The company broke up at nine.'

And so, my lord is scarcely out of chapel but his privations begin! Well. Let us hope that, in the course of his episcopacy, he incur no greater hardships, and that Dr Miley may come to be a bishop too in his time, when perhaps he will have a better opinion of the Bench.

The ceremony and feelings described are curious, I think, and more so perhaps to a person who was in England only yesterday, and quitted it just as their Graces, Lordships, and Reverences were sitting down to dinner. Among what new sights, ideas, customs, does the English traveller find himself after that brief six hours' journey from Holyhead!

There is but one part more of the papers to be looked at; and that is the most painful of all. In the law reports of the Tipperary special commission sitting at Clonmel, you read, that Patrick

Byrne is brought up for sentence, for the murder of Robert Hall, Esq.: and Chief Justice Doherty says, 'Patrick Byrne, I will not now recapitulate the circumstances of your enormous crime, but guilty as you are of the barbarity of having perpetrated with your hand the foul murder of an unoffending old man – barbarous, cowardly and cruel as that act was – there lives one more guilty man, and that is he whose diabolical mind hatched the foul conspiracy of which you were but the instrument and the perpetrator. Whoever that may be, I do not envy him his protracted existence. He has sent that aged gentleman without one moment's warning, to face his God: but he has done more, he has brought you, unhappy man, with more deliberation and more cruelty, to face your God, *with the weight of that man's blood upon you.* I have now only to pronounce the sentence of the law:' – it is the usual sentence, with the usual prayer of the judge, that the Lord may have mercy upon the convict's soul.

Timothy Woods, a young man of twenty years of age, is then tried for the murder of Michael Laffan. The Attorney-General states the case: – On the 19th of May last, two assassins dragged Laffan from the house of Patrick Cummins, fired a pistol-shot at him, and left him dead as they thought. Laffan, though mortally wounded, crawled away after the fall, when the assassins still seeing him give signs of life, rushed after him, fractured his skull by blows of a pistol, and left him on a dunghill dead. There Laffan's body lay for several hours, and *nobody dared to touch it.* Laffan's widow found the body there two hours after the murder, and *an inquest was held on the body as it lay on the dunghill.* Laffan was driver on the lands of Kilnertin, which were formerly held by Pat Cummins, *the man who had the charge of the lands before Laffan was murdered*; and the latter was dragged out of Cummins's house in the presence of a witness who refused to swear to the murderers, and was shot in sight of another witness, James Meara, who with other men was on the road; and when asked whether he cried out, or whether he went to assist the deceased, Meara answers, *Indeed I did not, we would not interfere – it was no business of ours!*

Six more instances are given of attempts to murder, on which the judge, in passing sentence, comments in the following way:-

'The Lord Chief Justice addressed the several persons, and
said – It was now his painful duty to pronounce upon them
severally and respectively the punishment which the law and
the court awarded against them, for the crimes of which they
had been convicted. Those crimes were one and all of them of
no ordinary enormity – they were crimes which, in point of
morals, involved the atrocious guilt of murder; and if it had
pleased God to spare their souls from the pollution of that
offence, the court could not still shut its eyes to the fact, that
although death had not ensued in consequence of the crimes of
which they had been found guilty, yet it was not owing to
their forbearance that such a dreadful crime had not been
perpetrated. The prisoner, Michael Hughes, had been convicted of firing a gun at a person of the name of John Ryan
(Luke); his horse had been killed, and no one could say that the
balls were not intended for the prosecutor himself. The
prisoner had fired one shot himself, and then called on his
companion in guilt to discharge another. One of these shots
killed Ryan's mare, and it was by the mercy of God that the
life of the prisoner had not become forfeited by his own act.
The next culprit was John Pound, who was equally guilty of
the intended outrage perpetrated on the life of an unoffending
individual, that individual a female, surrounded by her little
children five or six in number, with a complete carelessness to
the probable consequences, while she and her family were
going, or had gone, to bed. The contents of a gun were
discharged through the door, which entered the panel in three
different places. The deaths resulting from this act might have
been extensive, but it was not a matter of any moment how
many were deprived of life. The woman had just risen from
her prayers, preparing herself to sleep, under the protection of
that arm which would shield the child and protect the
innocent, when she was wounded. As to Cornelius Flynn and
Patrick Dwyer, they likewise were the subjects of similar
imputations and similar observations. There was a very slight
difference between them, but not such as to amount to any
real distinction. They had gone upon a common, illegal
purpose, to the house of a respectable individual, for the
purpose of interfering with the domestic arrangements he
thought fit to make. They had no sort of right to interfere

with the disposition of a man's affairs; and what would be the consequences if the reverse were to be held? No imputation had ever been made upon the gentleman whose house was visited, but he was desired to dismiss another, under the pains and penalties of death, although that other was not a retained servant, but a friend who had come to Mr Hogan on a visit. Because this visitor used sometimes to inspect the men at work, the lawless edict issued that he should be put away. Good God! to what extent did the prisoners and such mis-guided men, intend to carry out their objects? Where was their dictation to cease? are they, and those in a similar rank, to take upon themselves to regulate how many, and what men a farmer should take into his employment? Were they to be the judges whether a servant had discharged his duty to his principal? or was it because a visitor happened to come, that the host should turn him away, under the pains and penalties of death? His lordship, after adverting to the guilt of the prisoners in this case – the last two persons convicted, Thos. Stapleton and Thos. Gleeson – said their case was so recently before the public, that it was sufficient to say they were morally guilty of what might be considered wilful and deliberate murder. Murder was most awful, because it could only be suggested by deliberate malice, and the act of the prisoners was the result of that base, malicious, and diabolical disposition. What was the cause of resentment against the unfortunate man who had been shot at, and so desperately wounded? Why he had dared to comply with the wishes of a just landlord; and because the landlord, for the benefit of his tenantry, proposed that the farms should be squared, those who acquiesced in his wishes were to be equally the victims of the assassin. What were the facts in this case? The two prisoners at the bar, Stapleton and Gleeson, sprung out at the man as he was leaving work, placed him on his knees, and without giving him a moment of preparation, commenced the work of blood, intending deliberately to despatch that unpre-pared and unoffending individual to eternity. What country was it that they lived in, in which such crimes could be perpetrated in the open light of day? It was not necessary that deeds of darkness should be shrouded in the clouds of night, for the darkness of the deeds themselves was considered a sufficient protection. He (the Chief Justice) was not aware of any solitary instance at the present commission, to show that the crimes committed were the consequences of poverty. Poverty should be no justification, however, it might be some little palliation, but on no trial at this commission did it appear that the crime could be attributed to distress. His lordship concluded a most impressive address, by sentencing the six prisoners called up, to transportation for life.

'The clock was near midnight as the court was cleared, and the whole of the proceedings were solemn and impressive in the extreme. The commission is likely to prove extremely beneficial in its results on the future tranquillity of the country.'

I confess, for my part, to that common cant and sickly sentimentality which, thank God! is felt by a great number of people now-a-days, and which leads them to revolt against murder, whether performed by a ruffian's knife or a hangman's rope; whether accompanied with a curse from the thief as he blows his victim's brains out, or a prayer from my lord on the bench in his wig and black cap. Nay, is all the cant and sickly sentimentality on our side, and might not some such charge be applied to the admirers of the good old fashion? Long ere this is printed, for instance, Byrne and Woods have been hanged:* sent 'to face their God,' as the Chief Justice says, 'with the weight of their victim's blood upon them,' – a just observation; and remember that it is *we who send them*. It is true that the judge hopes Heaven will have mercy upon their souls, but are such recommendations of particular weight because they come from the bench? Psha! If we go on killing people without giving them time to repent, let us at least give up the cant of praying for their souls' salvation. We find a man drowning in a well, shut the lid upon him, and heartily pray that he may get out. Sin has hold of him, as the two ruffians of Laffan yonder, and we stand aloof, and hope that he may

---

* The two men were executed pursuant to sentence, and both persisted solemnly in denying their guilt. There can be no doubt of it: but it appears to be a point of honour with these unhappy men to make no statement which may incriminate the witnesses who appeared on their behalf, and on their part perjured themselves equally.

escape. Let us give up the ceremony of condolence, and be honest, like the witness, and say, 'Let him save himself or not, it's no business of ours.' . . . Here a waiter, with a very broad, though insinuating accent says, 'Have you done with the Sandthers, sir, there's a gentleman waiting for't these two hours.' And so he carries off that strange picture of pleasure and pain, trade, theatres, schools, courts, churches, life and death, in Ireland, which a man may buy for a fourpenny-piece.

The papers being read, it became my duty to discover the town; and a handsomer town with fewer people in it, it is impossible to see on a summer's day. In the whole wide square of Stephen's Green, I think there were not more than two nursery-maids, to keep company with the statue of George I, who rides on horse-back in the middle of the garden, the horse having his foot up to trot, as if he wanted to go out of town too. Small troops of dirty children (too poor and dirty to have lodgings at Kingstown) were squatting here and there upon the sunshiny steps, the only clients at the thresholds of the professional gentlemen, who names figure on brass plates on the doors. A stand of lazy carmen, a policeman or two with clinking boot-heels, a couple of moaning beggars leaning against the rails, and calling upon the Lord, and a fellow with a toy and book stall, where the lives of St Patrick, Robert Emmett, and Lord Edward Fitzgerald, may be brought for double their value, were all the population of the Green.

At the door of the Kildare-street Club I saw eight gentlemen looking at two boys playing at leap-frog: at the door of the University six lazy porters, in jockey caps, were sunning themselves on a bench – a sort of blue-bottle race; and the Bank on the opposite side did not look as if sixpence-worth of change had been negotiated there during the day. There was a lad pretending to sell umbrellas under the colonnade, almost the only instance of trade going on; and I began to think of Juan Fernandez, or Cambridge in the long vacation. In the courts of the College, scarce the ghost of a gyp or the shadow of a bedmaker.

In spite of the solitude, the square of the College is a fine sight – a large ground, surrounded by buildings of various

ages and styles, but comfortable, handsome, and in good
repair; a modern row of rooms; a row that has been Elizabethan once; a hall and senate-house, facing each other, of the
style of George I; and a noble library, with a range of many
windows, and a fine manly, simple façade of cut stone. The
library was shut. The librarian, I suppose, is at the sea-side;
and the only part of the establishment which I could see, was
the museum, to which one of the jockey-capped porters
conducted me, up a wide, dismal staircase, (adorned with an
old pair of jack-boots, a dusty canoe or two, a few helmets,
and a South Sea Islander's armour), which passes through a
hall hung round with cobwebs, (with which the blue-bottles
are too wise to meddle), into an old mouldy room, filled with
dingy glass-cases, under which the articles of curiosity or
science, were partially visible. In the middle was a very *seedy*
camelopard, (the word has grown to be English by this time),
the straw splitting through his tight old skin, and the black
cobbler's-wax, stuffing the dim orifices of his eyes; other
beasts formed a pleasing group around him, not so tall, but
equally mouldy and old. The porter took me round to the
cases, and told me a great number of fibs concerning their
contents; there was the harp of Brian Borou, and the sword of
some one else, and other cheap old gimcracks with their
corollary of lies. The place would have been a disgrace to Don
Saltero. I was quite glad to walk out of it, and down the dirty
staircase again, about the ornaments of which the jockey-
capped gyp had more figments to tell; an atrocious one (I
forget what) relative to the pair of boots; near which – a fine
specimen of collegiate taste – were the shoes of Mr O'Brien,
the Irish giant. If the collection is worth preserving, – and
indeed the mineralogical specimens look quite as awful as
those in the British Museum, – one thing is clear, that the
rooms are worth sweeping. A pail of water costs nothing, a
scrubbing brush not much, and a charwoman might he hired
for a trifle, to keep the room in a decent state of cleanliness.

Among the curiosities, is a mask of the Dean – not the
scoffer and giber, not the fiery politician, nor the courtier of St
John and Harley, equally ready with servility and scorn; but
the poor old man, whose great intellect had deserted him, and
who died old, wild, and sad. The tall forehead is fallen away in

a ruin, the mouth has settled in a hideous vacant smile. Well, it was a mercy for Stella that she died first; it was better that she should be killed by his unkindness, than by the sight of his misery; which, to such a gentle heart as that, would have been harder still to bear.

The Bank, and other public buildings of Dublin, are justly famous. In the former, may still be seen the room which was the House of Lords formerly, and where the Bank directors now sit, under a clean marble image of George III. The House of Commons has disappeared, for the accommodation of clerks and cashiers. The interior is light, splendid, airy, well-furnished, and the outside of the building not less so. The Exchange, hard by, is an equally magnificent structure; but the genius of commerce has deserted it, for all its architectural beauty. There was nobody inside when I entered, but a pert statue of George III, in a Roman toga, simpering and turning out his toes; and two dirty children playing, whose hoop sticks caused great clattering echoes under the vacant sounding dome. The neighbourhood is not cheerful, and has a dingy, poverty-stricken look.

Walking towards the river, you have on either side of you, at Carlisle-bridge, a very brilliant and beautiful prospect. The Four Courts and their dome to the left, the Custom-house and its dome to the right; and in this direction seaward, a considerable number of vessels are moored, and the quays are black and busy with the cargoes discharged from ships. Seamen cheering, herring-women bawling, coal-carts loading – the scene is animated and lively. Yonder is the famous Corn Exchange; but the Lord Mayor is attending to his duties in Parliament, and little of note is going on. I had just passed his lordship's mansion, in Dawson-street, – a queer old dirty brick house, with dumpy urns at each extremity, and looking as if a storey of it had been cut off – a rasée-house. Close at hand, and peering over a paling, is a statue of our blessed sovereign George II. How absurd these pompous images look, of defunct majesties, for whom no breathing soul cares a halfpenny! It is not so with the effigy of William III, who has done something to merit a statue. At this minute the Lord Mayor has William's effigy under a canvas and is painting him of a bright green, picked out with yellow – his lordship's own livery.

The view along the quays to the Four Courts, has no small resemblance to a view along the quays at Paris, though not so lively as are even those quiet walks. The vessels do not come above-bridge, and the marine population remains constant about them, and about numerous dirty liquor-shops, eating-houses, and marine-store establishments, which are kept for their accommodation along the quay. As far as you can see, the shining Liffey flows away eastward, hastening (like the rest of the inhabitants of Dublin), to the sea.

In front of Carlisle-bridge, and not in the least crowded, though in the midst of Sackville-street, stands Nelson upon a stone pillar. The Post-office is on his right hand (only it is cut off); and on his left, Gresham's and the Imperial Hotel. Of the latter let me say (from subsequent experience), that it is ornamented by a cook who could dress a dinner by the side of M. Borel, or M. Soyé. Would there were more such artists in this ill-fated country! The street is exceedingly broad and handsome; the shops at the commencement, rich and spacious; but in Upper Sackville-street, which closes with the pretty building and gardens of the Rotunda, the appearance of wealth begins to fade somewhat, and the houses look as if they had seen better days. Even in this, the great street of the town, there is scarcely any one, and it is as vacant and listless as Pall Mall, in October. In one of the streets off Sackville-street, is the house and Exhibition of the Irish Academy, which I went to see, as it was positively to close at the end of the week. While I was there, two *other* people came in; and we had besides the money-taker and a porter, to whom the former was reading, out of a newspaper, those Tipperary murders which were mentioned in a former page. The echo took up the theme, and hummed it gloomily through the vacant place.

The drawings and reputation of Mr Burton are well known in England: his pieces were the most admired in the collection. The best draftsman is an imitator of Maclise, Mr Bridgeman, whose pictures are full of vigorous drawing, and remarkable too for their grace. I gave my catalogue to the two young ladies before mentioned, and have forgotten the names of other artists of merit, whose works decked the walls of the little gallery. Here, as in London, the Art-Union is making a stir; and se_ral of the pieces were marked as the property of members of that body. The possession of some of these, one would not be inclined to covet; but it is pleasant to see that people begin to buy pictures at all, and there will be no lack of artists presently, in a country where nature is so beautiful, and genius so plenty. In speaking of the fine arts and views of Dublin, it may be said, that Mr Petrie's designs for Curry's Guide-book of the City, are exceedingly beautiful, and above all, *trustworthy*; not common quality in a descriptive artist at present.

Having a couple of letters of introduction to leave, I had the pleasure to find the blinds down at one house, and the window in papers at another; and at each place the knock was answered in that leisurely way, by one of those dingy female lieutenants, who have no need to tell you that families are out of town. So the solitude became very painful, and I thought I would go back and talk to the waiter at the Shelburne, the only man in the whole kingdom that I knew. I had been accommodated with a queer little room, and dressing-room on the ground floor, looking towards the Green – a black-faced, good humoured chambermaid, had promised to perform a deal of scouring which was evidently necessary, (which fact she might have observed for six months back, only she is no doubt of an absent turn) and when I came back from the walk, I saw the little room was evidently enjoying itself in the sunshine, for it had opened its window, and was taking a breath of fresh air, as it looked out upon the Green. Here is a portrait of the little window.

As I came up to it in the street, its appearance made me burst out laughing, very much to the surprise of a ragged cluster of idlers lolling upon the steps next door; and I have drawn it here, not because it is a particularly picturesque or rare kind of window, but because as I fancy there is a sort of *moral* in it. You don't see such windows commonly in respectable English inns – windows leaning gracefully upon hearth brooms for support. Look out of that window without the hearth broom and it would

cut your head off; how the beggars would start that are always
sitting on the steps next door! Is it prejudice that makes one
prefer the English window, that relies on its own ropes and
ballast, (or lead if you like,) and does not need to be propped
by any foreign aid? or is this only a solitary instance of the
kind, and are there no other specimens in Ireland of the
careless dangerous extravagant hearth broom system?

In the midst of these reflections (which might have been
carried much farther, for a person with an allegorical turn
might examine the entire country through this window) a
most wonderful cab, with an immense prancing cab-horse,
was seen to stop at the door of the hotel, and Pat the waiter
tumbling into the room swiftly with a card in his hand, says
'Sir, the gentleman of this card is waiting for you at the door.'
Mon dieu! it was an invitation to dinner! and I almost leapt
into the arms of the man in the cab – so delightful was it to
find a friend in a place where, a moment before, I had been as
lonely as Robinson Crusoe.

The only drawback, perhaps, to pure happiness, when
riding in such a gorgeous equipage as this, was that we could
not drive up Regent Street, and meet a few creditors or
acquaintances, at least. However, Pat, I thought, was exceedingly awe-stricken by my disappearance in this vehicle,
which had evidently, too, a considerable effect upon some
other waiters at the Shelburne, with whom I was not as yet so
familiar. The mouldy camelopard at the Trinity College
'Musayum' was scarcely taller than the bay horse in the cab;
the groom behind was of a corresponding smallness. The cab
was of a lovely olive green, picked out white, high on high
springs, and enormous wheels, which, big as they were,
scarcely seemed to touch the earth; the little tiger swung
gracefully up and down, holding on by the hood, which was
of the material of which the most precious and polished boots
are made: – as for the *lining* – but here we come too near the
sanctity of private life; suffice that there was a kind friend
inside, who (though by no means of the fairy sort) was as
welcome as any fairy in the finest chariot. W—— had seen me
landing from the packet that morning, and was the very man
who in London, a month previous, had recommended me to
the Shelburne. These facts are not of much consequence to the

public, to be sure, except that an explanation was necessary of the miraculous appearance of the cab and horse.

Our course, as may be imagined, was towards the sea-side, for whither else should an Irishman at this season go? Not far from Kingstown is a house devoted to the purpose of festivity; it is called Salt-hill, stands upon a rising ground, commanding a fine view of the bay and the railroad, and is kept by persons bearing the celebrated name of Lovegrove. It is in fact a sea-Greenwich, and though there are no marine white-bait, other fishes are to be had in plenty, and especially the famous Bray trout, which does not ill deserve its reputation.

Here we met three young men, who may be called by the names of their several counties – Mr Galway, Mr Roscommon, and Mr Clare; and it seemed that I was to complain of solitude no longer: for one straightway invited me to his county, where was the finest salmon-fishing in the world; another said he would drive me through the county Kerry in his four-in-hand drag; and the third had some propositions of sport equally hospitable. As for going down to some races, on the Curragh of Kildare I think, which were to be held on the next and the three following days, there seemed to be no question about *that*. That a man should miss a race within forty miles, seemed to be a point never contemplated by these jovial sporting fellows.

Strolling about in the neighbourhood before dinner, we went down to the sea-shore, and to some caves which had lately been discovered there; and two Irish ladies, who were standing at the entrance of one of them, permitted me to take the following portraits, which were pronounced to be pretty accurate.

They said they had not acquiesced in the general Temperance movement that had taken place throughout the country; and, indeed, if the truth must be known, it was only under promise of a glass of whiskey apiece that their modesty could be so far overcome as to permit them to sit for their portraits. By the time they were done, a crowd of both sexes had gathered round, and expressed themselves quite ready to sit upon the same terms. But though there was great variety in their countenances, there was not much beauty; and besides, dinner was by this time ready, which has at certain periods a charm even greater than art.

The bay, which had been veiled in mist and grey in the morning, was now shining under the most beautiful clear sky, which presently became rich with a thousand gorgeous hues of sunset. The view was as smiling and delightful a one as can be conceived, – just such a one as should be seen *à travers* a good dinner, with no fatiguing sublimity or awful beauty in it – but brisk, brilliant, sunny, enlivening. In fact, in placing his banqueting-house here, Mr Lovegrove had, as usual, a brilliant idea. You must not have too much view, or a severe one, to give a relish to a good dinner; nor too much music, nor too quick, nor too slow, nor too loud; any reader who has dined at a *table d'hôte* in Germany will know the annoyance of this – a set of musicians immediately at your back will sometimes play you a melancholy polonaise: and a man with a good ear must perforce eat in time, and your soup is quite cold before it is swallowed; then, all of a sudden, crash goes a brisk gallop! and you are obliged to gulp your victuals at the rate of ten miles an hour. And in respect of conversation during a good dinner, the same rules of propriety should be consulted. Deep and sublime talk is as improper as sublime prospects. Dante and Champagne (I was going to say Milton and oysters, but that is a pun) are quite unfit themes of dinner-talk. Let it be light, brisk, not oppressive to the brain. Our conversation was, I recollect, just the thing. We talked about the last Derby the whole time, and the state of the odds for the St Leger; nor was the Ascot Cup forgotten; and a bet or two was gaily booked.

Meanwhile the sky, which had been blue and then red, assumed, towards the horizon, as the red was sinking under it, a gentle delicate cast of green. Howth Hill became of a darker purple, and the sails of the boats rather dim. The sea grew deeper and deeper in colour. The lamps at the railroad dotted the line with fire; and the light-houses of the bay began to flame. The trains to and from the city rushed flashing and hissing by – in a word, everybody said it was time to light a cigar, which was done, the conversation about the Derby still continuing.

'Put out that candle,' said Roscommon to Clare; which the latter instantly did by flinging the taper out of the window upon the lawn, which is a thoroughfare, and where a great laugh arose among half a score of beggar-boys, who had been under the window for some time past, repeatedly requesting the company to throw out sixpence between them.

Two other sporting young fellows had now joined the company; and as by this time claret began to have rather a mawkish taste, whiskey-and-water was ordered, which was drunk upon the *perron* before the house, whither the whole party adjourned, and where for many hours we delightfully tossed for sixpences – a noble and fascinating sport. Nor would these remarkable events have been narrated, had I not received express permission from the gentlemen of the party to record all that was said and done. Who knows but, a thousand years hence, some antiquary or historian may find a moral in this description of the amusement of the British youth at the present enlightened time?

HOT LOBSTER

P.S. – You take a lobster, about three feet long, if possible, remove the shell, cut or break the flesh of the fish in pieces not too small. Some one else meanwhile makes a mixture of mustard, vinegar, catsup, and lots of cayenne pepper. You produce a machine called a *dispatcher*, which has a spirit-lamp under it that is usually illuminated with whiskey. The lobster, the sauce, and near half a pound of butter are placed in the dispatcher, which is immediately closed. When boiling, the mixture is stirred up, the lobster being sure to heave about in the pan in a convulsive manner, while it emits a remarkably rich and agreeable odour through the apartment. A glass and a half of sherry is now thrown into the pan, and the contents served out hot, and eaten by the company. Porter is commonly drunk, and whiskey-punch afterwards, and the dish is fit for an emperor.

N.B.– You are recommended not to hurry yourself in getting up the next morning, and may take soda-water with advantage. – *Probatum est.*

CHAPTER II

A COUNTRY-HOUSE IN KILDARE – SKETCHES OF AN IRISH FAMILY AND FARM

It had been settled among my friends, I don't know for what particular reason, that the Agricultural Show at Cork was an exhibition I was specially bound to see; when, therefore, a gentleman, to whom I had brought a letter of introduction, kindly offered me a seat in his carriage, which was to travel by short day's journeys to that city, I took an abrupt farewell of Pat the waiter, and some other friends in Dublin, proposing to renew our acquaintance, however, upon some future day.

We started then one fine afternoon on the road from Dublin to Naas, which is the main southern road from the capital to Leinster and Munster, and met, in the course of the ride of a score of miles, a dozen of coaches very heavily loaded, and bringing passengers to the city. The exit from Dublin this way is not much more elegant than the outlet by way of Kingstown, for though the great branches of the city appear flourishing enough as yet, the small outer ones are in a sad state of decay. Houses drop off here and there, and dwindle woefully in size; we, are got into the back premises of the seemingly prosperous place, and it looks miserable, careless and deserted. We passed through a street which was thriving once, but has fallen since into a sort of decay, to judge outwardly, – St Thomas' Street. Emmett was hanged in the midst of it; and on pursuing the line of street, and crossing the great Canal, you come presently to a fine tall square building in the outskirts of the town, which is no more nor less than Kilmainham Jail or castle. Poor Emmett is the Irish darling still – his history is on every book-stall in the city, and yonder trim-looking brick jail a spot where Irishmen may go and pray. Many a martyr of theirs has appeared and died in front of it, – found guilty of 'wearing of the green.'

24

There must be a fine view from the jail windows, for we presently come to a great stretch of brilliant green country, leaving the Dublin hills lying to the left, picturesque in their outline, and of wonderful colour. It seems to me to be quite a different colour to that in England – different-shaped clouds – different shadows and lights. The country is well tilled, well peopled; the hay-harvest on the ground, and the people taking advantage of the sunshine to gather it in; but in spite of everything, green meadows, white villages and sunshine, the place has a sort of sadness in the look of it.

The first town we passed, as appears by reference to the Guide-book, is the little town of Rathcoole; but in the space of three days Rathcoole has disappeared from my memory, with the exception of a little low building which the village contains, and where are the quarters of the Irish constabulary. Nothing can be finer than the trim, orderly and soldierlike appearance of this splendid corps of men.

One has glimpses all along the road of numerous gentlemen's places, looking extensive and prosperous, of a few mills by streams here and there, but though the streams run still, the mill-wheels are idle for the chief part; and the road passes more than one long low village, looking bare and poor, but neat and whitewashed. It seems as if the inhabitants were determined to put a decent look upon their poverty. One or two villages there were evidently appertaining to gentlemen's seats; these are smart enough, especially that of Johnstown, near Lord Mayo's fine domain, where the houses are of the Gothic sort, with pretty porches, creepers and railings. Noble purple hills, to the left and right, keep up, as it were, an accompaniment to the road.

As for the town of Naas, the first after Dublin, that I have seen, what can be said of it but that it looks poor, mean, and yet somehow cheerful? There was a little bustle in the small shops, a few cars were jingling along the broadest street of the town – some sort of dandies and military individuals were lolling about right and left; and I saw a fine Court-house, where the assizes of Kildare county are held.

But by far the finest, and I think the most extensive edifice in Naas, was a haystack in the inn-yard, the proprietor of which did not fail to make me remark its size and splendour. It was of such dimensions as to strike a cockney with respect and pleasure; and here standing just as the new crops were coming in, told a tale of opulent thrift and good husbandry. Are there many more such haystacks, I wonder, in Ireland? The crops along the road seemed healthy, though rather light: wheat and oats plenty, and especially flourishing: hay and clover not so good; and turnips (let the important remark be taken at its full value) almost entirely wanting.

The little town, as they call it, of Kilcullen, tumbles down a hill and struggles up another; the two being here picturesquely divided by the Liffey, over which goes an antique bridge. It boasts, moreover, of a portion of an abbey wall, and a piece of round tower, both on the hill summit, and to be seen (says the Guide-book) for many miles round. Here we saw the first public evidences of the distress of the country. There was no trade in the little place, and but few people to be seen, except a crowd round a meal-shop, where meal is distributed once a week by the neighbouring gentry. There must have been some hundreds of persons waiting about the doors; women for the most part: some of their children were to be found loitering about the bridge much farther up the street: but it was curious to note, amongst these undeniably-starving people, how healthy their looks were. Going a little farther we saw women pulling weeds and nettles in the hedges, on which dismal sustenance the poor creatures live, having no bread, no potatoes, no work – well! these women did not look thinner or more unhealthy than many a well-fed person. A company of English lawyers, now, look more cadaverous than these starving creatures.

Stretching away from Kilcullen bridge, for a couple of miles or more, near the fine house and plantations of the Latouche family, is to be seen a much prettier sight, I think, than the finest park and mansion in the world. This is a tract of excessively green land, dotted over with brilliant white cottages, each with its couple of trim acres of garden, where you see thick potato ridges covered with blossom, great blue plots of comfortable cabbages, and such pleasant plants of the poor man's garden. Two or three years since, the land was a marshy common, which had never since the days of the Deluge fed any being bigger than a snipe, and into which the poor people descended, draining and cultivating, and rescuing the marsh from the water, and raising their cabins and setting up their little enclosures of two or three acres upon the land which they had thus created. 'Many of 'em has passed months in jail for that,' said my informant (a groom on the back seat of my host's phaeton); for it appears that certain gentlemen in the neighbourhood looked upon the titles of these new colonists with some jealousy, and would have been glad to depose them, but there were some better philosophers among the surrounding gentry, who advised that instead of discouraging the settlers it would be best to help them; and the consequence has been, that there are now two hundred flourishing little homesteads upon this rescued land, and as many families in comfort and plenty.

Just at the confines of this pretty rustic republic, our pleasant afternoon's drive ended; and I must begin this tour by a monstrous breach of confidence by first describing what I saw.

Well then, we drove through a neat lodge gate, with no stone lions or supporters, but riding well on its hinges, and looking fresh and white; and passed by a lodge, not Gothic, but decorated with flowers and evergreens, with clean windows, and a sound slate roof; and then went over a trim road, through a few acres of grass, adorned with plenty of young firs, and other healthy trees, under which were feeding a dozen of fine cows or more. The road led up to a house, or rather a congregation of rooms, built seemingly, to suit the owner's convenience, and increasing with his increasing wealth, or whim, or family. This latter is as plentiful as everything else about the place; and as the arrows increased, the good-natured, lucky father has been forced to multiply the quivers.

First came out a young gentleman, the heir of the house, who, after greeting his papa, began examining the horses with much interest; while three or four servants, quite neat and well drest, and, wonderful to say, without any talking, began to occupy themselves with the carriage, the passengers, and the trunks. Meanwhile, the owner of the house had gone into the hall, which is snugly furnished as a morning-room, and where one, two, three, young ladies came in to greet him. The young ladies having concluded their embraces, performed (as I am bound to say from experience, both in London and Paris) some very appropriate and well-finished curtsies to the strangers arriving; and these three young persons were presently succeeded by some still younger, who came without any curtsies at all, but bounding and jumping, and shouting out 'Papa' at the top of their voices, they fell forthwith upon that worthy gentleman's person, taking possession this of his knees, that of his arms, that of his whiskers, as fancy or taste might dictate.

'Are there any more of you?' says he, with perfect good humour; and, in fact, it appeared that there were some more in the nursery, as we subsequently had occasion to see.

Well, this large happy family are lodged in a house than which a prettier or more comfortable is not to be seen even in England; of the furniture of which it may be in confidence said, that each article is only made to answer one purpose:–thus, that chairs are never called upon to exercise the versatility of their genius by propping up windows; that chests of drawers are not obliged to move their unwieldy persons in order to act as locks to doors; that the windows are not variegated by paper, or adorned with wafers, as in other places which I have seen: in fact, that the place is just as comfortable as a place can be.

And if these comforts and reminiscences of three days' date are enlarged upon at some length, the reason is simply this:–this is written at what is supposed to be the best inn at one of the best towns of Ireland, Waterford. Dinner is just over; it is assize week, and the *table d'hôte* was surrounded for the chief part by English attorneys – the councillors (as the bar are pertinaciously called) dining up stairs in private. Well, on going to the public room, and being about to lay down my hat on the sideboard, I was obliged to pause – out of regard to a fine thick coat of dust, which had been kindly left to gather for some days past, I should think, and which it seemed a shame to misplace. Yonder is a chair basking quietly in the sunshine; some round object has evidently reposed upon it (a hat or plate probably), for you see a clear circle of black horsehair in the middle of the chair, and dust all round it. Not one of those dirty napkins that the four waiters carry, would wipe away the grime from the chair, and take to itself a little dust more! The people in the room are shouting out for the waiters, who cry, 'Yes, sir,' peevishly, and don't come; but stand bawling and jangling, and calling each other names, at the sideboard. The dinner is plentiful and nasty – raw ducks, raw peas, on a crumpled table-cloth, over which a waiter has just spirted a pint of obstreperous cider. The windows are open, to give free view of a crowd of old beggar-women, and of a fellow playing a cursed Irish-pipe. Presently this delectable apartment fills with choking peat-smoke; and on asking what is the cause of this agreeable addition to the pleasures of the place, you are told they are lighting a fire in a back-room.

Why should lighting a fire in a back-room fill a whole enormous house with smoke? Why should four waiters stand and *jaw* and gesticulate among themselves, instead of waiting on the guests? Why should ducks be raw, and dust lie quiet in places where a hundred people pass daily? All these points make one think very regretfully of neat, pleasant, comfortable, prosperous H—— town, where the meat was cooked, and the rooms were clean, and the servants didn't talk. Nor need it be said here, that it is as cheap to have a house clean as dirty, and that a raw leg of mutton costs exactly the same sum as one *cuit à point*. And by this moral earnestly hoping that all Ireland may profit, let us go back to H——, and the sights to be seen there.

There is no need to particularise the chairs and tables any farther, nor to say what sort of conversation and claret we had; nor to set down the dishes served at dinner. If an Irish gentleman does not give you a more hearty welcome than an Englishman, at least he has a more hearty manner of welcoming you; and while the latter reserves his fun and humour (if he possess those qualities) for his particular friends, the former is ready to laugh and talk his best with all the world, and give way entirely to his mood. And it would be a good opportunity here for a man who is clever at philosophising, to expound various theories upon the modes of hospitality practised in various parts of Europe. In a couple of hours' talk, an Englishman will give you his notions on trade, politics, the crops; the last run with the hounds, or the weather: it requires a long sitting, and a bottle of wine at the least, to induce him

to laugh cordially, or to speak unreservedly; and if you joke
with him before you know him, he will assuredly set you down
as a low impertinent fellow. In two hours, and over a pipe, a
German will be quite ready to let loose the easy floodgates of his
sentiment, and confide to you many of the secrets of his soft
heart. In two hours a Frenchman will say a hundred and twenty
smart, witty, brilliant, false things, and will care for you as
much then as he would if you saw him every day for twenty
years, that is, not one single straw; and in two hours an
Irishman will have allowed his jovial humour to unbutton, and
gambolled and frolicked to his heart's content. Which of these,
putting *Monsieur* out of the question, will stand by his friend
with the most constancy, and maintain his steady wish to serve
him? That is a question which the Englishman (and I think with
a little of his ordinary cool assumption) is disposed to decide in
his own favour; but it is clear, that for a stranger the Irish ways
are the pleasantest, for here he is at once made happy and at
home, or at ease rather; for home is a strong word, and implies
much more than any stranger can expect, or even desire to
claim.

Nothing could be more delightful to witness than the evident
affection which the children and parents bore to one another,
and to their parents, and the cheerfulness and happiness of their
family parties. The father of one lad went with a party of his
friends and family, on a pleasure party, in a handsome
coach-and-four. The little fellow sate on the coach-box and
played with the whip very wistfully for some time: the sun was
shining, the horses came out in bright harness, with glistening
coats; one of the girls brought a geranium to stick in papa's
button-hole, who was to drive. But although there was room in
the coach, and though papa said he should go if he liked, and
though the lad longed to go – as who wouldn't? – he jumped off
the box, and said, he would not go: mama would like him to
stop at home and keep his sister company; and so down he went
like a hero. Does this story appear trivial to any one who reads
this? If so, he is a pompous fellow, whose opinion is not worth
the having; or he has no children of his own; or he has forgotten
the day when he was a child himself; or he has never repented of
the surly selfishness with which he treated brothers and sisters,
after the habit of young English gentlemen.

'That's a list that uncle keeps of his children,' said the same young fellow, seeing his uncle reading a paper; and to understand this joke, it must be remembered, that the children of the gentleman called uncle, came into the breakfast-room by half-dozens: 'That's a *rum* fellow,' said the eldest of these latter to me, as his father went out of the room, evidently thinking his papa was the greatest wit and wonder in the whole world. And a great merit, as it appeared to me, on the part of these worthy parents was, that they consented not only to make, but to take jokes from their young ones: nor was the parental authority in the least weakened by this kind familiar intercourse.

A word with regard to the ladies so far. Those I have seen appear to the full as well educated and refined, and far more frank and cordial, than the generality of the fair creatures on the other side of the channel. I have not heard anything about poetry, to be sure, and in only one house have seen an album; but I have heard some capital music, of an excellent family sort – that sort which is used, namely, to set young people dancing, which they have done merrily for some nights. In respect of drinking, among the gentry, teetotalism does not, thank heaven! as yet appear to prevail; but although the claret has been invariably good, there has been no improper use of it.★ Let all English be recommended to be very careful of whiskey, which experience teaches to be a very deleterious drink. Natives say that it is wholesome, and may be some-times seen to use it with impunity; but the whiskey-fever is naturally more fatal to strangers than inhabitants of the country; and whereas an Irishman will sometimes imbibe a half-dozen tumblers of the poison, two glasses will often be found sufficient to cause headaches, heartburns, and fevers, to a person newly arrived in the country. The said whiskey is always to be had for the asking, but is not produced at the bettermost sort of tables.

Before setting out on our second day's journey, we had time to accompany the well-pleased owner of H—— town, over

★The only instances of intoxication that I have heard of as yet, has been on the part of two 'cyouncillors,' undeniably drunk and noisy yesterday after the bar dinner at Waterford.

some of his fields and out-premises. Nor can there be a
pleasanter sight to owner or stranger. Mr P—— farms four
hundred acres of land about his house; and employs on this
estate no less than a hundred and ten persons. He says there is
full work for every one of them; and to see the elaborate state
of cultivation in which the land was, it is easy to understand
how such an agricultural regiment were employed. The estate
is like a well-ordered garden – we walked into a huge field of
potatoes, and the landlord made us remark that there was not a
single weed between the furrows; and the whole formed a vast
flower-bed of a score of acres. Every bit of land up to the
hedge-side was fertilised and full of produce: the space left for
the plough having afterwards been gone over, and yielding its
fullest proportion of 'fruit.' In a turnip-field were a score or
more of women and children, who were marching through
the ridges, removing the young plants where two or three had
grown together, and leaving only the most healthy. Every
individual root in the field was thus the object of culture; and
the owner said that this extreme cultivation answered his
purpose, and that the employment of all these hands, (the
women and children earn 6d. and 8d. a day all the year round,)
which gained him some reputation as a philanthropist,
brought him profit as a farmer too; for his crops were the best
that land could produce. He has further the advantage of a
large stock for manure, and does everything for the land
which art can do.

Here we saw several experiments in manuring. An acre of
turnips prepared with bone-dust; another with 'Murray's
Composition,' whereof I do not pretend to know the ingredi-
ents; another with a new manure called Guano. As far as
turnips and a first year's crop went, the Guano carried the day.
The plants on the Guano acre looked to be three weeks in
advance of their neighbours, and were extremely plentiful and
healthy. I went to see this field two months after the above
passage was written; the Guano acre still kept the lead; the
bone-dust run Guano very hard; and Composition was clearly
distanced.

Behind the house is a fine village of corn and hay-ricks, and
a street of out-buildings, where all the work of the farm is
prepared. Here were numerous people coming with pails for

buttermilk, which the good-natured landlord made over to them. A score of men or more were busied about the place; some at a grindstone, others at a forge – other fellows busied in the cart-houses and stables, all of which were as neatly kept as in the best farm in England. A little further on was a flower-garden, a kitchen-garden, a hot-house just building, a kennel of fine pointers and setters; – indeed a noble feature of country neatness, thrift, and plenty.

We went into the cottages and gardens of several of Mr P——'s labourers, which were all so neat, that I could not help fancying they were pet cottages erected under the landlord's own superintendence, and ornamented to his order. But he declared that it was not so; that the only benefit his labourers got from him was constant work, and a house rent-free; and that the neatness of the gardens and dwellings was of their own doing. By making them a present of the house, he said, he made them a present of the pig and live stock, with which almost every Irish cotter pays his rent, so that each workman could have a bit of meat for his support; – would that all labourers in the empire had as much! With regard to the neatness of the houses, the best way to ensure this, he said, was for the master constantly to visit them – to awaken as much emulation as he could amongst the cottagers, so that each should make his place as good as his neighbour's – and to take them good-humouredly to task if they failed in the requisite care.

And so this pleasant day's visit ended. A more practical person would have seen, no doubt, and understood much more than a mere citizen could, whose pursuits have been very different from those noble and useful ones here spoken of. But a man has no call to be a judge of turnips or live stock, in order to admire such an establishment as this, and heartily to appreciate the excellence of it. There are some happy organisations in the world which possess the great virtue of *prosperity*. It implies cheerfulness, simplicity, shrewdness, perseverance, honesty, good health. See how, before the good-humoured resolution of such characters, ill-luck gives way, and fortune assumes their own smiling complexion! Such men grow rich without driving a single hard bargain; their condition being to make others prosper along with themselves. Thus, his very charity, another informant tells me, is one of the causes of my host's good fortune. He might have three pounds a year from each of forty cottages, but instead prefers a hundred healthy workmen; or he might have a fourth of the number of workmen, and a farm yielding a produce proportionately less, but instead of saving the money of their wages, prefers a farm the produce of which, as I have heard from a gentlemen whom I take to be good authority, is unequalled elsewhere.

Besides the cottages, we visited a pretty school, where children of an exceeding smallness were at their work, – the children of the catholic peasantry. The few protestants of the district do not attend the national school, nor learn their alphabet or their multiplication table in company with their little Roman catholic brethren. The clergyman who lives hard by the gate of H—— town, in his communication with his parishioners cannot fail to see how much misery is relieved and how much good is done by his neighbour: but though the two gentlemen are on good terms, the clergyman will not break bread with his catholic fellow-christian. There can be no harm, I hope, in mentioning this fact, as it is rather a public than a private matter; and, unfortunately, it is only a stranger that is surprised by such a circumstance, which is quite familiar to residents of the country. There are catholic inns and

 protestant inns in the towns; catholic coaches and protestant coaches on the the roads; nay, in the north, I have since heard of a high-church coach and a low-church coach, adopted by travelling christians of either party.

CHAPTER III

FROM CARLOW TO WATERFORD

The next morning being fixed for the commencement of our journey towards Waterford, a carriage made its appearance in due time before the hall door; an amateur stage-coach, with four fine horses, that were to carry us to Cork. The crew of the 'drag,' for the present, consisted of two young ladies, and two who will not be old, please heaven! for these thirty years; three gentlemen whose collected weights might amount to fifty-four stone; and one of smaller proportions, being as yet only twelve years old: to these were added a couple of grooms, and a lady's-maid. Subsequently we took in a dozen or more passengers, who did not seem in the slightest degree to inconvenience the coach or the horses; and thus was formed a tolerably numerous amd merry party. The governor took the reins, with his geranium in his button-hole, and the place on the box was quarrelled for without ceasing, and taken by turns.

Our day's journey lay through a country more picturesque, though by no means so prosperous and well cultivated as the district through which we had passed on our drive from Dublin. This trip carried us through the county of Carlow, and the town of that name; a wretched place enough, with a fine court-house, and a couple of fine churches; the protestant church, a noble structure; and the catholic cathedral, said to be built after some continental model. The catholics point to the structure with considerable pride: it was the first, I believe, of the many handsome cathedrals for their worship which have been built of late years in this country by the noble contributions of the poor man's penny and by the untiring energies and sacrifices of the clergy. Bishop Doyle, the founder of the church, has the place of honour within it; nor, perhaps did any christian pastor ever merit the affection of his flock more than

that great and high-minded man. He was the best champion
the catholic church and cause ever had in Ireland: in learning,
and admirable kindness and virtue, the best example to the
clergy of his religion: and if the country is now filled with
schools, where the humblest peasant in it can have the benefit
of a liberal and wholesome education, it owes this great boon
mainly to his noble exertions, and to the spirit which they
awakened.

As for the architecture of the cathedral, I do not fancy a
professional man would find much to praise in it: it seems to
me overloaded with ornaments, nor were its innumerable
spires and pinnacles the more pleasing to the eye because some
of them were of the perpendicular. The interior is quite plain,
not to say bare and unfinished. Many of the chapels in the
country that I have since seen are in a similar condition; for
when the walls are once raised, the enthusiasm of the subs-
cribers to the building seems somewhat characteristically, to
grow cool, and you enter at a porch that would suit a palace,
with an interior scarcely more decorated than a barn. A wide
large floor, some confession-boxes against the blank walls
here and there, with some humble pictures at the 'stations,'
and the statue, under a mean canopy of red woollen stuff,
were the chief furniture of the cathedral.

The severe homely features of the good bishop were not
very favourable subjects for Mr Hogan's chisel; but a figure of
prostrate, weeping Ireland, kneeling by the prelate's side, and
for whom he is imploring protection, has much beauty. In the
chapels of Dublin and Cork some of this artist's works may be
seen, and his countrymen are exceedingly proud of him.

Connected with the catholic cathedral is a large tumble-
down looking divinity college: there are upwards of a hundred
students here, and the college is licensed to give degrees in arts
as well as divinity; at least so the officer of the church said, as
he showed us the place through the bars of the sacristy-
windows, in which apartment may be seen sundry crosses, a
pastoral letter of Dr Doyle, and a number of ecclesiastical
vestments formed of laces, poplins, and velvets, handsomely
laced with gold. There is a convent by the side of the
cathedral, and, of course, a parcel of beggars all about, and
indeed all over the town, profuse in their prayers and invo-

cations of the Lord, and whining flatteries of the persons whom they address. One wretched old tottering hag began whining the Lord's prayer as a proof of her sincerity, and blundered in the very midst of it, and left us thoroughly disgusted after the very first sentence.

It was market-day in the town, which is tolerably full of poor-looking shops, and streets being thronged with donkey-carts, and people eager to barter their small wares. Here and there were picture-stalls, with huge hideous coloured engravings of the Saints; and indeed the objects of barter upon the banks of the clear bright river Barrow seemed scarcely to be of more value than the articles which change hands, as one reads of, in a town of African huts and traders on the banks of the Quarra. Perhaps the very bustle and cheerfulness of the people served only, to a Londoner's eyes, to make it look the more miserable. It seems as if they had no *right* to be eager about such a parcel of wretched rags and trifles as were exposed to sale.

There are some old towers of a castle here, looking finely from the river; and near the town is a grand modern residence belonging to Colonel Bruen, with an oak-park on one side of the road, and a deer park on the other. These retainers of the Colonel's lay, in their rushy green enclosures, in great numbers and seemingly in flourishing condition.

The road from Carlow to Leighlin-bridge is exceedingly beautiful; noble purple hills rising on either side, and the broad silver Barrow flowing through rich meadows of that astonishing verdure which is only to be seen in this country. Here and there was a country-house, or a tall mill by a stream-side: but the latter buildings were for the most part empty, the gaunt windows gaping without glass, and their great wheels idle. Leighlin-bridge, lying up and down a hill by the river, contains a considerable number of pompous-looking warehouses, that looked for the most part to be doing no more business than the mills on the Carlow road, but stood by the roadside staring at the coach, as it were, and basking in the sun, swaggering, idle, insolvent, and out at elbows. There are one or two very pretty modest, comfortable looking country places about Leighlin-bridge, and on the road thence to a miserable village called the Royal Oak, a beggarly sort of bustling place.

Here stands a dilapidated hotel and posting-house: and indeed on every road, as yet, I have been astonished at the great movement and stir; – the old coaches being invariably crammed, cars jingling about equally full, and no want of gentlemen's carriages to exercise the horses of the Royal Oak and similar establishments. In the time of the rebellion, the landlord of this Royal Oak, a great character in those parts, was a fierce United Irishman. One day it happened that Sir John Anderson came to the inn, and was eager for horses on. The landlord who knew Sir John to be a Tory, vowed and swore he had no horses; that the judges had the last going to Kilkenny; that the yeomanry had carried off the best of them; that he could not give a horse for love or money. 'Poor Lord Edward!' said Sir John, sinking down in a chair, and clasping his hands, 'my poor dear misguided friend, and must you die for the loss of a few hours and the want of a pair of horses?'

'Lord *what*?' says the landlord.

'Lord Edward Fitzgerald,' replied Sir John; 'the Government has seized his papers, and got scent of his hiding-place; if I can't get to him before two hours, Sirr will have him.'

'My dear Sir John,' cried the landlord; 'it's not two horses but it's eight I'll give you, and may the judges go hang for me! Here, Larry! Tim! First and second pair for Sir John Anderson; and long life to you, Sir John, and the Lord reward you for your good deed this day!'

Sir John, my informant told me, had invented this predicament of Lord Edward's in order to get the horses; and by way of corroborating the whole story, pointed out an old chaise which stood at the inn-door with its window broken, a great crevice in the panel, some little wretches crawing underneath the wheels, and two huge blackguards lolling against the pole, – 'and that,' says he, 'is no doubt the very post-chaise Sir John Anderson had.' It certainly looked ancient enough.

Of course, as we stopped for a moment in the place, troops of slatternly, ruffianly-looking fellows assembled round the carriage, dirty heads peeped out of all the dirty windows, beggars came forward with a joke and a prayer, and troops of children raised their shouts and halloos. I confess, with regard to the beggars, that I have never yet had the slightest sentiment of compassion for the very oldest or dirtiest of them, or been inclined to give them a penny; they come crawling round you with lying prayers and loathsome compliments, that make the stomach turn; they do not even disguise that they are lies; for, refuse them, and the wretches turn off with a laugh and a joke, a miserable grinning cynicism that creates distrust and indifference, and must be, one would think, the very best way to close the purse, not to open it, for objects so unworthy.

How do all these people live? one can't help wondering; – these multifarious vagabonds, without work or workhouse, or means of subsistence? The Irish Poor Law Report says that there are twelve hundred thousand people in Ireland, a sixth of the population, who have no means of livelihood but charity, and whom the state, or individual members of it, must maintain. How *can* the state support such an enormous burthen; or the twelve hundred thousand be supported? What a strange history it would be, could one but get it true, – that of the manner in which a score of these beggars have maintained themselves for a fortnight past!

Soon after quitting the Royal Oak, our road branches off to the hospitable house where our party, consisting of a dozen persons, was to be housed and fed for the night. Fancy the look which an English gentleman of moderate means would assume, at being called on to receive such a company! A pretty road of a couple of miles, thickly grown with ash and oak trees, under which the hats of coach passengers suffered some danger, leads to the house of D——. A young son of the house, on a white pony, was on the look-out, and great cheering and shouting took place among the young people as we came in sight.

Trotting away by the carriage-side, he brought us through a gate with a pretty avenue of trees leading to the pleasure-grounds of the house – a handsome building commanding noble views of river, mountains, and plantations. Our entertainer only rents the place; so I may say, without any imputation against him, that the house was by no means so handsome within as without, – not that the want of finish in the interior made our party the less merry, or the host's entertainment less hearty and cordial.

The gentleman who built and owns the house, like many other proprietors in Ireland, found his mansion too expensive for his means, and has relinquished it. I asked what his income might be, and no wonder that he was compelled to resign his house; which a man with four times the income in England, would scarcely venture to inhabit. There were numerous sitting-rooms below; a large suite of rooms above, in which our large party, with their servants, disappeared without any seeming inconvenience, and which already accommodated a family of at least a dozen persons, and a numerous train of domestics. There was a great court-yard surrounded by capital offices, with stabling and coach-houses sufficient for a half-dozen of country gentlemen. An English squire of ten thousand a year might live in such a place – the original owner, I am told, had not many more hundreds.

Our host has wisely turned the chief part of the pleasure-ground round the house, into a farm; nor did the land look a bit the worse, as I thought, for having such rich crops of potatoes growing in place of grass, and fine plots of waving wheat and barley. The care, skill, and neatness everywhere exhibited, and the immense luxuriance of the crops, could not fail to strike even a cockney; and one of our party, a very well-known practical farmer, told me that there was at least five hundred pounds worth of produce upon the little estate of some sixty acres, of which only five-and-twenty were under the plough.

As at H—— town, on the previous day, several men and women appeared sauntering in the grounds, and as the master came up, asked for work, or sixpence, or told a story of want. There are lodge-gates at both ends of the demesne; but it appears the good natured practice of the country admits a beggar as well as any other visitor. To a couple our landlord gave money, to another a job of work; another he sent roughly out of the premises: and I could judge thus what a continual tax upon the Irish gentlemen these travelling paupers must be, of whom his ground is never free.

There loitering about the stables and out-houses, were several people who seemed to have acquired a sort of right to be there: women and children who had a claim upon the buttermilk; men who did an odd job now and then; loose

hangers-on of the family: and in the lodging-houses and inns I have entered, the same sort of ragged vassals are to be found; in a house however poor, you are sure to see some poorer dependant who is a stranger, taking a meal of potatoes in the kitchen; a Tim or Mike loitering hard by, ready to run on a message, or carry a bag. This is written, for instance, at a lodging over a shop at Cork. There sits in the shop a poor fellow quite past work, but who totters up and down stairs to the lodgers, and does what little he can for his easily-won bread. There is another fellow outside who is sure to make his bow to anybody issuing from the lodging, and ask if his honour wants an errand done? Neither class of such dependants exist with us. What housekeeper in London is there will feed an old man of seventy that's good for nothing, or encourage such a disreputable hanger-on as yonder shuffling, smiling cad?

Nor did Mr M——'s 'irregulars' disappear with the day; for

when, after a great deal of merriment, and kind, happy dancing and romping of young people, the fineness of the night suggested the propriety of smoking a certain cigar (it is never more acceptable than at that season), the young squire voted that we should adjourn to the stables for the purpose, where accordingly the cigars were discussed. There were still the inevitable half-dozen hangers-on; one came grinning with a lantern, all nature being in universal blackness except his grinning face; another ran obsequiously to the stables to show a favourite mare – I think it was a mare – though it may have been a mule, and your humble servant not much the wiser. The cloths were taken off; the fellows with the candles crowded about; and the young squire bade me admire the beauty of her fore-leg, which I did with the greatest possible gravity. Did you ever see such a fore-leg as that in your life? says the young squire, and further discoursed upon the horse's points, the amateur grooms joining in chorus.

There was another young squire of our party, a pleasant gentlemanlike young fellow, who danced as prettily as any Frenchman, and who had ridden over from a neighbouring house: as I went to bed, the two lads were arguing whether young Squire B—— should go home or stay at D—— that night. There was a bed for him – there was a bed for everybody, it seemed, and a kind welcome too. How different was all this to the ways of a severe English house!

Next morning the whole of our merry party assembled round a long, jovial breakfast-table, stored with all sorts of good things; and the biggest and joviallest man of all, who had just come in fresh from a walk in the fields, and vowed that he was as hungry as a hunter, and was cutting some slices out of an inviting ham on the side-table, suddenly let fall his knife and fork with dismay. 'Sure, John, don't you know it's Friday,' cried a lady from the table; and back John came with a most lugubrious queer look on his jolly face, and fell to work upon bread and butter, as resigned as possible, admidst no small laughter, as may be well imagined. On this I was bound, as a Protestant, to eat a large slice of pork, and discharged that duty nobly, and with much self-sacrifice.

The famous 'drag' which had brought us so far, seemed to be as hospitable and elastic as the house which we now left, for the coach accommodated, inside and out, a considerable party from the house, and we took our road leisurely, in a cloudless, scorching day, towards Waterford. The first place we passed through was the little town of Gowran, near which is a grand, well-ordered park, belonging to Lord Clifden, and where his mother resides, with whose beautiful face, in Lawrence's pictures, every reader must be familiar. The kind English lady has done the greatest good in the neighbourhood, it is said, and the little town bears marks of her beneficence, in its neatness, prettiness, and order. Close by the church there are the ruins of a fine old abbey here, and a still finer one a few miles on, at Thomastown, most picturesquely situated amidst trees and meadow, on the river Nore. The place within, however, is dirty and ruinous – the same wretched suburbs, the same squalid congregation of beggarly loungers, that are to be seen elsewhere. The monastic ruin is very fine, and the road hence to Thomastown, rich with varied cultivation and beautiful verdure, pretty gentlemen's mansions shining among the trees on either side of the way. There was one place along this rich tract that looked very strange and ghastly – a huge old pair of gate pillars, flanked by a ruinous lodge, and a wide road winding for a mile up a hill. There had been a park once, but all the trees were gone; thistles were growing in the yellow sickly land, and rank thin grass on the road. Far away you saw in this desolate tract a ruin of a house: many a butt of claret has been emptied there, no doubt, and many a pretty party come out with hound and horn. But what strikes the Englishman with wonder is not so much, perhaps, that an owner of the place should have been ruined and a spendthrift, as that the land should lie there useless ever since. If one is not successful with us another man will be, or another will try, at least. Here lies useless a great capital of hundreds of acres of land; barren, where the commonest effort might make it productive, and looking as if for a quarter of a century past no soul ever looked or cared for it. You might travel five hundred miles through England and not see such a spectacle.

A short distance from Thomastown is another abbey; and presently, after passing through the village of Knocktopher, we came to a posting-place called Ballyhale, of the *moral* aspect of which, the following scrap taken in the place will give a notion.

A dirty, old, contented, decrepit idler was lolling in the sun at a shop-door, and hundreds of population of the dirty, old, decrepit, contented place were employed in the like way. A dozen of boys were playing at pitch and toss; the other male and female beggars were sitting on a wall looking into a stream; scores of raggamuffins, of course, round the carriage; and beggars galore at the door of the little ale-house or hotel.

A gentleman's carriage changed horses as we were baiting here. It was a rich sight to see the cattle, and the way of starting them: Halloo! Yoop, Hoop! a dozen ragged ostlers and amateurs running by the side of the miserable old horses, the postilion shrieking, yelling, and belabouring them with his whip. Down goes one horse among the new laid stones; the postilion has him up with a cut of the whip and a curse, and takes advantage of the start caused by the stumble to get the brute into a gallop, and to go down the hill. 'I know it for a fact,' a gentleman of our party says, 'that no horses *ever* got out of Ballyhale without an accident of some kind.'

'Will your honour like to come and see a big pig?' here asked a man of the above gentleman, well known as a great farmer and breeder. We all went to see the big pig, not very fat as yet, but, upon my word, it is as big as a pony. The country round is, it appears, famous for the breeding of such, especially a district called the Welsh mountains, through which we had to pass on our road to Waterford.

This is a curious country to see, and has curious inhabitants: for twenty miles there is no gentleman's house: gentlemen dare not live there. The place was originally tenanted by a clan of Welshes; hence its name; and they maintain themselves in their occupancy of the farms in Tipperary fashion, by simply putting a ball into the body of any man who would come to take a farm over any one of them. Some of the crops in the fields of the Welsh country seemed very good, and the fields well tilled; but it is common to see by the side of one field that is well cultivated, another that is absolutely barren; and the whole tract is extremely wretched. Appropriate histories and reminiscences accompany the traveller; at a chapel near Mullinavat is the spot where sixteen policemen were murdered in the tithe campaign; farther on you come to a lime-kiln, where the guard of a mail-coach was seized and *roasted alive*. I saw here the first hedge-school I have seen; a crowd of half-savage looking lads and girls looked up from their studies in the ditch, their college or lecture-room being in a mud cabin hard by.

And likewise, in the midst of this wild tract, a fellow met us who was trudging the road with a fish-basket over his shoulder, and who stopped the coach, hailing two of the gentlemen in it by name, both of whom seemed to be much amused by his humour. He was a handsome rogue, a poacher, or salmon-taker, by profession, and presently poured out such a flood of oaths, and made such a monstrous display of grinning wit and blackguardism, as I have never heard equalled by the best Billingsgate practitioner, and as it would be more than useless to attempt to describe. Blessings, jokes, and curses, trolled off the rascal's lips with a volubility which caused his Irish audience to shout with laughter, but which were quite beyond a Cockney. It was a humour so purely national as to be understood by none but natives, I should think. I recollect the same feeling of perplexity while sitting, the only Englishman, in a company of jocular Scotchmen. They bandied about puns, jokes, imitations, and applauded with shrieks of laughter – what, I confess, appeared to me the most abominable dulness – nor was the salmon-taker's jocularity any better. I think it rather served to frighten than to amuse; and I am not sure but that I looked out for a band of jocular cut-throats of his sort, to come up at a given guffaw, and playfully rob us all round. However, he went away quite peaceably, calling down for the party the benediction of a great number of saints, who must have been somewhat ashamed to be addressed by such a rascal.

Presently we caught sight of the valley through which the Suire flows, and descended the hill towards it, and went over the thundering old wooden bridge to Waterford.

CHAPTER IV

FROM WATERFORD TO CORK

The view of the town, from the bridge and the heights above it, is very imposing; as is the river both ways. Very large vessels sail up almost to the doors of the houses, and the quays are flanked by tall red warehouses, that look at a little distance as if a world of business might be doing within them. But as you get into the place, not a soul is there to greet you except the usual society of beggars, and a sailor or two, or a green-coated policeman sauntering down the broad pavement. We drove up to the Coach Inn, a huge, handsome, dirty building, of which the discomforts have been pathetically described elsewhere. The landlord is a gentleman and considerable horse proprietor, and though a perfectly well-bred, active and intelligent man, far too much of a gentleman to play the host well, at least as an Englishman understands that character.

Opposite the town is a tower of questionable antiquity and undeniable ugliness; for though the inscription says it was built in the year one thousand and something, the same documents adds that it was rebuilt in 1819 – to either of which dates the traveller is thus welcomed. The quays stretch for a considerable distance along the river, poor patched-windowed, mouldy-looking shops forming the basement-storey of most of the houses. We went into one, a jeweller's to make a purchase – it might have been of a gold watch for anything the owner knew; but he was talking with a friend in his back parlour, gave us a look as we entered, allowed us to stand some minutes in the empty shop, and at length to walk out without being served. In another shop a boy was lolling behind a counter, but could not say whether the articles we wanted were to be had; turned out a heap of drawers, and could not find them; and finally went for the master, who could not come. True commercial independence, and an easy way enough of life.

In one of the streets leading from the quay is a large, dingy, Catholic chapel, of some pretensions within; but, as usual, there had been a failure for want of money, and the front of the chapel was unfinished, presenting the butt-end of a portico, and walls on which the stone coating was to be laid. But a much finer ornament to the church than any of the questionable gewgaws which adorned the ceiling was the piety, stern, simple, and unaffected, of the people within. Their whole soul seemed to be in their prayers, as rich and poor knelt indifferently on the flags. There is of course an Episcopal cathedral, well and neatly kept, and a handsome Bishop's palace: near it was a convent of nuns, and a little chapel-bell clinking melodiously. I was prepared to fancy something romantic of the place; but as we passed the convent gate, a shoeless slattern of a maid opened the door – the most dirty and unpoetical of housemaids.

Assizes were held in the town, and we ascended to the Court-house through a steep street, a sort of rag-fair, but more villainous and miserable than any rag-fair in St Giles's: the houses and stock of the Seven Dials look as if they belonged to capitalists when compared with the scare-crow wretchedness of the goods here hung out for sale. Who wanted to buy such things? I wondered. One would have thought that the most part of the articles had passed the possibility of barter for money, even out of the reach of the half-farthings coined of late. All the street was lined with wretched hucksters and their merchandise of gooseberries, green apples, children's dirty cakes, cheap crockeries, brushes, and tin-ware; among which objects the people were swarming about busily.

Before the court is a wide street, where a similar market was held, with a vast number of donkey-carts urged hither and thither, and great shrieking, chattering, and bustle. It is five hundred years ago since a poet who accompanied Richard II in his voyage hither spoke of '*Watreforde ou moult vilaine et orde y sont la gente.*' They don't seem to be much changed now, but remain faithful to their ancient habits.

About the court-house swarms of beggars of course were collected, varied by personages of a better sort; grey-coated farmers, and women with their picturesque blue cloaks, who had trudged in from the country probably. The court-house is as beggarly and ruinous as the rest of the neighbourhood; smart-looking policemen kept order about it, and looked very hard at me as I ventured to take a sketch.

The figures as I saw them were accurately so disposed. The man in the dock, the policeman seated easily above him, the woman looking down from a gallery. The man was accused of stealing a sack of wool, and, having no counsel, made for himself as adroit a defence as any one of the counsellors (they are without robes or wigs here, by the way) could have made for him. He had been seen examining a certain sack of wool in a coffee-shop at Dungarvan, and next day was caught sight of in Waterford market, standing under an archway from the rain, with the sack by his side.

'Wasn't there twenty other people under the arch?' said he to a witness, a noble-looking beautiful girl – the girl was obliged to own there were. 'Did you see me touch the wool, or stand nearer to it than a dozen of the dacent people there?' and the girl confessed she had not. 'And this it is, my lord,' says he to the bench, 'they attack

me because I am poor and ragged, but they never think of
charging the crime on a rich farmer.'

But alas for the defence! another witness saw the prisoner
with his legs round the sack, and being about to charge him
with the theft, the prisoner fled into the arms of a policeman,
to whom his first words were, 'I know nothing about the
sack.' So as the sack had been stolen, as he had been seen
handling it four minutes before it was stolen, and holding it
for sale the day after, it was concluded that Patrick Malony
had stolen the sack, and he was accommodated with eighteen
months accordingly.

In another case we had a woman and her child on the table;
and others followed, in the judgment of which it was impossible not to admire the extreme leniency, acuteness, and
sensibility of the judge presiding, Chief Justice Pennefather:-
the man against whom all the liberals in Ireland, and every one
else who has read his charge too, must be angry, for the
ferocity of his charge against a Belfast newspaper editor. It
seems as if no parties here will be dispassionate when they get
to a party question, and that natural kindness has no claim,
when Whig and Tory come into collision.

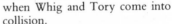

The juryman is here placed on a
table instead of a witnessbox; nor
was there much farther peculiarity
to remark, except in the dirt of the
Court, the absence of the barris-
terial wig and gown, and the great
coolness with which a fellow who
seemed a sort of clerk, usher, and
Irish interpreter to the court,
recommended a prisoner, who
was making rather a long defence,
to be quiet. I asked him why the
man might not have his say.
'Sure,' says he, 'he's said all he has
to say, and there's no use in any
more;' but there was no use in
attempting to convince Mr Usher
that the prisoner was best judge

on this point; in fact the poor devil shut his mouth at the admonition, and was found guilty with perfect justice.

A considerable poor-house has been erected at Waterford, but the beggars of the place as yet prefer their liberty, and less certain means of gaining support. We asked one who was calling down all the blessings of all the saints and angels upon us, and telling a most piteous tale of poverty, why she did not go to the poor-house. The woman's look at once changed from a sentimental whine to a grin. 'Dey owe two hundred pounds at dat house,' said she, 'and faith, an honest woman can't go dere;' with which wonderful reason ought not the most squeamish to be content?

After describing, as accurately as words may, the features of a landscape, and stating that such a mountain was to the left, and such a river or town to the right, and putting down the situations and names of the villages, and the bearings of the roads, it has no doubt struck the reader of books of travels that the writer has not given him the slightest idea of the country, and that he would have been just as wise without perusing the letter-press landscape through which he has toiled. It will be as well then, under such circumstances, to spare the public any lengthened description of the road from Waterford to Dungarvan, which was the road we took, followed by benedictions delivered gratis from the beggarhood of the former city. Not very far from it you see the dark plantations of the magnificent domain of Curraghmore, and pass through a country, blue, hilly, and bare, except where gentlemen's seats appear with their ornaments of wood. Presently, after leaving Waterford, we came to a certain town called Kilmacthomas, of which all the information I have to give is, that it is situated upon a hill and river, and that you may change horses there. The road was covered with carts of sea-weed, which the people were bringing for manure from the shore some four miles distant; and beyond Kilmacthomas we beheld the Cummeragh Mountains, 'often named in maps the Nennavoulagh,' either of which names the reader may select at pleasure.

Thence we came to 'Cushcam,' at which village be it known that the turnpike-man kept the drag a very long time waiting.

'I think the fellow must be writing a book,' said the
coachman, with a most severe look of drollery at a cockney
tourist, who tried, under the circumstances, to blush, and not
to laugh. I wish I could relate or remember half the mad jokes
that flew about the jolly Irish crew on top of the coach, and
which would have made a journey through the Desert jovial.
When the 'pike-man had finished his composition (that of a
turnpike-ticket, which he had to fill), we drove on to Dungarvan; the two parts of which town, separated by the river
Colligan, have been joined by a causeway three hundred yards
along, and a bridge erected at an enormous outlay by the Duke
of Devonshire. In former times, before his Grace spent his
eighty thousand pounds upon the causeway, this wide estuary
was called 'Dungarvan Prospect,' because the ladies of the
country, walking over the river at low water took off their
shoes and stockings (such as had them), and tucking up their
clothes, exhibited – what I have never seen, and cannot,
therefore, be expected to describe. A large and handsome
Catholic chapel, a square with some pretensions to regularity
of building, a very neat and comfortable inn, and beggars and
idlers still more numerous than at Waterford, were what we
had leisure to remark in half-an-hour's stroll through the
town.

Near the prettily situated village of Cappoquin is the
Trappist-house of Mount Meilleraie, of which we could only
see the pinnacles. The brethren were presented some years
since with a barren mountain, which they have cultivated
most successfully. They have among themselves workmen to
supply all their frugal wants, ghostly tailors and shoemakers,
spiritual gardeners and bakers, working in silence, and serving
Heaven after their way. If this reverend community, for fear
of the opportunity of sinful talk, choose to hold their tongues,
the next thing will be to cut them out altogether, and so render
the danger impossible – if, being men of education and
intelligence, they incline to turn butchers and cobblers, and
smother their intellects by base and hard menial labour; who
knows but one day a sect may be more pious still, and
rejecting even butchery and bakery as savouring too much of
worldly convenience and pride, take to a wild-beast life at
once? Let us concede that suffering, and mental and bodily

debasement, are the things most agreeable to Heaven, and there is no knowing where such Piety may stop. I was very glad we had not time to see the grovelling place; and as for seeing shoes made or fields tilled by reverend amateurs, we can find cobblers and plough-boys to do the work better.

By the way, the Quakers have set up in Ireland a sort of monkery of their own. Not far from Carlow we met a couple of cars, drawn by white horses, and holding white quakers and quakeresses, in white hats, clothes, shoes, with wild maniacal-looking faces, bumping along the road. Let us hope that we may soon get a community of Fakeers and howling Dervises into the country. It would be a refreshing thing to see such ghostly men in one's travels, standing at the corners of roads, and praising the Lord by standing on one leg, or cutting and hacking themselves with knives like the prophets of Baal. Is it not as pious for a man to deprive himself of his leg as of his tongue, and to disfigure his body with the gashes of a knife, as with the hideous white raiment of the illuminated quakers?

While these reflections were going on, the beautiful Blackwater river suddenly opened before us, and driving along it for three miles through some of the most beautiful, rich country ever seen, we came to Lismore. Nothing can be certainly more magnificent than this drive. Parks and rocks covered with the grandest foliage; rich, handsome seats of gentlemen in the midst of fair lawns, and beautiful bright plantations and shrubberies; and at the end, the graceful spire of Lismore church, the prettiest I have seen in, or, I think, out of Ireland. Nor in any country that I have visited have I seen a view more noble – it is too rich and peaceful to be what is called romantic, but lofty, large, and *generous*, if the term may be used; the river and banks as fine as the Rhine; the castle not as large, but as noble and picturesque as Warwick. As you pass the bridge, the banks stretch away on either side in amazing verdure, and the castle-walks remind one somewhat of the dear old terrace of St Germains, with its groves, and long grave avenues of trees.

The salmon-fishery of the Blackwater is let, as I hear, for a thousand a year. In the evening, however, we saw some gentlemen who are likely to curtail the profits of the farmer of

the fishery – a company of ragged boys, to wit – whose
occupation, it appears, is to poach. These young fellows were
all lolling over the bridge, as the moon rose rather mistily, and
pretended to be deeply enamoured of the view of the river.
They answered the questions of one of our party with the
utmost innocence and openness, and one would have supposed the lads were so many Arcadians, but for the arrival of
an old woman, who suddenly coming up among them,
poured out, upon one and all, a volley of curses, both deep and
loud, saying, that perdition would be their portion, and
calling them 'shchamers,' at least a hundred times. Much to
my wonder, the young men did not reply to the voluble old
lady for some time, who then told us the cause of her anger:
She had a son, – 'Look at him there, the villain.' The lad was
standing, looking very unhappy. 'His father, that's now dead,
paid a fistful of money to bind him 'prentice at Dungarvan:
but these shchamers followed him there; made him break his
indentures, and go poaching and thieving and shchaming with
them.' The poor old woman shook her hands in the air, and
shouted at the top of her deep voice; there was something very
touching in her grotesque sorrow, nor did the lads make light
of it at all, contenting themselves with a surly growl, or an
oath, if directly appealed to by the poor creature.

So, cursing and raging, the woman went away. The son, a
lad of fourteen, evidently the fag of the big bullies round about
him, stood dismally away from them, his head sunk down. I
went up and asked him, 'Was that his mother?' He said, 'Yes.'
'Was she good and kind to him when he was at home?' He
said, 'O yes.' 'Why not come back to her?' I asked him; but he
said, 'he couldn't.' Whereupon, I took his arm and tried to
lead him away by main force; but he said, 'Thank you, sir, but
I can't go back,' and released his arm. We stood on the bridge
some minutes longer, looking at the view; but the boy,
though he kept away from his comrades, would not come. I
wonder what they have done together, that the poor boy is
past going home? The place seemed to be so quiet and
beautiful, and far away from London, that I thought crime
couldn't have reached it; and yet, here it lurks somewhere
among six boys of sixteen, each with a stain in his heart, and
some black history to tell. The poor widow's yonder was the

only family about which I had a chance of knowing anything in this remote place; nay, in all Ireland; and, God help us, hers was a sad lot! – A husband gone dead, – an only child gone to ruin. It is awful to think that there are eight millions of stories to be told in this island. Seven million nine hundred and ninety-nine thousand nine hundred and ninety-eight more lives than I, and all brother Cockneys know nothing about. Well, please God, they are not all like this.

That day, I heard *another* history. A little old disreputable man in tatters, with a huge steeple of a hat, came shambling down the street, one among the five hundred blackguards there. A fellow standing under the sun portico (a sort of swaggering, chattering, cringing *touter*, and master of cere-monies to the gutter), told us something with regard to the old disreputable man. His son had been hanged the day before at Clonmel, for one of the Tipperary murders. That blackguard in our eyes instantly looked quite different from all other blackguards – I saw him gesticulating at the corner of a street, and watched him with wonderful interest.

The church with the handsome spire, that looks so graceful among the trees, is a cathedral church, and one of the neatest kept and prettiest edifices I have seen in Ireland. In the old grave-yard Protestants and Catholics lie together – that is, not together; for each has a side of the ground, where they sleep, and so occupied, do not quarrel. The sun was shining down upon the brilliant grass – and I don't think the shadows of the Protestant graves were any longer or shorter than those of the Catholics? Is it the right or the left side of the grave-yard which is nearest heaven I wonder? Look, the sun shines upon both alike, 'and the blue sky bends over all.'

Raleigh's house is approached by a grave old avenue, and well-kept wall, such as is rare in this country: and the court of the castle within has the solid, comfortable, quiet look, equally rare. It is like one of our colleges at Oxford: there is a side of the quadrangle with pretty ivy-covered gables; another part of the square is more modern; and by the main body of the castle is a small chapel exceedingly picturesque. The interior is neat and in excellent order; but it was unluckily done up some thirty years ago (as I imagine from the style), before our architects had learned Gothic, and all the ornamen-

tal work is consequently quite ugly and out of keeping. The
church has probably been arranged by the same hand. In the
castle are some plainly-furnished chambers, one or two good
pictures, and a couple of oriel windows, the views from which
up and down the river are exceedingly lovely. You hear
praises of the Duke of Devonshire as a landlord, wherever you
go among his vast estates: it is a pity that, with such a noble
residence as this, and with such a wonderful country round
about it, his Grace should not inhabit it more.

Of the road from Lismore to Fermoy it does not behove me
to say much, for a pelting rain came on very soon after we
quitted the former place, and accompanied us almost without
ceasing to Fermoy. Here we had a glimpse of a bridge across
the Blackwater, which we had skirted in our journey from
Lismore. Now enveloped in mist and cloud – now, spanned
by a rainbow; at another time, basking in sunshine. Nature
attired the charming prospect for us in a score of different
ways; and it appeared before us like a coquettish beauty who
was trying what dress in her wardrobe might most become
her. At Fermoy we saw a vast barrack, and an overgrown inn,
where, however, good fare was provided; and thence hastening came by Rathcormack, and Watergrass Hill, famous
for the residence of Father Prout, whom my friend, the Rev.
Francis Sylvester, has made immortal; from which descending
we arrived at the beautiful wooded village of Glanmire, with
its mills and steeples, and streams, and neat school-houses,
and pleasant country residences. This brings us down upon
the superb stream which leads from the sea to Cork.

The view for three miles on both sides is magnificently
beautiful. Fine gardens, and parks, and villas, cover the shore
on each bank; the river is full of brisk craft moving to the city
or out to sea; and the city finely ends the view, rising upon
two hills on either side of the stream. I do not know a town to
which there is an entrance more beautiful, commodious, and
stately.

Passing by numberless handsome lodges, and, nearer the
city, many terraces in neat order, the road conducts us near a
large tract of some hundred acres, which have been reclaimed
from the sea, and are destined to form a park and pleasure-
ground for the citizens of Cork. In the river, and up to the

bridge, some hundreds of ships were lying; and a fleet of steam-boats opposite the handsome house of the St George's Steam Packet Company. A church stands prettily on the hill above it, surrounded by a number of new habitations very neat and white. On the road is a handsome Roman Catholic chapel, or a chapel which will be handsome as soon as the necessary funds are raised to complete it. But, as at Waterford, the chapel has been commenced, and the money has failed, and the fine portico which is to decorate it one day, as yet only exists on the architect's paper. Saint Patrick's bridge, over which we pass, is a pretty building; and Patrick-street, the main street of the town, has an air of business and cheerfulness, and looks densely thronged.

As the carriage drove up to those neat, comfortable, and extensive lodgings which Mrs Mac O'Boy has to let, a magnificent mob was formed round the vehicle, and we had an opportunity of at once making acquaintance with some of the dirtiest rascally faces that all Ireland presents. Besides these professional rogues and beggars, who make a point to attend on all vehicles, every body else seemed to stop too, to see that wonder, a coach and four horses. People issued from their shops, heads appeared at windows. I have seen the Queen pass in state in London, and not bring together a crowd near so great as that which assembled in the busiest street of the second city of the kingdom, just to look at a green coach and four bay horses. Have they nothing else to do? – or is it that they *will* do nothing but stare, swagger, and be idle in the streets.

CHAPTER V

CORK – THE AGRICULTURAL SHOW – FATHER MATHEW

A man has no need to be an agriculturist in order to take a warm interest in the success of the Irish Agricultural Society, and to see what vast good may result from it to the country. The National Education scheme – a noble and liberal one, at least as far as a stranger can see, which might have united the Irish people, and brought peace into this most distracted of all countries – failed unhappily of one of its greatest ends. The Protestant clergy have always treated the plan with bitter hostility: and I do believe, in withdrawing from it, have struck the greatest blow to themselves as a body, and to their own influence in the country, which has been dealt to them for many a year. Rich, charitable, pious, well-educated, to be found in every parish in Ireland, had they chosen to fraternise with the people and the plan, they might have directed the educational movement; they might have attained the influence which is now given over entirely to the priest; and when the present generation, educated in the National Schools, were grown up to manhood, they might have had an interest in almost every man in Ireland. Are they as pious, and more polished, and better educated, than their neighbours, the priests? There is no doubt of it; and by constant communion with the people, they would have gained all the benefits of the comparison, and advanced the interests of their religion far more than now they can hope to do. Look at the National School: throughout the country it is commonly by the chapel side – it is a Catholic school, directed and fostered by the priest; and as no people are more eager for learning, more apt to receive it, or more grateful for kindness, than the Irish, he gets all the gratitude of the scholars who flock to the school, and all the future influence over them, which naturally and justly comes to him. The Protestant wants to better the condition of these people: he says that the woes of the country are owing to its prevalent religion; and in order to carry his plans of amelioration into effect, he obstinately refuses to hold communion with those whom he is desirous to convert to what he believes are sounder principles and purer doctrines. The clergyman will reply, that points of principle prevented him: with this fatal doctrinal objection, it is not, of course, the province of a layman to meddle; but this is clear, that the parson might have had an influence over the country, and he would not; that he might have rendered the Catholic population friendly to him, and he would not: but instead, has added one cause of estrangement and hostility more to the many which already existed against him. This is one of the attempts at union in Ireland, and one can't but think with the deepest regret and sorrow of its failure.

Mr O'Connell and his friends set going another scheme for advancing the prosperity of the country, – the notable project of home manufacturers, and of a coalition against foreign importation. This was a union certainly, but a union of a different sort to that noble and peaceful one which the National Education Board proposed. It was to punish England, while it pretended to secure the independence of Ireland, by shutting out our manufactures from the Irish markets, which were one day or other, it was presumed, to be filled by native produce. Large bodies of tradesmen and private persons in Dublin and other towns in Ireland associated together, vowing to purchase no articles of ordinary consumption or usage, but what were manufactured in the country. This bigoted, old-world scheme of restriction – not much more liberal than Swing's crusade against the threshing machines, or the coalitions in England against machinery, failed, as it deserved to do. For the benefit of a few tradesmen, who might find their account in selling at dear rates their clumsy and imperfect manufactures, it was found impossible to tax a people that are already poor enough; nor did the party take into account the cleverness of the merchants across the sea, who were by no means disposed to let go their Irish customers. The famous Irish frieze uniform which was to distinguish these patriots, and which Mr O'Connell lauded so loudly and so simply, came over made at half-price from Leeds and Glasgow, and was retailed as real Irish by many worthies who had been first to join the union. You may still see shops here and there with their pompous announcement of 'Irish Manufactures;' but the scheme is long gone to ruin – it could not stand against the vast force of English and Scotch capital and machinery, any more than the Ulster spinning-wheel against the huge factories and steam-engines which one may see about Belfast.

The scheme of the Agricultural Society is a much more feasible one; and if, please God, it can be carried out, likely to give not only prosperity to the country, but union likewise in a great degree. As yet, Protestants and Catholics concerned in it, have worked well together; and it is a blessing to see them meet upon *any* ground without heartburning and quarrelling. Last year, Mr Purcell, who is well known in Ireland as the principal main coach contractor for the country, – who himself employs more workmen in Dublin than perhaps any other person there, and has also more land under cultivation than most of the great landed proprietors in the country, – wrote a letter to the newspapers, giving his notions of the fallacy of the exclusive-dealing system, and pointing out at the same time how he considered the country might be benefited – by agricultural improvement, namely. He spoke of the neglected state of the country, and its amazing natural fertility; and, for the benefit of all, called upon the landlords and landholders to use their interest and develop its vast agricultural resources. Manufactures are at best but of slow growth, and demand not only time, but capital; meanwhile, until the habits of the people should grow to be such as to render manufactures feasible, there was a great neglected treasure, lying under their feet, which might be the source of prosperity to all. He pointed out the superior methods of husbandry employed in Scotland and England, and the great results obtained upon soils naturally much poorer; and, taking the Highland Society for an example, the establishment of which had done so much for the prosperity of Scotland, he proposed the formation in Ireland of a similar association.

The letter made an extraordinary sensation throughout the country. Noblemen and gentry of all sides took it up; and numbers of these wrote to Mr Purcell, and gave him their cordial adhesion to the plan. A meeting was held, and the Society formed: subscriptions were set on foot, headed by the Lord-Lieutenant (Fortescue) and the Duke of Leinster, each with a donation of 200*l.*; and the trustees had soon 5000*l.* at their disposal; with, besides, an annual revenue of 1000*l.* The subscribed capital is funded; and political subjects strictly excluded. The Society has a show yearly in one of the principal towns of Ireland; it corresponds with the various local agricultural associations throughout the country; encourages the formation of new ones; and distributes prizes and rewards. It has further in contemplation to establish a large Agricultural school for farmers' sons; and has formed in Dublin an Agricultural Bazaar and Museum.

It was the first meeting of the Society which we were come to see at Cork. Will it be able to carry its excellent intentions into effect? Will the present enthusiasm of its founders and members continue? Will one political party or another get the upper hand in it? One can't help thinking of these points with some anxiety – of the latter especially: as yet, happily, the clergy of either side have kept aloof, and the union seems pretty cordial and sincere.

There are in Cork, as no doubt in every town of Ireland sufficiently considerable to support a plurality of hotels, some especially devoted to the Conservative and Liberal parties. Two dinners were to be given apropos of the Agricultural meeting; and in order to conciliate all parties, it was determined that the Tory landlord should find the cheap ten-shilling dinner for one thousand, the Whig landlord the genteel guinea dinner for a few select hundreds.

I wish Mr Cuff, of the Freemasons' Tavern, could have been at Cork to take a lesson from the latter gentleman; for he would have seen that there are means of having not merely enough to eat, but enough of the very best, for the sum of a guinea; that persons can have not only wine, but good wine; and, if inclined (as some topers are on great occasions) to pass to another bottle, – a second, a third, or a fifteenth bottle, for what I know, is very much at their service. It was a fine sight to see Mr Mc'Dowall presiding over an ice-well, and extracting the bottles of Champagne. With what calmness he did it! How the corks popped, and the liquor fizzed, and the agriculturalists drank the bumpers off! And how good the wine was too – the greatest merit of all! Mr Mc'Dowall did credit to his liberal politics by his liberal dinner.

'Sir,' says a waiter whom I asked for currant jelly for the haunch – (there were a dozen such smoking on various parts of the table – think of that, Mr Cuff!) – 'Sir,' says the waiter, 'there's no jelly, but I've brought you *some very fine lobster sauce.*' I think this was the most remarkable speech of the evening, not excepting that of my Lord Bernard, who, to three hundred gentlemen, more or less connected with farming, had actually the audacity to quote the words of the great agricultural poet of Rome –

'O fortunatos nimium sua si,' &c.

How long are our statesmen in England to continue to back their opinions by the Latin grammar? Are the Irish agriculturalists so *very* happy, if they did but know it, at least those out of doors? Well, those within were jolly enough. Champagne and claret, turbot and haunch, are gifts of the *justissima tellus*, with which few husbandmen will be disposed to quarrel; – no more let us quarrel either with eloquence after dinner.

If the Liberal landlord has shown his principles in his dinner, the Conservative certainly showed his; by conserving as much profit as possible for himself. We sat down one thousand to some two hundred and fifty cold joints of meat. Every man was treated with a pint of wine, and very bad too, so that there was the less cause to grumble because more was not served. Those agriculturalists who had a mind to drink whiskey and water, had to pay extra for their punch. Nay, after shouting in vain for half-an-hour to a waiter for some cold water, the unhappy writer could only get it by promising a shilling. The sum was paid on delivery of the article; but as everybody round was thirsty too, I got but a glassful from the decanter, which only served to make me long for more. The waiter (the rascal!) promised more, but never came near us afterwards: he had got his shilling, and so left us in a hot room, surrounded by a thousand hot fellow-creatures, one of them making a dry speech. The agriculturalists were not on this occasion *nimium fortunati.*

To have heard a nobleman, however, who discoursed the meeting, you would have fancied that we were the luckiest mortals under the broiling July sun. He said he could conceive nothing more delightful than to see 'on proper occasions,' – 'mind, *on proper occasions!*' – 'the landlord mixing with his tenantry; and to look around him at a scene like this, and see *the condescension* with which the gentry mingled with the farmers!' Prodigious condescension truly! This neat speech seemed to me an oratoric slap on the face to about nine hundred and seventy persons present; and being one of the latter, I began to hiss by way of acknowledgment of the compliment, and hoped that a strong party would have destroyed the harmony of the evening, and done likewise. But not one hereditary bondsman would join in the compliment – and they were quite right too. The old lord who talked about condescension is one of the greatest and kindest landlords in Ireland. If he thinks he condescends by doing his duty and mixing with men as good as himself, the fault lies with the latter. Why are they so ready to go down on their knees to my lord? A man can't help 'condescending' to another who will persist in kissing his shoe-strings. They respect rank in England – the people seem almost to adore it here.

As an instance of the intense veneration for lords which distinguishes this county of Cork, I may mention what occurred afterwards. This members of the Cork Society gave a dinner to their guests of the Irish Agricultural Association. The founder of the latter, as Lord Downshire stated, was Mr Purcell: and as it was agreed on all hands that the Society so founded was likely to prove of the greatest benefit to the country, one might have supposed that any compliment paid to it might have been paid to it through its founder. Not so. The Society asked the lords to dine, and Mr Purcell to meet the lords.

After the grand dinner came a grand ball, which was indeed one of the gayest and prettiest sights ever seen; nor was it the less agreeable, because the ladies of the city mixed with the ladies from the country, and vied with them in grace and beauty. The charming gaiety and frankness of the Irish ladies have been noted and admired by every foreigner who has had the good fortune to mingle in their society; and I hope it is not detracting from the merit of the upper classes, to say that the lower are not a whit less pleasing. I never saw in any country such a general grace of manner and *ladyhood*. In the midst of their gaiety, too, it must be remembered that they are the chastest of women, and that no country in Europe can boast of such a general purity.

In regard of the Munster ladies, I had the pleasure to be present at two or three evening parties at Cork, and must say that they seem to excel the English ladies not only in wit and vivacity, but in the still more important article of the toilette. They are as well dressed as French women, and incomparably handsomer; and if ever this book reaches a thirtieth edition, and I can find out better words to express admiration, they shall be inserted here. Among the ladies' accomplishments, I may mention that I have heard in two or three private families such fine music as is rarely to be met with out of a capital. In one house we had a supper and songs afterwards, in the old honest fashion. Time was in Ireland when the custom was a common one; but the world grows languid as it grows genteel; and I fancy it requires more than ordinary spirit and courage now for a good old gentleman, at the head of his kind family table, to strike up a good old family song.

The delightful old gentleman who sung the song here mentioned could not help talking of the temperance movement with a sort of regret, and said that all the fun had gone out of Ireland since Father Mathew banished the whiskey from it. Indeed, any stranger going amongst the people can perceive that they are now anything but gay. I have seen a great number of crowds and meetings of people in all parts of Ireland, and found them all gloomy. There is nothing like the merry-making one reads of in the Irish novels. Lever and Maxwell must be taken as chroniclers of the old times – the pleasant but wrong old times – for which one can't help having an antiquarian fondness.

On the day we arrived at Cork, and as the passengers descended from 'the drag,' a stout, handsome, honest-looking man, of some two-and-forty years, was passing by, and received a number of bows from the crowd around. It was

Theobald Mathew

with whose face a thousand little print-shop windows had already rendered me familiar. He shook hands with the master of the carriage very cordially, and just as cordially with the master's coachman, a disciple of temperance, as at least half Ireland is at present. The day after the famous dinner at MacDowall's, some of us came down rather late, perhaps in consequence of the events of the night before – (I think it was Lord Bernard's quotation from Virgil, or else the absence of the currant jelly for the venison, that occasioned a slight headache among some of us, and an extreme longing for soda-water,) – and there was the Apostle of Temperance seated at the table drinking tea. Some of us felt a little ashamed of ourselves, and did not like to ask somehow for the soda-water in such an awful presence as that. Besides, it would have been a confession to a Catholic priest, and, as a Protestant, I am above it.

The world likes to know how a great man appears even to a valet-de-chambre, and I suppose it is one's vanity that is flattered in such rare company to find the great man quite as unassuming as the very smallest personage present; and so like to other mortals, that we would not know him to be a great man at all, did we not know his name, and what he had done. There is nothing remarkable in Mr Mathew's manner, except that it is exceedingly simple, hearty, and manly, and that he does not wear the down-cast, demure look which, I know not why, certainly characterises the chief part of the gentlemen of his profession. Whence comes that general scowl which darkens the faces of the Irish priesthood? I have met a score of these reverend gentlemen in the country, and not one of them seemed to look or speak frankly, except Mr Mathew, and a couple more. He is almost the only man, too, that I have met in Ireland, who, in speaking of public matters, did not talk as a partisan. With the state of the country, of landlord, tenant, and peasantry, he seemed to be most curiously and intimately acquainted; speaking of their wants, differences, and the means of bettering them, with the minutest practical knowledge. And it was impossible in hearing him, to know, but from previous acquaintance with his character, whether he was Whig or Tory, Catholic or Protestant. Why does not Government make a Privy Councillor of him? – that is, if he would honour the Right Honourable body by taking a seat amongst them. His knowledge of the people is prodigious, and their confidence in him as great; and what a touching attachment that is which these poor fellows show to anyone who has their cause at heart – even to anyone who says he has!

Avoiding all political questions, no man seems more eager than he for the practical improvement of this country. Leases and rents, farming improvements, reading societies, music societies – he was full of these, and of his schemes of temperance above all. He never misses a chance of making a convert, and has his hand ready and a pledge in his pocket for sick or poor. One of his disciples in a livery coat came into the room with a tray – Mr Mathew recognised him, and shook him by the hand directly; so he did with the strangers who were presented to him; and not with a courtly popularity-hunting air, but, as it seemed, from sheer hearty kindness, and a desire to do every one good.

When breakfast was done – (he took but one cup of tea, and says that, from having been a great consumer of tea and refreshing liquids before, a small cup of tea, and one glass of water at dinner, now serve him for his day's beverage) – he took the ladies of our party to see his burying-ground – a new and handsome cemetery, lying a little way out of the town, and where, thank God! Protestants and Catholics may lie together, without clergymen quarrelling over their coffins.

It is a handsome piece of ground, and was formerly a botanic garden; but the funds failed for that undertaking, as they have for a thousand other public enterprises in this poor disunited country; and so it has been converted into a *hortus siccus* for us mortals. There is already a pretty large collection. In the midst is a place for Mathew himself – honour to him living or dead! – Meanwhile, numerous stately monuments have been built, flowers planted here and there over dear remains, and the garden in which they lie is rich, green, and beautiful. Here is a fine statue, by Hogan, of a weeping genius that broods over the tomb of an honest merchant and clothier of the city. He took a liking to the artist, his fellow townsman, and ordered his own monument, and had the gratification to see it arrive from Rome a few weeks before his death. A prettier thing even than the statue is the tomb of a little boy, which has been shut in by a large and curious *grille* of iron-work. The father worked it, a blacksmith, whose darling the child was, and he spent three years in hammering out this mausoleum. It is the beautiful story of the pot of ointment, told again at the poor blacksmith's anvil; and who can but like him for placing this fine gilded cage over the body of his poor little one? Presently you come to a Frenchwoman's tomb, with a French epitaph, by a French husband, and a pot of artificial flowers in a niche – a wig, and a pot of rouge, as it were, just to make the dead look passably well. It is *his* manner of showing his sympathy for an immortal soul that has passed away. The poor may be buried here for nothing; and here, too, once more, THANK GOD! each may rest without priests or parsons scowling hell-fire at his neighbour unconscious under the grass.

CHAPTER VI

CORK – THE URSULINE CONVENT

There is a large Ursuline convent at Blackrock, near Cork, and a lady who had been educated there was kind enough to invite me to join a party to visit the place. Was not this a great privilege for a heretic? I have peeped into convent chapels abroad, and occasionally caught glimpses of a white veil or black gown; but to see the pious ladies in their own retreat was quite a novelty – much more exciting than the exhibition of Long Horns and Short Horns, by which we had to pass on our road to Blackrock.

The three miles' ride is very pretty. As far as nature goes, she has done her best for the neighbourhood, and the noble hills on the opposite coast of the river, studded with innumerable pretty villas, and garnished with fine trees and meadows, the river itself dark blue, under a brilliant cloudless heaven, and lively with its multiplicity of gay craft, accompany the traveller along the road, except here and there where the view is shut out, by fine avenues of trees, a beggarly row of cottages, or a villa wall. Rows of dirty cabins, and smart bankers' country houses, meet one at every turn; nor do the latter want for fine names, you may be sure. The Irish grandiloquence displays itself finely in the invention of such; and, to the great inconvenience, I should think, of the postman, the names of the houses appear to change with the tenants, for I saw many old houses with new placards in front, setting forth the *last* title of the house.

I had the box of the carriage (a smart vehicle that would have done credit to the ring), and found the gentleman by my side very communicative. He named the owners of the pretty mansions and lawns visible on the other side of the river: they appear almost all to be merchants, who have made their fortunes in the city. In the like manner, though the air of the town is extremely fresh and pure to a pair of London lungs, the Cork shopkeeper is not satisfied with it, but contrives for himself a place (with an euphonious name, no doubt) in the suburbs of the city. These stretch to a great extent along the beautiful, liberal-looking banks of the stream.

I asked the man about the Temperance, and whether he was a temperance man? He replied by pulling a medal out of his waistcoat pocket, saying that he always carried it about with him for fear of temptation. He said that he took the pledge two years ago, before which time, as he confessed, he had been a sad sinner in the way of drink. 'I used to take,' said he, 'from eighteen to twenty glasses of whiskey a day; I was always at the drink; I'd be often up all night at the public; I was turned away by my present master on account of it;' – and all of a sudden he resolved to break off. I asked him whether he had not at first experienced ill health from the suddenness of the change in his habits; but he said – and let all persons meditating a conversion from liquor remember the fact – that the abstinence never affected him in the least, but that he went on growing better and better in health every day, stronger and more able of mind and body.

The man was a Catholic, and in speaking of the numerous places of worship along the road as we passed, I'm sorry to confess dealt some rude cuts with his whip, regarding the Protestants. Coachman as he was, the fellow's remarks seemed to be correct; for it appears that the religious world of Cork is of so excessively enlightened a kind, that one church will not content one pious person; but that, on the contrary, they will be at Church of a morning, at Independent Church of an afternoon, at a Darbyite congregation of an evening, and so on, gathering excitement or information from all sources by which they could come at. Is not this the case? are not some of the ultra-serious as eager after a new preacher, as the ultra-worldly for a new dancer? don't they talk and gossip about him as much? Though theology from the coach-box is rather questionable, (after all, the man was just as much authorised to propound his notions as many a fellow from an amateur pulpit,) yet he certainly had the right here, as far as his charge against certain Protestants went.

The reasoning from it was quite obvious, and I'm sure was in the man's mind, though he did not utter it, as we drove by this time into the convent gate. 'Here,' says coachman, 'is *our* church. *I* don't drive my master and mistress from church to chapel, from chapel to conventicle, hunting after new preachers every Sabbath. I bring them every Sunday and set them down at the same place, where they know that everything they hear *must* be right. Their fathers have done the same thing before them; and the young ladies and gentlemen will come here too; and all the new-fangled doctors and teachers may go roaring through the land, and still here we come regularly, not caring a whit for the vagaries of others, knowing that we ourselves are in the real old right original way.'

I am sure this is what the fellow meant by his sneer at the Protestants, and their gadding from one doctrine to another; but there was no call and no time to have a battle with him, as by this time we had entered a large lawn covered with haycocks, and prettily, as I think, ornamented with a border of blossoming potatoes, and drove up to the front door of the convent. It is a huge old square house, with many windows, having probably been some flaunting squire's residence; but the nuns have taken off somewhat from its rakish look, by flinging out a couple of wings with chapels, or buildings like chapels, at either end.

A large, lofty, clean, trim hall was open to a flight of steps, and we found a young lady in the hall, playing, instead of a pious sonata – which I vainly thought was the practice in such godly seminaries of learning – that abominable rattling piece of music called *la Violette*, which it has been my lot to hear executed by other young ladies; and which (with its like) has always appeared to me to be constructed upon this simple fashion – to take a tune, and then, as it were, to fling it down and upstairs. As soon as the young lady playing 'the Violet' saw us, she quitted the hall, and retired to an inner apartment, where she resumed that delectable piece at her leisure. Indeed there were pianos all over the educational part of the house.

We were shown into a gay parlour, (where hangs a pretty drawing, representing the melancholy old convent which the Sisters previously inhabited in Cork,) and presently Sister No. Two-Eight made her appearance – a pretty and graceful lady, thus attired.

"'Tis the prettiest nun of the whole house,' whispered the lady who had been educated at the convent; and, I must own, that slim, gentle, and pretty as this young lady was, and calculated with her kind smiling face and little figure, to frighten no one in the world, a great six-foot Protestant could not help looking at her with a little tremble. I had never been in a nun's company before; I'm afraid of such – I don't care to own – in their black mysterious robes and awful veils. As priests in gorgeous vestments, and little rosy incense-boys in red, bob their heads and knees up and down before altars, or  clatter silver pots full of smoking odours, I feel I don't know what sort of thrill and secret creeping terror. Here I was, in a room with a real live nun, pretty and pale – I wonder has she any of her sisterhood immured in *oubliettes* down below; is her poor little, weak, delicate body scarred all over with scourgings, iron-collars, hair-shirts? What has she had for dinner to-day? – as we passed the refectory there was a faint sort of vapid nunlike vegetable smell, speaking of fasts and wooden platters; and I could picture to myself silent sisters eating their meal – a grim old yellow one in the reading-desk, croaking out an extract from a sermon for their edification.

But is it policy, or hypocrisy, or reality? These nuns affect extreme happiness and content with their condition; a smiling beatitude, which they insist belongs peculiarly to them, and about which the only doubtful point is the manner in which it is produced before strangers. Young ladies educated in convents have often mentioned this fact, how the nuns persist in declaring and proving to them their own extreme enjoyment of life.

Were all the smiles of that kind-looking Sister Two-Eight

perfectly sincere? Whenever she spoke her face was lighted up
with one. She seemed perfectly radiant with happiness, trip-
ping lightly before us, and distributing kind compliments to
each, which made me in a very few minutes forget the
introductory fright which her poor little presence had occasioned.

She took us through the hall, (where was the vegetable
savour before mentioned,) and showed us the contrivance by
which the name of Two-Eight was ascertained. Each nun has a
number, or a combination of numbers, prefixed to her name:
and a bell is pulled a corresponding number of times, by
which each sister knows when she is wanted. Poor souls! are
they always on the look-out for the bell, that the ringing of it
should be supposed infallibly to awaken their attention?

From the hall the sister conducted us through ranges of
apartments, and I had almost said avenues of pianofortes,
whence here and there a startled pensioner would rise, *hinnuleo
similis*, at our approach, seeking a *pavidam matrem*, in the
person of a demure old stout mother hard by. We were taken
through a hall decorated with series of pictures of Pope Pius
VI, – wonderful adventures, truly, in the life of the gentle old
man. In one you see him gracefully receiving a Prince and
Princess of Russia (tremendous incident!). The Prince has a
pigtail, the Princess powder and a train, the Pope a – but never
mind, we shall never get through the house at this rate.

Passing through Pope Pius's gallery, we came into a long,
clean, lofty passage, with many little doors on each side; and
here I confess my heart began to thump again. These were the
doors of the cells of the Sisters. Bon Dieu! and is it possible
that I shall see a nun's cell? Do I not recollect the nun's cell in
'The Monk,' or in 'The Romance of the Forest?' or, if not
there, at any rate, in a thousand noble romances, read in early
days of half-holiday perhaps – romances at twopence a
volume.

Come in, in the name of the saints! Here is the cell. I took
off my hat, and examined the little room with much curious
wonder and reverence. There was an iron bed, with comfortable curtains of green serge. There was a little clothes-chest of
yellow-wood, neatly cleaned, and a wooden chair beside it,
and a desk on the chest, and about six pictures on the wall –

little religious pictures: a saint with gilt paper round him; the Virgin showing on her breast a bleeding heart, with a sword run through it; and the other sad little subjects, calculated to make the inmate of the cell think of the sufferings of the saints and martyrs of the church. Then there was a little crucifix, and a wax-candle on the ledge; and here was the place where the poor black-veiled things were to pass their lives for ever!

After having seen a couple of these little cells, we left the corridors in which they were, and were conducted with a sort of pride on the nun's part, I thought, into the grand room of the convent – a parlour with pictures of saints and a gay paper, and a series of small fineries, such only as women very idle know how to make: there were some portraits in the room, one an atrocious daub of an ugly old woman, surrounded by children still more hideous. Somebody had told the poor nun that this was a fine thing, and she believed it – Heaven bless her! – quite implicitly; nor is the picture of the ugly old Canadian woman the first reputation that has been made this way.

Then from the fine parlour we went to the museum. I don't know how we should be curious of such trifles; but the chronicling of small-beer is the main business of life – people only differing, as Tom Moore wisely says in one of his best poems, about their own peculiar tap. The poor nun's little collection of gimcracks was displayed in great state; there were spars in one drawer; and I think a Chinese shoe and some Indian wares in another; and some medals of the Popes, and a couple of score of coins; and a clean glass case, full of antique works of French theology of the distant period of Louis XV, to judge by the bindings – and this formed the main part of the museum. 'The chief objects were gathered together by a single nun,' said the sister with a look of wonder; as she went prattling on, and leading us hither and thither, like a child showing her toys.

What strange mixture of pity and pleasure is it which comes over you sometimes, when a child takes you by the hand, and leads you up solemnly to some little treasure of its own – a feather or a string of glass beads? I declare I have often looked at such with more delight than at diamonds; and felt the same sort of soft wonder examining the nun's little treasure-chamber. There was something touching in the very poverty of it: – had it been finer, it would not have been half so good.

And now we had seen all the wonders of the house but the chapel, and thither we were conducted; all the ladies of our party kneeling down as they entered the building, and saying a short prayer.

This, as I am on sentimental confessions, I must own affected me too. It was a very pretty and tender sight. I should have liked to kneel down too, but was ashamed; our northern usages not encouraging – among men at least – that sort of abandonment of dignity. Do any of us dare to sing psalms at church? and don't we look with rather a sneer at a man who does?

The chapel had nothing remarkable in it except a very good organ, as I was told, for we were allowed only to see the exterior of that instrument, our pious guide with much pleasure removing an oil-cloth which covered the mahogany. At one side of the altar is a long high *grille*, through which you see a hall, where the nuns have their stalls, and sit in chapel time; and beyond this hall is another small chapel, with a couple of altars, and one beautiful print in one of them – a German Holy Family – a prim, mystical, tender piece, just befitting the place.

In the *grille* is a little wicket and a ledge before it. It is to this wicket that women are brought to kneel; and a bishop is in the chapel on the other side, and takes their hands in his, and receives their vows. I had never seen the like before, and own that I felt a sort of shudder at looking at the place. There rest the girl's knees as she offers herself up, and forswears the sacred affections which God gave her; there she kneels and denies for ever the beautiful duties of her being – no tender maternal yearnings – no gentle attachments are to be had for her or from her, – there she kneels and commits suicide upon her heart. O honest Martin Luther! thank God, you came to pull that infernal, wicked, unnatural altar down – that cursed Paganism! Let people, solitary, worn out by sorrow or oppressed with extreme remorse, retire to such places: fly and beat your breasts in caverns and wildernesses, O women, if you will, but be Magdalens first. It is shameful that any young girl, with any vocation, however seemingly strong, should be allowed to bury herself in this small tomb of a few acres. Look at yonder nun, – pretty, smiling, graceful, and young, – what has God's world done to *her*, that she should run from it, or she done to the world, that she should avoid it? What call has she to give up all her duties and affections; and would she not be best serving God with a husband at her side, and a child on her knee?

The sights in the house having been seen, the nun led us through the grounds and gardens. There was the hay in front, a fine yellow corn-field at the back of the house, and a large melancholy-looking kitchen garden, in all of which places the nuns, for certain hours in the day, are allowed to take recreation. 'The nuns here are allowed to amuse themselves more than ours at New Hall,' said a little girl who is educated at that English Convent; 'do you know that here the nuns may make hay?' What a privilege is this! We saw none of the black sisterhood availing themselves of it however: the hay was neatly piled into cocks and ready for housing; so the poor souls must wait until next year before they can enjoy this blessed sport once more.

Turning into a narrow gate with the nun at our head, we found ourselves in a little green, quiet inclosure – it was the burial ground of the convent. The poor things know the places where they are to lie; she who was with us talked smilingly of being stretched there one day, and pointed out the resting-place of a favourite old sister who had died three months back, and been buried in the very midst of the little ground. And here they come to live and die. The gates are open, but they never go out. All their world lies in a dozen acres of ground; and they sacrifice their lives in early youth, many of them passing from the grave up-stairs in the house to the one scarcely narrower in the churchyard here; and are seemingly not unhappy.

I came out of the place quite sick; and looking before me, – there, thank God! was the blue spire of Monkstown church soaring up into the free sky – a river in front rolling away to the sea – liberty, sunshine, all sorts of glad life and motion, round about: and I couldn't but thank heaven for it, and the Being whose service is freedom, and who has given us affections that we may use them – not smother and kill them;

and a noble world to live in, that we may admire it and Him who made it – not shrink from it, as though we dared not live there, but must turn our backs upon it and its bountiful Provider.

And, in conclusion, if that most cold-blooded and precise of all personages, the respectable and respected English reader, may feel disposed to sneer at the above sentimental homily, or to fancy that it has been written for effect – let him go and see a convent for himself. I declare I think for my part, that we have as much right to permit Sutteeism in India, as to allow women in the United Kingdom to take these wicked vows, or Catholic bishops to receive them; and that government has as good a right to interpose in such cases, as the police has to prevent a man from hanging himself, or the doctor to refuse a glass of prussic acid to any one who may have a wish to go out of the world.

CHAPTER VII

CORK

Amidst the bustle and gaieties of the Agricultural meeting, the working-day aspect of the city was not to be judged of: but I passed a fortnight in the place afterwards, during which time it settled down to its calm and usual condition. The flashy French and plated-goods shops, which made a show for the occasion of the meeting, disappeared; you were no longer crowded and jostled by smart male and female dandies in walking down Patrick-street or the Mall: the poor little theatre had scarcely a soul in its bare benches; I went once, but the dreadful brassband of a dragoon regiment blew me out of doors. This music could be heard much more pleasantly at some distance off in the street.

One sees in this country many a grand and tall iron gate leading into a very shabby field covered with thistles; and the simile to the gate will in some degree apply to this famous city of Cork, – which is certainly not a city of palaces, but of which the outlets are magnificent. That towards Killarney leads by the Lee – the old avenue of Mardyke, and the rich green pastures stretching down to the river – and as you pass by the portico of the county-gaol, as fine and as glancing as a palace, you see the wooded heights on the other side of the fair stream, crowded with a thousand pretty villas and terraces, presenting every image of comfort and prosperity. The entrance from Cove has been mentioned before; nor is it easy to find anywhere a nobler, grander, and more cheerful scene.

Along the quays up to Saint Patrick's-bridge there is a certain bustle. Some forty ships may be lying at anchor along the walls of the quay: and its pavements are covered with goods of various merchandize; here a cargo of hides; yonder a company of soldiers, their kits, and their Dollies, who are taking leave of the red-coats at the steamer's side. Then you shall see a fine, squeaking, shrieking drove of pigs embarking by the same conveyance, and insinuated into the steamer by all sorts of coaxing, threatening, and wheedling. Seamen are singing and yeehoing on board; grimy colliers smoking at the liquor-shops along the quay; and as for the bridge – there is a crowd of idlers on *that*, you may be sure, sprawling over the balustrade for ever and ever, with long ragged coats, steeple hats, and stumpy doodeens.

Then along the coal-quay you may see a clump of jingle-drivers, who have all a word for your honour; and in Patrick-street, at three o'clock, when 'the Rakes of Mallow' gets under weigh (a cracked old coach with the paint rubbed off, some smart horses, and an exceedingly dingy harness) – at three o'clock, you will be sure to see at least forty persons waiting to witness the departure of the said coach; so that the neighbourhood of the inn has an air of some bustle.

At the other extremity of the town, if it be assize time, you will see some five hundred persons squatting in the court-house, or buzzing and talking within; the rest of the respectable quarter of the city is pretty free from anything like bustle. There is no more life in Patrick-street than in Russell-square of a sunshiny day; and as for the Mall, it is as lonely as the chief street of a German Residenz.

I have mentioned the respectable quarter of the city – for there are quarters in it swarming with life, but of such a frightful kind as no pen need care to describe; alleys where the odours and rags and darkness are so hideous, that one runs frightened away from them. In some of them, they say, not the policeman, only the priest, can penetrate. I asked a Roman Catholic clergyman of the city to take me into some of these haunts, but he refused very justly; and indeed a man may be quite satisfied with what he can see in the mere outskirts of the districts, without caring to penetrate further. Not far from the quays is an open space where the poor hold a market or bazaar. Here is liveliness and business enough; ragged women chattering and crying their beggarly wares; ragged boys gloating over dirty apple and pie-stalls; fish frying, and raw and stinking; clothes-booths, where you might buy a wardrobe for scarecrows; old nails, hoops, bottles, and marine wares; old battered furniture, that has been sold against starvation. In the streets round about this place, on a sunshiny day all the black gaping windows and mouldy steps are covered with squatting lazy figures – women, with bare breasts, nursing babies, and leering a joke as you pass by – ragged children paddling everywhere. It is but two minutes walk out of Patrick-street, where you come upon a fine flashy shop of plated goods, or a grand French emporium of dolls, walking-sticks, carpet-bags, and perfumery. The markets hard by have a rough, old-fashioned, cheerful look; its a comfort after the misery to hear a red butcher's wife crying after you to buy an honest piece of meat.

The poor-house, newly established, cannot hold a fifth part of the poverty of this great town; the richer inhabitants are untiring in their charities, and the Catholic clergyman before mentioned took me to see a delivery of rice, at which he presides every day until the potatoes shall come in. This market, over which he presides so kindly, is held in an old bankrupt warehouse, and the rice is sold considerably under the prime cost to hundreds of struggling applicants who come when lucky enough to have wherewithal to pay.

That the city contains much wealth is evidenced by the number of handsome villas round about it, where the rich merchants dwell; but the warehouses of the wealthy provision merchants make no show to the stranger walking the streets; and of the retail shops, if some are spacious and handsome, most look as if too big for the business carried on within. The want of ready-money was quite curious. In three of the principal shops I purchased articles, and tendered a pound in exchange – not one of them had silver enough; and as for a five-pound note, which I presented at one of the topping booksellers, his boy went round to various places in vain, and finally set forth to the bank, where change was got. In another small shop I offered half-a-crown to pay for a sixpenny article – it was all the same. 'Tim,' says the good woman, 'run out in a hurry and fetch the gentleman change.' Two of the shopmen, seeing an Englishman, were very particular to tell me in what years they themselves had been in London. It seemed a merit in these gentlemen's eyes to have once dwelt in that city; and I see in the papers continually ladies advertising as governesses, and specifying particularly that they are 'English ladies.'

I received six 5*l.* post-office orders; I called four times on as
many different days at the post-office before the capital could
be forthcoming, getting on the third application 20*l.* (after
making a great clamour, and vowing that such things were
unheard-of in England), and on the fourth call the remaining
10*l.* I saw poor people who may have come from the country
with their orders, refused payment of an order of some 40*s.*;
and a gentleman who tendered a pound note in payment of a
foreign letter, told to 'leave his letter and pay some other
time.' Such things could not take place in the hundred and
second city in England; and as I do not pretend to doctrinise at
all, I leave the reader to draw his own deductions with regard
to the commercial condition and prosperity of the second city
in Ireland.

Half-a-dozen of the public buildings I saw were spacious
and shabby beyond all Cockney belief. Adjoining the Imperial
Hotel is a great, large, handsome, desolate reading-room,
which was founded by a body of Cork merchants and
tradesmen, and is the very picture of decay. Not Palmyra –
not the Russell Institution in Great Coram-street – present
more melancholy appearances of faded greatness. Opposite
this is another institution, called the Cork Library, where
there are plenty of books and plenty of kindness to the
stranger; but the shabbiness and faded splendour of the place
are quite painful. There are three handsome Catholic churches
commenced of late years; not one of them is complete. Two
want their porticoes; the other is not more than thirty feet
from the ground; and according to the architectural plan was
to rise as high as a cathedral. There is an institution, with a fair
library of scientific works; a museum, and a drawing-school
with a supply of casts. The place is in yet more dismal
condition than the library. The plasters are spoiled incurably
for want of a sixpenny feather-brush; the dust lies on the
walls, and nobody seems to heed it. Two shillings a year
would have repaired much of the evil which has happened to
this institution; and it is folly to talk of inward dissensions and
political differences as causing the ruin of such institutions.
Kings or law don't cause or cure dust and cobwebs; but
indolence leaves them to accumulate, and imprudence will not
calculate its income, and vanity exaggerates its own powers,

and the fault is laid upon that tyrant of a sister kingdom. The whole country is filled with such failures; swaggering beginnings that could not be carried through; grand enterprises begun dashingly, and ending in shabby compromises or downright ruin.

I have said something in praise of the manners of the Cork ladies: in regard of the gentlemen, a stranger too must remark the extraordinary degree of literary taste and talent amongst them, and the wit and vivacity of their conversation. The love for literature seems to an Englishman doubly curious. What, generally speaking, do a company of grave gentlemen and ladies in Baker-street know about it? Who ever reads books in the City, or how often does one hear them talked about at a Club? The Cork citizens are the most book-loving men I ever met. The town has sent to England a number of literary men of reputation too, and is not a little proud of their fame. Everybody seemed to know what Maginn was doing, and that Father Prout had a third volume ready, and what was Mr Croker's last article in the *Quarterly*. The young clerks and shopmen seemed as much *au fait* as their employers, and many is the conversation I heard about the merits of this writer or that – Dickens, Ainsworth, Lover, Lever.

I think, in walking the streets and looking at the ragged urchins crowding there, every Englishman must remark that the superiority of intelligence is here, and not with us. I never saw such a collection of bright-eyed, wild, clever, eager faces. Mr Maclise has carried away a number of them in his memory; and the lovers of his admirable pictures will find more than one Munster countenance under a helmet in company of Macbeth, or in a slashed doublet alongside of Prince Hamlet, or in the very midst of Spain in company with Signor Gil Blas. Gil Blas himself came from Cork, and not from Oviedo.

I listened to two boys almost in rags: they were lolling over the quay balustrade, and talking about *one of the Ptolemys*! and talking very well too. One of them had been reading in 'Rollin,' and was detailing his information with a great deal of eloquence and fire. Another day, walking in the Mardyke, I followed three boys, not half so well-dressed as London errand-boys: one was telling the other about Captain Ross's voyages, and spoke with as much brightness and intelligence as the best-read gentleman's son in England could do. He was as much of a gentleman too, the ragged young student; his manner as good, though perhaps more eager and emphatic; his language was extremely rich, too, and eloquent. Does the reader remember his school days, when half-a-dozen lads in the bed rooms took it by turns to tell stories? how poor the language generally was, and how exceedingly poor the imagination! Both of those ragged Irish lads had the making of gentlemen, scholars, orators, in them. Apropos of love of reading, let me mention here a Dublin story. Dr Lever, the celebrated author of 'Harry Lorrequer,' went into Dycer's stables to buy a horse. The groom who brought the animal out, directly he heard who the gentleman was, came out and touched his cap, and pointed to a little book in his pocket in a pink cover. '*I can't do without it, sir,*' says the man. It was 'Harry Lorrequer.' I wonder does any one of Mr Rymell's groom take in 'Pickwick,' or would they have any curiosity to see Mr Dickens, should he pass that way?

The Corkagians are eager for a Munster University; asking for, and having a very good right to, the same privilege which has been granted to the chief city of the north of Ireland. It would not fail of being a great benefit to the city and to the country too, which would have no need to go so far as Dublin for a school of letters and medicine; nor Whig and Catholic, for the most part, to attend a Tory and Protestant University. The establishing of an open college in Munster would bring much popularity to any ministry that should accord such a boon. People would cry out, 'Popery and Infidelity,' doubtless, as they did when the London University was established; as the same party in Spain would cry out, 'Atheism and Heresy.' But the time, thank God! is gone by in England when it was necessary to legislate for *them*; and Sir Robert Peel, in giving his adherence to the National Education scheme, has sanctioned the principle of which this so much longed-for college would only be a consequence.

The medical charities and hospitals are said to be very well arranged, and the medical men of far more than ordinary skill. Other public institutions are no less excellent. I was taken over the Lunatic Asylum, where everything was conducted with admirable comfort, cleanliness, and kindness; and as for the county gaol, it is so neat, spacious, and comfortable, that we can only pray to see every cottager in the country as cleanly, well lodged, and well fed, as the convicts are. They get a pound of bread and a pint of milk twice a day: there must be millions of people in this wretched country, to whom such food would be a luxury that their utmost labours can never by possibility procure for them; and in going over this admirable institution, where everybody is cleanly, healthy, and well-clad, I could not but think of the rags and filth of the horrid starvation market before mentioned; so that the prison seemed almost a sort of premium for vice. But the people like their freedom, such as it is, and prefer to starve and be ragged as they list. They will not go to the poor-houses, except at the greatest extremity, and leave them on the slightest chance of existence elsewhere.

Walking away from this palace of a prison, you pass amidst all sorts of delightful verdure, cheerful gardens, and broad green luscious pastures down to the beautiful river Lee. On one side the river shines away towards the city with its towers and purple steeples: on the other it is broken by little waterfalls, and bound in by blue hills, an old castle towering in the distance, and innumerable parks and villas lying along the pleasant wooded banks. How beautiful the scene is, how rich and how happy! Yonder, in the old Mardyke avenue, you hear the voices of a score of children, and along the bright green meadows, where the cows are feeding, the gentle shadows of the clouds go playing over the grass. Who can look at such a charming scene but with a thankful swelling heart?

In the midst of your pleasure, three beggars have hobbled up, and are howling supplications to the Lord. One is old and blind, and so diseased and hideous, that straightway all the pleasure of the sight round about vanishes from you – that livid ghastly face interposing between you and it. And so it is throughout the south and west of Ireland; the traveller is haunted by the face of the popular starvation. It is not the exception, it is the condition of the people. In this fairest and richest of countries, men are suffering and starving by mil-lions. There are thousands of them at this minute stretched in the sunshine at their cabin doors with no work, scarcely any food, no hope seemingly. Strong countrymen are lying in bed *'for the hunger'* – because a man lying on his back does not need so much food as a person a-foot. Many of them have torn up the unripe potatoes from their little gardens, to exist now, and must look to winter, when they shall have to suffer starvation and cold too. The epicurean, and traveller for pleasure, had better travel anywhere than here; where there are miseries that one does not dare to think of; where one is always feeling how helpless pity is, and how hopeless relief, and is perpetually made ashamed of being happy.

I have just been strolling up a pretty little height called Grattan's Hill, that overlooks the town and the river, and where the artist that comes Cork-wards may find many subjects for his pencil. There is a kind of pleasure ground at the top of this eminence – a broad walk that draggles up to a ruined wall, with a ruined niche in it, and a battered stone bench. On the side that shelves down to the water are some beeches, and opposite them a row of houses from which you see one of the prettiest prospects possible – the shining river with the craft along the quays, and the busy city in the distance, the active little steamers puffing away towards Cove, the farther bank crowned with rich woods, and pleasant-looking country-houses, – perhaps they are tumbling rickety and ruinous as those houses close by us, but you can't see the ruin from here.

What a strange air of forlorn gaiety there is about the place! – the sky itself seems as it if did not know whether to laugh or cry, so full is it of clouds and sunshine. Little fat, ragged, smiling children are clambering about the rocks, and sitting on mossy door-steps, tending other children yet smaller, fatter, and more dirty. 'Stop till I get you a posy,' (pronounced *pawawawsee*) cries one urchin to another. 'Tell me who is it ye love, Jooly,' exclaims another, cuddling a red-faced infant with a very dirty nose. More of the same race are perched about the summer-house, and two wenches with large purple feet are flapping some carpets in the air. It is a wonder the carpets will bear this kind of treatment at all, and do not be off at once to mingle with the elements. I never saw things that hung to life by such a frail thread.

This dismal pleasant place is a suburb of the second city in Ireland, and one of the most beautiful spots about the town. What a prim, bustling, active, green-railinged, tea-gardened, gravel-walked place would it have been in the five-hundredth town in England! – but you see the people can be quite as happy in the rags and without the paint, and I hear a great deal more heartiness and affection from these children than from their fat little brethren across the Channel.

If a man wanted to study ruins here is a house close at hand, not forty years old no doubt, but yet as completely gone to wrack as Netley Abbey. It is quite curious to study that house; and a pretty ruinous fabric of improvidence, extravagance, happiness, and disaster may the imagination build out of it! In the first place, the owners did not wait to finish it before they went to inhabit it! This is written in just such another place; – a handsome drawing-room with a good carpet, a lofty marble mantelpiece, and no paper to the walls. The door is prettily painted white and blue, and though not six weeks old, a great piece of the wood-work is off already (Peggy uses it to prevent the door from banging to); and there are some fine chinks in every one of the panels, by which my neighbour may see all my doings.

A couple of score of years, and this house will be just like yonder place on Grattan's Hill.

Like a young prodigal, the house begins to use its constitution too early; and when it should yet (in the shape of carpenters and painters) have all its masters and guardians to watch and educate it, my house on Grattan's Hill must be a man at once, and enjoy all the privileges of strong health! I would lay a guinea they were making punch in that house before they could keep the rain out of it! that they had a dinner party and ball before the floors were firm or the wainscots painted, and a fine tester-bed in the best room, where my lady might catch cold in state, in the midst of yawning chimneys, creaking window-sashes, and smoking plaster.

Now look at the door of the coach-house, with its first coat of paint seen yet, and a variety of patches to keep the feeble barrier together. The loft was arched once, but a great corner has tumbled at one end, leaving a gash that unites the windows with the coach-house door. Several of the arch-stones are removed, and the whole edifice is about as rambling and disorderly as – as the arrangement of this book, say. Very tall tufts of mouldy moss are on the drawing-room windows, with long white heads of grass. As I am sketching this; – *honk!* – a great lean sow comes trampling through the slush within the court-yard, breaks down the flimsy apparatus of rattling boards and stones which had passed for the gate, and walks with her seven squeaking little ones to disport on the grass on the hill.

The drawing-room of the tenement mentioned just now, with its pictures and pulleyless windows, and lockless doors, was tenanted by a friend who lodged there with a sick wife and a couple of little children; one of whom was an infant in arms. It is not, however, the lodger, who is an Englishman, but the kind landlady and her family, who may well be described here – for their like are hardly to be found on the other side of the Channel. Mrs Fagan is a young widow who has seen better days, and that portrait over the grand mantelpiece is the picture of her husband that is gone, a handsome young man, and well to do at one time as a merchant. But the widow (she is as pretty, as lady-like, as kind, and as neat as ever widow could be) has little left to live upon but the rent of her lodgings and her furniture, of which we have seen the best in the drawing-room.

She has three fine children of her own; there is Minny, and Katey, and Patsey, and they occupy indifferently the dining-room on the ground-floor or the kitchen opposite: where in the midst of a great smoke sits an old nurse by a copper of potatoes which is always bubbling and full. Patsey swallows quantities of them that's clear – his cheeks are as red and shining as apples, and when he roars, you are sure that his lungs are in the finest condition. Next door to the kitchen is the pantry, and there is a bucket-full of the before-mentioned fruit, and a grand service of china for dinner and dessert. The kind young widow shows them with no little pride, and says with reason that there are few lodging-houses in Cork that can match such china as that. They are relics of the happy old times when Fagan kept his gig and horse, doubtless, and had his friends to dine – the happy prosperous days which she has exchanged for poverty and the sad black gown.

Patsey, Minny, and Katey have made friends with the little English people up-stairs; the elder of whom, in the course of a month, has as fine a Munster brogue as ever trolled over the lips of any born Corkagian. The old nurse carries out the whole united party to walk, with the exception of the English baby, that jumps about in the arms of a countrywoman of her own. That is, unless one of the four Miss Fagans take her; for four of them there are, four *other* Miss Fagans, from eighteen downwards to fourteen: – handsome, fresh, lively, dancing bouncing girls. You may always see two or three of them smiling at the parlour window, and they laugh and turn away their heads when any young fellow looks and admires them.

Now, it stands to reason that a young widow of five-and-twenty can't be the mother of four young ladies of eighteen downwards, and, if anybody wants to know how they come to be living with the poor widow their cousin, the answer is, they are on a visit. Peggy the maid says, their papa is a gentleman of property, and can 'spend his eight hundred a year.'

Why don't they remain with the old gentleman then, instead of quartering on the poor young widow, who has her own little mouths to feed? The reason is, the old gentleman has gone and *married his cook*; and the daughters have quitted him in a body, refusing to sit down to dinner with a person who ought by rights to be in the kitchen. The whole family (the Fagans are of good family) take the quarrel up, and here are the young people under shelter of the widow.

Four merrier, tender-hearted girls are not to be found in all Ireland; and the only subject of contention amongst them is, which shall have the English baby; they are nursing it, and singing to it, and dandling it by turns all day long. When they are not singing to the baby, they are singing to an old piano; such an old, wiry, jingling, wheezy piano! It has plenty of work, playing jigs and song accompaniments between meals, and acting as a sideboard at dinner. I am not sure that it is at rest at night either; but have shrewd suspicion that it is turned into a four-post bed. And for the following reason:-

Every afternoon, at four o'clock, you see a tall old gentleman walking leisurely to the house. He is dressed in a long great coat with huge pockets, and in the huge pockets are sure to be some big apples for all the children – the English child amongst the rest, and she generally has the biggest one. At seven o'clock, you are sure to hear a deep voice shouting PAGGY, in an awful tone – it is the old gentleman calling for his 'materials;' which Peggy brings without any farther ado; and a glass of punch is made, no doubt, for everybody. Then the party separates: the children and the old nurse have long since trampled up-stairs. Peggy has the kitchen for her sleeping apartment; and the four young ladies make it out somehow in the back drawing-room. As for the old gentleman, he reposes in the parlour; and it must be some-where about the piano, for there is no furniture in the room except that, a table, a few old chairs, a work-box, and a couple of albums.

The English girl's father met her in the street one day, talking confidentially with a tall old gentleman in a great-coat. 'Who's your friend?' says the Englishman afterwards to the little girl. 'Don't you know him, papa?' said the child in the purest brogue. 'Don't you know him? – THAT'S UNCLE JAMES!' And so it was: in this kind, poor, generous, bare-backed house, the English child found a set of new relations; little rosy brothers and sisters to play with, kind women to take the place of the almost dying mother, a good old Uncle James to bring her home apples and care for her – one and all ready to share their little pittance with her, and to give her a place in their simple friendly hearts. God Almighty bless the widow and her mite, and all the kind souls under her roof!

How much goodness and generosity – how much purity, fine feeling, nay happiness, may dwell amongst the poor whom we have been just looking at! Here, thank God, is an instance of this happy and cheerful poverty: and it is good to look, when one can, at the heart that beats under the thread-bare coat, as well as the tattered old garment itself. Well, please Heaven, some of those people whom we have been looking at, are as good, and not much less happy: but though they are accustomed to their want, the stranger does not reconcile himself to it quickly; and I hope no Irish reader will be offended at my speaking of this poverty, not with scorn or ill-feeling, but with hearty sympathy and good-will.

One word more regarding the Widow Fagan's house. When Peggy brought in coals for the drawing-room fire, she carried them – in what do you think? 'In a coal-scuttle, to be sure,' says the English reader, down on you as sharp as a needle.

No, you clever Englishman, it wasn't a coal-scuttle.

'Well, then, it was in a fire-shovel,' says that brightest of wits, guessing again.

No, it *wasn't* a fire-shovel, you heaven-born genius: and you might guess from this until Mrs Snooks called you up to coffee, and you would never find out. It was in something which I have already described in Mrs Fagan's pantry.

'Oh, I have you now it, was the bucket where the potatoes were: the thlatternly wetch!' says Snooks.

Wrong again – Peggy brought up the coals – in a CHINA PLATE!

Snooks turned quite white with surprise, and almost chokes himself with his port. 'Well,' says he, 'of all the *wum* countwith that I ever wead of, hang me if Ireland ithn't the *wummetht*. Coalth in a plate! Mawyann, do you hear that? In Ireland they alwayth thend up their coalth in a plate!'

CHAPTER VIII

FROM CORK TO BANTRY; WITH AN ACCOUNT OF THE CITY OF SKIBBEREEN

That light four-inside four-horse coach, 'the Skibbereen Perseverance,' brought me fifty-two miles to-day, for the sum of three-and sixpence, through a country which is as usual some-what difficult to describe. We issued out of Cork by the western road, in which, as the guide-book says, there is something very imposing. 'The magnificence of the county courthouse, the extent, solidity, and characteristic sternness of the county gaol,' were visible to us for a few minutes; when, turning away southward from the pleasant banks of the stream, the road took us towards Bandon, through a country that is bare and ragged looking, but yet green and pretty; and it always seems to me, like the people, to look cheerful in spite of its wretchedness, or, more correctly, to look tearful and cheerful at the same time.

The coach, like almost every other public vehicle I have seen in Ireland, was full to the brim and over it. What can send these restless people travelling and hurrying about from place to place as they do? I have heard one or two gentlemen hint that they had 'business' at this place or that; and found afterwards that one was going a couple of score of miles to look at a mare, another to examine a setter-dog, and so on. I did not make it my business to ask on what errand the gentlemen on the coach were found, though two of them, seeing an Englishman, very good-naturedly began chalking out a route for him to take, and showing a sort of interest in his affairs which is not with us generally exhibited. The coach, too, seemed to have the elastic hospitality of some Irish houses; it accommodated an almost impossible number. For the greater part of the journey the little guard sat on the roof among the carpet-bags, holding in one hand a huge tambour frame, in the other a band-box marked 'Foggarty, Hatter;' (what is there more ridiculous in the name of Foggarty than in that of Smith? and yet, had Smith been the name, I never should have laughed at or remarked it); presently by his side clambered a green-coated policeman with his carbine, and we had a talk about the vitriol throwers at Cork, and the sentence just passed upon them. The populace has decidedly taken part with the vitriol throwers; parties of dragoons were obliged to surround the avenues of the court; and the judge who sentenced them was abused as he entered his carriage, and called an old villain, and many other opprobious names.

This case the reader very likely remembers. A saw-mill was established at Cork, by which some four hundred sawyers were thrown out of employ. In order to deter the proprietors of this and all other mills from using such instruments farther, the sawyers determined to execute a terrible vengeance, and cast lots among themselves which of their body should fling vitriol into the faces of the mill-owners. The men who were chosen by the lot were to execute this horrible office on pain of death, and did so, — frightfully burning and blinding one of the gentlemen owning the mill. Great rewards were offered for the apprehension of the criminals, and at last one of their own body came forward as an approver, and the four principal actors in this dreadful outrage were sentenced to be transported for life. Crowds of the ragged admirers of these men were standing round 'the magnificent county court-house' as we passed the building. Ours is a strange life indeed. What a history of poverty and barbarity, and crime and even kindness, was that by which we passed before the magnificent county court-house, at eight miles an hour! What a chapter might a philosopher write on them! Look yonder at those two hundred ragged fellow-subjects of yours; they are kind, good, pious, brutal, starving. If the priest tells them, there is scarce any penance they will not perform, there is scarcely any pitch of misery which they have not been known to endure, nor any degree of generosity of which they are not capable: but if a man comes among these people, and can afford to take land over their heads, or if he invents a machine which can work more economically than their labour, they will shoot the man down without mercy, murder him, or put him to horrible tortures, and glory almost in what they do. There stand the men; they are only separated from us by a few paces; they are as fond of their mothers and children as we are; their gratitude for small kindnesses shown to them is extraordinary; they are Christians as we are; but, interfere with their interests, and they will murder you without pity.

It is not revenge so much which these poor fellows take, as a brutal justice of their own. Now, will it seem a paradox to say in regard to them and their murderous system, that the way to put an end to the latter, is to *kill them no more*? Let the priest be able to go amongst them and say, the law holds a man's life so sacred, that it will on *no account* take it away. No man, nor no body of men, has a right to meddle with human life; not the Commons of England any more than the Commons of Tipperary. This may cost two or three lives, probably, until such time as the system may come to be known and understood; but which will be the greatest economy of blood in the end?

By this time the vitriol-men were long passed away, and we began next to talk about the Cork and London steam-boats; which are made to pay on account of the number of paupers whom the boats bring over from London, at the charge of that city. The passengers found here, as in everything else almost which I have seen as yet, another instance of the injury which England inflicts on them. 'As long as these men are strong and can work,' says one, 'you keep them; when they are in bad health, you fling them upon us.' Nor could I convince him, that the agricultural gentlemen were perfectly free to stay at home if they liked: that we did for them what was done for English paupers – sent them, namely, as far as possible on the way to their parishes; nay, that some of them (as I have seen with my own eyes) actually saved a bit of money during the harvest, and took this cheap way of conveying it and themselves to their homes again. But nothing would convince the gentleman, that there was not some wicked scheming on the part of the English in the business; and, indeed, I find upon almost every other subject, a peevish and puerile suspiciousness, which is worthy of France itself.

By this time we came to a pretty village called Innishannon, upon the noble banks of the Bandon river; leading for three miles by a great number of pleasant gentlemen's seats to Bandon town. A good number of large mills were on the banks of the stream; and the chief part of them, as in Carlow, useless. One mill we saw, was too small for the owner's great speculations; and so he built another and larger one: the big mill cost him 10,000*l.*, for which his brothers went security; and, a lawsuit being given against the mill-owner, the two mills stopped, the two brothers went off, and yon fine old house, in the style of Anne, with terraces and tall chimneys, one of the oldest country-houses I have seen in Ireland, is now inhabited by the natural son of the mill-owner, who has more such interesting progeny. Then we came to a tall, comfortable house, in a plantation; opposite to which was a stone castle, in its shrubberies on the other side of the road. The tall house in the plantation shot the opposite side of the road in a duel, and nearly killed him; on which the opposite side of the road built this castle, *in order to plague* the tall house. They are good friends now, but the opposite side of the road ruined himself in building his house. I asked, Is the house finished? – '*A good deal of it is,*' was the answer. – And then we came to a brewery, about which was a similar story of extravagance and ruin; but, whether before or after entering Bandon, does not matter.

We did not, it appears, pass through the best part of Bandon: I looked along one side of the houses in the long street through which we went, to see if there was a window without a broken pane of glass, and can declare on my conscience, that every single window had three broken panes: there we changed horses, in a market-place surrounded, as usual, by beggars: then we passed through a suburb, still more wretched and ruinous than the first street, and which, in very large letters, is called DOYLE STREET: and the next stage was at a place called Dunmanway.

Here it was market-day, too, and, as usual, no lack of attendants: swarms of peasants in their blue cloaks, squatting by their stalls here and there. – There is a little, miserable, old market-house; where a few women were selling buttermilk; another, bullocks' hearts, liver, and such like scraps of meat; another had dried mackerel on a board; and plenty of people huckstering of course. Round the coach came crowds of raggery, and blackguards fawning for money. I wonder who

gives them any? I have never seen any one give yet; and were they not even so numerous that it would be impossible to gratify them all, there is something in their cant and supplications to the Lord so disgusting to me, that I could not give a halfpenny.

In regard of pretty faces, male or female, this road is very unfavourable. I have not seen one for fifty miles; though as it was market-day all along the road, we have had the opportunity to examine vast numbers of countenances. The women are, for the most part, stunted, short, with flat Tartar faces; and the men no handsomer. Every woman has bare legs, of course; and as the weather is fine, they are sitting outside their cabins, with the pig, and the geese, and the children sporting around.

Before many doors we saw a little flock of these useful animals, and the family pig almost everywhere. You might see him browsing and poking along the hedges, his fore and hind leg attached with a wisp of hay, to check his propensity to roaming. Here and there were a small brood of turkeys;

now and then a couple of sheep or a single one grazing upon a scanty field, of which the chief crop seemed to be thistles and stone; and, by the side of the cottage, the potato-field always.

The character of the landscape for the most part is bare and sad, except here and there in the neighbourhood of the towns, where people have taken a fancy to plant, and where nature has helped them, as it almost always will in this country. If we saw a field with a good hedge to it, we were sure to see a good crop inside. Many a field was there that had neither crop nor hedge. We passed by and over many pretty streams, running bright through brilliant emerald meadows; and I saw a thousand charming pictures, which want as yet an Irish Berghem. A bright road winding up a hill; on it a country cart, with its load stretching a huge shadow; the before-mentioned emerald pastures and silver rivers in the fore-ground; a noble sweep of hills rising up from them, and contrasting their magnificent purple with the green; in the extreme distance the clear cold outline of some far-off mountains, and the white clouds tumbled about in the blue sky overhead. It has no doubt struck all persons who love to look at nature, how different the skies are in different countries. I fancy Irish or French clouds are as characteristic as Irish or French landscapes. It would be well to have a Daguerreotype and get a series of each. Some way beyond Dunmanna the road takes us through a noble savage country of rocks and heath. Nor must the painter forget long black tracts of bog here and there, and the water glistening brightly at the places where the turf has been cut away. Add to this, and chiefly by the banks of rivers, a ruined old castle or two: some were built by the Danes, it is said. The O'Connors the O'Mahonys, the O'Driscolls, were lords of many others, and their ruined towers may be seen here and along the sea.

Near Dunmanna that great coach, 'the Skibbereen Industry,' dashed by us at seven miles an hour; a wondrous vehicle. There were gaps between every one of the panels; you could see daylight through-and-through it. Like our machine it was full, with three complementary sailors on the roof, as little harness as possible to the horses, and as long stages as horses can well endure – ours were each eighteen-mile stages. About eight miles from Skibbereen a one-horse car met us, and carried away an offshoot of passengers to Bantry. Five passengers and their luggage, and a very wild, steep road; all this had one poor little pony to overcome! About the towns there were some show of gentlemen's cars, smart and well appointed, and on the road great numbers of country carts; an army of them met us coming from Skibbereen, and laden with gray sand for manure.

Before you enter the city of Skibbereen, the tall new Poor-house presents itself to the eye of the traveller; of the common model, being a bastard-Gothic edifice, with a profusion of cottage-ornée (is cottage masculine or feminine in French ?) of cottage-ornée roofs, and pinnacles, and insolent-looking stacks of chimneys. It is built for 900 people, but as yet not more than 400 have been induced to live in it, the beggars preferring the freedom of their precarious trade to the dismal certainty within its walls. Next we come to the chapel, a very large respectable-looking building of dark-gray stone; and presently, behold, by the crowd of blackguards in waiting, the 'Skibbereen Perseverance' has found its goal, and you are inducted to the 'Hotel' opposite.

Some gentlemen were at the coach besides those of lower degree. Here was a fat fellow with large whiskers, a geranium, and a cigar; yonder a tall handsome old man that I would swear was a dragoon on half-pay. He had a little cap, a Taglioni coat, a pair of beautiful spaniels, and a pair of knee-breeches which showed a very handsome old leg; and his object seemed to be to invite everybody to dinner as they got off the coach – no doubt he has seen the 'Skibbereen Perseverance' come in ever since it was a 'Perseverance.' It is wonderful to think what will interest men in prisons or country towns!

There is a dirty coffee-room, with a strong smell of whiskey; indeed three young 'materialists' are employed at the moment: and I hereby beg to offer an apology to three other gentlemen – the Captain, another, and the gentleman of the geranium, who had caught hold of a sketching-stool which is my property, and were stretching it, and sitting upon it, and wondering, and talking of it, when the owner came in, and they bounced off to their seats like so many school-boys. Dirty as the place was this was no reason why it should not produce an exuberant dinner of trouts and Kerry mutton; after which Dan the Waiter, holding up a dingy decanter, asks how much whiskey I'd have.

That calculation need not be made here; and if a man sleeps well has he any need to quarrel with the appointments of his bed-room, and spy out the deficiences of the land? As it was Sunday, it was impossible for me to say what sort of shops 'the active and flourishing town' of Skibbereen contains. There were some of the architectural sort, viz. with gilt letters and cracked mouldings, and others into which I thought I saw the cows walking, but it was only into their little cribs and paddocks at the back of the shops. There is a trim Wesleyan chapel, without any broken windows; a neat church standing modestly on one side; the lower street crawls along the river to a considerable extent, having by-streets and boulevards of cabins here and there.

The people came flocking into the place by hundreds, and you saw their blue cloaks dotting the road and the bare open plains beyond. The men came with shoes and stockings to-day, the women all bare-legged, and many of them might be seen washing their feet in the stream, before they went up to the chapel. The street seemed to be lined on either side with blue cloaks, squatting along the doorways as is their wont. Among these, numberless cows were walking to and fro, and pails of milk passing, and here and there a hound or two went stalking about. Dan, the waiter, says they are hunted by the handsome old Captain who was yesterday inviting everybody to dinner.

Anybody at eight o'clock of a Sunday morning in summer may behold the above scene from a bridge just outside the town. He may add to it the river, with one or two barges lying idle upon it; a flag flying at what looks like a customhouse; bare country all around; and the chapel before him, with a swarm of the dark figures round about it.

I went into it, not without awe (for, as I confessed before, I always feel a sort of tremor on going into a Catholic place of worship: the candles, and altars, and mysteries, the priest, and his robes, and nasal chaunting, and wonderful genuflexions, will frighten me as long as I live). The chapel yard was filled with men and women; a couple of shabby old beadles were at the gate, with copper shovels to collect money; and inside the chapel four or five hundred people were on their knees, and scores more of the blue-mantles came in, dropping their curtsies as they entered, and then taking their places on the flags.

And now the pangs of hunger beginning to make themselves felt, it became necessary for your humble servant (after making several useless applications to a bell, which properly declined to work on Sundays) to make a personal descent to the inn-kitchen, where was not a bad study for a painter. It was a huge room, with a peat fire burning, and a staircase walking up one side of it, on which stair was a damsel in a partial though by no means picturesque dishabille. The cook had just come in with a great frothing pail of milk, and sat with her arms folded; the hostler's boy sat dangling his legs from the table, the hostler was dandling a noble little boy of a year old, at whom Mrs Cook likewise grinned delighted. Here, too, sat Mr Dan, the waiter; and no wonder the breakfast was delayed, for all three of these worthy domestics seemed delighted with the infant.

He was handed over to the gentleman's arms for the space of thirty seconds; the gentleman being the father of a family, and of course an amateur.

'Say Dan for the gentleman,' says the delighted Cook.

'Dada,' says the baby; at which the assembly grinned with joy: and Dan promised I should have my breakfast 'in a hurry.'

But of all the wonderful things to be seen in Skibbereen, Dan's pantry is the most wonderful – every article within is a make-shift, and has been ingeniously perverted from its original destination. Here lie bread, blacking, fresh-butter, tallow-candles, dirty knives – all in the same cigar-box, with snuff, milk, cold bacon, brown-sugar, broken tea-cups, and bits of soap. No pen can describe that establishment, as no English imagination could have conceived it. But lo! the sky has cleared after a furious fall of rain – (in compliance with Dan's statement to that effect 'that the weather would be fine') – and a car is waiting to carry us to Loughine.

Although the description of Loughine can make but a poor figure in a book, the ride thither is well worth the traveller's

short labour. You pass by one of the cabin-streets out of the
town, into a country which for a mile is rich with grain,
though bare of trees; then through a boggy bleak district,
from which you enter into a sort of sea of rocks, with patches
of herbage here and there. Before the traveller, almost all the
way, is a huge pile of purple mountain, on which, as one
comes nearer, one perceives numberless waves and breaks, as
you see small waves on a billow in the sea – then clambering
up a hill, we look down upon a bright green flat of land with
the lake beyond it, girt round by gray melancholy hills. The
water may be a mile in extent – a cabin tops the mountain here
and there; gentlemen have erected one or two anchorite
pleasure-houses on the banks, as cheerful as a summer-house
would be on Salisbury plain. I felt not sorry to have seen this
lonely lake, and still happier to leave it. There it lies with crags
all round it, in the midst of desolate plains: it escapes
somewhere to the sea; its waters are salt: half a dozen boats lie
here and there upon its banks, and we saw a small crew of
boys plashing about and swimming in it, laughing and
yelling. It seemed a shame to disturb the silence so.

The crowd of swaggering 'gents' (I don't know the corresponding phrase in the Anglo-Irish vocabulary to express a
shabby dandy) awaiting the Cork mail, which kindly goes
twenty miles out of its way to accommodate the town of
Skibbereen, was quite extraordinary. The little street was
quite blocked up with shabby gentlemen, and shabby beggars,
awaiting this daily phenomenon. The man who had driven us
to Loughine, did not fail to ask for his fee as driver; and then,
having received it, came forward in his capacity of boots and
received another remuneration. The ride is desolate, bare, and
yet beautiful. There are a set of hills that keep one company
the whole way; they were partially hidden in a gray sky,
which flung a general hue of melancholy too over the green
country through which we passed. There was only one
wretched village along the road, but no lack of population;
ragged people who issued from their cabins as the coach
passed, or were sitting by the way-side. Everybody seems
sitting by the way-side here: one never sees this general repose
in England – a sort of ragged lazy contentment. All the
children seem to be on the watch for the coach; waited very

knowingly and carefully their opportunity, and then hung on by scores behind. What a pleasure to run over flinty roads with bare feet, to be whipped off, and to walk back to the cabin again! These were very different cottages to those neat ones I had seen in Kildare. The wretchedness of them is quite painful to look at; many of the potato-gardens were half dug up, and it is only the first week in August, near three months before the potato is ripe and at full growth; and the winter still six months away. There were chapels occasionally, and smart new-built churches – one of them has a congregation of ten souls, the coachman told me. Would it not be better that the clergyman should receive them in his room, and that the Church building-money should be bestowed otherwise?—

At length, after winding up all sorts of dismal hills speckled with wretched hovels, a ruinous mill every now and then, black bog-lands, and small winding streams, breaking here and there into little falls, we come upon some ground well tilled and planted, and descending (at no small risk, from stumbling horses) a bleak long hill, we see the water before us, and turning to the right by the handsome little park of Lord Bearhaven, enter Bantry. The harbour is beautiful. Small mountains in green undulations rising on the opposite side; great gray ones further back; a pretty island in the midst of the water, which is wonderfully bright and calm. A handsome yacht, and two or three vessels with their Sunday colours out were lying in the bay. It looked like a sea-port scene at a theatre, gay, cheerful, neat, and picturesque. At a little distance the town, too, is very pretty. There are some smart houses on the quays, a handsome court-house as usual, a fine large hotel, and plenty of people flocking round the wonderful coach.

The town is most picturesquely situated, climbing up a wooded hill, with numbers of neat cottages here and there, an ugly church with an air of pretension, and a large grave Roman Catholic chapel, the highest point of the place. The main street was as usual thronged with the squatting blue cloaks, carrying on their eager trade of buttermilk and green apples, and such cheap wares. With the exception of this street and the quay, with their whitewashed and slated houses, it is a town of cabins. The wretchedness of some of them is quite curious; I tried to make a sketch of a row which lean against an old wall, and are built upon a rock that tumbles about in the oddest and most fantastic shapes, with a brawling waterfall dashing down a channel in the midst. These are it appears, the beggars' houses; any one may build a lodge against that wall, rent free, and such places were never seen! As for drawing them, it was in vain to try; one might as well make a sketch of a bundle of rags. An ordinary pig-stye in England is really more comfortable. Most of them were not six feet long or five feet high, built of stones huddled together, a hole being left for the people to creep in at, a ruined thatch to keep out some little portion of the rain. The occupiers of these places sat at their doors in tolerable contentment, or the children came down and washed their feet in the water. I declare I believe a Hottentot kraal has more comforts in it: even to write of the place makes one unhappy, and the words move slow. But in the midst of all this misery there is an air of actual cheerfulness; and go but a few score yards off, and these wretched hovels lying together look really picturesque and pleasing.

CHAPTER IX

RAINY DAYS AT GLENGARIFF

A smart two-horse car takes the traveller thrice a week from Bantry to Killarney, by way of Glengariff and Kenmare. Unluckily, the rain was pouring down furiously as we passed to the first-named places, and we had only opportunity to see a part of the astonishing beauty of the country. What sends picturesque tourists to the Rhine and Saxon Switzerland? within five miles round the pretty inn of Glengariff there is a country of the magnificence of which no pen can give an idea. I would like to be a great prince, and bring a train of painters over to make, if they could, and according to their several capabilities, a set of pictures of the place. Mr Creswick would find such rivulets and waterfalls, surrounded by a luxuriance of foliage and verdure that only his pencil can imitate. As for Mr Catermole, a red-shanked Irishman should carry his sketching-books to all sorts of wild noble heights, and vast, rocky valleys, where he might please himself by piling crag upon crag, and by introducing, if he had a mind, some of the wild figures which peopled this country in old days. There is the Eagles' Nest, for instance, regarding which the Guide-book gives a pretty legend. The Prince of Bantry being conquered by the English soldiers, fled away, leaving his Princess and children to the care of a certain faithful follower of his, who was to provide them with refuge and food. But the whole country was overrun by the conquerors; all the flocks driven away by them, all the houses ransacked, and the crops burnt off the ground, and the faithful servitor did not know where he should find a meal or a resting-place for the unhappy Princess O'Donovan.

He made, however, a sort of shed by the side of a mountain, composing it of sods and stones so artfully that no one could tell but that it was a part of the hill itself; and here, having

speared or otherwise obtained a salmon, he fed their Highnesses for the first day; trusting to Heaven for a meal when the
salmon should be ended.

The Princess O'Donovan and her princely family soon
came to an end of the fish: and cried out for something more.

So the faithful servitor, taking with him a rope and his little
son Shamus, mounted up to the peak where the eagles rested;
and, from the spot to which he climbed, saw their nest and the
young eaglets in it, in a cleft below the precipice.

'Now,' said he, 'Shamus my son, you must take these thongs
with you, and I will let you down by the rope,' (it was a straw-rope
which he had made himself, and though it might be considered a
dangerous thread to hang by in other countries, you'll see plenty of
such contrivances in Ireland to the present day).

'I will let you down by the rope, and you must tie the
thongs round the necks of the eaglets not so as to choke them,
but to prevent them from swallowing much.' So Shamus
went down and did as his father bade him, and came up again
when the eaglets were doctored.

Presently the eagles came home; one bringing a rabbit and the other a grouse. These they dropped into the nest for the young ones; and soon after went away in quest of other adventures.

Then Shamus went down into the eagles' nest again, gutted the grouse and rabbit, and left the garbage to the eaglets (as was their right), and brought away the rest. And so the Princess and Princes had game that night for their supper. How long they lived in this way, the Guide-book does not say: but let us trust that the Prince, if he did not come to his own again, was at least restored to his family, and decently mediatised: and, for my part, I have very little doubt but that Shamus, the gallant young eagle robber, created a favourable impression upon one of the young Princesses, and (after many adventures in which he distinguished himself,) was accepted by her Highness for a husband, and by her princely parents for a gallant son-in-law.

And here, while we are travelling to Glengariff, and ordering painters about with such princely liberality, (by the way Mr Stanfield should have a boat in the bay, and paint both rock and sea at his ease,) let me mention a wonderful, awful incident of real life which occurred on the road. About four miles from Bantry, at a beautiful wooded place, hard by a mill and waterfall, up rides a gentleman to the car with his luggage, going to Killarney races. The luggage consisted of a small carpet-bag and a pistol-case. About two miles further on, a fellow stops the car: 'Joe,' says he, 'my master is going to ride to Killarney, so you please to take his luggage.' The luggage consisted of a small carpet-bag, and – a pistol-case as before. Is this a gentleman's usual travelling baggage in Ireland?

As there is more rain in this country than in any other, and as therefore, naturally, the inhabitants should be inured to the weather, and made to despise an inconvenience which they cannot avoid, the travelling-conveyances are arranged so that you may get as much practice in being wet as possible. The traveller's baggage is stowed in a place between the two rows of seats, and which is not inaptly called the well, as in a rainy season you might possibly get a bucket full of water out of that orifice. And I confess, I saw, with a horrid satisfaction, the pair of pistol-cases lying in this moist aperture, with water

pouring above them, and lying below them; nay, prayed that
all such weapons might one day be consigned to the same fate.
But as the waiter at Bantry, in his excessive zeal to serve me,
had sent my portmanteau back to Cork by the coach, instead
of allowing me to carry it with me to Killarney, and as the rain
had long since begun to insinuate itself under the seat-cushion,
and through the waterproof apron of the car, I dropped off at
Glengariff, and dried the only suit of clothes I had by the
kitchen-fire. The inn is very pretty; some thorn-trees stand
before it, where many bare-legged people were lolling in spite
of the weather. A beautiful bay stretches out before the house,
the full tide washing the thorn-trees; mountains rise on either
side of the little bay, and there is an island, with a castle on it,
in the midst, near which a yacht was moored. But the
mountains were hardly visible for the mist, and the yacht,
island, and castle looked as if they had been washed against the
flat gray sky in Indian-ink.

The day did not clear up sufficiently to allow me to make
any long excursion about the place, or indeed, to see a very
wide prospect round about it: at a few hundred yards, most of
the objects were enveloped in mist; but even this, for a lover of
the picturesque, had its beautiful effect, for you saw the hills in
the foreground pretty clear, and covered with their wonderful
green, while immediately behind them rose an immense blue
mass of mist and mountain that served to *relieve* (to use the
painter's phrase) the nearer objects. Annexed to the hotel is a
flourishing garden, where the vegetation is so great that the
landlord told me it was all he could do to check the trees from
growing: round about the bay, in several places, they come
clustering down to the water edge, nor does the salt water
interfere with them.

Winding up a hill to the right, as you quit the inn, is the
beautiful road to the cottage and park of Lord Bantry. One or
two parties, on pleasure bent, went so far as the house, and
were partially consoled for the dreadful rain which presently
poured down upon them, by wine, whiskey, and
refreshments, which the liberal owner of the house sent out to
them. I myself had only got a few hundred yards when the
rain overtook me, and sent me for refuge into a shed, where a
blacksmith had arranged a rude furnace and bellows, and

where he was at work with a rough gilly to help him, and, of course, a lounger or two to look on.

The scene was exceedingly wild and picturesque, and I took out a sketch-book and began to draw. The blacksmith was at first very suspicious of the operation which I had commenced, nor did the poor fellow's sternness at all yield until I made him a present of a shilling to buy tobacco, when he, his friend, and his son, became good-humoured, and said their little say. This was the first shilling he had earned these three years: he was a small farmer, but was starved out, and had set up a forge here, and was trying to get a few pence. What struck me was the great number of people about the place. We had at least twenty visits while the sketch was being made; cars, and single and double horsemen, were continually passing; between the intervals of the shower a couple of ragged old women would creep out from some hole, and display baskets of green apples for sale: wet or not, men and women were lounging up and down the road. You would have thought it was a fair, and yet there was not even a village at this place, only the inn and posthouse, by which the cars to Tralee pass thrice a-week.

The weather, instead of mending, on the second day was worse than ever. All the view had disappeared now under a rushing rain, of which I never saw anything like the violence. We were visited by five maritime, nay buccaneering, looking gentlemen, in mustachios, with fierce caps and jackets, just landed from a yacht: and then the car brought us three Englishmen wet to the skin, and thirsting for whiskey-and-water.

And with these three Englishmen, a great scene occurred, such as we read of in Smollett's and Fielding's inns. One was a fat old gentleman from Cambridge, who, I was informed, was a fellow of a college in that university, but who, I shrewdly suspect★ to be butler or steward of the same. The younger men burly, manly, good-humoured fellows of seventeen stone, were the nephews of the elder, who, says one, 'could draw a check for his thousand pounds.'

★ The suspicion turned out to be very correct. The gentleman is the respected cook of C——, as I learned afterwards from a casual Cambridge man.

Two-and-twenty years before, on landing at the Pigeon-House at Dublin, the old gentleman had been cheated by a carman, and his firm opinion seemed to be that all carmen, nay, all Irishmen, were cheats.

And a sad proof of this depravity speedily showed itself: for having hired a three-horse car at Killarney, which was to carry them to Bantry, the Englishmen saw, with immense indignation, after they had drunk a series of glasses of whiskey, that the three-horse car had been removed, a one-horse vehicle standing in its stead.

Their wrath no pen can describe. 'I tell you they are all so,' shouted the elder. 'When I landed at the Pigeon-House'. . . 'Bring me a post-chaise,' roars the second. 'Waiter, get some more whiskey,' exclaims the third; 'if they don't send us on with three horses, I'll stop here for a week.' Then issuing, with his two young friends, into the passage, to harangue the populace assembled there, the elder Englishman began a speech about dishonesty, 'd—d rogues and thieves, Pigeon-House; he was a gentleman, and wouldn't be done, d—n his eyes, and everybody's eyes.' Upon the affrighted landlord, who came to interpose, they all fell with great ferocity: the elder man swearing, especially, that he 'would write to Lord Lansdowne regarding his conduct, likewise to Lord Bandon, also to Lord Bantry: he was a gentleman; he'd been cheated in the year 1815, on his first landing at the Pigeon-House: and, d—n the Irish, they were all alike.' After roaring and cursing for half an hour, a gentleman at the door, seeing the meek bearing of the landlord, who stood quite lost and powerless in the whirlwind of rage that had been excited about his luckless ears, said, 'if men cursed and swore in that way in his house, he would know how to put them out.'

'Put *me* out,' says one of the young men, placing himself before the fat old blasphemer, his relative. 'Put *me* out, my fine fellow;' but it was evident the Irishman did not like his customer. 'Put *me* out,' roars the old gentleman, from behind his young protector; '——my eyes, who are *you*, sir? who *are* you, sir? I insist on knowing who you are.'

'And who are you?' asks the Irishman.

'Sir, I'm a gentleman, and *pay my way* – and as soon as I get into Bantry, I swear I'll write a letter to Lord Bandon Bantry, and complain of the treatment I have received here.'

Now, as the unhappy landlord had not said one single word, and as, on the contrary, to the annoyance of the whole house, the stout old gentleman from Cambridge had been shouting, raging and cursing for two hours, I could not help, like a great ass as I was, coming forward, and (thinking the landlord might be a tenant of Lord Bantry's) saying, 'Well, sir, if you write and say the landlord has behaved ill, I will write to say that he has acted with extraordinary forbearance and civility.'

O fool! to interfere in disputes, where one set of the disputants have drunk half-a-dozen glasses of whiskey in the middle of the day! No sooner had I said this, than the other young man came and fell upon me, and in the course of a few minutes found leisure to tell me 'that I was no gentleman; that I was ashamed to give my name, or say where I lived; that I was a liar, and didn't live in London, and couldn't mention the name of a single respectable person there; that he was a merchant and tradesman, and hid his quality from no one;' and finally, 'that though bigger than himself, there was nothing he would like better than that I should come out on the green, and stand to him like a man.'

This invitation, although repeated several times, I refused with as much dignity as I could assume; partly because I was sober and cool, while the other was furious and drunk; also because I felt a strong suspicion that in about ten minutes the man would manage to give me a tremendous beating, which I did not merit in the least; thirdly, because a victory over him would not have been productive of the least pleasure to me; and lastly, because there was something really honest and gallant in the fellow coming out to defend his old relative. Both of the younger men would have fought like tigers for this disreputable old gentleman, and desired no better sport. The last I heard of the three, was that they and the driver made their appearance before a magistrate in Bantry; and a pretty story will the old man have to tell to his club at the Hoop or the Red Lion, of those swindling Irish, and the ill-treatment he met with in their country.

As for the landlord, the incident will be a blessed theme of conversation to him for a long time to come. I heard him discoursing of it in the passage during the rest of the day, and next morning when I opened my window and saw with much delight the bay clear and bright as silver, except where the green hills were reflected in it, the blue sky above, and the purple mountains round about with only a few clouds veiling their peaks – the first thing I heard, was the voice of Mr Eccles repeating the story to a new customer.

'I thought thim couldn't be gintlemin,' was the appropriate remark of Mr Tom the waiter, 'from the way in which they took their whishky – raw with cold wather, widout *mixing or inything.*' Could an Irish waiter give a more excellent definition of the ungenteel?

At nine o'clock in the morning of the next day, the unlucky car which had carried the Englishmen to Bantry came back to Glengariff, and as the morning was very fine, I was glad to take advantage of it, and travel some five-and-thirty English miles to Killarney.

CHAPTER X

FROM GLENGARIFF TO KILLARNEY

The Irish car seems accommodated for any number of persons: it appeared to be full when we left Glengariff, for a traveller from Bearhaven, and the five gentlemen from the yacht, took seats upon it with myself, and we fancied it was impossible more than seven should travel by such a conveyance; but the driver showed the capabilities of his vehicle presently. The journey from Glengariff to Kenmare is one of astonishing beauty; and I have seen Killarney since, and am sure that Glengariff loses nothing by comparison with this most famous of lakes. Rock, wood, and sea, stretch around the traveller – a thousand delightful pictures: the landscape is at first wild without being fierce, immense woods and plantations enriching the valleys – beautiful streams to be seen everywhere.

Here again I was surprised at the great population along the road; for one saw but few cabins, and there is no village between Glengariff and Kenmare. But men and women were on banks and in fields; children, as usual, came trooping up to the car; and the jovial men of the yacht had great conversations with most of the persons whom we met on the road. A merrier set of fellows it were hard to meet. 'Should you like anything to drink, sir?' says one commencing the acquaintance; 'we have the best whiskey in the world, and plenty of porter in the basket.' Therewith the jolly seamen produced a long bottle of grog, which was passed round from one to another; and then began singing, shouting, laughing roaring for the whole journey, 'British sailors have a knack, pull away ho, boys! Hurroo! my fine fellow, does your mother know you're out? Hurroo, Tim Herlihy! you're *a fluke*, Tim Herlihy.' One man sang on the roof, one *hurrooed* to the echo, another apostrophised the aforesaid Herlihy as he

passed grinning on a car; a third had a pocket-handkerchief
flaunting from a pole, with which he performed exercises in
the face of any horseman whom we met; and great were their
yells as the ponies shied off at the salutation, and the riders
swerved in their saddles. In the midst of this rattling chorus
we went along: gradually the country grew wilder and more
desolate, and we passed through a grim mountain region,
bleak and bare; the road winding round some of the innumerable hills, and once or twice, by means of a tunnel,
rushing boldly through them. One of these tunnels, they say,
is a couple of a hundred yards long; and a pretty howling, I
need not say, was made through that pipe of rock by the jolly
yacht's crew. 'We saw you sketching in the black-smith's shed
at Glengariff,' says one, 'and we wished we had you on board.
Such a jolly life we led of it!' – They roved about the coast,
they said, in their vessel; they feasted off the best of fish,
mutton, and whiskey; they had Gamble's turtle-soup on
board, and fun from morning till night, and *vice versâ*.
Gradually it came out that there was not, owing to the
tremendous rains, a dry corner in their ship: that they slung
two in a huge hammock in the cabin, and that one of their
crew had been ill, and shirked off. What a wonderful thing
pleasure is! to be wet all day and night; to be scorched and
blistered by the sun and rain; to beat in and out of little
harbours, and to exceed diurnally upon whiskey-punch –
faith, London, and an arm-chair at the club, are more to the
tastes of some men.

After much mountain-work of ascending and descending
(in which latter operation, and by the side of precipices that
make passing cocknies rather squeamish, the carman drove
like mad to the hooping and screeching of the red-rovers;) we
at length came to Kenmare, of which all that I know is that it
lies prettily in a bay or arm of the sea; that it is approached by a
little hanging-bridge, which seems to be a wonder in these
parts; that it is a miserable little place when you enter it; and
that, finally, a splendid luncheon of all sorts of meat and
excellent cold salmon may sometimes be had for a shilling at
the hotel of the place. It is a great vacant house, like the rest of
them, and would frighten people in England; but after a few
days one grows used to the Castle Rackrent style. I am not

sure that there is not a certain sort of comfort to be had in these rambling rooms, and among these bustling, blundering waiters, which one does not always meet with in an orderly English house of entertainment.

After discussing the luncheon, we found the car with fresh horses, beggars, idlers, policemen, &c., standing round, of course; and now the miraculous vehicle, which had held hitherto seven with some difficulty, was called upon to accommodate thirteen.

A pretty noise would our three Englishmen of yesterday, nay any other Englishman, for the matter of that, have made, if coolly called upon to admit an extra party of four into a mail-coach! The yacht's crew did not make a single objection: a couple clambered up on the roof, where they managed to locate themselves with wonderful ingenuity, perched upon hard wooden chests, or agreeably reposing upon the knotted ropes which held them together: one of the new passengers scrambled between the driver's legs, where he held on somehow, and the rest were pushed and squeezed astonishingly in the car.

Now, the fact must be told, that five of the new passengers (I don't count a little boy besides) were women, and very pretty, gay, frolicksome, lively, kind-hearted, innocent women too; and for the rest of the journey there was no end of laughing and shouting, and singing, and hugging, so that the caravan presented the appearance which is depicted in the frontispiece of this work.

Now it may be a wonder to some persons, that with such a cargo the carriage did not upset, or some of us did not fall off to which the answer is that we *did* fall off. A very pretty woman fell off, and showed a pair of never-mind-what-coloured garters, and an interesting English traveller fell off too; but Heaven bless you! these cars are made to fall off from; and considering the circumstances of the case and in the same company, I would rather fall off than not. A great number of polite allusions and genteel inquiries were, as may be imagined, made by the jolly boat's crew. But though the lady affected to be a little angry at first, she was far too good-natured to be angry long, and at last fairly burst out laughing with the passengers. We did not fall off again, but held on very tight, and just as we were reaching Killarney, saw somebody else fall off from another car. But in this instance the gentleman had no lady to tumble with.

For almost half the way from Kenmare, this wild, beautiful road commands views of the famous lake and vast blue mountains about Killarney. Turk, Tomies, and Mangerton, were clothed in purple, like kings in mourning; great, heavy clouds were gathered round their heads, parting away every now and then, and leaving their noble features bare. The lake lay for some time underneath us, dark and blue, with dark misty islands in the midst. On the right-hand side of the road, would be a precipice covered with a thousand trees, or a green rocky flat, with a reedy mere in the midst, and other mountains rising as far as we could see. I think of that diabolical tune in Der Freischutz, while passing through this sort of country. Every now and then, in the midst of some fresh country or inclosed trees, or at a turn of the road, you lose the sight of the great, big, awful mountain; but, like the aforesaid tune in Der Freischutz, it is always there close at hand. You feel that it keeps you company. And so it was that we rode by dark old Mangerton, then presently past Mucruss, and then through two miles of avenues of lime-trees, by numerous lodges and gentlemen's seats, across an old bridge, where you see the mountains again and the lake, until by Lord Kenmare's house, a hideous row of houses informed us that we were at Killarney.

Here my companion suddenly let go my hand, and, by a certain uneasy motion of the waist, gave me notice to withdraw the other too; and so we rattled up to the Kenmare Arms: and so ended, not without a sigh on my part, one of the merriest six-hour rides that five yachtmen, one cockney, five women and a child, the carman, and a countryman with an alpeen, ever took in their lives.

As for my fellow companion, she would hardly speak the next day, but all the five maritime men made me vow and promise that I would go and see them at Cork, where I should have horses to ride, the fastest yacht out of the harbour to sail in, and the best of whiskey, claret, and welcome. Amen, and may every single person who buys a copy of this book meet with the same deserved fate.

The town of Killarney was in a violent state of excitement with a series of horse-races, hurdle-races, boat-races, and stag-hunts by land and water, which were taking place, and attracted a vast crowd from all parts of the kingdom. All the inns were full, and lodgings cost five shillings a-day, nay, more in some places; for though my landlady, Mrs Macgilli-cuddy, charges but that sum, a leisurely old gentleman whom I never saw in my life before, made my acquaintance by stopping me in the street, yesterday, and said he paid a pound a day for his two bed-rooms.

The old gentleman is eager for company; and, indeed, when a man travels alone, it is wonderful how little he cares to select his society; how indifferent company pleases him; how a good fellow delights him; how sorry he is when the time for parting comes, and he has to walk off alone, and begin the friendship-hunt over again.

The first sight I witnessed at Killarney was a race-ordinary, where for a sum of twelve shillings, any man could take his share of turbot, salmon, venison, and beef, with port, and sherry, and whiskey-punch at discretion. Here were the squires of Cork and Kerry, one or two Englishmen, whose voices amidst the rich humming brogue round about, sounded quite affected (not that they were so, but there seems a sort of impertinence in the shrill high-pitched tone of the English voice here): at the head of the table, near the chairman, sat some brilliant young dragoons, neat, solemn, dull, with huge moustachios, and boots polished to a nicety.

And here of course the conversation was of the horse, horsy. How Mr This had refused fifteen hundred guineas for a horse, which he bought for a hundred; how Bacchus was the best horse in Ireland; which horses were to run at Something races; and how the Marquis of Waterford gave a plate or a purse. We drank 'the Queen,' with hip, hip, hurra. The 'winner of the Kenmare stakes,' hurray. Presently the gentleman next me rose and made a speech; he had brought a mare down, and won the stakes, a hundred and seventy guineas, and I looked at him with a great deal of respect. Other toasts ensued, and more talk about horses; nor am I in the least disposed to sneer at gentlemen who like sporting and talk about it; for I do believe that the conversation of a dozen fox-hunters is just as clever as that of a similar number of merchants, barristers, or literary men. But to this trade, as to all others, a man must be bred; if he has not learnt it thoroughly or in early life, he will not readily become a proficient afterwards, and when therefore the subject is broached, had best maintain a profound silence.

A young Edinburgh cockney, with an easy self-confidence that the reader may have perhaps remarked in others of his calling and nation, and who evidently knew as much of sporting matters as the individual who writes this, proceeded nevertheless to give the company his opinions, and greatly astonished them all, for these simple people are at first willing to believe that a stranger is sure to be a knowing fellow, and did not seem inclined to be undeceived even by this little pert grinning Scotsman. It was good to hear him talk of Haddington, Musselburgh – and Heaven knows what strange outlandish places, as if they were known to all the world. And here would be a good opportunity to enter into a dissertation upon natural characteristics; to show that the bold swaggering Irishman is really a modest fellow, while the canny Scot is a most brazen one; to wonder why the inhabitant of one country is ashamed of it, which is in itself so fertile and beautiful, and has produced more than its fair proportion of men of genius, valour, and wit; whereas it never enters into the head of a Scotchman to question his own equality (and something more) at all: but that such discussions are quite unprofitable, nay, that exactly the contrary propositions may be argued to just as much length. Has the reader ever tried with a dozen of Mr Tocqueville's short crisp philosophic apophthegms and taken the converse of them? The one or other set of propositions will answer equally well, and it is the best way to avoid all such. Let the above passage, then, simply be understood to say, that on a certain day, the writer met a vulgar little Scotchman – not that all Scotchmen are vulgar; – that this little pert creature prattled about his country as if he and it were ornaments to the world, which the latter is, no doubt; and that one could not but contrast his behaviour with that of great big stalwart simple Irishmen, who asked your opinion of their country with as much modesty as if you – because an Englishman – must be somebody, and they the dust of the earth.

Indeed, this want of self-confidence at times becomes quite painful to the stranger: if in reply to their queries, you say you like the country, people seem really quite delighted. – Why should they? Why should a stranger's opinion who doesn't know the country, be more valued than a native's who does? – Suppose an Irishman in England were to speak in praise or abuse of the country, would one be particularly pleased or annoyed? One would be glad that the man liked his trip, but as for his good or bad opinion of the country, the country stands on its own bottom, superior to any opinion of any man or men.

I must beg pardon of the little Scotchman for reverting to him (let it be remembered that there were *two* Scotchmen at Killarney, and that I speak of the other one), but I have seen no specimen of that sort of manners in any Irishman since I have been in the country. I have met more gentlemen here than in any place I ever saw, gentlemen of high and low ranks, that is to say, men shrewd and delicate of perception, observant of society, entering into the feelings of others, and anxious to set them at ease or to gratify them; of course exaggerating their professions of kindness, and in so far insincere; but the very exaggeration seems to be a proof of a kindly nature, and I wish in England we were a little more complimentary. In Dublin, a lawyer left his chambers, and a literary man his books, to walk the town with me – the town, which they must know a great deal too well, for pretty as it is, it is but a small place after all, not like that great bustling, changing, struggling world, the Englishman's capital. Would a London man leave his business to trudge to the Tower or the Park with a stranger? We would ask him to dine at the club, or to eat whitebait at Lovegrove's and think our duty done, neither caring for him, nor professing to care for him; and we pride ourselves on our honesty accordingly. Never was honesty more selfish. And so a vulgar man in England disdains to flatter his equals, and chiefly displays his character of snob by assuming as much as he can for himself, swaggering and showing off in his coarse, dull, stupid way.

'I am a gentlemen, and pay my way,' as the old fellow said at Glengariff. I have not heard a sentence near so vulgar from any man in Ireland. Yes, by the way, there was another

Englishman at Cork; a man in a middling, not to say humble, situation of life. When introduced to an Irish gentleman, his formula seemed to be, 'I think, sir, I have met you somewhere before.' 'I am sure, sir, I have met you before,' he said, for the second time in my hearing, to a gentleman of great note in Ireland. 'Yes, I have met you at Lord X ——'s.' 'I don't know my Lord X,' replied the Irishman. 'Sir,' says the other, '*I shall have great pleasure in introducing you to him.*' Well, the good-natured simple Irishman thought this gentleman a very fine fellow. There was only one, of some dozen who spoke about him, that found out Snob. I suppose the Spaniards lorded it over the Mexicans in this way: their drummers passing for generals among the simple red men, their glass beads for jewels, and their insolent bearing for heroic superiority.

Leaving then the race-ordinary (that little Scotchman with his airs has carried us the deuce knows how far out of the way), I came home just as the gentlemen of the race were beginning to 'mix,' that is to forsake the wine for the punch. At the lodgings I found my five companions of the morning with a bottle of that wonderful whiskey of which they spoke; and which they had agreed to exchange against a bundle of Liverpool cigars: so we discussed them, the whiskey, and other topics in common. Now there is no need to violate the sanctity of private life, and report the conversation which took place, the songs which were sung, the speeches which were made, and the other remarkable events of the evening. Suffice it to say, that the English traveller gradually becomes accustomed to whiskey-punch (in moderation, of course), and finds the beverage very agreeable at Killarney; against which I recollect a protest was entered at Dublin.

But after we had talked of hunting, racing, regatting, and all other sports, I came to a discovery which astonished me, and for which these honest kind fellows are mentioned publicly here. The portraits, or a sort of resemblance of four of them, may be seen in the foregoing drawing of the car. The man with the straw hat and handkerchief tied over, it is the captain of an Indiaman; three others, with each a pair of moustachios, sported yacht-costumes, jackets, club-anchor-buttons, and so forth; and, finally, one on the other side of the car (who cannot be seen on account of the portmanteaus, otherwise the likeness would be perfect), was dressed with a coat and a hat in the ordinary way. One with the gold band and moustachios is a gentleman of property, the other three are attorneys, every man of them. Two in large practice in Cork and Dublin, the other, and owner of the yacht, under articles to the attorney of Cork. Now did any Englishman ever live with three attorneys for a whole day, without hearing a single syllable of law spoken? Did we ever see in our country attorneys with

moustachios; or, above all, an attorney's clerk the owner of a yacht of thirty tons? He is a gentleman of property too, the heir that is to a good estate; and has had a yacht of his own, he says, ever since he was fourteen years old. Is there any English boy of fourteen who commands a ship, with a crew of five men under him? We all agreed to have a boat for the stag-hunt on the lake next day; and I went to bed wondering at this strange country more than ever. An attorney with moustachios! What would they say of him in Chancery Lane?

CHAPTER XI

KILLARNEY – STAG-HUNTING ON THE LAKE

Mrs Macgillicuddy's house is at the corner of the two principal streets of Killarney-town, and the drawing room windows command each a street. Before one window is a dismal, ricketty building, with a slated face, that looks like an ex-town hall. There is a row of arches to the ground floor, the angles at the base of which seem to have mouldered or to have been kicked away. Over the centre arch is a picture with a flourishing yellow inscription above, importing that it is the meeting-place of the Total Abstinence Society. Total abstinence is represented by the figures of a gentleman in a blue coat and drab tights, with gilt garters, who is giving his hand to a lady; between them is an escutcheon surmounted with a cross and charged with religious emblems. Cupids float above the heads and between the legs of this happy pair, while an exceedingly small tea-table with the requisite crockery reposes against the lady's knee; a still, with Death's head and bloody-bones, filling up the naked corner near the gentleman. A sort of market is held here, and the place is swarming with blue cloaks, and groups of men talking; here and there is a stall with coarse linens, crockery, a cheese; and crowds of egg and milk-women are squatted on the pavement with their ragged customers or gossips; and the yellow-haired girl, on the next page, with a barrel containing nothing at all, has been sitting, as if for her portrait, this hour past.

Carts, cars, jingles, barouches, horses, and vehicles of all descriptions, rattle presently through the streets, for the town is crowded with company for the races and other sports, and all the world is bent to see the stag-hunt on the lake. Where the ladies of the Macgillicuddy family have slept, Heaven knows, for their house is full of lodgers. What voices you hear! 'Bring me some hot watah,' says a genteel, high-piped English voice.

'Hwhere's me hot wather,' roars a deep-toned Hibernian. See
over the way, three ladies in ringlets and green tabinet taking
their 'tay' preparatory to setting out. I wonder whether they
heard the sentimental songs of the law-marines last-night?
They must have been edified if they did.

My companions came, true to their appointment, and we
walked down to the boats, lying at a couple of miles from the

town, near the Victoria Inn, a handsome mansion, in pretty grounds, close to the lake, and owned by the patriotic Mr Finn. A nobleman offered Finn eight hundred pounds for the use of his house during the races, and, to Finn's eternal honour be it said, he refused the money, and said he would keep his house for his friends and patrons, the public. Let the Cork Steam Packet Company think of this generosity on the part of Mr Finn, and blush for shame; at the Cork Agricultural Show they raised their faces, and were disappointed in their speculation, as they deserved to be, by indignant Englishmen refusing to go at all.

The morning had been bright enough, but for fear of accidents we took our Mackintoshes, and at about a mile from the town found it necessary to assume those garments and wear them for the greater part of the day. Passing by the Victoria, with its beautiful walks, park, and lodge, we came to a little creek, where the boats were moored, and there was the wonderful lake before us, with its mountains, and islands, and trees. Unluckily, however, the mountains happened to be invisible; the islands looked like gray masses in the fog, and all that we could see for some time was the gray silhouette of the boat ahead of us, in which a passenger was engaged in a witty conversation with some boat still further in the mist.

Drumming and trumpeting was heard at a little distance, and presently we found ourselves in the midst of a fleet of boats upon the rocky shores of the beautiful little Innisfallen.

Here we landed for awhile, and the weather clearing up, allowed us to see this charming spot. Rocks, shrubs, and little abrupt rises and falls of ground, covered with the brightest emerald grass; a beautiful little ruin of a Saxon chapel, lying gentle, delicate, and plaintive on the shore; some noble trees round about it, and beyond, presently, the tower of Ross Castle, island after island appearing in the clearing sunshine, and the huge hills throwing their misty veils off, and wearing their noble robes of purple. The boats' crew were grouped about the place, and one large barge especially had landed some sixty people, being the Temperance band, with its drums, trumpets, and wives. They were marshalled by a grave old gentleman, with a white waistcoat and queue, a silver medal decorating one side of his coat, and a brass heart reposing on the other flap. The horns performed some Irish airs prettily; and, at length, at the instigation of a fellow who went swaggering about with a pair of whirling drumsticks, all formed together, and played Garryowen – the active drum, of course most dreadfully out of time.

Having strolled about the island for a quarter of an hour, it became time to take to the boats again, and we were rowed over to the wood opposite Sullivan's cascade, where the hounds had been laid in in the morning, and the stag was expected to take water. Fifty or sixty men are employed on the mountain to drive the stag lakewards, should he be inclined to break away: and the sport generally ends by the stag, a wild one, making for the water with the pack swimming afterwards; and here he is taken and disposed of, how I know not. It is rather a parade than a stag-hunt, but, with all the boats around and the noble view, must be a fine thing to see.

Presently steering his barge, the Erin, with twelve oars, and a green flag sweeping the water, came by the president of the sports, Mr John O'Connell, a gentleman who appears to be liked by rich and poor here, and by the latter especially is adored. 'Sure we'd dhrown ourselves for him,' one man told me, and proceeded to speak eagerly in his praise, and to tell numberless acts of his generosity and justice. – The justice is rather rude in this wild country sometimes, and occasionally the judges not only deliver the sentence but execute it, nor does anyone think of appealing to any more regular jurisdiction. The likeness of Mr O'Connell to his brother is very striking; one might have declared it was the Liberator sitting at the stern of the boat.

Some scores more boats were there, darting up and down in the pretty, busy waters. Here came a Cambridge boat; and where, indeed, will not the gentlemen of that renowned university be found? Yonder were the dandy dragoons, stiff, silent, slim, faultlessly appointed, solemnly puffing cigars.

Every now and then a hound would be heard in the wood, whereon numbers of voices, right and left, would begin to yell in chorus – Hurroo! Hoop! Yow, yow, yow! in accents the most shrill or the most melancholious; meanwhile the sun had had enough of the sport, the mountains put on their veils again, the islands retreated into the mist, the word went through the fleet to spread all umbrellas, and ladies took shares of Mackintoshes, and disappeared under the flaps of silk cloaks.

The wood comes down to the very edge of the water, and many of the crews thought fit to land and seek this green shelter. There you might see how the dandium summâ genus haesit ulmo, clambering up thither to hide from the rain, and many 'membra' in dabbled russia-ducks, cowering viridi sub arbuto; ad aquae lene caput. To behold these moist dandies the natives of the country came eagerly. Strange, savage faces might be seen peering from out of the trees; long-haired, bare-legged girls came down the hill, some with green apples and very sickly-looking plums; some with whiskey and goat's milk – a ragged boy had a pair of stag's horns to sell: the place swarmed with people. We went up the hill to see the noble cascade, and when you say that it comes rushing down over rocks and through tangled woods, alas! one has said all the dictionary can help you to, and not enough to distinguish this particular cataract from any other. This seen and admired, we came back to the harbour where the boats lay, and from which spot the reader might have seen the foregoing view of the lake – that is, you *would* see the lake, if the mist would only clear away.

But this for hours it did not seem inclined to do. We rowed up and down industriously for a period of time which seemed to me atrociously long. The bugles of the Erin had long since sounded 'Home, sweet home,' and the greater part of the fleet had dispersed. As for the stag-hunt, all I saw of it was four dogs, that appeared on the shore at different intervals; and a huntsman, in a scarlet coat, who similarly came and went: once or twice we were gratified by hearing the hounds, but at last it was agreed that there was no chance for the day, and we rowed off to Kenmare cottage, where, on the lovely lawn, or in a cottage adjoining, the gentry picnic; and where, with a handkerchief full of potatoes, we made as pleasant a meat as ever I recollect. Here a good number of the boats were assembled; here you might see cloths spread, and dinner going on; here were those wonderful officers, looking as if they had just stepped from bandboxes, with, by Heavens! not a shirt collar disarranged, nor a boot dimmed by the wet. An old piper was making a very feeble music, with a handkerchief spread over his face; and farther on a little smiling German boy was playing an accordion, and singing a ballad of Hauff's. I had a silver medal in my pocket, with Victoria on one side and Britannia on the other, and gave it him, for the sake of old times and his round friendly face. Oh, little German boy, many a night as you trudge lonely through this wild land, must you yearn after brüderlein and schwesterlein at home – yonder in stately Frankfurt city that lies by silver Mayn. – I thought of vineyards and sunshine, and the greasy clock in the theatre, and the railroad all the way to Wiesbaden, and the handsome Jew country-houses by the Bockenheimer-Thor. . . . 'Come along,' says the boatman, 'all the gintlemin are waiting for your honour;' and I found them finishing the potatoes, and we all had a draught of water from the lake, and so pulled to the middle, or Turk Lake, through the picturesque green rapid that floats under Brickeen bridge.

What is to be said about Turk lake? When there, we agreed that it was more beautiful than the large lake, of which it is not one-fourth the size – then, when we came back, we said, 'No, the large lake is the most beautiful;' and so, at every point we stopped at, we determined that that particular spot was the prettiest in the whole lake. The fact is, and I don't care to own it, they are too handsome. As for a man coming from his desk in London or Dublin, and seeing, 'the whole lakes in a day,' he is an ass for his pains: a child doing sums in addition might as well read the whole multiplication table, and fancy he had it by heart. We should look at these wonderful things leisurely and thoughtfully; and even then, blessed is he who understands them. I wonder what impression the sight made upon the three tipsy Englishmen at Glengariff? What idea of natural beauty belongs to an old fellow who says he is 'a gentleman, and pays his way?' What to a jolly fox-hunter, who had rather see a good 'screeching' run with the hounds, than the best landscape ever painted? And yet, they all come hither, and go through the business regularly, and would not miss seeing every one of the lakes, and going up every one of the hills – by which circumlocution the writer wishes ingenuously to announce that he will not see any more lakes, ascend any mountains or towers, visit any gaps of Dunloe, or any prospects whatever, except such as nature shall fling in his way in the course of a quiet reasonable walk.

In the middle lake we were carried to an island, where a ceremony of goats' milk and whiskey is performed by some travellers, and where you are carefully conducted to a spot that 'Sir Walter Scott admired more than all.' Whether he did or not, we can only say on the authority of the boatman; but the place itself was a quiet nook, where three waters meet, and indeed of no great picturesqueness when compared with the beauties around. But it is of a gentle, homely beauty – not like the lake, which is as a princess dressed out in diamonds and velvet for a drawing room, and knowing herself to be faultless too. As for Innisfallen, it was just as if she gave one smiling peep into the nursery before she went away, so quiet, innocent, and tender is that lovely spot; but, depend on it, if there is a lake fairy or princess, as Crofton Croker and other historians assert, she is of her nature a vain creature, proud of her person, and fond of the finest dresses to adorn it. May I confess, that I would rather, for a continuance, have a house facing a paddock, with a cow in it, than be always looking at this immense overpowering splendour. You would not, my dear brother Cockney from Tooley-street, – no, those brilliant eyes of thine were never meant to gaze at anything less bright than the sun. Your mighty spirit finds nothing too vast for its comprehension, spurns what is humble as unworthy, and only, like Foot's bear, dances to 'the genteelest of tunes.'

The long and short of the matter is, that on getting off the lake, after seven hours' rowing, I felt as much relieved as if I had been dining for the same length of time with her Majesty the Queen, and went jumping home as gaily as possible; but those marine lawyers insisted so piteously upon seeing Ross Castle, close to which we were at length landed, that I was obliged (in spite of repeated oaths to the contrary,) to ascend that tower, and take a bird's-eye view of the scene. Thank Heaven, I have neither tail nor wings, and have not the slightest wish to be a bird; that continual immensity of prospect which stretches beneath those little wings of theirs, must deaden their intellects, depend on it. Tomkins and I are not made for the immense. We can enjoy a little at a time, and enjoy that little very much; or if like birds, we are like the ostrich – not that we have fine feathers to our backs, but because we cannot fly. Press us too much, and we become flurried and run off, and bury our heads in the quiet bosom of dear mother earth, and so get rid of the din, and the dazzle, and the shouting.

Because we dined upon potatoes, that was no reason we should sup on buttermilk: well, well, salmon is good, and whiskey is good too.

CHAPTER XII

KILLARNEY – THE RACES – MUCROSS

The races were as gay as races could be, in spite of one or two untoward accidents that arrived at the close of the day's sport. Where all the people came from that thronged out of the town was a wonder; where all the vehicles, the cars, barouches, and shandrydans, the carts, the horse and donkey-men could have found stable and shelter, who can tell? Of all these equipages and donkeypages I had a fine view from Mrs Macgillicuddy's window, and it was pleasant to see the happy faces shining under the blue cloaks as the carts rattled by.

A very handsome young lady – I presume Miss Mac G—— who gives a hand to the drawing-room, and comes smiling in with the tea-pot; Miss Mac G, I say, appeared to day in a silk bonnet and stiff silk dress, with a brooch and a black mantle, as smart as any lady in the land, and looking as if she was accustomed to her dress too, which the housemaid on banks of Thames does not. Indeed, I have not met a more ladylike young person in Ireland than Miss Mac G; and, when I saw her in a handsome car on the course, I was quite proud of a bow.

Tramping thither, too, as hard as they could walk, and as happy and smiling as possible, were Mary the coachman's wife, of the day before, and Johanna with the child, and presently the other young lady – the man with the stick, you may be sure; he would toil a year for that day's pleasure: they are all mad for it; people walk for miles and miles round to the race; they come without a penny in their pockets, often, trusting to chance and charity, and that some worthy gentleman may fling them a sixpence. A gentleman told me that he saw on the course persons from his part of the country, who must have walked eighty miles for the sport.

For a mile and a half to the race-course there could be no

pleasanter occupation than looking at the happy multitudes who were thronging thither; and I am bound to say, that on rich or poor shoulders I never saw so many handsome faces in my life. In the carriages, among the ladies of Kerry, every second woman was handsome; and there is something peculiarly tender and pleasing in the looks of the young female peasantry, that is perhaps even better than beauty. Beggars had taken their stations along the road in no great numbers, for I suspect they were most of them on the ground, and those who remained were consequently of the oldest and ugliest. It is a shame that such horrible figures are allowed to appear in public, as some of the loathsome ones which belong to these unhappy people. On went the crowd, however, laughing and gay as possible; all sorts on fun passing from car to foot-passengers as the pretty girls came clattering by, and the 'boys' had a word for each. One lady, with long, flowing, auburn hair, who was turning away her head from some 'boys' very demurely, I actually saw, at a pause of the cart, kissed by one of them. She gave the fellow a huge box on the ear, and he roared out, 'O murther!' and she frowned for some time as hard as she could, whilst the ladies in the blue cloaks at the back of the car uttered a shrill rebuke in Irish. But in a minute the whole party was grinning, and the young fellow who had administered the salute may, for what I know, have taken another without the slap on the face, by way of exchange.

And here, lest the fair public may have a bad opinion of the personage who talks of kissing with such awful levity, let it be said, that with all this laughing, romping kissing, and the like, there are no more innocent girls in the world than the Irish girls; and that the women of our squeamish country are far more liable to err. One has but to walk through an English and Irish town, and see how much superior is the morality of the latter. That great terror-striker, the Confessional, is before the Irish girl, and, sooner or later, her sins must be told there.

By this time we are got upon the course, which is really one of the most beautiful spots that ever was seen: the lake and mountains lying along two sides of it, and of course visible from all. They were busy putting up the hurdles when we arrived – stiff bars and poles, four feet from the ground, with furze bushes over them. The grand stand was already full;

along the hedges sate thousands of the people, sitting at their ease doing nothing, and happy as kings. A daguerreotype would have been of great service to have taken their portraits, and I never saw a vast multitude of heads and attitudes so picturesque and lively. The sun lighted up the whole course and the lakes with amazing brightness, though behind the former lay a huge rack of the darkest clouds, against which the corn fields and meadows shone in the brightest green and gold, and a row of white tents was quite dazzling.

There was a brightness and intelligence about this immense Irish crowd, which I don't remember to have seen in an English one. The women in their blue cloaks, with red smiling faces peering from one end, and bare feet from the other, had seated themselves in all sorts of pretty attitudes of cheerful contemplation; and the men, who are accustomed to lie about, were doing so now with all their might – sprawling on the banks, with as much ease and variety as club-room loungers on their soft cushions, – or squatted leisurely among the green potatoes. The sight of so much happy laziness did one good to look on. Nor did the honest fellows seem to weary of this amusement. Hours passed on, and the gentlefolks (judging from our party) began to grow somewhat weary; but the finest peasantry in Europe never budged from their posts, and continued to indulge in talk, indolence, and conversation.

When we came to the row of white tents, as usual it did not look so brilliant or imposing as it appeared from a little distance, though the scene around them was animating enough. The tents were long humble booths stretched on hoops, each with its humble streamer or ensign without, and containing, of course, articles of refreshment within. But Father Mathew has been busy among the publicans, and the consequence is, that the poor fellows are now condemned for the most part to sell 'tay' in place of whiskey; for the concoction of which beverage, huge cauldrons were smoking in front of each hut-door, in round graves dug for the purpose and piled up with black smoking sod.

Behind this camp were the carts of the poor people, which were not allowed to penetrate into the quarter where the quality cars stood. And a little way from the huts again, you might see (for you could scarcely hear) certain pipers executing their melodies and inviting people to dance.

Anything more lugubrious than the drone of the pipe, or the jig danced to it, or the countenances of the dancers and musicians, I never saw. Round each set of dancers the people formed a ring, in the which the figurantes and coryphées went through their operations. The toes went in and the toes went out; then there came certain mystic figures of hands across, and so forth. I never saw less grace or seemingly less enjoyment, no not even in a quadrille. The people, however, took a great interest, and it was 'Well done, Tim!' 'Step out, Miss Brady!' and so forth during the dance.

Thimble-rig too obtained somewhat, though in a humble way. A ragged scoundrel, the image of Hogarth's Bad Apprentice, went bustling and shouting through the crowd with his dirty tray and thimble; and, as soon as he had taken his post, stated that this was the 'royal game of thimble,' and calling upon 'jintlemin' to come forward; and then a ragged fellow would be seen to approach, with as innocent an air as he could assume, and the bystanders might remark that the second ragged fellow almost always won. Nay, he was so benevolent, in many instances, as to point out to various people who had a mind to bet, under which thimble the pea actually was; meanwhile, the first fellow was sure to be looking away and taking to some one in the crowd. But somehow it generally happened, and how of course I can't tell, that any man who listened to the advice of rascal No. 2, lost his money. I believe it is so even in England.

Then you would see gentlemen with halfpenny roulette tables; and again, here were a pair (indeed they are very good portraits) who came forward disinterestedly with a table and a pack of cards, and began playing against each other for ten shillings a game, betting crowns as freely as possible.

Gambling, however, must have been fatal to both of these gentlemen, else might not one have supposed, that if they were in the habit of winning much, they would have treated themselves to better clothes? This, however, is the way with all gamblers, as the reader has, no doubt, remarked; for, look at a game of loo or *vingt et un*, played in a friendly way, and where you, and three or four others, have certainly lost three or four pounds: well, ask at the end of the game who has won? and you invariably find that nobody has. Hopkins has only

covered himself; Snooks has neither lost nor won; Smith has
won four shillings; and so on. Who gets the money? The devil
gets it, I dare say, and so, no doubt, he said laid hold of the
money of yonder gentleman in the handsome great-coat.

But, to the shame of the stewards be it spoken, they are
extremely averse to this kind of sport; and presently comes up
one, a stout old gentleman on a bay horse, wielding a huge
hunting-whip, at the sight of which all fly, amateurs, idlers,
professional men, and all. He is a rude customer to deal with,
that gentleman with the whip: just now he was clearing the
course, and cleared it with such a vengeance, that a whole troop
on a hedge retreated backwards into a ditch opposite, where was
rare kicking, and sprawling, and disarrangement of petticoats,
and cries of 'O murther!' 'Mother of God?' 'I'm kilt!' and so on.
But as soon as the horsewhip was gone, the people clambered
out of their ditch again, and were as thick as ever on the bank.

The last instance of the exercise of the whip shall be this. A groom rode insolently after a gentleman, and calling him names, and inviting him to fight. This the great flagellator hearing, rode up to the groom, lifted him gracefully off his horse, into the air, and on to the ground, and when there administered to him a severe and merited fustigation; after which he told the course-keepers to drive the fellow off the course, and enjoined the latter not to appear again at his peril.

As for the races themselves, I won't pretend to say that they were better or worse than other such amusements; or to quarrel with gentlemen who choose to risk their lives in manly exercise. In the first race there was a fall; one of the gentlemen was carried off the ground, and it was said *he was dead*. In the second race, a horse and man went over and over each other, and the fine young man (we had seen him five minutes before, full of life and triumph, clearing the hurdles on his grey horse, at the head of the race): – in the second heat of the second race, the poor fellow missed his leap, was carried away, stunned and dying; – and the bay-horse won.

I was standing, during the first heat of this race, (this is the second man the grey has killed – they ought to call him the Pale Horse,) by half-a-dozen young girls from the gentleman's village, and hundreds more of them were there, anxious for the honour of their village, the young squire, and the grey horse. Oh, how they hurra'd as he rode ahead; I saw these girls – they might be fourteen years old – after the catastrophe. 'Well,' says I, 'this is a sad end to the race.' '*And is it the pink jacket or the blue has won this time?*' says one of the girls. It was poor Mr C——'s only epitaph: and wasn't it a sporting answer? That girl ought to be a hurdle-racer's wife; and I would like, for my part, to bestow her upon the groom who won the race.

I don't care to confess that the accident to the poor young gentleman so thoroughly disgusted my feeling as a man and a Cockney, that I turned off the race-course short, and hired a horse for sixpence to carry me back to Miss Macgillicuddy. In the evening, at the inn (let no man who values comfort go to an Irish inn in race-time,) a blind old piper, with silvery hair, and of a most respectable, bard-like appearance, played a great deal too much for us after dinner. He played very well, and with very much feeling, ornamenting the airs with flourishes and variations that were very pretty indeed, and his pipe was by far the most melodious I have heard; but honest truth compels me to say, that the bad pipes are execrable, and the good inferior to a clarionet.

Next day, instead of going back to the race-course, a car drove me out to Mucross, where, in Mr Herbert's beautiful grounds, lies the prettiest little *bijou* of a ruined abbey ever seen – a little chapel with a little chancel, a little cloister, a little dormitory, and in the midst of the cloister a wonderful huge yew-tree which darkens the whole place. The abbey is famous in book and legend; nor could two young lovers, or artists in search of the picturesque, or picnic parties with the cold chicken and champagne in the distance, find a more charming place to while away a summer's day than in the park of Mr Herbert. But depend on it, for show-places and the due enjoyment of scenery, that distance of cold chickens and champagne is the most pleasing perspective one can have. I would have sacrificed a mountain or two for the above, and would have pitched Mangerton into the lake for the sake of a friend with whom to enjoy the rest of the landscape.

The walk through Mr Herbert's demesne carries you, through all sorts of beautiful avenues, by a fine house which he is building in the Elizabethan style, and from which, as from the whole road, you command the most wonderful rich views of the lake. The shore breaks into little bays, which the water washes; here and there are picturesque gray rocks to meet it, the bright grass as often, or the shrubs of every kind which bathe their roots in the lake. It was August, and the men before Turk Cottage were cutting a second crop of clover, as fine, seemingly, as a first crop elsewhere; a short walk from it brought us to a neat lodge, whence issued a keeper with a key, quite willing, for the consideration of sixpence, to conduct us to Turk Waterfall.

Evergreens and other trees, in their brightest livery; blue sky; roaring water, here black, and yonder, foaming of a dazzling white; rocks shining in the dark places, or frowning black against the light, all the leaves and branches keeping up a perpetual waving and dancing round about the cascade: what is the use of putting down all this? A man might describe the cataract of the Serpentine in exactly the same terms, and the reader be no wiser. Suffice it to say, that the Turk cascade is even handsomer than the before-mentioned waterfall of O'Sullivan, and that a man may pass half an hour there, and look, and listen, and muse, and not even feel the want of a companion, or so much as think of iced champagne. There is just enough of savageness in the Turk cascade to make the view *piquante*. It is not, at this season at least, by any means fierce, only wild; nor was the scene peopled by any of the rude, red-shanked figures that clustered about the trees of O'Sullivans' waterfall, – savages won't pay sixpence for the prettiest waterfall ever seen, so that this only was for the best of company.

The road hence to Killarney carries one through Mucross village, a pretty cluster of houses, where the sketcher will find abundant materials for exercising his art and puzzling his hand. There are not only noble trees, but a green common and an old watergate to a river lined on either side by beds of rushes, and discharging itself beneath an old mill-wheel. But the old mill-wheel was perfectly idle, like most men and mill-wheels in this country: by it is a ruinous house, and a fine garden of stinging nettles; opposite it, on the common, is another ruinous house, with another garden containing the same plant; and far away are sharp ridges of purple hills, which make as pretty a landscape as the eye can see. I don't know how it is, but throughout the country the men and the landscapes seem to be the same, and one and the other seem rugged, ruined, and cheerful.

Having been employed all day (making some abominable attempts at landscape-drawing, which shall not be exhibited here), it became requisite, as the evening approached, to recruit an exhausted Cockney stomach, which, after a very moderate portion of exercise, begins to sigh for beef-steaks in the most peremptory manner. Hard by is a fine hotel with a fine sign stretching along the road for the space of a dozen windows at least, and looking inviting enough. All the doors were open, and I walked into a great number of rooms, but the only person I saw was a woman with trinkets of arbutus, who offered me, by way of refreshment, a walking-stick or a card-rack. I suppose everybody was at the races; and an evilly disposed person might have laid *main-basse* upon the great coats which were there, and the silver-spoons, if by any miracle such things were kept – but Britannia metal is the favourite composition in Ireland; or else iron by itself; or else iron that has been silvered over; but that takes good care to peep out at all the corners of the forks; and, blessed is the traveller who has not other observations to make regarding his fork, besides the mere abrasion of the silver.

This was the last day's race, and on the next morning (Sunday), all the thousands who had crowded to the race, seemed trooping to the chapels, and the streets were blue with cloaks. Walking in to prayers, and without his board, came my young friend of the thimble-rig, and presently after sauntered in the fellow with the long coat, who had played at cards for sovereigns. I should like to hear the confession of himself and friend, the next time they communicate with his reverence.

The extent of this town is very curious, and I should imagine its population to be much greater than five thousand, which was the number, according to Miss Macgillicuddy. Along the three main streets are numerous arches, down every one of which runs an alley, intersected by other alleys, and swarming with people. A stream or gutter runs commonly down these alleys, in which the pigs and children are seen paddling about. The men and women loll at their doors or windows, to enjoy the detestable prospect. I saw two pigs under a fresh-made deal staircase, in one of the main streets near the Bridewell: two very well-dressed girls, with their hair in ringlets, were looking out of the parlour window: almost all the glass in the upper rooms was of course smashed, the windows patched here and there (if the people were careful), the wood-work of the door loose, the whitewash peeling off, – and the house evidently not two years old.

By the Bridewell is a busy potato-market, picturesque to the sketcher, if not very respectable to the merchant: here were the country carts and the country cloaks, and the shrill beggarly bargains going on – a world of shrieking, and gesticulating, and talk, about a pennyworth of potatoes.

All round the town miserable streets of cabins are stretched. You see people lolling at each door, women staring and

combing their hair, men with their little pipes, children whose rags hang on by a miracle, idling in a gutter. Are we to set all this down to absenteeism, and pity poor injured Ireland? Is the landlord's absence the reason why the house is filthy, and Biddy lolls in the porch all day? Upon my word, I have heard people talk as if, when Pat's thatch was blown off, the landlord ought to go fetch the straw and the ladder, and mend it himself. People need not be dirty if they are ever so idle; if they are ever so poor, pigs and men need not live together. Half an hour's work, and digging a trench, might remove that filthy dunghill from that filthy window. The smoke might as well come out of the chimney as out of the door. Why should not Tim do that, instead of walking a hundred and sixty miles to and from a race? The priests might do much more to effect these reforms, than even the landlords themselves: and I hope, now that the excellent Father Mathew has succeeded in arraying his clergy to work with him in the abolition of drunkenness, they will attack the monster Dirt with the same good-will, and surely with the same success.

CHAPTER XIII

TRALEE – LISTOWEL – TARBERT

I made the journey to Tralee next day, upon one of the famous Bianconi cars – very comfortable conveyances too – if the booking officers would only receive as many persons as the car would hold, and not have too many on the seats. For half an hour before the car left Killarney, I observed people had taken their seats: and, let all travellers be cautious to do likewise, lest, although they have booked their places, they be requested to mount on the roof, and accommodate themselves on a bandbox, or a pleasant deal trunk with a knotted rope, to prevent it from being slippery, while the corner of another box jolts against your ribs for the journey. I had put my coat on a place, and was stepping to it, when a lovely lady with great activity jumped up and pushed the cloak on the roof, and not only occupied my seat, but insisted that her husband should have the next one to her. So there was nothing for it but to make a huge shouting with the book-keeper, and call instantly for the taking down of my luggage, and vow my great gods that I would take a postchaise and make the office pay; on which, I am ashamed to say, some other person was made to give up a decently comfortable seat on the roof, which I occupied, the former occupant hanging on – Heaven knows where or how.

A company of young squires were on the coach, and they talked of horse-racing and hunting punctually for three hours, during which time I do believe they did not utter one single word upon any other subject. What a wonderful faculty it is! the writers of Natural Histories, in describing the noble horse, should say, he is made not only to run, to carry burdens, &c., but to be talked about. What would hundreds of thousands of dashing young fellows do with their tongues, if they had not this blessed subject to discourse on?

As far as the country went, there was here, to be sure, not much to be said. You pass through a sad-looking, bare, undulating country, with few trees, and poor stone hedges, and poorer crops; nor have I yet taken in Ireland so dull a ride. About half way between Tralee and Killarney is a wretched town, where horses are changed, and where I saw more hideous beggary than anywhere else, I think. And I was glad to get over this gloomy tract of country, and enter the capital of Kerry.

It has a handsome description in the guide-books; but, if I mistake not, the English traveller will find a stay of a couple of hours in the town quite sufficient to gratify his curiosity with respect to the place. There seems to be a great deal of poor business going on; the town thronged with people as usual; the shops large and not too splendid. There are two or three rows of respectable houses, and a mall, and the townspeople have the further privilege of walking in the neighbouring grounds of a handsome park, which the proprietor has liberally given to their use. Tralee has a newspaper, and boasts of a couple of clubs; the one I saw was a big white house, no windows broken, and looking comfortable. But the most curious sight of the town was the chapel, with the festival held there. It was the feast of the Assumption of the Virgin (let those who are acquainted with the calendar and the facts it commemorates say what the feast was, and when it falls), but all the country seemed to be present on the occasion, and the chapel and the large court leading to it were thronged with worshippers, such as one never sees in our country, where devotion is by no means so crowded as here. Here, in the court-yard, there were thousands of them on their knees, rosary in hand, for the most part praying, and mumbling, and casting a wistful look round as the strangers passed. In a corner was an old man groaning in the agonies of death or cholic, and a woman got off her knees to ask us for charity for the unhappy old fellow. In the chapel the crowd was enormous: the priest and his people were kneeling, and bowing, and humming, and chanting, and censer-rattling; the ghostly crew being attended by a fellow that I don't remember to have seen in Continental churches, a sort of catholic clerk, a black shadow to the parson, bowing his head when his reverence bowed, kneeling when he knelt, only three steps lower.

But we who wonder at copes and candlesticks, see nothing strange in surplices and beadles. A Turk, doubtless, would sneer equally at each, and have you to understand that the only reasonable ceremonial was that which took place at his mosque.

Whether right or wrong, in point of ceremony, it was evident the heart of devotion was there: the immense dense crowd moaned and swayed, and you heard a hum of all sorts of wild ejaculations, each man praying seemingly for himself, while the service went on at the altar. The altar candles flickered red in the dark, steaming place, and every now and then from the choir you heard a sweet female voice chanting Mozart's music, which swept over the heads of the people a great deal more pure and delicious than the best incense that ever smoked out of pot.

On the chapel floor, just at the entry, lay several people moaning, and tossing, and telling their beads. Behind the old woman was a font of holy water, up to which little children were clambering; and in the chapel-yard were several old women, with tin cans full of the same sacred fluid, with which the people, as they entered, aspersed themselves with all their might, flicking a great quantity into their faces, and making a curtsey and a prayer at the same time. 'A pretty prayer, truly!' says the parson's wife. 'What sad, sad, benighted superstition!' says the Independent minister's lady. Ah! ladies, great as your intelligence is, yet think, when compared with the Supreme One, what a little difference there is after all between your husbands' very best extempore oration, and the poor Popish creatures'! One is just as far off Infinite Wisdom as the other; and so let us read the story of the woman and her pot of ointment, that most noble and charming of histories; which equalises the great and the small, the wise and the poor in spirit, and shows that their merit before Heaven lies *in doing their best*.

When I came out of the chapel, the old fellow on the point of death was still howling and groaning in so vehement a manner, that I heartily trust he was an impostor, and that on receiving a sixpence he went home tolerably comfortable, having secured a maintenance for that day. But it will be long before I can forget the strange, wild scene, so entirely different

was it from the decent and comfortable observances of our
own church.

Three cars set off together from Tralee to Tarbert: three cars
full to overflowing. The vehicle before us contained nineteen
persons, half-a-dozen being placed in the receptacle called the
well, and one clinging on as if by a miracle at the bar behind.
What can people want at Tarbert? I wondered; or anywhere

else, indeed, that they rush about from one town to another in this inconceivable way. All the cars in all the towns seem to be thronged: people are perpetually hurrying from one dismal tumble-down town to another; and yet no business is done anywhere that I can see. The chief part of the contents of our three cars was discharged at Listowel, to which, for the greater part of the journey, the road was neither more cheerful nor picturesque than that from Killarney to Tralee. As, however, you reach Listowel, the country becomes better cultivated, the gentlemen's seats are more frequent, and the town itself, as seen from a little distance, lies very prettily on a river, which is crossed by a handsome bridge, which leads to a neat-looking square, which contains a smartish church, which is flanked by a big Roman Catholic chapel, &c. An old castle, gray and ivy-covered, stands hard by. It was one of the strongholds of the Lords of Kerry, whose burying-place (according to the information of the coachman) is seen at about a league from the town.

But pretty as Listowel is from a distance, it has, on a more intimate acquaintance, by no means the prosperous appearance which a first glance gives it. The place seemed like a scene at a country theatre, once smartly painted by the artist; but the paint has cracked in many places, the lines are worn away, and the whole piece only looks more shabby for the flaunting strokes of the brush which remain. And here, of course, came the usual crowd of idlers round the car: the epileptic idiot holding piteously out his empty tin snuff-box; the brutal idiot in an old soldier's coat, proffering his money-box, and grinning and clattering the single half-penny it contained; the old man with no eye-lids, calling upon you in the name of the Lord; the woman with a child at her hideous wrinkled breast; the children without number. As for trade, there seemed to be none; a great Jeremy-Didler-kind of hotel stood hard by, swaggering and out at elbows, and six pretty girls were smiling out of a beggarly straw-bonnet shop, dressed as smartly as any gentleman's daughters of good estate. It was good among the crowd of bustling, shrieking fellows, who were 'jawing' vastly and doing nothing, to see how an English bagman, with scarce any words, laid hold of an ostler, carried him off, *vi et armis*, in the midst of a speech, in which the latter was going to explain his immense activity and desire to serve, pushed him into a stable, from which he issued in a twinkling, leading the ostler and a horse; and had his bag on the car and his horse off in about two minutes of time, while the natives were still shouting round about other passengers' portmanteaus.

Some time afterwards, away we rattled on our own journey to Tarbert, having a postillion on the leader, and receiving, I must say, some graceful bows from the young bonnet-makeresses. But of all the roads over which human bones were ever jolted, the first part of this from Listowel to Tarbert deserves the palm. It shook us all into headaches; it shook some nails out of the side of a box I had; it shook all the cords loose in a twinkling, and sent the baggage bumping about the passengers' shoulders. The coachman at the call of another English bagman, who was a fellow-traveller, – the postillion at the call of the coachman, descended to re-cord the baggage. The English bagman had the whole mass of trunks and bags stoutly corded and firmly fixed in a few seconds; the coachman helped him as far as his means allowed; the postillion stood by with his hands in his pockets, smoking his pipe, and never offering to stir a finger. I said to him that I was delighted to see in a youth of sixteen that extreme activity and willingness to oblige, and that I would give him a handsome remuneration for his services at the end of the journey: the young rascal grinned with all his might, understanding the satiric nature of the address perfectly well; but he did not take his hands out of his pockets for all that, until it was time to get on his horse again, and then, having carried us over the most difficult part of the journey, removed his horse and pipe, and rode away with a parting grin.

The cabins along the road were not much better than those to be seen south of Tralee, but the people were far better clothed, and indulged in several places in the luxury of pig-styes. Near the prettily situated village of Ballylongford, we came in sight of the Shannon mouth; and a huge red round moon, that shone behind an old convent on the banks of the bright river, with dull green meadows between it and us, and white purple flats beyond, would be a good subject for the pencil of any artist whose wrist had not been put out of joint by the previous ten miles' journey.

The town of Tarbert, in the guide-books and topographical dictionaries, flourishes considerably. You read of its port, its corn and provision stores, &c., and of certain good hotels, for which as travellers, we were looking with a laudable anxiety. The town, in fact, contains about a dozen of houses, some hundreds of cabins, and two hotels, to one of which we were driven, and a kind landlady, conducting her half-dozen guests into a snug parlour, was for our ordering refreshment immediately, – which I certainly should have done, but for the ominous whisper of a fellow in the crowd as we descended, (of course a disinterested patron of the other house), who hissed into my ears, '*Ask to see the beds*,' which proposal, accordingly, I made before coming to any determination regarding supper.

The worthy landlady eluded my question several times with great skill and good-humour, but it became at length necessary to answer it, which she did by putting on as confident an air as possible, and leading the way up-stairs to a bed-room, where there was a good large comfortable bed, certainly.

The only objection to the bed, however, was that it contained a sick lady, whom the hostess proposed to eject without any ceremony, saying that she was a great deal better, and going to get up that very evening: however, none of us had the heart to tyrannise over lovely woman in so painful a situation, and the hostess had the grief of seeing four out of her five guests repair across the way to Brallaghan's or Gallagher's Hotel, – the name has fled from my memory, but it is the big hotel in the place, and unless the sick lady has quitted the other inn, which most likely she has done by this time, the English traveller will profit by this advice, and on arrival at Tarbert will have himself transported to Gallagher's at once.

The next morning a car carried us to Tarbert Point, where there is a pier not yet completed, and a Preventive-station, and where the Shannon steamers touch, that ply between Kilrush and Limerick. Here lay the famous river before us with low banks and rich pastures on either side.

CHAPTER XIV

LIMERICK

A capital steamer, which on this day was thronged with people, carried us for about four hours down the noble stream and landed us at Limerick Quay. The character of the landscape on either side the stream is not particularly picturesque, but large, liberal, and prosperous. Gentle sweeps of rich meadows and corn-fields cover the banks, and some, though not too many gentlemen's parks and plantations rise here and there. But the landscape was somehow more pleasing than if it had been merely picturesque; and, especially after coming out of that desolate county of Kerry, it was pleasant for the eye to rest upon this peaceful, rich, and generous scene. The first aspect of Limerick is very smart and pleasing; fine neat quays with considerable liveliness and bustle, a very handsome bridge (the Wellesley bridge) before the spectator, who, after a walk through two long and flourishing streets, stops at length at one of the best inns in Ireland – the large, neat, and prosperous one kept by Mr Cruise. Except at Youghal, and the poor fellow whom the Englishman belaboured at Glenga-riff, Mr Cruise is the only landlord of an inn I have had the honour to see in Ireland. I believe these gentlemen commonly (and very naturally) prefer riding with the hounds, or manly sports, to attendance on their guests; and the landladies, if they prefer to play the piano, or to have a game of cards in the parlour, only show a taste at which no one can wonder; for who can expect a lady to be troubling herself with vulgar chance-customers, or looking after Molly in the bed-room, or waiter-Tim in the cellar?

Now, beyond this piece of information regarding the excellence of Mr Cruise's hotel, which every traveller knows, the writer of this doubts very much whether he has anything to say about Limerick that is worth the trouble of saying or reading. I can't attempt to describe the Shannon, only to say that on board the steam-boat there was a piper and a bugler, a hundred of genteel persons coming back from donkey-riding and bathing at Kilkee, a couple of heaps of raw hides that smelt very foully, a score of women nursing children, and a lobster-vender, who vowed to me on his honour that he gave eightpence a-piece for his fish, and that he had boiled them only the day before; but when I produced the guide-book, and solemnly told him to swear upon that to the truth of his statement, the lobster-seller turned away, quite abashed, and would not be brought to support his previous assertion at all. Well, this is no description of the Shannon, as you have no need to be told, and other travelling cockneys will no doubt meet neither piper nor lobster-seller, nor raw hides; nor if they come to the inn where this is written, is it probable that they will hear, as I do at this present moment, two fellows with red whiskers, and immense pomp and noise and blustering with the waiter, conclude by ordering a pint of ale between them. All that one can hope to do is, to give a sort of notion of the movement and manners of the people, pretending by no means to offer a description of places, but simply an account of what one sees in them.

So that if any traveller after staying two days in Limerick should think fit to present the reader with forty or fifty pages of dissertation upon the antiquities and history of the place, upon the state of commerce, religion, education; the public may be pretty well sure that the traveller has been at work among the guide-books, and filching extracts from the topo-graphical and local works.

They say there are three towns to make one Limerick: there is the Irish town on the Clare side; the English town with its old castle, (which has sustained a deal of battering and blows from Danes, from fierce Irish kings, from English warriors who took an interest in the place, Henry Secundians, Eliza-bethians, Cromwellians, and *vice versâ*, Jacobites, King Willia-mites, – and nearly escaped being in the hands of the Robert Emmettites;) and finally the district called New-town-Pery. In walking through this latter tract, you are, at first, half led to believe that you are arrived in a second Liverpool, so tall are the warehouses and broad the quays: so neat and trim a street of near a mile which stretches before you. But even this mile-long street does not, in a few minutes, appear to be so wealthy and prosperous as it shows at first glance: for of the population that throng the streets, two-fifths are bare-footed women, and two-fifths more ragged men: and the most part of the shops which have a grand show with them, appear, when looked into, to be no better than they should be, being empty make-shift looking places, with their best goods outside.

Here, in this handsome street too, is a handsome club-house, with plenty of idlers, you may be sure, lolling at the portico; likewise you see numerous young officers, with very tight waists and absurd brass shell-epaulettes to their little absurd frock-coats, walking the pavement – the dandies of the street. Then you behold whole troops of pear, apple, and plum-women, selling very raw, green-looking fruit, which, indeed, it is a wonder that any one should eat and live: – the houses are bright red – the street is full and gay, carriages and cars in plenty go jingling by – dragoons in red are every now and then clattering up the street, and as upon every car which passes with ladies in it you are sure (I don't know how it is) to see a pretty one, the great street of Limerick is altogether a very brilliant and animated sight.

If the ladies of the place are pretty, indeed, the vulgar are scarcely less so. I never saw a greater number of kind, pleasing, clever looking faces among any set of people. There seem however, to be two sorts of physiognomies which are common; the pleasing and somewhat melancholy one before mentioned, and a square high-cheeked flat-nosed physiognomy, not uncommonly accompanied by a hideous staring head of dry, red hair. Except, however, in the latter case, the hair flowing loose and long is a pretty characteristic of the women of the country; many a fair one do you see at the door of the cabin, or the poor shop in the town, combing complacently that 'greatest ornament of female beauty,' as Mr Rowland justly calls it.

The generality of the women here seem also much better clothed than in Kerry; and I saw many a one going barefoot, whose gown was nevertheless a good one, and whose cloak was of fine cloth. Likewise it must be remarked, that the beggars in Limerick were by no means so numerous as those in Cork, or in many small places through which I have passed. There were but five, strange to say, round the mail-coach as we went away; and, indeed, not a great number in the streets.

The belles lettres seem to be by no means so well cultivated here as in Cork. I looked in vain for a Limerick guide-book: I saw but one good shop of books, and a little, trumpery, circulating library, which seemed to be provided with those immortal works of a year old, which, having been sold for half-a-guinea the volume at first, are suddenly found to be worth only a shilling. Among these, let me mention, with perfect resignation to the decrees of fate, the works of one Titmarsh: they were rather smartly bound by an enterprising publisher, and I looked at them in Bishop Murphy's library at Cork, in a book-shop in the remote little town of Ennis, and elsewhere, with a melancholy tenderness. Poor flowerets of a season! (and a very short season too,) let me be allowed to salute your scattered leaves with a passing sigh! . . . Besides the book-shops, I observed in the long, best street of Limerick a half-dozen of what are called French shops, with knick-knacks, German silver chimney-ornaments, and paltry finery. In the windows of these you saw a card with 'Cigars;' in the book-shop, 'Cigars;' at the grocer's, the whiskey-shop, 'Cigars:' everybody sells the noxious weed, or makes believe to sell it, and I know no surer indication of a struggling, uncertain trade, than that same placard of 'Cigars.' I went to buy some of the pretty Limerick gloves, (they are chiefly made, as I have since discovered, at Cork.) I think the man who sold them had a patent from the Queen, or His Excellency, or both, in his window: but, seeing a friend pass just as I entered the shop, he brushed past, and held his friend in conversation for some minutes in the street, – about the Killarney races, no doubt, or the fun going on at Kilkee. I might have swept away a bagful of walnut shells, containing the flimsy gloves; but instead walked out, making him a low bow, and saying I would call next week. He said, wouldn't I wait? and resumed his conversation; and, no doubt, by this way of doing business, is making a handsome independence. I asked one of the ten thousand fruit-women the price of her green pears. 'Twopence a-piece,' she said; and there were two little ragged beggars standing by, who were munching the fruit; a book shop-woman made me pay threepence for a bottle of ink which usually costs a penny; a potato-woman told me that her potatoes cost fourteen-pence a stone; and all these ladies treated the stranger with a leering, wheedling servility, which made me long to box their ears, were it not that the man who lays his hand upon a woman is an ——, &c., whom 'twere gross flattery to call a what-d'ye-call-'em. By the way, the man who played Duke Aranza at Cork, delivered the celebrated claptrap above aluded to as follows:-

> 'The man who lays his hand upon a woman,
> Save in the way of kindness, is a villain,
> Whom 'twere *a gross piece* of flattery to call a coward;'

and looked round calmly for the applause, which deservedly followed his new reading of the passage.

To return to the apple-women; – legions of ladies were employed through the town upon that traffic; there were really thousands of them, clustering upon the bridges, squatting down in doorways and vacant sheds for temporary markets, marching and crying their sour goods in all the crowded lanes of the city. After you get out of the main street, the handsome part of the town is at an end, and you suddenly find yourself in such a labyrinth of busy swarming poverty and squalid commerce as never was seen – no, not in Saint Giles's, where Jew and Irishman side by side exhibit their genius for dirt. Here every house almost was a half ruin, and swarming with people; in the cellars you looked down and saw a barrel of herrings, which a merchant was dispensing; or a sack of meal, which a poor dirty woman sold to people poorer and dirtier than herself; above was a tinman, or a shoemaker, or other craftsman, his batterd ensign at the door, and his small wares peering through the cracked panes of his shop. As for the ensign, as a matter of course, the name is never written in letters of the same size. You read

PAT^K HANLAHAⁿ
TAILOR

JAME^s HURL^{EY}
SHOE MAK^{er}

or some similar sign-board. High and low, in this country, they begin things on too large a scale. They begin churches too big and can't finish them; mills and houses too big, and are ruined before they are done; letters on sign-boards too big, and are up in a corner before the inscription is finished – there is something quite strange, really, in this general consistency.

Well, over James Hurley, or Pat Hanlahan, you will most likely see another board of another tradesman, with a window to the full as curious. Above Tim Carthy evidently lives another family; there are long-haired girls of fourteen at every one of the windows, and dirty children everywhere. In the cellars, look at them in dingy white night-caps over a bowl of stir-about; in the shop, paddling up and down the ruined steps, or issuing from beneath the black counter; up above, see the girl of fourteen is tossing and dandling one of them, and a pretty tender sight it is, in the midst of this filth and wretchedness, to see the women and children together. It makes a sunshine in the dark place, and somehow half reconciles one to it. Children are everywhere – look out of the nasty streets into the still more nasty back lanes; there they are, sprawling at every door and court, paddling in every puddle, and in about a fair proportion to every six children, an old woman; a very old, blear-eyed, ragged woman, who makes believe to sell something out of a basket, and is perpetually calling upon the name of the Lord. For every three ragged old women you will see two ragged old men, praying and moaning like the females; and there is no lack of young men, either, though I never could make out what they were about: they loll about the street, chiefly conversing in knots, and in every street you will be pretty sure to see a recruiting sergeant, with gay ribands in his cap, loitering about with an eye upon the other loiterers there. The buz, and hum, and chattering of this crowd is quite inconceivable to us in England, where a crowd is generally silent: as a person with a decent coat passes, they stop in their talk, and say, 'God bless you for a fine gentleman!' In these crowded streets, where all are beggers, the beggary is but small: only the very old and hideous venture to ask for a penny, otherwise the competition would be too great.

As for the buildings that one lights upon every now and then in the midst of such scenes as this, they are scarce worth the trouble to examine; occasionally you come on a chapel with sham gothic windows and a little belfry, one of the Catholic places of worship; then, placed in some quiet street, a neat looking dissenting meeting-house. Across the river yonder, as you issue out from the street, where the preceding sketch was taken, is a handsome hospital; near it the old cathedral, a barbarous old turreted edifice, of the fourteenth century, it is said; how different to the sumptuous elegance which characterises the English and Continental churches of the same period! Passing by it, and walking down other streets, – black, ruinous, swarming, dark, hideous, – you come upon the barracks and the walks of the old castle, and from it on to an old bridge, from which the view is a fine one. On one side are the gray bastions of the castle; beyond them, in the midst of the broad stream, stands a huge mill that looks like another castle; further yet is the handsome new Wellesley bridge, with some little craft upon the river, and the red warehouses of the new town looking prosperous enough. The Irish town stretches away to the right; there are pretty villas beyond it, and on the bridge are walking twenty-four young girls, in parties of four and five, with their arms round each other's waists, swaying to and fro, and singing or chattering, as happy as if they had shoes to their feet. Yonder you see a dozen pair of red legs glittering in the water, their owners being employed in washing their own or other people's rags.

The guide-book mentions that one of the aboriginal forests of the country is to be seen at a few miles from Limerick, and thinking that an aboriginal forest would be a huge discovery, and form an instructive and delightful feature of the present work, I hired a car in order to visit the same, and pleased myself with visions of gigantic oaks, Druids, Norma, wildernesses and awful gloom, which would fill the soul with horror. The romance of the place was heightened by a fact stated by the carman, viz., that until late years, robberies were very frequent about the wood, the inhabitants of the district being a wild lawless race. Moreover, there are numerous castles round about, – and for what can a man wish more than robbers, castles, and an aboriginal wood?

The way to these wonderful sights lies through the undulating grounds which border the Shannon, and though the view is by no means a fine one, I know few that are pleasanter than the sight of these rich, golden, peaceful plains, with the full harvest waving on them and just ready for the sickle. The hay harvest was likewise just being concluded, and the air loaded with the rich odour of the hay. Above the trees, to your left, you saw the mast of a ship, perhaps moving along, and every now and then caught a glimpse of the Shannon and the low grounds and plantations of the opposite county of Limerick. Not an unpleasant addition to the landscape too, was a sight which I do not remember to have witnessed often in this country, that of several small and decent farm-houses with their stacks and sheds and stables, giving an air of neatness and plenty that the poor cabin with its potato-patch does not present. Is it on account of the small farms that the land seems richer and better cultivated here, than in most other parts of the country? Some of the houses in the midst of the warm summer landscape had a strange appearance, for it is often the fashion to white-wash the roofs of the houses, leaving the slates of the walls of their natural colour; hence, and in the evening especially, contrasting with the purple sky, the house-tops often looked as if they were covered with snow.

According to the guide-books' promise, the castles began soon to appear; at one point we could see three of these ancient mansions in a line, each seemingly with its little grove of old trees, in the midst of the bare but fertile country. By this time, too, we had got into a road so abominably bad and rocky, that I began to believe more and more with regard to the splendour of the aboriginal forest, which must be most aboriginal and ferocious indeed when approached by such a savage path. After travelling through a couple of lines of wall with plantations on either side, I at length became impatient as to the forest, and, much to my disappointment, was told this was it. For the fact is, that though the forest has always been there, the trees have not, the proprietors cutting them regularly when grown to no great height; and the monarchs of the woods which I saw round about, would scarcely have afforded timber for a bed-post. Nor did any robbers make their appearance in this wilderness: with which disappointment, however, I was more willing to put up than with the former one.

But if the wood and the robbers did not come up to my romantic notions, the old castle of Bunratty fully answered them, and indeed should be made the scene of a romance, in three volumes at least.

'It is a huge, square tower, with four smaller ones at each angle; and you mount to the entrance by a steep flight of steps, being commanded all the way by the cross-bows of two of the Lord De Clare's retainers, the points of whose weapons may be seen lying upon the ledge of the little narrow *meurtrière* on each side of the gate. A venerable seneschal, with the keys of office, presently opens the little back postern, and you are admitted to the great hall – a noble chamber, *pardi*! some seventy feet in length, and thirty high. 'Tis hung round with a thousand trophies of war and chase, – the golden helmet and spear of the Irish king, the long yellow mantle he wore, and the huge brooch that bound it. Hugo De Clare slew him before the castle in 1305, when he and his kernes attacked it. Less successful in 1314, the gallant Hugo saw his village of Bunratty burned round his tower by the son of the slaughtered O'Neil; and, sallying out to avenge the insult, was brought back – a corpse! Ah! what was the pang that shot through the fair bosom of the *Lady Adela*, when she knew that 'twas the hand of *Redmond O'Neil* sped the shaft which slew her sire!

'You listen to this sad story, reposing on an oaken settle (covered with deer's skin taken in the aboriginal forest of Carclow hard by), and placed at the enormous hall-fire. Here sits Thonom an Diaoul, "Dark Thomas," the blind harper of the race of De Clare, who loves to tell the deeds of the lordly family. "Penetrating in disguise," he continues, "into the castle, Redmond of the golden locks sought an interview with the lily of Bunratty; but she screamed when she saw him under the disguise of the gleeman, and said, My father's blood is in the hall! At this, up started fierce Sir Ranulph. Ho, Bludyer! he cried to his squire, call me the hangman and Father John; seize me, vassals, yon villain, in gleeman's guise, and hang him on the gallows on the tower!

'"Will it please ye walk to the roof of the old castle, and see the beam on which the lords of the place execute the refractory?" "Nay, marry," say you, "by my spurs of knighthood, I have seen hanging enough in merry England, and care not to

see the gibbets of Irish kernes." The harper would have taken
fire at this speech, reflecting on his country; but luckily here
Gulph, your English squire, entered from the pantler (with
whom he had been holding a parley), and brought a manchet
of bread, and bade ye, in the Lord de Clare's name, crush a cup
of Ypocras, well spiced, *pardi*, and by the fair hands of the
Lady Adela.

'"The Lady Adela!" say you, starting up in amaze. "Is not
this the year of grace 1600, and lived she not three hundred
years syne?"

'"Yes, Sir Knight, but Bunratty tower hath *another lily*: will
it please you see your chamber?"

'So saying, the seneschal leads you up a winding stair in one
of the turrets, past one little dark chamber and another
without a fire-place, without rushes, (how different from the
stately houses of Nonsuch or Audley End!) and, leading you
through another vast chamber above the baronial hall, similar
in size, but decorated with tapestries and rude carvings, you
pass the little chapel ("Marry," says the steward, "many
would it not hold, and many do not come!") until at last you
are located in the little cell appropriated to you. Some rude
attempts have been made to render it fitting for the stranger;
but, though more neatly arranged than the hundred other little
chambers which the castle contains, in sooth 'tis scarce fitted
for the serving-man, much more for Sir Reginald, the English
knight.

'While you are looking at a bouquet of flowers, which lies
on the settle – magnolias, geraniums, the blue flowers of the
cactus, and in the midst of the bouquet, *one lily*; whilst you
wonder whose fair hands could have culled the flowers – hark
the horns are blowing at the drawbridge, and the warder lets
the portcullis down. You rush to your window, a stalwart
knight rides over the gate, the hoofs of his black courser
clanging upon the planks. A host of wild retainers wait round
about him; see, four of them carry a stag, that hath been slain,
no doubt, in the aboriginal forest of Carclow. By my fay! (say
you) 'tis a stag of ten.

'But who is that yonder on the gray palfrey, conversing so
prettily, and holding the sportive animal with so light a rein? –
a light green riding-habit and ruff, a little hat with a green

plume – sure it must be a lady, and a fair one. She looks up. O blessed Mother of Heaven, that look! those eyes, that smile, those sunny golden ringlets! It is, *it is* the Lady Adela: the lily of Bunrat.'

* * * *

If the reader cannot finish the other two volumes for him or herself, he or she never deserves to have a novel from a circulating library again: for my part, I will take my affidavit the English knight will marry the Lily at the end of the third volume, having previously slain the other suitor at one of the multifarious sieges of Limerick: and I beg to say, that the historical part of this romance has been extracted carefully from the guide-book: the topographical and descriptive portion being studied on the spot. A policeman shows you over it, halls, chapels, galleries, gibbets, and all. The huge old tower was, until late years, inhabited by the family of the proprietor, who built himself a house in the midst of it: but he has since built another in the park opposite, and half-a-dozen 'peelers,' with a commodity of wives and children, now inhabit Bunratty. On the gate where we entered were numerous placards, offering rewards for the apprehension of various country offenders; and a turnpike, a bridge, and a quay, have sprung up from the place which Red Redmond (or anybody else) burned.

On our road to Galway the next day, we were carried once more by the old tower, and for a considerable distance along the fertile banks of the Fergus lake, and a river which pours itself into the Shannon. The first town we come to is Castle Clare, which lies conveniently on the river, with a castle, a good bridge, and many quays and warehouses, near which a small ship or two were lying. The place was once the chief town of the county, but is wretched and ruinous now, being made up for the most part of miserable thatched cots, round which you see the usual dusky population. The drive hence to Ennis lies through a country which is by no means so pleasant as that rich one we have passed through, being succeeded 'by that craggy, bleak, pastoral district which occupies so large a portion of the limestone district of Clare.' Ennis, likewise, stands upon the Fergus, a busy, little, narrow-streeted, foreign-looking town, approached by half-a-mile of thatched cots, in which I am not ashamed to confess, that I saw some as pretty faces as over any half-mile of country I ever travelled in my life.

A great light of the Catholic church, who was of late a candlestick in our own communion, was on the coach with us, reading devoutly out of a breviary, on many occasions, along the road. A crowd of black coats and heads, with that indescribable look which belongs to the Catholic clergy, were evidently on the look-out for the coach; and as it stopped, one of them came up to me with a low bow, and asked if I was the Honourable and Reverend Mr S——? How I wish I had answered him I was! It would have been a grand scene. The respect paid to this gentleman's descent is quite absurd – the papers bandy his title about with pleased emphasis – the Galway paper calls him the *very* Reverend. There is something in the love for rank almost childish: witness the adoration of George IV; the pompous joy with which John Tuam records his correspondence with a great man; the continual my-lording of the Bishops, the Right-Honourabling of Mr O'Connell – which title his party-papers delight on all occasions to give him – nay, the delight of that great man himself when first he attained the dignity; he figured in his robes in the most good-humoured simple delight at having them, and went to church forthwith in them, as if such a man wanted a title before his name.

At Ennis, as well as everywhere else in Ireland, there were of course the regular number of swaggering-looking buckeens, and shabby-genteel idlers, to watch the arrival of the mail-coach. A poor old idiot, with his gray hair tied up in bows, and with a ribbon behind, thrust out a very fair soft hand with taper fingers, and told me, nodding his head very wistfully, that he had no father nor mother: upon which score he got a penny. Nor did the other beggars round the carriage who got none, seem to grudge the poor fellow's good fortune. I think when one poor wretch has a piece of luck, the others seem glad here: and they promise to pray for you just the same if you give as if you refuse.

The town was swarming with people; the little dark streets, which twist about in all directions, being full of cheap merchandise and its vendors. Whether there are many buyers, I can't say. This is written opposite the Market-place in Galway, and I have watched a stall a hundred times in the course of the last three hours, and seen no money taken: but at every place I come to, I can't help wondering at the numbers; it seems market-day everywhere – apples, pigs, and potatoes being sold all over the kingdom. There seem to be some good shops in those narrow streets; among others, a decent little library, where I bought, for eighteenpence, six volumes of works strictly Irish, that will serve for a half-hour's gossip on the next rainy day.

The road hence to Gort carried us at first by some dismal, lonely-looking, reedy lakes, through a melancholy country; an open village standing here and there, with a big chapel in the midst of it, almost always unfinished in some point or other. Crossing at a bridge near a place called Tubbor, the coachman told us we were in the famous county of Galway, which all readers of novels admire in the warlike works of Maxwell and Lever; and, dismal as the country had been in Clare, I think on the northern side of the bridge it was dismaller still – the stones not only appearing in the character of hedges, but strewing over whole fields in which sheep were browsing as well as they could.

We rode for miles through this stony, dismal district, seeing more lakes now and anon, with fellows spearing eels in the midst. Then we passed the plantations of Lord Gort's Castle of Loughcooter, and presently came to the town which bears his name, or *vice versâ*. It is a regularly-built little place, with a square and street; but it looked as if it wondered how the deuce it got into the midst of such a desolate country, and seemed to *bore* itself there considerably. It had nothing to do, and no society.

A short time before arriving at Oranmore, one has glimpses of the sea, which comes opportunely to relieve the dulness of the land. Between Gort and that place we passed through little but the most woeful country, in the midst of which was a village, where a horse-fair was held, and where (upon the word of the coachman) all the bad horses of the country were to be seen. The man was commissioned no doubt to buy for his employers, for two or three merchants were on the look-out for him, and trotted out their cattle by the side of the coach. A very good, neat-looking, smart-trotting, chesnut horse of seven years old, was offered by the owner for £8; a neat brown mare for £10, and a better (as I presume) for £14; but all *looked* very respectable, and I have the coachman's word for it that they were good serviceable horses. Oranmore, with an old castle in the midst of the village, woods, and park-plantations round about, and the bay beyond it, has a pretty and romantic look; and the drive, of about four miles thence to Galway, is the most picturesque part, perhaps, of the fifty miles' ride from Limerick. The road is tolerably wooded. You see the town itself, with its huge old church-tower stretching along the bay, 'backed by hills linking into the long chain of mountains which stretch across Connemara and the Joyce country.' A suburb of cots that seems almost endless has, however, an end at last among the houses of the town; and a little fleet of a couple of hundred fishing-boats was manoeuvring in the bright waters of the bay.

CHAPTER XV

GALWAY – KILROY'S HOTEL – GALWAY NIGHT'S ENTERTAINMENTS – FIRST NIGHT: AN EVENING WITH CAPTAIN FREENY

When it is stated that, throughout the town of Galway, you cannot get a cigar which costs more than twopence, Londoners may imagine the strangeness and remoteness of the place. The rain poured down for two days, after our arrival at Kilroy's Hotel. An umbrella under such circumstances is a poor resource: self-contemplation is far more amusing, especially smoking, and a game at cards, if any one will be so good as to play.

But there was no one in the Hotel coffee-room who was inclined for the sport. The company there, on the day of our arrival, consisted of two coach-passengers, – a Frenchman who came from Sligo, and ordered mutton-chops and *fraid potatoes* for dinner by himself, a turbot which cost two shillings, and in Billingsgate would have been worth a guinea, and a couple of native or inhabitant bachelors, who frequented the table d'hote.

By the way, besides these there were at dinner two turkeys (so that Mr Kilroy's two-shilling ordinary was by no means ill supplied); and, as a stranger, I had the honour of carving these animals, which were dispensed in rather a singular way. There are, as it is generally known, to two turkeys four wings. Of the four passengers, one ate no turkey, one had a pinion, another the remaining part of the wing, and the fourth gentleman took the other three wings for his share. Does everybody in Galway eat three wings when there are two turkeys for dinner? One has heard wonders of the country, – the dashing, daring, duelling, desperate, rollicking, whiskey-drinking people: but this wonder beats all. When I asked the Galway turkiphagus (there is no other word, for turkey was

158

invented long after Greece) 'if he would take a third wing?'
with a peculiar satiric accent on the words *third wing*, which
cannot be expressed in writing, but which the occasion fully
merited, I thought perhaps that, following the custom of the
country, where everybody, according to Maxwell and Lever,
challenges everybody else, – I thought the Galwagian would
call me out: but no such thing. He only said, 'If you plase, sir,'
in the blandest way in the world; and gobbled up the limb in a
twinkling.

As an encouragement, too, for persons meditating that
important change of condition, the gentleman was a tee-
totaller; he took but one glass of water to that intolerable deal
of bubbly-jock. Galway must be very much changed since the
days when Maxwell and Lever knew it. Three turkey-wings
and a glass of water! But the man cannot be the representative
of a class, that is clear: it is physically and arithmetically
impossible. They can't *all* eat three wings of two turkeys at
dinner; the turkeys could not stand it, let alone the men. These
wings must have been 'non usitatae (nec tenues) pennae:' but
no more of these flights: let us come to sober realities.

The fact is, that when the rain is pouring down in the
streets, the traveller has little else to remark except these
peculiarities of his fellow-travellers and inn-sojourners; and,
lest one should be led into farther personalities, it is best to
quit that water-drinking gormandizer at once, and retiring to a
private apartment, to devote one's self to quiet observation,
and the acquisition of knowledge, either by looking out of the
window and examining mankind, or by perusing books, and
so living with past heroes and ages.

As for the knowledge to be had by looking out of window,
it is this evening not much. A great wide blank, bleak,
water-whipped square lies before the bed-room window; at
the opposite side of which is to be seen the Opposition Hotel,
looking even more bleak and cheerless than that over which
Mr Kilroy presides. Large dismal warehouses and private
houses form three sides of the square; and in the midst is a bare
pleasure-ground surrounded by a growth of gaunt iron-
railings, the only plants seemingly in the place. Three triangular edifices that look somewhat like gibbets stand in the
paved part of the square, but the victims that are consigned to

their fate under these triangles are only potatoes, which are weighed there; and, in spite of the torrents of rain, a crowd of barefooted red-petticoated women, and men in gray coats and flower-pot hats, are pursuing their little bargains with the utmost calmness. The rain seems to make no impression on the males; nor do the women guard against it more than by flinging a petticoat over their heads, and so stand bargaining and chattering in Irish, their figures indefinitely reflected in the shining varnished pavement. Donkeys and pony-carts innumerable stand around, similarly reflected; and in the baskets upon these vehicles you see shoals of herrings lying. After a short space this prospect becomes somewhat tedious, and one looks to other sources of consolation.

The eighteen-pennyworth of little books purchased at Ennis in the morning, came here most agreeably to my aid; and indeed they afford many a pleasant hour's reading. Like the *Bibliothèque Grise*, which one sees in the French cottages in the Provinces, and the German Volksbuecher, both of which contain stores of old legends that are still treasured in the country, these yellow-covered books are prepared for the people chiefly; and have been sold for many long years before the march of knowledge began to banish Fancy out of the world, and gave us, in place of the old fairy tales, Penny Magazines, and similar wholesome works. Where are the little harlequin-backed story books, that used to be read by children in England some thirty years ago? Where such authentic narratives as 'Captain Bruce's Travels,' 'The Dreadful Adventures of Sawney Bean,' &c., which were commonly supplied to little boys at school, by the same old lady who sold oranges and alycompayne? – they are all gone out of the world, and replaced by such books as 'Conversations on Chemistry,' 'The Little Geologist,' 'Peter Parley's Tales about the Binomial Theorem,' and the like. The world will be a dull world some hundreds of years hence, when Fancy shall be dead, and ruthless Science (that has no more bowels than a steam-engine) has killed her.

It is a comfort, meanwhile, to come on occasions on some of the good old stories and biographies. These books were evidently written before the useful had attained its present detestable popularity. There is nothing useful *here*, that's certain: and a man will be puzzled to extract a precise moral out of the adventures of Mr James Freeny; or out of the legends in the Hibernian Tales; or out of the lamentable tragedy of the Battle of Aughrim, writ in most doleful Anglo-Irish verse. But, are we to reject all things that have not a moral tacked to them? 'Is there any moral shut within the bosom of the rose?' And yet, as the same noble poet sings, (giving a smart slap to the utility people the while,) 'useful applications lie in art and nature,' and every man may find a moral suited to his mind in them; or if not a moral, an occasion for moralising.

Honesty Freeny's adventures (let us begin with history and historic tragedy, and leave fancy for future consideration), if they have a moral, have that dubious one which the poet admits may be elicited from a rose; and which every man may select according to his mind. And surely this is a far better and more comfortable system of moralising than that in the fable-books, where you are obliged to accept the story with the inevitable moral corollary, that *will* stick close to it.

Whereas, in Freeny's life, one man may see the evil of drinking, another the harm of horse-racing, another the danger attendant on early marriage, a fourth the exceeding inconvenience as well as hazard of the heroic highwayman's-life – which a certain Ainsworth, in company with a certain Cruikshank, have represented as so poetic and brilliant, so prodigal of delightful adventure, so adorned with champagne, gold-lace, and brocade.

And the best part of worthy Freeny's tale is the noble naïveté and simplicity of the hero as he recounts his own adventures; and the utter unconsciousness that he is narrating anything wonderful. It is the way of all great men, who recite their great actions modestly, and as if they were matters of course; as indeed to them they are. A common tyro, having perpetrated a great deed, would be amazed and flurried at his own action; whereas, I make no doubt the Duke of Wellington, after a great victory, took his tea and went to bed just as quietly as he would after a dull debate in the House of Lords. And so with Freeny, – his great and charming characteristic is grave simplicity; he does his work; he knows his danger as well as another; but he goes through his fearful duty quite quietly and easily; and not with the least air of bravado, or the smallest notion that he is doing anything uncommon.

It is related of Carter, the Lion-King, that when he was a boy, and exceedingly fond of gingerbread-nuts, a relation gave him a parcel of those delicious cakes, which the child put in his pocket, just as he was called on to go into a cage with a very large and roaring lion. He had to put his head into the forest-monarch's jaws, and leave it there for a considerable time, to the delight of thousands, as is even now the case; and the interest was so much the greater, as the child was exceedingly innocent, rosy-cheeked, and pretty. To have seen that little flaxen head bitten off by the lion, would have been a far more pathetic spectacle than that of the decapitation of some grey-bearded, old unromantic keeper, who had served out raw-meat, and stirred up the animals with a pole, any time these twenty years: and the interest rose in consequence.

While the little darling's head was thus enjawed, what was the astonishment of everybody, to see him put his hand into his little pocket, take out a paper – from the paper a gingerbread-nut – pop that gingerbread-nut into the lion's mouth, then into his own, and so finish at least two-pennyworth of nuts!

The excitement was delirious: the ladies, when he came out of Chancery, were for doing what the lion had not done, and eating him up – with kisses. And the only remark the young hero made was, 'Uncle, them nuts wasn't so crisp as them I had t'other day.' He never thought of the danger, – he only thought of the nuts.

Thus it is with FREENY. It is fine to mark his bravery, and to see how he cracks his simple philosophic nuts in the jaws of innumerable lions.

At the commencement of the last century, honest Freeny's father was house steward in the family of Joseph Robbins, Esq., of Ballyduff; and, marrying Alice Phelan, a maid-servant in the same family, had issue JAMES, the celebrated Irish hero. At a proper age James was put to school, but being a nimble active lad, and his father's mistress taking a fancy to him, he was presently brought to Ballyduff, where she had a private tutor to instruct him, during the time which he could spare from his professional duty, which was that of pantry-boy in Mr Robbins's establishment. At an early age he began to neglect his duty; and although his father, at the excellent Mrs Robbins's suggestion, corrected him very severely, the bent of his genius was not to be warped by the rod, and he attended 'all the little country dances, diversions and meetings, and became what is called a good dancer, his own natural inclinations hurrying him (as he finely says), into the contrary diversions.'

He was scarce twenty years old when he married (a frightful proof of the wicked recklessness of his former courses), and set up in trade in Waterford; where, however, matters went so ill with him, that he was speedily without money, and £50 in debt. He had, he says, not any way of paying the debt, except by selling his furniture or his *riding-mare*, to both of which measures he was averse; for where is the gentleman in Ireland that can do without a horse to ride? Mr Freeny and his riding-mare became soon famous, insomuch that a thief in gaol warned the magistrates of Kilkenny to beware of a *one-eyed man with a mare.*

These unhappy circumstances sent him on the highway to seek a maintenance, and his first exploit was to rob a gentleman of fifty pounds; then to attack another, against whom he 'had *a secret disgust,* because this gentleman had prevented his former master from giving him a suit of clothes!'

Urged by a noble resentment against this gentleman, Mr Freeny, in company with a friend by the name of Reddy, robbed the gentleman's house, taking therein £70 in money, which was honourably divided among the captors.

'We then,' continues Mr Freeny, 'quitted the house with the booty, and came to Thomastown; but not knowing how to dispose of the plate, left it with Reddy, who said he had a friend from whom he would get cash for it. In some time afterwards I asked him for the dividend of the cash he got for the plate, but all the satisfaction he gave me was, that it was lost, which occasioned me to *have my own opinion of him.*'

Mr Freeny then robbed Sir William Fownes' servant of £14, in such an artful manner that everybody believed the servant had himself secreted the money; and no doubt the rascal was turned adrift, and starved in consequence – a truly comic incident, and one that could be used so as to provoke a great deal of laughter, in an historical work of which our champion should be the hero.

The next enterprise of importance is that against the house of Colonel Palliser, which Freeny thus picturesquely describes. Coming with one of his spies close up to the house, Mr Freeny watched the Colonel lighted to bed by a servant; and thus, as he cleverly says, could judge 'of the room the Colonel lay in.'

'Some time afterwards,' says Freeny, 'I observed a light upstairs, by which I judged the servants were going to bed, and soon after observed that the candles were all quenched, by which I assured myself they were all gone to bed. I then came back to where the men were, and appointed Bulger, Motley, and Commons to go in along with me; but Commons answered, that he never had been in any house before where there were arms; upon which I asked the coward what business he had there, and swore I would as soon shoot him as look at him, and at the same time cocked a pistol to his breast; but the rest of the men prevailed upon me to leave him at the back of the house, where he might run away when he thought proper.

'I then asked Grace where did he choose to be posted: he answered, 'That he would go where I pleased to order him,' for which I thanked him; we then immediately came up to the house, lighted our candles, put Houlahan at the back of the house to prevent any person from coming out that way, and placed Hacket on my mare, well armed, at the front, and I then broke one of the windows with a sledge, whereupon Bulger, Motley, Grace, and I got in, upon which I ordered Motley and Grace to go upstairs, and Bulger and I would stay below, where we thought the greatest danger would be; but I immediately, upon second consideration, for fear Motley or Grace should be daunted, desired Bulger to go up with them, and when he had fixed matters above, to come down, as I judged the Colonel lay below. I then went to the room where the Colonel was, and burst open the door; upon which he said, 'Odds-wounds! who's there?' to which I answered, 'A friend, sir;' upon which he said, 'You lie; by G——d, you are no friend of mine.' I then said that I was, and his relation also, and that if he viewed me close he would know me, and begged of him not to be angry; upon which I immediately seized a bullet gun and case of pistols, which I observed hanging up in his room. I then quitted his room, and walked round the lower part of the house, thinking to meet some of the servants, *whom* I thought would strive to make their escape from the men who were above, and meeting none of them, I immediately returned to the Colonel's room; where I no sooner entered than he desired me to go out for a villain, and asked why I bred such disturbance in his house at that time of night; at the same time I snatched his breeches from under his head, wherein I got a small purse of gold, and said, that abuse was not fit treatment for me who was his relation, and that it would hinder me of calling to see him again; I then demanded the key of his desk which stood in his room; he answered he had no key; upon which I said I had a very good key; at the same time giving it a stroke with the sledge, which burst it open, wherein I got a purse of ninety guineas, a four-pound piece, two moidores, some small gold, and a large glove, with twenty-eight guineas in silver.

'By this time Bulger and Motley came downstairs to me, after rifling the house above; we then observed a closet inside his room, which we soon entered, and got therein a basket wherein there was plate to the value of three hundred pounds.'

And so they took leave of Colonel Palliser, and rode away with their earnings.

The story, as here narrated, has that simplicity which is beyond the reach of all except the very highest art; and it is not high art certainly which Mr Freeny can be said to possess, but a noble nature rather, which leads him thus grandly to describe scenes wherein he acted a great part. With what a gallant determination does he inform the coward Commons, that he would shoot him '*as soon as look at him;*' and how dreadful he must have looked (with his one eye) as he uttered that sentiment! But he left him, he says with a grim humour, at the back of the house, 'where he might run away when he thought proper.' The Duke of Wellington must have read Mr Freeny's history in his youth (his Grace's birthplace is not far from the scene of the other gallant Irishman's exploit), for the Duke acted in precisely a similar way by a Belgian Colonel at Waterloo.

It must be painful to great and successful commanders to think how their gallant comrades and lieutenants, partners of their toil, their feelings, and their fame, are separated from them by time, by death, by estrangement, nay sometimes by treason. Commons is off, disappearing noiseless into the deep night, whilst his comrades perform the work of danger; and Bulger, – BULGER, who in the above scene acts so gallant a part, and in whom Mr Freeny places so much confidence – actually went away to England, carrying off 'some plate, some shirts, a gold watch, and a diamond ring' of the Captain's; and, though he returned to his native country, the valuables did not return with him, on which the Captain swore he would blow his brains out. As for poor Grace, he was hanged, much to his leader's sorrow, who says of him that he was 'the faithfullest of his spies.' Motley was sent to Naas gaol for the very robbery: and though Captain Freeny does not mention his ultimate fate, 'tis probable he was hanged too. Indeed, the warrior's life is a hard one, and over misfortunes like these the feeling heart cannot but sigh.

But, putting out of the question the conduct and fate of the Captain's associates, let us look to his own behaviour as a leader. It is impossible not to admire his serenity, his dexterity, that dashing impetuosity in the moment of action, and that aquiline *coup d'oeil* which belongs to but few generals. He it is who leads the assault, smashing in the window with a sledge; he bursts open the Colonel's door, who says (naturally enough), 'Odds-wounds! who's there?' 'A friend, sir,' says Freeny. 'You lie; by G——d, you are no friend of mine,' roars the military blasphemer. 'I then said that I was, *and his relation also*, and that if he viewed me close he would know me, and begged of him not to be angry; *upon which I immediately seized* a brace of pistols which I observed hanging up in his room.' That is something like presence of mind: none of your brutal braggadocio work, but neat, wary, nay sportive bearing in the face of danger. And again, on the second visit to the Colonel's room, when the latter bids him 'go out for a villain, and not breed a disturbance,' what reply makes Freeny? '*At the same time I snatched his breeches* from under his head.' A common man would never have thought of looking for them in such a place at all. The difficulty about the key he resolves in quite an

Alexandrian manner; and, from the specimen we already have
had of the Colonel's style of speaking, we may fancy how
ferociously he lay in bed and swore, after Captain Freeny and
his friends had disappeared with the ninety guineas, the
moidores, the four-pound piece, and the glove with twenty-
eight guineas in silver.

As for the plate, he hid it in a wood; and then, being out of
danger, he sat down and paid everybody his deserts. By the
way, what a strange difference of opinion is there about a
man's *deserts*! Here sits Captain Freeny with a company of
gentlemen, and awards them a handsome sum of money, for
an action which other people would have remunerated with a
halter. Which are right? perhaps both: but at any rate, it will be
admitted that the Captain takes the humane view of the
question.

The greatest enemy Captain Freeny had was Counsellor
Robbins, a son of his old patron, and one of the most
determined thief-pursuers the country ever knew. But though
he was untiring in his efforts to capture (and of course to hang)
Mr Freeny, and though the latter was strongly urged by his
friends to blow the Counsellor's brains out; yet, to his
immortal honour, it is said he refused that temptation,
agreeable as it was, declaring that he had eaten too much of
that family's bread ever to take the life of one of them, and
being besides quite aware that the Counsellor was only acting
against him in a public capacity. He respected him in fact, like
an honourable though terrible adversary.

How deep a stratagem-inventor the Counsellor was, may
be gathered from the following narration of one of his plans.

'Counsellor Robbins finding his brother had not got intelligence that was sufficient to carry any reasonable foundation
for apprehending us, walked out as if merely for exercise, till
he met with a person whom he thought he could confide in,
and desired the person to meet him at a private place appointed
for that purpose, which they did; and he told that person he
had a very good opinion of him, from the character received
from his father of him, and from his own knowledge of him,
and hoped that the person would then show him that such
opinion was not ill-founded. The person assuring the
Counsellor he would do all in his power to serve and oblige

him, the Counsellor told him how greatly he was concerned
to hear the scandalous character that part of the country
(which had formerly been an honest one) had lately fallen into.
That it was said that a gang of robbers who disturbed the
country lived thereabouts; the person told him he was afraid
what he said was too true; and, on being asked whom he
suspected, he named the same four persons Mr Robbins had,
but said, he dare not, for fear of being murdered, be too
inquisitive, and therefore could not say anything material; the
Counsellor asked him if he knew where there was any private
ale to be sold; and he said, Moll Burke, who lived near the end
of Mr Robbins's avenue, had a barrel or half a barrel. The
Counsellor then gave the person a moidore, and desired him
to go to Thomastown and buy two or three gallons of
whiskey, and bring it to Moll Burke's, and invite as many as
he suspected to be either principals or accessories, to take a
drink, and make them drink very heartily, and when he found
they were fuddled, and not sooner, to tell some of the hastiest,
that some other had said some bad things of them, so as to
provoke them to abuse and quarrel with each other; and then,
probably, in their liquor and passion, they might make some
discoveries of each other, as may enable the Counsellor to get
some one of the gang to discover and accuse the rest.

'The person accordingly got the whiskey and invited a good
many to drink; but the Counsellor being then at his brother's,
a few only went to Moll Burke's, the rest being afraid to
venture while the Counsellor was in the neighbourhood;
among those who met, there was one Moll Brophy, the wife
of Mr Robbins's smith, and one Edmund or Edward Stapleton, otherwise Gaul, who lived thereabouts; and when they
had drank plentifully, the Counsellor's spy told Moll Brophy,
Gaul had said she had gone astray with some persons or other;
she then abused Gaul, and told him he was one of Freeny's
accomplices, for that he, Gaul, had told her he had seen
Colonel Palliser's watch with Freeny, and that Freeny had told
him, Gaul, that John Welsh and the two Graces had been with
him at the robbery.

'The company on their quarrel broke up, and the next
morning the spy met the Counsellor at the place appointed, at
a distance from Mr Robbins's house, to prevent suspicion, and

there told the Counsellor what intelligence he had got; the
Counsellor not being then a justice of the peace, got his
brother to send for Moll Brophy to be examined; but when
she came, she refused to be sworn or to give any evidence, and
thereupon the Counsellor had her tied and put on a car in
order to be carried to gaol on a mittimus from Mr Robbins,
for refusing to give evidence on behalf of the Crown. When
she found she would really be sent to gaol, she submitted to be
sworn, and the Counsellor drew from her what she had said
the night before, and something further, and desired her not to
tell any body what she had sworn.'

But if the Counsellor was acute, were there not others as
clever as he? For when, in consequence of the information of
Mrs Brophy, some gentlemen who had been engaged in the
burglarious enterprises in which Mr Freeny obtained so much
honour, were seized and tried, Freeny came forward with the
best of arguments in their favour. Indeed, it is fine to see these
two great spirits matched one against the other, – the
Counsellor, with all the regular force of the country to back
him, – the Highway-General with but the wild resources of
his gallant genius, and with cunning and bravery for his chief
allies.

'I lay by for a considerable time after, and concluded within
myself to do no more mischief till after the assizes, when I
would hear how it went with the men who were then in
confinement. Some time before the assizes Counsellor Robbins came to Ballyduff, and told his brother that he believed
Anderson and Welsh were guilty, and also said he would
endeavour to have them both hanged, of which I was
informed.

'Soon after, I went to the house of one George Roberts,
who asked me if I had any regard for those fellows who were
then confined (meaning Anderson and Welsh). I told him I had
a regard for one of them; upon which he said, he had a friend
who was a man of power and interest, – that he would save
either of them, provided I would give him five guineas. I told
him I would give him ten, and the first gold watch I could get;
whereupon he said that it was of no use to speak to his friend
without the money or value, for that he was a mercenary man;
on which I told Roberts I had not so much money at that time,

but that I would give him my watch as a pledge to give his friend. I then gave him my watch, and desired him to engage that I would pay the money which I promised to pay, or give value for it in plate, in two or three nights after, upon which he engaged that his friend would act the needful; when we appointed a night to meet, and we accordingly met; and Roberts told me that his friend agreed to save Anderson and Welsh from the gallows; whereupon I gave him a plate tankard, value £10, a large ladle, value £4, with some table-spoons; and the assizes of Kilkenny, in Spring, 1748, coming on soon after, Counsellor Robbins had Welsh transmitted from Naas to Kilkenny, in order to give evidence against Anderson and Welsh; and they were tried for Mrs Mounford's robbery, on the evidence of John Welsh and others; the physic working well, six of the jury were for finding them guilty, and six more for acquitting them; and the other six finding them peremptory and that they were resolved to starve the others into compliance, as they say they may do by law, were for their own sakes obliged to comply with them, and they were acquitted; on which Counsellor Robbins began to smoke the affair, and suspect the operation of gold dust, which was well applied for my comrades, and thereupon left the court in a rage, and swore he would for ever quit the country, since he found people were not satisfied with protecting and saving the rogues they had under themselves, but must also show that they could and would oblige others to have rogues under them whether they would or no.'

Here Counsellor Robbins certainly loses that greatness which has distinguished him in his former attack on Freeny; the Counsellor is defeated and loses his temper. Like Napoleon, he is unequal to reverses, but in adverse fortune his presence of mind deserts him.

But what call had he to be in a passion at all? It may be very well for a man to be in a rage because he is disappointed of his prey: so is the hawk when the dove escapes, in a rage; but let us reflect that, had Counsellor Robbins had his will, two honest fellows would have been hanged; and so let us be heartily thankful that he was disappointed, and that these men were acquitted by a jury of their countrymen. What right had the Counsellor, forsooth, to interfere with their verdict? Not against Irish juries at least does the old satire apply, 'And culprits hang that jurymen may dine?' At Naas, on the contrary, the jurymen starve in order that the culprits might be saved – a noble and humane act of self-denial.

In another case, stern justice, and the law of self-preservation, compelled Mr Freeny to take a very different course with respect to one of his ex-associates. In the former instance we have seen him pawning his watch, giving up tankard, tablespoons – all for his suffering friends; here we have his method of dealing with traitors.

One of his friends, by the name of Anderson, was taken prisoner, and condemned to be hanged, which gave Mr Freeny, he says, 'a great shock;' but presently this Anderson's fears were worked upon by some traitors within the gaol, and

'He then consented to discover; but I had a friend in gaol at the same time, one Patrick Healy, who daily insinuated to him that it was of no use or advantage to him to discover anything, as he received sentence of death; and that, after he had made a discovery, to leave him as he was, without troubling themselves about a reprieve. But notwithstanding, he told the gentlemen that there was a man *blind of an eye, who had a bay mare,* that lived at the other side of Thomastown bridge, *whom* he assured them would be very troublesome in that neighbourhood after his death. When Healy discovered what he told the gentlemen, he one night took an opportunity, and made Dooling fuddled, and prevailed upon him to take his oath he never would give the least hint about me any more. He also told him the penalty that attended infringing upon his oath; but more especially as he was at that time near his end, which had the desired effect; for he never mentioned my name, nor even anything relative to me;' and so went out of the world repenting of his meditated treason.

What further exploits Mr Freeny performed may be learned by the curious in his history; they are all, it need scarcely be said, of a similar nature to that noble action which has already been described. His escapes from his enemies were marvellous; his courage in facing them equally great. He is attacked by whole 'armies,' through which he makes his way; wounded, he lies in the woods for days together with three bullets in his leg, and in this condition manages to escape several 'armies' that have been marched against him. He is supposed to be dead, or travelling on the Continent, and suddenly makes his appearance in his old haunts, advertising his arrival by robbing ten men on the highway in a single day; and, so terrible is his courage, or so popular his manners, that he describes scores of labourers looking on while his exploits were performed, and not affording the least aid to the roadside traveller whom he vanquished.

But numbers always prevail in the end: what could Leonidas himself do against an army? The gallant band of brothers led by Freeny were so pursued by the indefatigable Robbins and his myrmidons, that there was no hope left for them, and the Captain saw that he must succumb.

He reasoned, however, with himself (with his usual keen logic), and said: 'My men must fall, – the world is too strong for us, and, to-day, or to-morrow, – it matters scarcely when, they must yield. They will be hanged for a certainty, and thus will disappear the noblest company of knights the world has ever seen.

'But as they will certainly be hanged, and no power of mine can save them, is it necessary that I should follow them too to the tree; and will James Bulger's fate be a whit more agreeable to him, because James Freeny dangles at his side? To suppose so, would be to admit that he was actuated by a savage feeling of revenge, which I know belongs not to his generous nature.'

In a word, Mr Freeny resolved to turn king's evidence; for though he swore (in a communication with the implacable Robbins) that he would rather die than betray Bulger, yet when the Counsellor stated that he must then die, Freeny says, 'I promised to submit, and *understood that Bulger should be set.*'

Accordingly some days afterwards (although the Captain carefully avoids mentioning that he had met his friends with any such intentions as those indicated in the last paragraph), he and Mr Bulger came together: and, strangely enough, it was agreed that the one was to sleep while the other kept watch; and, while thus employed, the enemy came upon them. But let Freeny describe for himself the last passages of his history.

'We then went to Welsh's house, with a view not to make any delay there; but, taking a glass extraordinary after supper, Bulger fell asleep. Welsh in the mean time told me, his house was the safest place I could get in that neighbourhood, and while I remained there I would be very safe, provided that no person knew of my coming there, (I had not acquainted him that Breen knew of my coming that way.) I told Welsh that as Bulger was asleep, I would not go to bed till morning: upon which Welsh and I stayed up all night, and in the morning Welsh said, that he and his wife had a call to Callen, it being market-day. About nine o'clock I went and awoke Bulger, desiring him to get up and guard me whilst I slept, as I guarded him all night; he said he would, and then I went to bed charging him to watch close, for fear we should be surprised. I put my blunderbuss and two cases of pistols under my head, and soon fell fast alseep. In two hours after the servant-girl of the house, seeing an enemy coming into the yard, ran up to the room where we were, and said that there were an hundred men coming into the yard; upon which Bulger immediately awoke me, and, taking up my blunder-buss, he fired a shot towards the door, which wounded Mr Burgess, one of the sheriffs of Kilkenny, of which wound he died. They concluded to set the house on fire about us, which they accordingly did; upon which I took my fusee in one hand, and a pistol in the other, and Bulger did the like, and as we came out of the door, we fired on both sides, imagining it to be the best method of dispersing the enemy, who were on both sides of the door. We got through them, but they fired after us, and as Bulger was leaping over a ditch, he received a shot in the small of the leg, which rendered him incapable of running; but getting into a field, where I had the ditch between me and the enemy, I still walked slowly with Bulger, till I thought the enemy were within shot of the ditch, and then wheeled back to the ditch, and presented my fusee at them; they all drew back and went for their horses to ride round, as the field was wide and open, and without cover except the ditch. When I discovered their intention I stood in the middle of the field, and one of the gentlemen's servants (there were fourteen in number) rode foremost towards me, upon which I told the son of a coward, I believed he had no more than five pounds a year from his master, and that I would put him in such a condition, that his master would not maintain him afterwards; to which he answered, that he had no view of doing us any harm, but that he was commanded by his master to ride so near us; and then immediately rode back to the enemy, who were coming towards him. They rode almost within shot of us, and I observed they intended to surround us in the field, and prevent me from having any recourse to the ditch again. Bulger was at this time so bad with the wound, that he could not go one step without leaning on my shoulder. At length, seeing the enemy coming within shot of me, I laid down my fusee, and stripped off my coat and waistcoat, and running towards them, cried out, 'You sons of cowards, come on, and I will blow your brains out;' on which they returned back, and then I walked easy to the place where I left my clothes, and put them on, and Bulger and I walked leisurely some distance further. The enemy came a second time, and I occasioned them to draw back as before, and then we walked to Lord Dysart's deer-park wall. I got up the wall and helped Bulger up: the enemy who still pursued us, though not within shot, seeing us on the wall, one of them fired a random shot at us to no purpose. We got safe over the wall, and went from thence into my Lord Dysart's wood, where Bulger said he would remain, thinking it a safe place, but I told him he would be safer any where else, for the army of Kilkenny and Callen would be soon about the wood, and that he would be taken if he staid there. Besides, as I was very averse to betraying him at all, I could not bear the thoughts of his being taken in my company by any party but Lord Carrick's. I then brought him about half a mile beyond the wood, and left him there in a break of briars, and looking towards the wood, I saw it surrounded by the army. There was a cabin near that place where I fixed Bulger; he said he would go to it at night, and he would send for some of his friends to take care of him. It was then almost two o'clock, and we were four hours going to that place, which was about two miles from Welsh's house. Imagining that there were spies fixed on all the fords and by-roads between that place and the mountain, I went towards the bounds of the county Tipperary, where I arrived about night-fall, and going to a cabin, I asked whether there was any drink sold near that place? The man of the house said there was not; and as I was very much fatigued, I sat down, and there refreshed myself

with what the cabin afforded. I then begged of the man to sell
me a pair of his brogues and stockings as I was then
bare-footed, which he accordingly did. I quitted the house,
went through Kinsheenah and Poulacoppal, and having so
many thorns in my feet, I was obliged to go bare-footed, and
went to Sleedelagh, and through the mountains, till I came
within four miles of Waterford, and going into a cabin, the
man of the house took eighteen thorns out of the soles of my
feet, and I remained in and about that place for some time
after.

'In the mean time, a friend of mine was told that it was
impossible for me to escape death, for Bulger had turned
against me, and that his friends and Stack were resolved upon
my life; but the person who told my friend so, also said, that if
my friend would set Bulger and Breen, I might get a pardon
through the Earl of Carrick's means and Counsellor Robbins's
interest. My friend said, that he *was sure I would not consent to
such a thing, but the best way was to do it unknown to me*; and my
friend accordingly set Bulger, who was taken by the Earl of
Carrick and his party, and Mr Fitzgerald, and six of
Counsellor Robbins's soldiers, and committed to Kilkenny
jail; he was three days in jail before I heard he was taken, being
at that time twenty miles distant from the neighbourhood, nor
did I hear from him or see him since I left him near Lord
Dysart's wood, *till a friend* came and told me it was to preserve
my life and to fufil my articles, that Bulger was taken.'

* * * *

'Finding I was suspected, I withdrew to a neighbouring wood,
and concealed myself there till night, and then went to
Ballyduff to Mr Fitzgerald and surrendered myself to him, till
I could write to my Lord Carrick, which I did immediately, and
gave him an account of what I escaped, or that I would
have gone to Ballilynch and surrendered myself there to him,
and begged his lordship to send a guard for me, to conduct me
to his house, which he did, and I remained there for a few
days.

'He then sent me to Kilkenny jail; and at the summer assizes
following, James Bulger, Patrick Hacket, otherwise Bristeen,

Martin Millea, John Stack, Felix Donelly, Edmund Kenny, and James Larrasy, were tried, convicted, and executed; and at spring assizes following, George Roberts was tried for receiving Colonel Palliser's gold watch, knowing it to be stolen, but was acquitted on account of exceptions taken to my pardon, which prevented my giving evidence. At the following assizes, when I had got a new pardon, Roberts was again tried for receiving the tankard, ladle, and silver spoons from me, knowing them to be stolen, and was convicted and executed. At the same assizes, John Reddy, my instructor, and Martin Millea, were also tried, convicted, and executed.'

And so they were all hanged – James Bulger, Patrick Hacket, or Bristeen, Patrick Millea, John Stack, and Felix Donelly, and Edmund Kenny, and James Larrasy, with Roberts who received the Colonel's watch, the tankard, ladle, and the silver spoons, were all convicted and executed. Their names drop naturally into blank verse. It is hard upon poor George Roberts too; for the watch he received was no doubt in the very inexpressibles which the Captain himself took from the Colonel's head.

As for the captain himself, he says that, on going out of jail, Counsellor Robbins and Lord Carrick proposed a subscription for him; in which, strangely, the gentlemen of the county would not join; and so that scheme came to nothing, and so he published his memoirs in order to get himself a little money.

Many a man has taken up the pen under similar circumstances of necessity. But what became of Captain Freeny afterwards, does not appear. Was he an honest man ever after? Was he hanged for subsequent misdemeanours? It matters little to him now, though perhaps one cannot help feeling a little wish that the latter fate may have befallen him.

Whatever his death was, however, the history of his life has been one of the most popular books ever known in this country. It formed the class-book in those rustic universities, which are now rapidly disappearing from among the hedges of Ireland. And lest any English reader should, on account of its lowness, quarrel with the introduction here of this strange picture of wild courage and daring, let him be reconciled by the moral at the end, which, in the persons of Bulger and the rest, hangs at the beam before Kilkenny jail.

CHAPTER XVI

MORE RAIN IN GALWAY – A WALK THERE – AND THE SECOND GALWAY NIGHT'S ENTERTAINMENT

Seven hills has Rome, seven mouths has Nilus' stream,
Around the Pole seven burning planets gleam.
Twice equal these is Galway, Connaught's Rome:
Twice seven illustrious tribes here find their home.★
Twice seven fair towers the city's ramparts guard,
Each house within is built of marble hard,
With lofty turret flanked, twice seven the gates,
Through twice seven bridges water permeates.
In the High Church are twice seven altars raised,
At each a holy saint and patron's praised.
Twice seven the Convents, dedicate to heaven, –
Seven for the female sex – for Godly fathers seven.†

Having read in Hardiman's History the quaint inscription in Irish Latin, of which the above lines are a version, and looked admiringly at the old plans of Galway which are to be found in

★ By the help of an Alexandrine, the names of these famous families may also be accommodated to verse.

'Athey, Blake, Bodkin, Browne, Deane, Dorsey, Frinche,
Joyce, Morech, Skereth, Fonte, Kirowan, Martin, Lynche.'

† If the rude old verses are not very remarkable in quality, in *quantity* they are still more deficient, and take some dire liberties with the laws laid down in the Gradus and the Grammar.

'Septem ornant montes Romam, septem ostia Nilum,
    Tot rutilis stellis splendet in axe Polus.
Galvia, Polo Niloque bis aequas. Roma Conachtae,
    Bis septem illustres has colit illa tribus.
Bis urbis septem defendunt moenia turres,

the same work, I was in hopes to have seen in the town some considerable remains of its former splendour, in spite of a warning to the contrary which the learned historiographer gives.

The old city certainly has some relics of its former stateliness; and, indeed, is the only town in Ireland I have seen, where an antiquary can find much subject for study, or a lover of the picturesque an occasion for using his pencil. It is a wild, fierce, and most original old town. Joyce's castle in one of the principal streets, a huge square gray tower, with many carvings and ornaments, is a gallant relic of its old days of prosperity, and gives one an awful idea of the tenements which the other families inhabited, and which are designed in the interesting plate which Mr Hardiman gives in his work. The Collegiate Church, too, is still extant without its fourteen altars, and looks to be something between a church and a castle, and as if it should be served by templars with sword and helmet, in place of mitre and crosier. The old houses in the main street are like fortresses; the windows look into a court within; there is but a small low door, and a few grim windows peering suspiciously into the street.

Then there is Lombard-street, otherwise called Deadman's-lane, with a raw-head and cross-bones, and a 'memento mori' over the door where the dreadful tragedy of the Lynches was acted in 1493. If Galway is the Rome of Connaught, James Lynch Fitzstephen, the Mayor, may be considered as the Lucius Junius Brutus thereof. Lynch had a son who went to Spain as master of one of his father's ships, and being of an extravagant wild turn, there contracted debts, and drew bills, and alarmed his father's correspondent, who sent a clerk and nephew of his own back in young Lynch's ship to Galway, to settle accounts. On the fifteenth day, young Lynch threw the

---

Intus et en duro est marmore quaeque domus.
Bis septem portae sunt, castra et culmina circum,
   Per totidem pontûm permeat unda vias.
Principe bis septem fulgent altaria templo,
   Quaevis patronae est ara dicata suo.
Et septem sacrata Deo coenobia, patrum,
   Foeminei et sexus, tot pia tecta tenet.'

Spaniard overboard: coming back to his own country, reformed his life a little, and was on the point of marrying one of the Blakes, Burkes, Bodkins, or others; when a seaman who had sailed with him, being on the point of death, confessed the murder in which he had been a participator.

Hereon the father, who was chief magistrate of the town, tried his son, and sentenced him to death: and when the clan Lynch rose in a body to rescue the young man, and avert such a disgrace from their family, it is said that Fitzstephen Lynch hung the culprit with his own hand. A tragedy called 'The Warden of Galway,' has been written on the subject, and was acted a few nights before my arrival.

The waters of Lough Corrib, which 'permeate' under the bridges of the town, go rushing and roaring to the sea with a noise and eagerness only known in Galway; and along the banks you see all sorts of strange figures washing all sorts of wonderful rags, with red petticoats and redder shanks standing in the stream. Pigs are in every street, the whole town shrieks with them. There are numbers of idlers on the bridges, thousands in the streets, humming and swarming in and out of dark old ruinous houses; congregated round numberless apple-stalls, nail-stalls, bottle-stalls, pigs'foot stalls; in queer old shops, that look to be two centuries old; loitering about warehouses, ruined or not; looking at the washer-women washing in the river, or at the fish-donkeys, or at the potato-stalls, or at a vessel coming into the quay, or at the boats putting out to sea.

That boat at the quay, by the little old gate, is bound for Arranmore; and one next to it has a freight of passengers for the cliffs of Mohir, on the Clare Coast; and as the sketch is taken, a hundred of people have stopped in the street to look on, and are buzzing behind in Irish, telling the little boys in that language, who will persist in placing themselves exactly in the front of the designer, to get out of his way, which they do for some time; but at length curiosity is so intense that you are entirely hemmed in, and the view rendered quite invisible. A sailor's wife comes up, who speaks English, with a very wistful face, and begins to hint, that them black pictures are very bad likenesses, and very dear too for a poor woman, and how much would a painted one cost, does his honour think?

and she has her husband that is going to sea to the West Indies to-morrow; and she'd give anything to have a picture of him. So I made bold to offer to take his likeness for nothing. But he never came, except one day at dinner, and not at all on the next day, though I staid on purpose to accommodate him. It is true that it was pouring with rain, and as English waterproof cloaks are not waterproof in *Ireland*, the traveller who has but one coat must of necessity respect it, and had better stay where he is, unless he prefers to go to bed while he has his clothes dried at the next stage.

The houses in the fashionable street where the club-house stands (a strong building, with an agreeable Old Bailey look,) have the appearance of so many little Newgates. The Catholic chapels are numerous, unfinished, and ugly. Great warehouses and mills rise up by the stream, or in the midst of unfinished streets here and there; and handsome convents with their gardens, justice-houses, barracks, and hospitals adorn the large, poor, bustling, rough-and-ready looking town. A man who sells hunting-whips, gunpowder, guns, fishing-tackle, and brass and iron ware, has a few books on his counter, and a lady in a bye-street, who carries on the profession of a milliner, eked out her stock in a similar way. But there were no regular book-shops that I saw, and when it came on to rain, I had no resource but the Hedge-School volumes again. They, like Patrick Spelman's sign (which was faithfully copied in the town,) present some very rude flowers of poetry, and 'entertainment' of an exceedingly humble sort: but such shelter is not to be despised when no better is to be had; nay, possibly its novelty may be piquant to some readers, as an admirer of Shakespeare will occasionally condescend to listen to Mr Punch, or an epicure to content himself with a homely dish of beans and bacon.

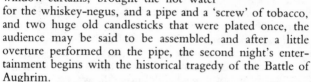

When Mr Kilroy's waiter has drawn the window-curtains, brought the hot water for the whiskey-negus, and a pipe and a 'screw' of tobacco, and two huge old candlesticks that were plated once, the audience may be said to be assembled, and after a little overture performed on the pipe, the second night's entertainment begins with the historical tragedy of the Battle of Aughrim.

Though it has found its way to the West of Ireland, the Battle of Aughrim is evidently by a Protestant author; a great enemy of Popery and wooden shoes; both of which principles, incarnate in the person of Saint Ruth, the French General commanding the troops sent by Louis XIV to the aid of James II., meet with a woeful downfall at the conclusion of the piece. It must have been written in the reign of Queen Anne, judging from some loyal compliments which are paid to that sovereign in the play, which is also modelled upon Cato.

The Battle of Aughrim is written from beginning to end in decasyllabic verse of the richest sort; and introduces us to the chiefs of William and James's army. On the English side we have Baron de Ginckle, three Generals, and two Colonels; on the Irish, Monsieur Saint Ruth, two Generals, two Colonels, and an English gentleman of fortune, a volunteer, and son of no less a person than Sir Edmonbury Godfrey.

There are two ladies – Jemima, the Irish Colonel Talbot's daughter, in love with Godfrey; and Lucinda, lady of Colonel Herbert, in love with her lord; and the deep nature of the tragedy may be imagined when it is stated that Colonel Talbot is killed, Colonel Herbert is killed, Sir Charles Godfrey is killed, and Jemima commits suicide, as resolved not to survive her adorer. St Ruth is also killed, and the remaining Irish heroes are taken prisoners or run away. Among the supernumeraries there is likewise a dreadful slaughter.

The author, however, though a Protestant is an Irishman, (there are peculiarities in his pronunciation which belong only to that nation,) and as far as courage goes, he allows the two parties to be pretty equal. The scene opens with a martial sound of kettle-drums and trumpets in the Irish camp, near Athlone. That town is besieged by Ginckle, and Monsieur St Ruth (despising his enemy with a confidence often fatal to Generals) meditates an attack on the besiegers' lines, if, by any chance, the besieged garrison be not in a condition to drive them off.

After discoursing on the posture of affairs, and letting General Sarsfield and Colonel O'Neil know his hearty contempt of the English and their General, all parties, after protestations of patriotism, indulge in hopes of the downfall of William. St Ruth says he will drive the wolves and lions' cubs away. O'Neil declares he scorns the revolution, and, like great Cato, smiles at persecution. Sarsfield longs for the day 'when our Monks and Jesuits shall return, and holy incense on our altars burn.' – When

'*Enter* a Post.

Post. With important news I from Athlone am sent,
Be pleased to lead me to the General's tent.
    Sars. Behold the General there. Your message tell.
    St Ruth. Declare your message. Are our friends all well?
    Post. Pardon me, sir, the fatal news I bring,
Like vulture's poison every heart shall sting.
Athlone is lost without your timely aid,
At six this morning an assault was made,
When under shelter of the British cannon,
Their grenadiers in armour took the Shannon,
Led by brave Captain Sandy's, who *with fame,
Plunged to his middle in the rapid stream*:
He led them through, and with undaunted ire
He gained the bank in spite of all our fire;

Being bravely followed by his grenadiers
Though bullets flew like hail about their ears,
And by this time they enter uncontrolled.
  St Ruth. Dare all the force of England be so bold,
T' attempt to storm so brave a town, when I
With all Hibernia's sons of war am nigh?
Return: and if the Briton's dare pursue,
Tell them St Ruth is near, and *that will do*.
  Post. Your aid would do much better than your name.
  St Ruth. Bear back this answer, friend, from whence
you came.
[*Exit* Post.'

The picture of brave Sandys 'who with fame, plunged to his
middle in the rapid strame:' is not a bad image on the part of
the Post: and St Ruth's reply, 'Tell them St Ruth is near, and
that will do,' characteristic of the vanity of his nation. But
Sarsfield knows Britons better, and pays a merited
compliment to their valour.

  '*Sars*. Send speedy succours and their fate prevent,
You know not yet what Britons dare attempt.
I know the English fortitude is such,
To boast of nothing, though they hazard much.
No force on earth their fury can repel,
Nor would they fly from all the devils in hell.'

Another officer arrives – Athlone is really taken, St. Ruth
gives orders to retreat to Aughrim, and Sarsfield, in a rage,
first challenges him, and then vows he will quit the army. 'A
gleam of horror does my vitals *damp*,' says the Frenchman (in a
figure of speech, more remarkable for vigour than logic;). 'I
fear Lord Lucan has forsook the camp?' But not so: after a
momentary indignation, Sarsfield returns to his duty, and ere
long is reconciled with his vain and vacillating chief.
  And now the love intrigue begins. Godfrey enters – and
states Sir Charles Godfrey is his lawful name – he is an
Englishman, and was on his way to join Ginckle's camp,
when Jemima's beauty overcame him: he asks Colonel Talbot
to bestow on him the lady's hand. The Colonel consents,

and in Act II, on the plain of Aughrim, at 5 o'clock in the morning, Jemima enters and proclaims her love. The lovers have an interview, which concludes by a mutual confession of attachment, and Jemima says, 'Here, take my hand. 'Tis true the gift is small, but when I can, I'll give you heart and all.' The lines show finely the agitation of the young person. She meant to say, take *my heart*, but she is longing to be married to him, and the words slip out as it were unawares. Godfrey cries in raptures –

'Thanks to the Gods! who such a present gave,
Such radiant graces ne'er could man *receive* (*resave*);
For who on earth has e'er such transports known?
What is the Turkish monarch on his throne,
Hemmed round *with rusty swords* in pompous state?
Amidst his court no joys can be so great.
Retire with me, my soul no longer stay!
In public view, the General moves this way.'

'Tis, indeed, the General, who, reconciled with Sarsfield, straightway, according to his custom, begins to boast about what he will do.

'Thrice welcome to my heart, thou best of friends!
The rock on which our holy faith depends;
May this our meeting as a tempest make
The vast foundations of Britannia shake,
Tear up their orange plant, and overwhelm
The strongest bulwarks of the British realm!
Then shall the Dutch and Hanoverian fall,
And James shall ride in triumph to Whitehall,
Then to protect our faith he will maintain
An inquisition here like that in Spain.
    Sars. Most bravely urged, my Lord! your skill I own,
Would be *unparalleled* – had you saved Athlone.'

– 'Had you saved Athlone!' Sarsfield has him there: and the contest of words might have provoked quarrels still more fatal; but alarms are heard: the battle begins, and St Ruth (still confident) goes to meet the enemy, exclaiming, 'Athlone was sweet, but Aughrim shall be sour.' The fury of the Irish is redoubled on hearing of Talbot's heroic death: the Colonel's corpse is presently brought in, and to it enters Jemima, who bewails her loss in the following pathetic terms.

> '*Jemima.* Oh! – he is dead! – my soul is all on fire,
> Witness ye gods! – he did with fame expire.
> For Liberty a sacrifice was made,
> And fell, like Pompey, by some *villain's* blade.
> There lies a breathless corse, whose soul ne'er knew
> A thought but what was always just and true;
> Look down from Heaven, God of peace and love,
> Waft him with triumph to the throne above;
> And Oh! ye winged guardians of the skies
> Tune your sweet harps, and sing his obsequies!
> Good friends, stand off – whilst I embrace the ground
> Whereon he lies – and bathe each mortal wound,
> With brinish tears, that like to torrents run
> From these sad eyes. Oh Heavens! I'm undone.
>   [*Falls down on the body.*

> '*Enter Sir Charles Godfrey. He raises her.*

> '*Sir Char.* Why do these precious eyes like fountains flow,
> *To drown the radiant Heaven that lies below?*
> Dry up your tears, – I trust his soul ere this,
> Has reached the mansions of eternal bliss,
> Soldiers – bear hence the body out of sight.
>   [*They bear him off.*

> '*Jem.* Oh stay – ye murderers, cease to kill me quite:
> See how he glares! – and see again he flies!
> The clouds fly open, and he mounts the skies.
> Oh! See his blood, it shines refulgent bright,
> I see him yet – I cannot lose him quite,
> But still pursue him on – and – *lose my sight.*'

The gradual disappearance of the Colonel's soul is now finely indicated, and so is her grief, when showing the body to Sir Charles, she says – 'Behold the mangled cause of all my woes.' The sorrow of youth, however, is but transitory; and when her lover bids her dry her *gushish* tears, she takes out her pocket-handkerchief with the elasticity of youth, and consoles herself for the father in the husband.

Act III represents the English camp: Ginckle and his Generals discourse: the armies are engaged: in Act IV the English are worsted in spite of their valour, which Sarsfield greatly describes. 'View' says he——

> 'View how the foe like an impetuous flood
> Breaks through the smoke, the water, and – the mud!'

It becomes exceedingly hot. Colonel Earles says,

> 'In vain Jove's lightnings issue from the sky
> For death more sure from British *ensigns* fly,
> Their messengers of death much blood have spilled,
> And full three hundred of the Irish killed.'

(A description of war. – Herbert.)

> 'Now bloody colours wave in their pride,
> *And each proud hero does his beast bestride.*'

General Dorrington's description of the fight is, if possible, still more noble.

> '*Dor.* Haste, noble friends, and save your lives by flight,
> For 'tis but madness if you stand to fight;
> Our cavalry the battle have forsook,
> And death appears in each dejected look,
> Nothing but dread confusion can be seen,
> For severed heads and trunks o'erspread the green;
> The fields, the vales, the hills, and vanquished plain,
> For five miles round are covered with the slain;
> Death in each quarter does the eye alarm,
> Here lies a leg, and there a shattered arm.
> There heads appear, which, cloven by mighty bangs,
> And severed quite, on either shoulder hangs,
> This is the awful scene, my Lords! Oh fly
> The impending danger, for your fate is nigh.'

Which party, however, is to win – the Irish or English?
Their heroism is equal, and young Godfrey especially, on the
Irish side, is carrying all before him; when he is interrupted in
the slaughter by *the ghost of his father*; of old Sir Edmonbury,
whose monument we may see in Westminster Abbey. Sir
Charles, at first, doubts about the genuineness of this venerable old apparition; and thus puts a case to the ghost:–

'Were ghosts in heaven, in heaven they there would stay,
Or if in hell, *they could not get away.*'

A clincher, certainly, as one would imagine; but the ghost
jumps over the horns of the fancied dilemma, by saying that
he is not at liberty to state where he comes from.

'*Ghost*. Where visions rest, or souls imprisoned dwell,
By Heavens's command, we are forbid to tell;
But in the obscure grave – where corpse decay,
Moulder in dust and putrify away, –
No rest is there; for the immortal soul
Takes its full flight and flutters round the pole;
Sometimes I hover over the Euxine sea,
From pole to sphere, until the judgment day;
Over the Thracian Bosphorus do I float,
And pass the Stygian lake in Charon's boat,
O'er Vulcan's fiery court, and sulph'rous cave,
And ride like Neptune on a briny wave;
List to the blowing noise of Etna's flames,
And court the shades of Amazonian dames;
Then take my flight up to the gleamy moon,
Thus do I wander till the day of doom.
Proceed I dare not, or I would unfold
A horrid tale would make your blood run cold,
Chill all your nerves and sinews in a trice
Like whispering rivulets congealed to ice.
    Sir Char. Ere you depart me, ghost, I here demand,
You'd let me know your last divine command!'

The ghost says, that the young man must die in the battle,
that it will go ill for him if he die in the wrong cause; and,

therefore, that he had best go over to the Protestants – which poor Sir Charles (not without many sighs for Jemima) consents to do. He goes off then, saying –

'I'll join my countrymen, and yet proclaim
Nassau's great title to the *crimson plain.*'

In Act V, that desertion turns the fate of the day. Sarsfield enters with his sword drawn, and acknowledges his fate. 'Aughrim,' exclaims Lord Lucan,

'Aughrim is now no more, St Ruth is dead,
And all his guards are from the battle fled.
As he rode down the hill he met his fall,
And died a victim to a cannon ball.'

And he bids the Frenchman's body to

— 'lie, like Pompey in his gore,
Whose hero's blood encircles the Egyptian shore.'

'Four hundred Irish prisoners we have got,' exclaims an English General, 'and seven thousand lyeth on the spot.' In fact, they are entirely discomfited, and retreat off the stage altogether; while, in the moment of victory, poor Sir Charles Godfrey enters, wounded to death, according to the old gentleman's prophecy. He is racked by bitter remorse; he tells his love of his treachery, and declares 'no crocodile was ever more unjust.' His agony increases, the 'optic nerves grow dim and lose their sight, and all his veins are now exhausted quite;' and he dies in the arms of his Jemima, who stabs herself in the usual way.

And so every one being disposed of, the drums and trumpets give a great peal; the audience huzzas; and the curtain falls on Ginckle, and his friends exclaiming –

'May all the gods th' auspicious evening bless,
Who crowns Great Britain's *arrums* with success!'

And questioning the prosody, what Englishman will not join in the sentiment?

In the interlude the band (the pipe) performs a favourite air. Jack the waiter and candle-snuffer looks to see that all is ready: and after the dire business of the tragedy, comes in to sprinkle the stage with water (and perhaps a little whiskey in it). Thus all things being arranged: the audience takes its seat again, and the afterpiece begins.

Two of the little yellow volumes purchased at Ennis are entitled, The Irish and Hibernian Tales. The former are modern, and the latter of an ancient sort; and so great is the superiority of the old stories over the new, in fancy, dramatic interest, and humour, that one can't help fancying Hibernia must have been a very superior country to Ireland.

These Hibernian novels too, are evidently intended for the hedge-school universities. They have the old tricks and some of the old plots that one has read in many popular legends of almost all countries, European and Eastern: successful cunning is the great virtue applauded; and the heroes pass through a thousand wild extravagant dangers, such as could only have been invented when art was young and faith was large. And as the honest old author of the tales says 'they are suited to the meanest as well as the highest capacity, tending both to improve the fancy and enrich the mind,' let us conclude the night's entertainment by reading one or two of them, and reposing after the doleful tragedy which has been represented. The 'Black Thief' is worthy of the Arabian Nights, I think, – as wild and odd as an Eastern tale.

It begins, as usual, with a king and a queen who lived once on a time in the south of Ireland, and had three sons: but the queen being on her death-bed, and fancying her husband might marry again, and unwilling that her children should be under the jurisdiction of any other woman, besought his majesty to place them in a tower at her death, and keep them there safe until the young princes should come of age.

The queen dies – the king of course marries again, and the new queen, who bears a son too, hates the offspring of the former marriage, and looks about for means to destroy them.

'At length the queen *having got some business with the hen-wife*, went herself to her, and after a long conference passed, was taking leave of her, when the hen-wife prayed, that if ever she should come back to her again, she might break her neck. The queen greatly incensed at such a daring insult from one of her meanest subjects, to make such a prayer on her, demanded immediately the reason, or she would have her put to death. "It was worth your while, madam," says the hen-wife, "to pay me well for it, for the reason I prayed so on you concerns you much." "What must I pay you?" asked the queen. "You must give me," says she, "the full of a pack of wool: and I have an ancient crock which you must fill with butter; likewise a barrel which you must fill for me full of wheat." "How much wool will it take to the pack?" says the queen. "It will take seven herds of sheep," said she, "and their increase for seven years." "How much butter will it take to fill your crock?" "Seven dairies," said she, "and the increase for seven years." "And how much will it take to fill the barrel you have?" says the queen. "It will take the increase of seven barrels of wheat for seven years." "That is a great quantity," says the queen, "but the reason must be extraordinary, and before I want it, I will give you all you demand."'

The hen-wife acquaints the queen with the existence of the three sons, and giving her majesty an enchanted pack of cards, bids her to get the young men to play with her with these cards, and on their losing, to inflict upon them such a task as must infallibly end in their ruin. All young princes are set upon such tasks, and it is a sort of opening of the pantomime, before the tricks and activity begin. The queen went home, and 'got speaking' to the king 'in regard of his children, and *she broke it off* to him in a very polite and engaging manner, so that he could see no muster or design it.' The king agreed to bring his sons to court, and at night, when the royal party 'began to sport, and play at all kinds of diversions,' the queen cunningly challenged the three princes to play cards. They lose, and she sends them in consequence to bring her back the Knight of the Glen's wild steed of bells.

On their road (as wandering young princes, Indian or Irish, always do) they meet with the Black Thief of Kone, who tells them what they must do. But they are caught in the attempt, and brought 'into that dismal part of the palace where the Knight kept a furnace always boiling, in which he threw all offenders that ever came in his way, which in a few minutes would entirely consume them. "Audacious villains!" says the Knight of the Glen, "how dare you attempt so bold an action as to steel my steed? see now the reward of your folly; for your greater punishment, I will not boil you all together, but one after the other, so that he that survives may witness the dire afflictions of his unfortunate companions." So saying, he ordered his servants to stir up the fire. "We will boil the eldest-looking of these young men first," says he, "and so on to the last, which will be this *old champion* with the black cap. He seems to be the captain, looks as if he had come through many toils." – "I was as near death once as this prince is yet" says the Black Thief, "and escaped: and so will he too." "No, you never were," said the Knight, "for he is within two or three minutes of his latter end." "But," says the Black Thief, "I was within one moment of my death, and I am here yet." "How was that?" says the Knight; "I would be glad to hear it, for it seems to be impossible." "If you think, sir Knight," says the Black Thief, "that the danger I was in surpassed that of this young man, will you pardon him his crime?" "I will," says the Knight, "so go on with your story."

'"I was, sir," says he, "a very wild boy in my youth, and came through many distresses; once in particular, as I was on my rambling, I was benighted, and could find no lodging. At length I came to an old kiln, and being much fatigued, I went up and lay on the ribs. I had not been long there, when I saw three witches coming in with three bags of gold. Each put their bags of gold under their heads, as if to sleep. I heard the one say to the other, that if the Black Thief came on them while they slept, he would not leave them a penny. I found by their discourse that everybody had got my name into their mouth, though I kept silent as death during their discourse. At length they fell fast asleep, and then I stole softly down, and seeing some turf *convenient*, I placed one under each of their heads, and off I went with their gold as fast as I could."

'"I had not gone far," continued the Thief of Sloan, "until I saw a greyhound, a hare, and a hawk, in pursuit of me, and began to think it must be the witches that had taken that metamorphose, in order that I might not escape them unseen either by land or water. Seeing they did not appear in any formidable shape, I was more than once resolved to attack them, thinking that with my broad-sword I could easily destroy them. But considering again that it was perhaps still in their power to become so, I gave over the attempt, and climbed with difficulty up a tree, bringing my sword in my hand, and all the gold along with me. However, when they came to the tree they found what I had done, and, making further use of their hellish art, one of them was changed into a smith's anvil, and another into a piece of iron, of which the third one soon made a hatchet. Having the hatchet made, she fell to cutting down the tree, and in course of an hour it began to shake with me."'

This is very good and original. The 'boiling' is in the first fee-faw-fum style, and the old allusion to 'the old champion in the black cap,' has the real Ogresque humour. Nor is that simple contrivance of the honest witches without its charm: for if, instead of wasting their time, the one in turning herself into an anvil, the other into a piece of iron, and so hammering out a hatchet at considerable labour and expense – if either of them had turned herself into a hatchet at once, they might have chopped down the Black Thief before cock-crow, when they were obliged to fly off, and leave him in possession of the bags of gold.

The eldest prince is ransomed by the Knight of the Glen, in consequence of this story: and the second prince escapes on account of the merit of a second story; but the great story of all is of course reserved for the youngest Prince.

'I was one day on my travels,' says the Black Thief, 'and I came into a large forest, where I wandered a long time, and could not get out of it: at length I came to a large castle, and fatigue obliged me to call in the same, where I found a young woman and a child sitting on her knee, and she crying; I asked her what made her cry, and where the lord of the castle was, for I wondered greatly that I saw no stir of servants, or any person about the place. "It is well for you," says the young woman, "that the lord of this castle is not at home at present; for he is a monstrous giant, with but one eye on his forehead, who lives on human flesh; he brought me this child, says she (I do not know where he got it), and ordered me to make it into a pie, and I cannot help crying at the command." I told her, that if she knew of any place convenient, that I could leave the child safely, I would do it, rather than that it should be buried in the bowels of such a monster. She told of a house a distance off, where I would get a woman who would take care of it. "But what will I do in regard of the pie?" "Cut a finger off it," said I, "and I will bring you in a young wild pig out of the forest, which you may dress as if it was the child, and put the finger in a certain place, that if the giant doubts any thing about it, you may know where to turn it over at first, and when he sees it he will be fully satisfied that it is made of the child." She agreed to the plan I proposed; and, cutting off the child's finger, by her direction, I soon had it at the house she told me of and brought her the little pig in the place of it: she then made ready the pie; and after eating and drinking heartily myself, I was just taking my leave of the young woman when we observed the giant coming through the castle gates. "Lord bless me!" said she, "what will you do now? run away and lie down among the dead bodies that he has in the room (showing me the place), and strip off your clothes that he may not know you from the rest, if he has occasion to go that way." I took her advice, and laid myself down among the rest, as if dead, to see how he would behave. The first thing I heard was him calling for his pie: when she set it down before him, he swore it smelt like swine's flesh; but, knowing where to find the finger, she immediately turned it up, which fairly convinced him of the contrary. The pie only served to sharpen his appetite, and I heard him sharpen his knife, and saying he must have a collop or two, for he was not near satisfied. But what was my terror, when I heard the giant groping among the bodies, and, fancying myself, cut the half of my hip off, and took it with him to be roasted. You may be certain I was in great pain; but the fear of being killed prevented me from making any complaint. However, when he had eat all, he began to drink hot liquors in great abundance, so that in a short time he could not hold up his head, but threw himself on a large creel he had made for the purpose, and fell fast asleep. *Whenever* I heard him snoring, bad as I was, I went up and caused the woman to bind my wound with a handkerchief; and taking the giant's spit, I reddened it in the fire, and ran it through the eye, but was not able to kill him. However, I left the spit sticking in his head, and took to my heels; but I soon found he was in pursuit of me, although blind; and, having an enchanted ring, he threw it at me, and it fell on my big toe, and remained fastened to it. The giant then called to the ring, where it was, and to my great surprise it made him answer on my foot, and he, guided by the same, made a leap at me, which I had the good luck to observe, and fortunately escaped the danger. However, I found running was of no use in saving me, as long as I had the ring on my foot; so I took my sword and cut off the toe it was fastened on, and threw both into a large fish-pond that was convenient. The giant called again to the ring, which, by the power of enchantment, always made answer; but, he not knowing what I had done, imagined it was still on some part of me, and made a violent leap to seize me, when he went into the pond, over head and ears, and was drowned. "Now, sir Knight," said the Thief of Sloan, "you see what dangers I came through and always escaped; but, indeed, I am lame for want of my toe ever since."'

And now remains but one question to be answered, viz., How is the Black Thief himself to come off? This difficulty is solved in a very dramatic way, and with a sudden turn in the narrative that is very wild and curious.

'My lord and master, says an old woman that was listening all the time, that story is but too true, as I well know; *for I am the very woman that was in the giant's castle, and you, my lord, the child that I was to make into a pie*, and this is the very man that saved your life, which you may know by the want of your finger that was taken off, as you have heard, to deceive the giant.'

That fantastical way of bearing testimony to the previous tale, by producing an old woman who says the tale is not only true, but she was the very old woman who lived in the giant's castle, is almost a stroke of genius. It is fine to think that the simple chronicler found it necessary to have a proof for his story, and he was no doubt perfectly contented with the proof found.

'The Knight of the Glen, greatly surprised at what he had heard the old woman tell, and knowing he wanted his finger from his childhood, began to understand that the story was true enough. "And is this my dear deliverer?" says he. "O brave fellow, I not only pardon you all, but I will keep you with myself while you live; where you shall feast like princes, and have every attendance that I have myself." They all returned thanks on their knees, and the Black Thief told him the reason they attempted to steal the steed of Bells, and the necessity they were under in going home. "Well," says the Knight of the Glen, "if that's the case, I bestow you my steed rather than this brave fellow should die; so you may go when you please; only remember to call and see me betimes, that we may know each other well." They promised they would, and with great joy they set off for the king their father's palace, and the Black Thief along with them. The wicked Queen was standing all this time on the tower, and hearing the bells ringing at a great distance off, knew very well it was the princes coming home, and the steed with them, and through spite and vexation precipitated herself from the tower, and was shattered to pieces. The three princes lived happy and well during their father's reign, always keeping the Black Thief along with them; but how they did after the old king's death is not known.'

Then we come upon a story that exists in many a European language, of the man cheating Death; then to the history of the Apprentice Thief, who of course cheated his masters; which, too, is an old tale, and may have been told very likely among those Phoenicians, who were the fathers of the Hibernians, for whom these tales were devised. A very curious tale is there, concerning Manus O'Malaghan and the fairies: – 'In the parish of Ahoghill, lived Manus O'Malaghan. *As he was searching for a calf that had strayed*, he heard many people talking. Drawing near, he distinctly heard them repeating, one after the other, "Get me a horse, get me a horse;" and "Get me a horse too," says Manus. Manus was instantly mounted on a steed surrounded with a vast crowd, who galloped off, taking poor Manus with them. In a short time, they suddenly stopped in a large wide street, asking Manus if he knew where he was? "Faith," says he, "I do not." "You are *in Spain*," said they.'

Here we have again the wild mixture of the positive and the fanciful. The chronicler is careful to tell us why Manus went out searching for a calf, and this positiveness prodigiously increases the reader's wonder at the subsequent events. And the question and answer of the mysterious horsemen is fine: 'Don't you know where you are? *in Spain.*' A vague solution, such as one has of occurrences in dreams sometimes.

The history of Robin the Blacksmith is full of these strange flights of poetry. He is followed about 'by a little boy in a green jacket,' who performs the most wondrous feats of the blacksmith's art, as follows:

'Robin was asked to do something who wisely shifted it saying he would be very sorry not to give the honour of the first trick to his lordship's smith; at which he was called forth to the bellows. When the fire was well kindled, to the great surprise of all present he blew a great shower of wheat out of the fire, which fell through all the shop. They then demanded of Robin to try what he could do. "Pho!" said Robin, as if he thought nothing of what was done; "come," said he to the boy, "I think I showed you something like that." The boy goes then to the bellows and blew out a great flock of pigeons, who soon devoured all the grain, and then disappeared.

'The Dublin smith, sorely vexed that such a boy as him should outdo him, goes a second time to the bellows, and blew a fine trout out of the hearth, who jumped into a little river that was running by the shop door, and was seen no more at that time.

'Robin then said to the boy, "Come, you must bring us yon trout back again, to let the gentlemen see we can do something." Away the boy goes, and blew a large otter out of the hearth, who immediately leaped into the river, and in a short time returned with it in his mouth, and then disappeared. All present allowed, that it was a folly to attempt a competition any further.'

The boy in the green jacket was one 'of a kind of small beings called Fairies;' and not a little does it add to the charm of these wild tales to feel, as one reads them, that the writer must have believed in his heart a great deal of what he told. You see the tremor, as it were, and a wild look of the eyes, as the story-teller sits in his nook, and recites, and peers wistfully round, lest the beings he talks of be really at hand.

Let us give a couple of the little tales entire. They are not so fanciful as those before mentioned, but of the comic sort, and suited to the first kind of capacity mentioned by the author in his preface.

DONALD AND HIS NEIGHBOURS

'Hudden and Dudden and Donald O'Neary, were near neighbours in the barony of Ballinconlig, and ploughed with three bullocks; but the two former, envying the present prosperity of the latter, determined to kill his bullock, to prevent his farm being properly cultivated and laboured, that, going back in the world, he might be induced to sell his lands, which they meant to get possession of. Poor Donald, finding his bullock killed, immediately skinned it, and throwing his skin over his shoulder, with the fleshy side out, set off to the next town with it, to dispose of it to the best advantage. Going along the road a magpie flew on the top of the hide, and began picking it, chattering all the time. This bird had been taught to speak and imitate the human voice, and Donald, thinking he understood some words it was saying, put round his hand and caught hold of it. Having got possession of it, he put it under his great coat, and so went on to the town. Having sold the hide, he went into an inn to take a dram; and, following the landlady into the cellar, he gave the bird a squeeze, which caused it to chatter some broken accents that surprised her very much. "What is that I hear?" said she to Donald: "I think it is talk, and yet I do not understand." "Indeed," said Donald, "it is a bird I have that tells me everything, and I always carry it with me to know when there is any danger. Faith," says he, "it says you have far better liquor than you are giving me." "That is strange," said she, going to another cask of better quality, and asking him if he would sell the bird. "I will," said Donald, "if I get enough for it." "I will fill your hat with silver if you leave it with me." Donald was glad to hear the news, and taking the silver, set off, rejoicing at his good luck. He had not been long home when he met with Hudden and Dudden. "Ha!" said he, "you thought you did me a bad turn, but you could not have done me a better; for, look here, what I have got for the hide," showing them the hatful of silver; "you never saw such a demand for hides in your life as there is

at present." Hudden and Dudden that very night killed their
bullocks, and set out the next morning to sell their hides. On
coming to the place they went through all the merchants, but
could only get a trifle for them; at last they had to take what
they could get, and came home in a great rage, and vowing
revenge on poor Donald. He had a pretty good guess how
matters would turn out; and his bed being under the kitchen
window, he was afraid they would rob him, or perhaps kill
him when asleep; and on that account, when he was going to
bed, he left his old mother in his bed, and lay down in her
place, which was in the other side of the house; and they,
taking the old woman for Donald, choked her in the bed; but
he making some noise, they had to retreat, and leave the
money behind them, which grieved them very much. However, by day-break, Donald got his mother on his back, and
carried her to town. Stopping at a well, he fixed his mother,
with her staff, as if she was stooping for a drink, and then
went into a public-house convenient, and called for a dram. "I
wish," said he to a woman that stood near him, "you would
tell my mother to come in; she is at yon well trying to get a
drink, and she is hard in hearing; if she does not observe you,
give her a little shake, and tell her that I want her." The
woman called her several times, but she seemed to take no
notice: at length she went to her and shook her by the arm; but
when she let her go again, she tumbled on her head into the
well, and, as the woman thought, was drowned. She, in great
fear and surprise at the accident, told Donald what had
happened. "O mercy," said he, "what is this?" – he ran and
pulled her out of the well, weeping and lamenting all the time,
and acting in such a manner that you would imagine that he
had lost his senses. The woman, on the other hand, was far
worse than Donald; for his grief was only feigned, but she
imagined herself to be the cause of the old woman's death.
The inhabitants of the town, hearing what had happened,
agreed to make Donald up a good sum of money for his loss,
as the accident happened in their place; and Donald brought a
greater sum home with him than he got for the Magpie. They
buried Donald's mother; and as soon as he saw Hudden and
Dudden, he showed them the last purse of money he had got.
"You thought to kill me last night," said he, "but it was good

for me it happened on my mother, for I got all that purse for her, to make gunpowder."

'That very night Hudden and Dudden killed their mothers, and the next morning set off with them to town. On coming to the town, with their burden on their backs, they went up and down crying, "Who will buy old wives for gunpowder?" so that everyone laughed at them, and the boys at last clodded them out of the place. They then saw the cheat, and vowing revenge on Donald, buried the old women, and set off in pursuit of him. Coming to his house, they found him sitting at his breakfast, and seizing him, put him in a sack, and went to drown him in a river at some distance. As they were going along the highway, they raised a hare, which they saw had but three feet, and, throwing off the sack, ran after her, thinking by appearance she would be easily taken. In their absence there came a drover that way, and, hearing Donald singing in the sack, wondered greatly what could be the matter. "What is the reason," said he, "that you are singing, and you confined?" "Oh, I am going to heaven," said Donald; "and in a short time I expect to be free from trouble." "O dear," said the drover, "what will I give you if you let me to your place?" "Indeed I do not know," said he, "it would take a good sum." "I have not much money," said the drover, "but I have twenty head of fine cattle, which I will give you to exchange places with me." "Well, well," says Donald, "I don't care if I should; loose the sack and I will come out." In a moment the drover liberated him, and went into the sack himself: and Donald drove home the fine heifers, and left them in his pasture.

'Hudden and Dudden having caught the hare, returned, and getting the sack on one of their backs, carried Donald, as they thought, to the river, and threw him in, where he immediately sunk. They then marched home, intending to take immediate possession of Donald's property; but how great was their surprise, when they found him safe at home before them, with such a fine herd of cattle, whereas they knew he had none before? "Donald," said they, "what is all this! We thought you were drowned, and yet you are here before us." "Ah!" said he, "if I had but help along with me, when you threw me in, it would have been the best job ever I met with; for of all the sight of cattle and gold that ever was seen, is there, and no one to own them; but I was not able to manage more than what you see, and I could show you the spot where you might get hundreds." They both swore they would be his friend, and Donald accordingly led them to a very deep part of the river, and lifting up a stone, "Now," said he, "watch this," throwing it into the stream; "there is the very place, and go in one of you first, and if you want help, you have nothing to do but call." Hudden jumping in and sinking to the bottom, rose up again, and making a bubbling noise as those do that are drowning, attempting to speak, but could not. "What is that he is saying now?" says Dudden. "Faith," says Donald, "he is calling for help – don't you hear him?" "Stand about," said he, running back, "till I leap in; I know how to do better than any of you." Dudden, to have the advantage of him, jumped in off the bank, and was drowned along with Hudden; and this was the end of Hudden and Dudden.'

THE SPAEMAN

'A poor man in the north of Ireland was under the necessity of selling his cow, to help to support his family. Having sold his cow, he went into an inn, and called for some liquor; having drank pretty heartily, he fell asleep, and when he awoke he found he had been robbed of his money. Poor Roger was at a loss to know how to act; and, as is often the case, when the landlord found that his money was gone, he turned him out of doors. The night was extremely dark, and the poor man was compelled to take up his lodgings in an uninhabited house at the end of the town.

'Roger had not remained long here, until he was surprised by the noise of three men, whom he observed making a hole, and, depositing something therein, closed it carefully up again, and then went away. The next morning, as Roger was walking towards the town, he heard that a cloth shop had been robbed to a great amount, and that a reward of thirty pounds was offered to any person who could discover the thieves. This was joyful news to Roger, who recollected what he had been witness to the night before; he accordingly went to the shop, and told the gentleman that for the reward he would recover the goods, and secure the robbers, provided he got six stout men to attend him; all which was thankfully granted him.

'At night Roger and his men concealed themselves in the old house, and in a short time after the robbers came to the spot for the purpose of removing their booty; but they were instantly seized and carried into the town, prisoners, with the goods. Roger received the reward and returned home, well satisfied with his good luck. Not many days after, it was noised over the country, that this robbery was discovered by the help of one of the best Spaemen to be found, in so much that it reached the ears of a worthy gentleman of the county of Derry, who made strict inquiry to find him out. Having at length discovered his abode, he sent for Roger, and told him he was every day losing some valuable article, and, as he was famed for discovering lost things, if he could find out the same, he should be handsomely rewarded. Poor Roger was put to a stand, not knowing what answer to make, as he had not the smallest knowledge of the like. But recovering himself a little, he resolved to humour the joke; and, thinking he would make a good dinner and some drink of it, told the gentleman he would try what he could do, but that he must have a room to himself for three hours, during which time he must have three bottles of strong ale and his dinner; all which the gentleman told him he should have. No sooner was it made known that the Spaeman was in the house, than the servants were all in confusion, wishing to know what would be said.

'As soon as Roger had taken his dinner, he was shown into an elegant room, where the gentleman sent him a quart of ale by the butler. No sooner had he set down the ale, than Roger said, "There comes one of them;" intimating the bargain he had made with the gentleman for the three quarts, which the butler took in a wrong light, and imagined it was himself. He went away in great confusion, and told his wife. "Poor fool," said she, "the fear makes you think it is you he means; but I will attend in your place, and hear what he will say to me." According she carried the second quart: but no sooner had she opened the door than Roger cried, "There comes two of them." The woman, no less surprised than her husband, told him the Spaeman knew her too. "And what will we do?" said he; "we will be hanged." "I will tell you what we must do," said she, "we must send the groom the next time, and if he is known, we must offer him a good sum not to discover on us." The butler went to William and told him the whole story, and that he must go next to see what he would say to him, telling him at the same time what to do, in case he was known also. When the hour was expired, William was sent with the third quart of ale, which, when Roger observed, he cried out, "There is the third and last of them;" at which he changed colour, and told him "that if he would not discover on them, they would show him where they were all concealed, and give him five pounds besides." Roger, not a little surprised at the discovery he had made, told him "if he recovered the goods, he would follow them no further."

'By this time the gentleman called Roger to know how he had succeeded. He told him "he could find the goods but that the thief was gone." "I will be well satisfied," said he, "with the goods, for some of them are very valuable." "Let the butler come along with me, and the whole shall be recovered." He accordingly conducted Roger to the back of the stables, where the articles were concealed, – such as silver cups, spoons, bowls, knives, forks, and a variety of other articles of great value.

'When the supposed Spaeman brought back the stolen goods, the gentleman was so highly pleased with Roger, that he insisted on his remaining with him always, as he supposed he would be perfectly safe as long as he was about his house. Roger gladly embraced the offer, and in a few days took possession of a piece of land, which the gentleman had given to him in consideration of his great abilities.

'Some time after this, the gentleman was relating to a large company the discovery Roger had made, and that he could tell anything: one of the gentlemen said he would dress a dish of meat, and bet for fifty pounds that he could not tell what was in it, and he would allow him to taste it. The bet being taken and the dish dressed, the gentleman sent for Roger, and told the bet that was depending on him. Poor Roger did not know what to do; at last he consented to the trial. The dish being produced, he tasted it, but could not tell what it was; at last, seeing he was fairly beat, he said, "Gentlemen, it is folly to talk: the fox may run a while, but he is caught at last;" – allowing with himself that he was found out. The gentleman that had made the bet then confessed that it was a fox he had dressed in the dish; at which they all shouted out in favour of the Spaeman, – particularly his master, who had more confidence in him than ever.

'Roger then went home, and so famous did he become, that no one dared take anything but what belonged to them, fearing that the Spaeman would discover on them.'

And so we shut up the Hedge-school Library, and close the Galway Night's Entertainments. They are not quite so genteel as Almack's, to be sure; but many a lady who has her opera-box in London has listened to a piper in Ireland.

Apropos of pipers: here is a young one that I caught and copied to-day. He was paddling in the mud, shining in the sun careless of his rays, and playing his little tin-music as happy as Mr Cooke with his oboe.

Perhaps the above verses and tales are not unlike my little Galway musician. They are grotesque and rugged; but they are pretty and innocent-hearted too; and as such, polite persons may deign to look at them for once in a way. While we have Signor Costa, in a white neckcloth, ordering opera-bands to play for us the music of Donizetti, which is not only sublime but genteel; of course such poor little operatives as he who plays the wind instrument yonder, cannot expect to be heard often: but is not this Galway? and how far is Galway from the Haymarket?

CHAPTER XVII

FROM GALWAY TO BALLYNAHINCH

The Clifden car which carries the Dublin letters into the heart of Connemara, conducts the passenger over one of the most wild and beautiful districts that it is ever the fortune of a traveller to examine; and I could not help thinking, as we passed through it, at how much pains and expense honest English Cockneys are, to go and look after natural beauties far inferior, in countries which, though more distant, are not a whit more strange than this one. No doubt, ere long, when people know how easy the task is, the rush of London tourism will come this way; and I shall be very happy if these pages shall be able to awaken in one bosom, beating in Tooley-street or the Temple, the desire to travel towards Ireland next year.

After leaving the quaint old town behind us, and ascending one or two small eminences to the north-westward, the traveller, from the car, gets a view of the wide sheet of Lough Corrib shining in the sun, as we saw it, with its low dark banks stretching round it. If the view is gloomy, at least it is characteristic: nor are we delayed by it very long; for though the lake stretches northwards into the very midst of the Joyce country (and is there in the close neighbourhood of another huge lake, Lough Mask, which again is near to another sheet of water), yet from this road henceforth, after keeping company with it for some five miles, we only get occasional views of it, passing over hills and through trees, by many rivers and smaller lakes, which are dependent upon that of Corrib. Gentlemen's seats, on the road from Galway to Moycullen, are scattered in great profusion – perhaps there is grass growing on the gravel walk, and the iron gates of the tumble-down old lodges are rather rickety; but for all that, the places look comfortable, hospitable, and spacious; and as for the shabbiness and want of finish here and there, the English eye grows quite accustomed to it in a month; and I find the bad condition of the Galway houses by no means so painful as that of the places near Dublin. At some of the lodges, as we pass, the mail carman, with a warning shout, flings a bag of letters; I saw a little party looking at one which lay there in the road, crying. Come, take me! but nobody cares to steal a bag of letters in this country, I suppose, and the carman drove on without any alarm. Two days afterwards, a gentleman with whom I was in company, left on a rock his book of fishing-flies; and I can assure you there was a very different feeling expressed about the safety of *that*.

In the first part of the journey, the neighbourhood of the road seemed to be as populous as in other parts of the country – troops of red-petticoated peasantry peering from their stone-cabins – yelling children following the car, and crying, 'Lash, lash!' It was Sunday, and you would see many a white chapel among the green bare plains to the right of the road, the courtyard blackened with a swarm of cloaks. The service seems to continue (on the part of the people) all day. Troops of people, issuing from the chapel, met us at Moycullen, and ten miles further on, at Oughterard, their devotions did not yet seem to be concluded.

A more beautiful village can scarcely be seen than this. It stands upon Lough Corrib, the banks of which are here, for once at least, picturesque and romantic: and a pretty river, the Feogh, comes rushing over rocks and by woods, until it passes the town and meets the lake. Some pretty buildings in the village stand on each bank of this stream, a Roman Catholic chapel with a curate's neat lodge, a little church, on one side of it; a fine court-house of gray stone on the other. And here it is that we get into the famous district of Connemara, so celebrated in Irish stories, so mysterious to the London tourist. 'It presents itself,' says the Guide-book, 'under every possible combination of heathy moor, bog, lake, and mountain. Extensive mossy plains, and wild pastoral valleys, lie embosomed among the mountains, and support numerous herds of cattle and horses, for which the district has been long celebrated. These wild solitudes, which occupy by far the greater part of the centre of the country, are held by a hardy and ancient race of grazing farmers, who live in a very primitive state, and, generally speaking, till little beyond what supplies their immediate wants. For the first ten miles the country is comparatively open; and the mountains on the left, which are not of great elevation, can be distinctly traced as they rise along the edge of the heathy plain.

'Our road continues along the Feogh River, which expands itself into several considérable lakes, and at five miles from Oughterard we reach Lough Bofin, which the road also skirts. Passing in succession Lough-a-preaghan, the lakes of Ander-ran and Shindella, at ten miles from Oughterard we reach Slyme and Lynn's Inn, or Half-way House, which is near the shore of Loughonard. Now, as we advance towards the group of Binabola, or the Twelve Pins, the most gigantic scenery is displayed.'

But the best guide-book that ever was written cannot set the view before the mind's eye of the reader, and I won't attempt to pile up big words in place of these wild mountains, over which the clouds as they passed, or the sunshine as it went and came, cast every variety of tint, light, and shadow; nor can it be expected that long, level sentences, however smooth and shining, can be mde to pass as representations of those calm lakes by which we took our way. All one can do is to lay down the pen and ruminate, and cry 'beautiful!' once more; and to the reader say, 'Come and see!'

Wild and wide as the prospect around us is, it has somehow a kindly, friendly look, differing in this from the fierce loneliness of some similar scenes in Wales that I have viewed. Ragged women and children come out of rude stone huts to see the car as it passes. But it is impossible for the pencil to give due raggedness to the rags, or to convey a certain picturesque mellowness of colour that the garments assume. The sexes, with regard to raiment, do not seem to be particular. There were many boys on the road in the national red petticoat, having no other covering for their lean, brown legs; as for shoes, the women eschew them almost entirely; and I saw a peasant trudging from mass in a handsome scarlet cloak, a fine blue cloth gown, turned up to show a new lining, of the same colour, and a petticoat quite white and neat, in a dress of which the cost must have been at least 10*l.*; and her husband walked in front carrying her shoes and stockings.

The road had conducted us for miles through the vast property of the gentleman to whose house I was bound, Mr Martin, the member for the county; and the last and prettiest part of the journey was round the lake of Ballynahinch, with tall mountains rising immediately above us on the right, pleasant woody hills on the opposite side of the lake, with the roofs of the houses rising above the trees; and in an island in the midst of the water a ruined old castle, that cast a long, white reflection into the blue waters where it lay. A land-pirate used to live in that castle, one of the peasants told me, in the time of 'Oliver Cromwell.' And a fine fastness it was for a robber, truly; for there was no road through these wild countries in his time – nay, only thirty years since, this lake was at three days' distance of Galway. Then comes the question, What, in a country where there were no roads and no travellers, and where the inhabitants have been wretchedly poor from time immemorial – what was there for the land-pirate to rob? But let us not be too curious about times so early as those of Oliver Cromwell. I have heard the name many times from the Irish peasant, who still has an awe of the grim, resolute Protector.

The builder of Ballynahinch House has placed it to command a view of a pretty melancholy river that runs by it, through many green flats, and picturesque rocky grounds; but from the lake it is scarcely visible. And so, in like manner, I fear it must remain invisible to the reader too, with all its kind inmates, and frank, cordial hospitality, unless he may take a fancy to visit Galway himself, when, as I can vouch, a very small pretext will make him enjoy both.

It will, however, be only a small breach of confidence to say, that the major-domo of the establishment (who has adopted accurately the voice and manner of his master, with a severe dignity of his own, which is quite original), ordered me on going to bed 'not to move in the morning till he called me,' at the same time expressing a hearty hope that I should 'want nothing more that evening.' Who would dare, after such peremptory orders, not to fall asleep immediately, and in this way disturb the repose of Mr J——n M——ll——y?

There may be many comparisons drawn between English and Irish gentlemen's houses; but perhaps the most striking point of difference between the two is the immense following of the Irish House, such as would make an English house-keeper crazy almost. Three comfortable, well-clothed, good-humoured fellows walked down with me from the car, persisting in carrying one a bag, another a sketching-stool, and so on: walking about the premises in the morning, sundry others were visible in the courtyard and near the kitchen door; in the grounds a gentleman, by name Mr Marcus C——rr, began discoursing to me regarding the place, the planting, the fish, the grouse, and the Master, being himself, doubtless, one of the irregulars of the house. As for maids, there were half a score of them skurrying about the house; and I am not ashamed to confess that some of them were exceedingly good-looking. And if I might venture to say a word more, it would be respecting Connemara breakfasts; but this would be an entire and flagrant breach of confidence, and, to be sure, the dinners were just as good.

One of the days of my three days' visit was to be devoted to the lakes; and as a party had been arranged for the second day after my arrival, I was glad to take advantage of the society of a gentleman staying in the house, and ride with him to the neighbouring town of Clifden.

The ride thither from Ballynahinch is surprisingly beautiful; and as you ascend the high ground from the two or three rude stone huts, which face the entrance gates of the house, there are views of the lake and the surrounding country, which the best parts of Killarney do not surpass, I think, although the Connemara lakes do not possess the advantage of wood, which belongs to the famous Kerry landscape.

But the cultivation of the country is only in its infancy as yet, and it is easy to see how vast its resources are, and what capital and cultivation may do for it. In the green patches among the flocks, and the mountain sides, wherever crops were grown, they flourished; plenty of natural wood is springing up in various places; and there is no end to what the planter may do, and to what time and care may effect. The carriage road to Clifden is but ten years old; as it has brought the means of communication into the country, the commerce will doubtless follow it; and in fact, in going through the whole kingdom, one can't but be struck with the idea that not one hundredth part of its capabilities are yet brought into action, or even known perhaps, and that, by the easy and certain progress of time, Ireland will be poor Ireland no longer.

For instance, we rode by a vast green plain, skirting a lake and river, which is now useless almost for pasture, and which a little draining will convert into thousands of acres of rich productive land. Streams and falls of water dash by everywhere: – they have only to utilise this water power for mills and factories; and hard by are some of the finest bays in the world, where ships can deliver and receive foreign and home produce. At Roundstone especially, where a little town has been erected, the bay is said to be unexampled for size, depth, and shelter; and the Government is now, through the rocks and hills on their wild shore, cutting a coast-road to Bunown, the most westerly part of Connemara, whence there is another good road to Clifden. Among the charges which the Repealers bring against the Union, they should include at least this – they would never have had these roads but for the Union, roads which are as much at the charge of the London tax-payer as of the most ill-used Milesian in Connaught.

A string of small lakes follow the road to Clifden, with mountains on the right of the traveller for the chief part of the way. A few figures at work in the bog-lands – a red petticoat passing here and there – a goat or two browsing among the stones – or a troop of ragged whitey-brown children, who came out to gaze at the car, form the chief society on the road: – the first house at the entrance to Clifden, is a gigantic poorhouse – tall, large, ugly, comfortable, it commands the town, and looks almost as big as everyone of the houses therein. The town itself is but of a few years' date, and seems to thrive in its small way. Clifden Castle is a fine château in the neighbourhood, and belongs to another owner of immense lands in Galway – Mr D'Arcy.

Here a drive was proposed along the coast to Bunown, and I was glad to see some more of the country, and its character. Nothing can be wilder – we passed little lake after lake, lying a few furlongs inwards from the shore. There were rocks everywhere, some patches of cultivated land here and there, nor was there any want of inhabitants along this savage coast.

There were numerous cottages, if cottages they may be called, and women, and above all, children in plenty. Here is one of the former – her attitude as she stood gazing at the car. To depict the multiplicity of her rags, would require a month's study.

At length we came in sight of a half-built edifice, which is approached by a rocky, dismal, gray road, guarded by two or three broken gates, against which rocks and stones were piled, which were to be removed to give an entrance to our car. The gates were closed so laboriously, I presume to prevent the egress of a single black consumptive pig, far gone in the family way – a teeming skeleton – that was cropping the thin dry grass that grew upon a round hill, which rises behind this most dismal castle of Bunown.

If the traveller only seeks for strange sights, this place will repay his curiosity. Such a dismal house is not to be seen in all England: or, perhaps, such a dismal situation. The sea lies before and behind, and on each side, likewise, are rocks and copper-coloured meadows, by which a few trees have made an attempt to grow. The owner of the house had, however, begun to add to it, and there, unfinished, is a whole apparatus of turrets, and staring raw stone and mortar, and fresh ruinous carpenters' work – and then the courtyard! – tumbled-down out-houses, staring empty pointed windows, and new-smeared plaster cracking from the walls – a black heap of turf, a mouldy pump, a wretched old coal-skuttle emptily sunning itself in the midst of this cheerful scene? There was an old Gorgon, who kept the place, and who was in perfect unison with it – Venus herself would become bearded, blear-eyed, and haggard, if left to be the housekeeper of this dreary place.

In the house was a comfortable parlour inhabited by the Priest who has the painful charge of the district. Here were his books and his breviaries, his reading-desk with the cross engraved upon it, and his portrait of Daniel O'Connell the Liberator, to grace the walls of his lonely cell. There was a dead crane hanging at the door on a gaff; his red fish-like eyes were staring open, and his eager grinning bill – a rifle ball had passed through his body, and this was doubtless the only game about the place: for we saw the sportsman who had killed the bird, hunting vainly up the round hill for other food for powder. This gentleman had had good sport, he said, shooting seals upon a neighbouring island, four of which animals he had slain.

Mounting up the round hill, we had a view of the Sline lights – the most westerly point in Ireland.

Here too was a ruined sort of summer-house, dedicated DEO HIBERNLIAE LIBERATORI. When these lights were put up, I am told the proprietor of Bunown was recommended to apply for compensation to Parliament, inasmuch as there would be no more *wrecks* on the coast; from which branch of commerce the inhabitants of the district used formerly to derive a considerable profit. Between these Sline lights and America nothing lies but the Atlantic. It was beautifully blue and bright on this day, and the sky almost cloudless; but I think the brightness only made the scene more dismal, it being of that order of beauties which cannot bear the full light, but require a cloud or a curtain to set them off to advantage. A pretty story was told me by the gentleman who had killed the seals. The place where he had been staying for sport was

almost as lonely as this Bunown, and inhabited by a priest too –
a young, lively, well-educated man. 'When I came here first,'
the priest said, '*I cried for two days;*' but afterwards he grew to like
the place exceedingly, his whole heart being directed towards it,
his chapel, and his cure. Who would not honour such
missionaries – the virtues they silently practise, and the
doctrines they preach? After hearing that story, I think Bunown
looked not quite so dismal, as it is inhabited they say, by such
another character. What a pity it is that John Tuam, in the next
county of Mayo, could not find such another hermitage to learn
modesty in, and forget his Graceship, his Lordship, and the
sham titles by which he sets such store.

A moon as round and bright as any moon that ever shone, and
riding in a sky perfectly cloudless, gave us a good promise of a
fine day for the morrow, which was to be devoted to the lakes in
the neighbourhood of Ballynahinch; one of which, Lough Ina,
is said to be of exceeding beauty. But no man can speculate upon
Irish weather. I have seen a day beginning with torrents of rain,
that looked as if a deluge was at hand, clear up in a few minutes,
without any reason, and against the prognostications of the
glass and all other weather-prophets; so in like manner, after the
astonishingly fine night there came a villainous dark day;
which, however, did not set in fairly for rain, until we were an
hour on our journey, with a couple of stout boatmen rowing us
over Ballynahinch Lake. Being, however, thus fairly started,
the water began to come down, not in torrents certainly, but in
that steady, creeping, insinuating mist, of which we scarce
know the luxury in England, and which, I am bound to say, will
wet a man's jacket as satisfactorily as a cataract would do.

It was just such another day as that of the famous stag-hunt at
Killarney, in a word; and as, in the first instance, we went to see
the deer killed, and saw nothing thereof, so, in the second case,
we went to see the landscape with precisely the same good
fortune. The mountains covered their modest beauties in
impenetrable veils of clouds; and the only consolation to the
boat's crew was, that it was a remarkably good day for
trout-fishing, which amusement some people are said to prefer
to the examination of landscapes, however beautiful.

O you, who laboriously throw flies in English rivers, and
catch, at the expiration of a hard day's walking, casting, and

wading, two or three feeble little brown trouts of two or three ounces in weight, how would you rejoice to have but an hour's sport in Derryclear or Ballynahinch, where you have but to cast and lo! a big trout springs at your fly, and, after making a vain struggling, splashing, and plunging for a while, is infallibly landed in the net and thence into the boat. The single rod in the boat, caught enough fish in an hour to feast the crew, consisting of five persons, and the family of a Herd of Mr Martin's, who has a pretty cottage on Derryclear Lake, inhabited by a cow and its calf, a score of fowls, and I don't know how many sons and daughters.

Having caught enough trout to satisfy any moderate appetite, like true sportsmen the gentlemen on board our boat became eager to hook a salmon. Had they hooked a few salmons, no doubt they would have trolled for whales, or for a mermaid, one of which finny beauties the waterman swore he had seen on the shore of Derryclear, he with Jim Mullen being above on a rock, the mermaid on the shore directly beneath them, visible to the middle, and as usual 'racking her hair.' It was fair hair, the boatman said; and he appeared as convinced of the existence of the mermaid, as he was of the trout just landed in the boat.

In regard of mermaids, there is a gentleman living near Killala Bay, whose name was mentioned to me, and who declares solemnly, that one day, shooting on the sands there, he saw a mermaid, and determined to try her with a shot. So he drew the small-charge from his gun, and loaded it with ball, that he always had by him for seal-shooting, fired, and hit the mermaid through the breast. The screams and moans of the creature, whose person he describes most accurately, were the most horrible heart-rending noises that he ever, he said, heard; and not only were they heard by him but by the fishermen along the coast, who were furiously angry against Mr A——n, because, they said, the injury done to the mermaid would cause her to drive all the fish away from the bay for years to come.

But we did not, to my disappointment, catch a single glimpse of one of these interesting beings, nor of the great sea-horse which is said to inhabit these waters, nor of any fairies (of whom the stroke-oar, Mr Marcus, told us not to

speak, for they didn't like bein' spoken of); nor even of a
salmon, though the fishermen produced the most tempting
flies. The only animal of any size that was visible, we saw
while lying by a swift black river, that comes jumping with
innumerable little waves into Derryclear, and where the
salmon are especially suffered to 'stand'; this animal was an
eagle – a real wild eagle, with gray wings and a white head and
belly: it swept round us, within gun-shot reach, once or twice,
through the leaden sky, and then settled on a gray rock and
began to scream its shrill, ghastly, aquiline note.

The attempts on the salmon having failed, the rain continuing to fall steadily, the herd's cottage before named was
resorted to: when Marcus, the boatman, commenced forthwith to gut the fish, and taking down some charred turf-ashes
from the blazing fire, on which about an hundred-weight of
potatoes were boiling, he – Marcus – proceeded to grill on the
floor some of the trout, which we afterwards ate with
immeasurable satisfaction. They were such trouts, as, when
once tasted, remain for ever in the recollection of a commonly
grateful mind – rich, flaky, creamy, full of flavour – a Parisian
gourmand would have paid ten francs for the smallest *cooleen*
among them; and, when transported to his capital, how
different in flavour would they have been! – how inferior to
what they were as we devoured them, fresh from the fresh
waters of the lake, and jerked as it were from the water to the
gridiron! The world had not had time to spoil those innocent
beings before they were gobbled up with pepper and salt, and
missed, no doubt, by their friends. I should like to know more
of their '*set*'. But enough of this: my feelings overpower me:
suffice it to say, they were red or salmon trouts – none of your
white-fleshed brown-skinned river fellows.

When the gentlemen had finished their repast, the boatmen
and the family set to work upon the ton of potatoes, a number
of the remaining fish, and a store of other good things; then
we all sat round the turf-fire in the dark cottage, the rain
coming down steadily outside, and veiling everything except
the shrubs and verdure immediately about the cottage. The
Herd, the Herd's wife, and a nondescript female friend, two
healthy young herdsmen in corduroy rags, the herdsman's
daughter paddling about with bare feet, a stout black-eyed

wench with her gown over her head and a red petticoat not quite so good as new, the two boatmen, a badger just killed and turned inside out, the gentlemen, some hens cackling and flapping about among the rafters, a calf in a corner cropping green meat and occasionally visited by the cow, her mamma, formed the society of the place. It was rather a strange picture; but as for about two hours we sat there, and maintained an almost unbroken silence, and as there was no other amusement but to look at the rain, I began, after the enthusiasm of the first half-hour, to think that after all London was a bearable place, and that for want of a turf-fire and a bench in Connemara, one *might* put up with a sofa and a newspaper, in Pall-Mall.

This, however, is according to tastes; and I must say that Mr Marcus betrayed a most bitter contempt for all Cockney tastes, awkwardness, and ignorance: and very right too. The night, on our return home, all of a sudden cleared; but though the fishermen – much to my disgust, at the expression of which, however, the rascals only laughed – persisted in making more casts for trout, and trying back in the dark upon the spots which we had visited in the morning, it appeared the fish had been frightened off by the rain: and the sportsmen met with such indifferent success that at about ten o'clock we found ourselves at Ballynahinch. Dinner was served at eleven; and, I believe, there was some whiskey-punch afterwards, recommended medicinally and to prevent the ill effects of the wetting; but that is neither here nor there.

The next day the Petty Sessions were to be held at Roundstone, a little town which has lately sprung up near the noble bay of that name. I was glad to see some specimens of Connemara litigation, as also to behold at least one thousand beautiful views that lie on the five miles of road between the town and Ballynahinch. Rivers and rocks, mountains and sea, green plains and bright skies, how (for the hundred-and-fiftieth time) can pen-and-ink set you down? But if Berghem could have seen those blue mountains, and Karel du Jardin could have copied some of these green airy plains, with their brilliant little coloured groups of peasants, beggars, horsemen, many an Englishman would know Connemara upon canvas, as he does Italy or Flanders now.

CHAPTER XVIII

ROUNDSTONE PETTY-SESSIONS

'The temple of august Themis,' as a Frenchman would call the Sessions-room at Roundstone, is an apartment of some twelve feet square, with a deal table and a couple of chairs for the accommodation of the magistrates, and a testament with a paper cross pasted on it to be kissed by the witnesses and complainants who frequent the court. The law-papers, warrants, &c., are kept on the Sessions-clerk's bed in an adjoining apartment, which commands a fine view of the court-yard, where there is a stack of turf, a pig, and a shed beneath which the magistrates' horses were sheltered during the sitting. The Sessions-clerk is a gentleman 'having,' as the phrase is here, both the English and Irish languages, and interpreting for the benefit of the worshipful bench.

And if the Cockney reader suppose that in this remote country spot, so wild, so beautiful, so distant from the hum and vice of cities, quarrelling is not, and Litigation never shows her snaky head, he is very much mistaken. From what I saw, I would recommend my ingenious young attorney whose merits are not appreciated in the Metropolis, to make an attempt upon the village of Roundstone, where as yet, I believe, there is no solicitor, and where an immense and increasing practice might speedily be secured. Mr O'Connell, who is always crying out 'Justice for Ireland', finds strong supporters among the Roundstonians, whose love of justice for themselves is inordinate. I took down the plots of the five first little litigious dramas which were played before Mr Martin and the stipendiary magistrate.

Case 1 – A boy summoned a young man for beating him so severely that he kept his bed for a week, thereby breaking an engagement with his master, and losing a quarter's wages.

The defendant stated, in reply, that the plaintiff was

engaged – in a field, through which defendant passed with another person – setting two little boys to fight; on which defendant took plaintiff by the collar and turned him out of the field. A witness who was present swore that defendant never struck plaintiff at all, nor kicked him, nor ill-used him, further than by pushing him out of the field.

As to the loss of his quarter's wages, the plaintiff ingeniously proved that he had afterwards returned to his master, that he had worked out his time, and that he had in fact received already the greater part of his hire. Upon which the case was dismissed, the defendant quitting court without a stain upon his honour.

Case 2 was a most piteous and lamentable case of killing a cow; the plaintiff stepped forward with many tears and much gesticulation to state the fact, and also to declare that she was in danger of her life from the defendant's family.

It appeared on the evidence that a portion of the defendant's respectable family are at present undergoing the rewards which the law assigns to those who make mistakes in fields with regard to the ownership of sheep which sometimes graze there. The defendant's father, O'Damon, for having appropriated one of the fleecy bleaters of O'Meliboeus, was at present past beyond sea to a country where wool, and consequently mutton, is so plentiful, that he will have the less temptation. Defendant's brothers tread the Ixionic wheel for the same offence. Plaintiff's son had been the informer in the case, hence the feud between the families, the threats on the parts of the defendants, the murder of the innocent cow.

But upon investigation of the business, it was discovered, and on the plaintiff's own testimony, that the cow had not been killed, nor even been injured, but that the defendant had flung two stones at it, which *might* have inflicted great injury had they hit the animal with greater force in the eye or in any delicate place.

Defendants admitted flinging the stones, but alleged as a reason that the cow was trespassing on their grounds, which plaintiff did not seem inclined to deny. Case dismissed. – Defendant retires with unblemished honour; on which his mother steps forward, and lifting up her hands with tears and shrieks, calls upon God to witness that the defendant's own brother-in-law had sold to her husband the very sheep on account of which he had been transported.

Not wishing probably to doubt the justice of the verdict of an Irish jury, the magistrate abruptly put an end to the lamentation and oaths of the injured woman by causing her to be sent out of court, and called the third cause on.

This was a case of thrilling interest and a complicated nature, involving two actions, which ought each perhaps to have been gone into separately, but were taken together. In the first place Timothy Horgan brought an action against Patrick Dolan for breach of contract in not remaining with him for the whole of six months during which Dolan had agreed to serve Horgan. Then Dolan brought an action against Horgan for not paying him his wages for six months' labour done – the wages being two guineas.

Horgan at once and with much candour withdrew his charge against Dolan, that the latter had not remained with him for six months; nor can I understand to this day, why in the first place he swore to the charge, and why afterwards he withdrew it. But immediately advancing another charge against his late servant, he pleaded that he had given him a suit of clothes which should be considered as a set-off against part of the money claimed.

Now such a suit of clothes of poor Dolan had, was never seen, I will not say merely on an English scarecrow, but on an Irish beggar. Strips of rags fell over the honest fellow's great brawny chest, and the covering on his big brown legs hung on by a wonder. He held out his arms with a grim smile, and told his Worship to look at the clothes – the argument was irresistible, Horgan was ordered to pay forthwith: – he ought to have been made to pay another guinea for clothing a fellow-creature in rags so abominable.

And now came a case of trespass, in which there was nothing interesting but the attitude of the poor woman who trespassed, and who meekly acknowledged the fact. She stated, however, that she only got over the wall as a short cut home; but the wall was eight feet high, with a ditch too; and I fear there were cabbages or potatoes in the enclosure. They fined her a sixpence, and she could not pay it, and went to gaol for three days, where she and her baby, at any rate, will get a meal.

Last on the list which I took down, came a man who will make the fortune of the London attorney, that I hope is on his way hither. A rather old curly-headed man, with a sly smile perpetually lying on his face (the reader may give whatever interpretation he please to the 'lying'), — he comes before the Court almost every fortnight they say, with a complaint of one kind or other. His present charge was against a man for breaking into his court-yard, and wishing to take possession of the same. It appeared however that he, the defendant, and another lived in  a row of houses – the plaintiff's house was, however, first built, and as his agreement specified that the plot of ground behind his house should be his likewise, he chose to imagine that the plot of ground behind all the three houses was his, and built his turf-stack against his neighbour's window. The magistrates of course pronounced against this ingenious discoverer of wrongs, and he left the court still smiling and twisting round his little wicked eyes, and declaring solemnly that he would put in an *appale*. If one could have purchased a kicking at a moderate price off that fellow's back, it would have been a pleasant little piece of self-indulgence, and I confess I longed to ask him the price of the article.

And so, after a few more such great cases, the court rose; and I had leisure to make moral reflections, if so minded – and sighing to think that cruelty and falsehood, selfishness and rapacity, dwell not in crowds alone, but flourish all the world over: sweet flowers of human nature, they bloom in all climates and seasons, and are just as much at home in a hot-house in Thavies' Inn, as on a lone mountain, or a rocky sea-coast in Ireland, where never a tree will grow!

We walked along this coast after the judicial proceedings were over, to see the country, and the new road that the Board of Works is forming – such a wilderness of rocks I never saw! the district for miles is covered with huge stones, shining white in patches of green, with the Binabola on one side of the spectator, and the Atlantic running in and out of a thousand little bays on the other. The country is very hilly, or wavy rather, being a sort of ocean petrified; and the engineers have hard work with these numerous abrupt little ascents and descents, which they equalise as best they may, by blasting, cutting, filling cavities, and levelling eminences. Some hundreds of men were employed at this work, busy with their hand-barrows, their picking, and boring. Their pay is eighteen-pence a day.

There is little to see in the town of Roundstone, except a Presbyterian Chapel in process of erection, that seems big enough to accommodate the Presbyterians of the county; and a sort of lay-convent, being a community of brothers of the third order of Saint Francis. They are all artisans and workmen, taking no vows but living together in common, and undergoing a certain religious regimen. Their work is said to be very good, and all are employed upon some labour or other. On the front of this unpretending little dwelling is an inscription with a great deal of pretence, stating, that the establishment was founded with the approbation of 'His Grace, the most Reverend the Lord Archbishop of Tuam.'

The most Reverend Dr MacHale is a clergyman of great learning, talents, and honesty, but His Grace the Lord Archbishop of Tuam strikes me as being no better than a mountebank; and some day I hope even his own party will laugh this humbug down. It is bad enough to be awed by big titles at all, but to respect sham ones! O stars and garters! We shall have his Grace the Lord Chief-Rabbi next, or his Lordship the Arch-Imaum.

CHAPTER XIX

CLIFDEN TO WESTPORT

On leaving Ballynahinch, (with sincere regret, as any lonely tourist may imagine, who is called upon to quit the hospitable friendliness of such a place and society) my way lay back to Clifden again, and thence through the Joyce country, by the Killery mountains, to Westport, in Mayo. The road, amounting in all to four-and-forty Irish miles, is performed in cars, in different periods of time, according to your horse and your luck. Sometimes, both being bad, the traveller is two days on the road; sometimes a dozen hours will suffice for the journey, which was the case with me, though I confess to having found the twelve hours long enough. After leaving Clifden, the friendly look of the country seemed to vanish; and, though picturesque enough, was a thought too wild and dismal for eyes accustomed to admire a hop-garden in Kent, or a view of rich folly meadows in Surrey, with a clump of trees and a comfortable village spire. 'Ingis,' the Guide-book says, 'compares the scenes to the Norwegian Fiords.' Well, the Norwegian Fiords must, in this case, be very dismal sights! and I own that the wildness of Hampstead Heath (with the imposing walls of Jack Straw's Castle rising stern in the midst of the green wilderness), are more to my taste than the general views of yesterday.

We skirted by lake after lake, lying lonely in the midst of lonely boglands, or bathing the sides of mountains robed in sombre rifle green. Two or three men, and as many huts, you see in the course of each mile, perhaps; as toiling up the bleak hills, or jingling more rapidly down them, you pass through this sad region. In the midst of the wilderness, a chapel stands here and there, solitary on the hill-side; or a ruinous, useless school-house, its pale walls contrasting with the general surrounding hue of sombre purple and green. But though the

country looks more dismal than Connemara, it is clearly more
fertile: we passed miles of ground that evidently wanted but
little cultivation to make them profitable; and along the
mountain sides, in many places, and over a great extent of Mr
Blake's country especially, the hills were covered with a thick,
natural plantation, that may yield a little brushwood now, but
might in fifty years' time bring thousands of pounds of
revenue to the descendants of the Blakes. This spectacle of a
country going to waste is enough to make the cheerfullest
landscape look dismal; it gives this wild district a woeful look
indeed. The names of the lakes by which we came I noted
down in a pocket-book as we passed along; but the names
were Irish, the car was rattling, and the only name readable in
the catalogue is Letterfrack.

The little hamlet of Leenane is at twenty miles' distance
from Clifden; and to arrive at it, you skirt the mountain along
one side of a vast pass, through which the ocean runs from
Killery Bay, separating the mountains of Mayo from the
mountains of Galway. Nothing can be more grand and
gloomy than this pass; and as for the character of the scenery,
it must, as the Guide-book says, 'be seen to be understood.'
Meanwhile, let the reader imagine huge, dark mountains, in
their accustomed livery of purple and green, a dull gray sky
above them, an estuary silver bright below: in the water lies a
fisherman's boat or two; a pair of sea-gulls, undulating with
the little waves of the water; a pair of curlews wheeling
overhead, and piping on the wing, and on the hill-side a
jingling car, with a cockney in it, oppressed by, and yet
admiring, all these things. Many a sketcher and tourist, as I
found, has visited this picturesque spot; for the hostess of the
inn had stories of English and American painters, and of
illustrious book-writers too, travelling in the service of our
Lords of Paternoster Row.

The landlord's son of Clifden, a very intelligent young
fellow, was here exchanged for a new carman, in the person of
a raw Irisher of twenty years of age, 'having' little English,
and dressed in that very pair of pantaloons which Humphrey
Clinker was compelled to cast off some years since, on acount
of the offence which they gave to Mrs Tabitha Bramble. This
fellow, emerging from among the boats, went off to a field to

seek for the black horse, which the landlady assured me was quite fresh, and had not been out all day, and would carry me to Westport in three hours. Meanwhile I was lodged in a neat little parlour, surveying the Mayo side of the water, with some cultivated fields and a show of a village at the spot where the estuary ends, and above them lodges and fine dark plantations, climbing over the dark hills that lead to Lord Sligo's seat of Delphi. Presently, with a curtsey, came a young woman, who sold worsted socks at a shilling a pair, and whose portrait is here given.

It required no small pains to entice this rustic beauty to stand, while a sketch should be made of her. Nor did any compliments or cajolements, on my part or the landlady's, bring about the matter; it was not until money was offered that the lovely creature consented. I offered (such is the ardour of the real artist) either to give her sixpence, or to purchase two pairs of her socks, if she would stand still for five minutes. On which she said she would prefer selling the socks. Then she stood still for a moment in the corner of the room; then she turned her face towards the corner, and the other part of her person towards the artist, and exclaimed in that attitude, 'I must have a shilling more.' Then I told her to go to the deuce. Then she made a proposition, involving the stockings and sixpence, which was similarly rejected; and finally, the above splendid design was completed at the price first stated.

However, as we went off, this timid little love barred the door for a moment, and said that 'I ought to give her another shilling, that a gentleman would give her another shilling,' and so on – she might have trod the London streets for ten years, and not have been more impudent and more greedy.

By this time the famous fresh horse was produced, and the driver, by means of a wraprascal, had covered a great part of the rags of his lower garment. He carried a whip and a stick, the former lying across his knees ornamentally, the latter being for service, and as his feet were directly under the horse's tail, he had full command of the brute's back, and belaboured it for six hours without ceasing.

What little English the fellow knew, he uttered with a howl, roaring into my ear answers, which, for the most part, were wrong, to various questions put to him. The lad's voice was so hideous, that I asked him if he could sing, on which forthwith he began yelling the most horrible Irish ditty, of which he told me the title, that I have forgotten. He sang three stanzas, certainly keeping a kind of tune, and the latter lines of each verse were in rhyme; but when I asked him the meaning of the song, he only roared out its Irish title.

On questioning the driver further, it turned out that the horse, warranted fresh, had already performed a journey of eighteen miles that morning, and the consequence was, that I had full leisure to survey the country through which we passed. There were more lakes, more mountains, more bog, and an excellent road through this lonely district, though few only of the human race enlivened it. At ten miles from Leenane, we stopped at a road-side hut, where the driver pulled out a bag of oats, and borrowing an iron pot from the good people, half filled it with corn, which the poor, tired, galled, bewhipped, black horse began eagerly to devour. The young charioteer himself hinted very broadly his desire for a glass of whiskey, which was the only kind of refreshment that this remote house of entertainment supplied.

In the various cabins I have entered, I have found talking a vain matter; the people are suspicious of the stranger within their wretched gates, and are shy, sly, and silent. I have, commonly, only been able to get half-answers in reply to my questions, given in a manner that seemed plainly to intimate that the visit was unwelcome. In this rude hostel, however, the landlord was a little less reserved, offered a seat at the turf fire, where a painter might have had a good subject for his skill. There was no chimney, but a hole in the roof, up which a small portion of the smoke ascended, (the rest preferring an egress by the door, or else to remain in the apartment altogether); and this light from above lighted up as rude a set of figures as ever were seen. There were two brown women, with black eyes and locks, the one knitting stockings on the floor, the other 'racking' (with that natural comb which five horny fingers supply) the elf-locks of a dirty urchin between her knees. An idle fellow was smoking his pipe by the fire, and by his side sate a stranger, who had been made welcome to the shelter of the place, a sickly well-looking man, whom I mistook for a deserter at first, for he had evidently been a soldier.

But there was nothing so romantic as desertion in his history. He had been in the dragoons, but his mother had purchased his discharge: he was married, and had lived comfortably in Cork for some time, in the glass-blowing business. Trade failing at Cork, he had gone to Belfast to seek for work. There was no work at Belfast; and he was so far on his road home again; sick, without a penny in the world, a hundred and fifty miles to travel, and a starving wife and children to receive him at his journey's end. He had been thrown off a caravan that day, and had almost broken his back in the fall. Here was a cheering story! I wonder where he is now: how far has the poor starving lonely man advanced over that weary desolate road, that in good health, and with a horse to carry me, I thought it a penalty to cross? What would one do under such circumstances, with solitude and hunger for present company, despair and starvation at the end of the vista? There are a score of lonely lakes along the road which he has to pass; would it be well to stop at one of them, and fling into it the wretched load of cares which that poor broken back has to carry? Would the world he would light on *then* be worse for him, than that he is pining in now? Heaven help us: and on this very day, throughout the three kingdoms, there are a million such stories to be told! Who dare doubt of Heaven after that? of a place where there is at last a welcome to the heart-stricken prodigal, and a happy home to the wretched.

The crumbs of oats which fell from the mouth of the feasting Dives of a horse, were battled for outside the door, by a dozen Lazaruses in the shape of fowls, and a lanky young pig, who had been grunting in an old chest in the cabin, or in a miserable recess of huddled rags and straw, which formed the couch of the family, presently came out and drove the poultry away, picking up, with great accuracy, the solitary grains lying about, and more than once trying to shove his snout into the corn pot, and share with the wretched old galled horse. Whether it was that he was refreshed by his meal, or that the car-boy was invigorated by his glass of whiskey, or inflamed by the sight of eighteen-pence, which munificent sum was tendered to the soldier, I don't know, but the remaining eight miles of the journey were got over in much quicker time, although the road was exceedingly bad and hilly for the greatest part of the way to Westport. However, by running up the hills at the pony's side, the animal, fired with emulation, trotted up them too, descending them with the proverbial surefootedness of his race, the car and he bouncing over the rocks and stones at the rate of at least four Irish miles an hour.

At about five miles from Westport, the cultivation became much more frequent. There were plantations upon the hills, yellow corn and potatoes in plenty in the fields, and houses thickly scattered. We had the satisfaction, too, of knowing that future tourists will have an excellent road to travel over in this district; for by the side of the old road which runs up and down a hundred little rocky steeps, according to the ancient plan, you see a new one running for several miles – the latter way being conducted not over the hills but around them, and, considering the circumstances of the country, extremely broad and even. The car-boy presently yelled out 'REEK, REEK!' with a shriek perfectly appalling. This howl was to signify that we were in sight of that famous conical mountain so named, and from which St Patrick, after inveigling thither all the venomous reptiles in Ireland, precipitated the whole noisome race into Clew Bay. The road also for several miles was covered with people, who were flocking in hundreds from Westport market, in cars and carts, on horseback single and double, and on foot.

And presently, from an eminence, I caught sight not only of a fine view, but of the most beautiful view I ever saw in the world, I think; and to enjoy the splendour of which I would travel a hundred miles in that car with that very horse and driver. The sun was just about to set, and the country round about and to the east was almost in twilight. The mountains were tumbled about in a thousand fantastic ways, and swarming with people. Trees, corn-fields, cottages made the scene indescribably cheerful; noble woods stretched towards the sea, and abutting on them, between two highlands lay the smoking town. Hard by was a large Gothic building – it is but a poor-house; but it looked like a grand castle in the gray evening – but the bay, and the Reek, which sweeps down to the sea, and a hundred islands in it, were dressed up in gold and purple, and crimson, with the whole cloudy west in a flame. Wonderful, wonderful! . . . The valleys in the road to Leenane, have lost all glimpses of the sun ere this; and I suppose there is not a soul to be seen in the black landscape, or by the shores of the ghastly lakes, where the poor glass-blower from the whiskey-shop is faintly travelling now.

CHAPTER XX

WESTPORT

Nature has done much for this pretty town of Westport; and after Nature, the traveller ought to be thankful to Lord Sligo, who has done a great deal too. In the first place, he has established one of the prettiest, comfortablest inns in Ireland, in the best part of his little town, stocking the cellars with good wines, filling the house with neat furniture, and lending, it is said, the whole to a landlord gratis, on condition that he should keep the house warm, and furnish the larder, and entertain the traveller. Secondly, Lord Sligo has given up, for the use of the townspeople, a beautiful little pleasure-ground about his house: 'You may depand upon it,' said a Scotchman at the inn, 'that they've right of pathway through the groonds, and that the Marquess couldn't shut them oot:' which is a pretty fair specimen of charity in this world – this kind world, that is always ready to encourage and applaud good actions, and find good motives for the same. I wonder how much would induce that Scotchman to allow poor people to walk in *his* park, if he had one!

In the midst of this pleasure-ground, and surrounded by a thousand fine trees, dressed up in all sorts of verdure, stands a pretty little church; paths through the wood lead pleasantly down to the bay; and, as we walked down to it on the day after our arrival, one of the green fields was suddenly black with rooks, making a huge cawing and clanging as they settled down to feed. The house, a handsome massive structure, must command noble views of the bay, over which all the colours of Titian were spread, as the sun set behind its purple islands.

Printer's ink will not give these wonderful hues; and the reader will make his picture at his leisure. That conical mountain to the left is Croagh-Patrick; it is clothed in the most magnificent violet-colour, and a couple of round clouds were

229

exploding as it were, from the summit, that part of them towards the sea, lighted up the most delicate gold and rose-colour. In the centre is the Clare island, of which the edges were bright cobalt, whilst the middle was lighted up with a brilliant scarlet tinge, such as I would have laughed at in a picture, never having seen in nature before, but looked at now with wonder and pleasure until the hue disappeared as the sun went away. The islands in the bay (which was of a gold colour) looked like so many dolphins and whales basking there. The rich park-woods stretched down to the shore; and the immediate foreground consisted of a yellow corn-field, whereon stood innumerable shocks of corn, casting immense long purple shadows over the stubble. The farmer, with some little ones about him, was superintending his reapers; and I heard him say to a little girl, 'Nory, I love you the best of all my children!' Presently, one of the reapers coming up, says, 'It's always the custom in these parts to ask strange gentlemen to give something to drink the first day of reaping; and we'd like to drink your honour's health in a bowl of coffee.' 'O fortunatos nimium!' The Cockney takes out sixpence, and thinks that he never passed such a pleasant half-hour in all his life as in that corn-field, looking at that wonderful bay.

A car which I had ordered presently joined me from the town, and going down a green lane very like England, and across a causeway near a building, where the carman proposed to show me 'me Lard's caffin that he brought from Rome, and a mighty big caffin entirely,' we came close upon the water and the Port. There was a long, handsome pier (which, no doubt, remains at this present minute), and one solitary cutter lying alongside it, which may not be there now. There were about three boats lying near the cutter, and six sailors, with long shadows, lolling about the pier. As for the warehouses, they are enormous; and might accommodate, I should think, not only the trade of Westport, but of Manchester too. There are huge streets of these houses, ten stories high, with cranes, owners' names, &c., marked Wine Stores, Flour Stores, Bonded Tobacco Warehouses, and so forth. The six sailors that were singing on the pier, no doubt, are each admirals of as many fleets of a hundred sail, that bring wines and tobacco from all quarters of the world to fill these enormous warehouses. These dismal mausoleums, as vast as pyramids, are the places where the dead trade of Westport lies buried – a trade that, in its lifetime, probably was about as big as a mouse. Nor is this the first nor the hundredth place to be seen in this country, which sanguine builders have erected to accommodate an imaginary commerce. Mill-owners over-mill themselves, merchants over-warehouse themselves, squires over-castle themselves, little tradesmen about Dublin and the cities over-villa and over-gig themselves, and we hear sad tales about hereditary bondage and the accursed tyranny of England.

Passing out of this dreary, pseudo-commercial port, the road lay along the beautiful shores of Clew Bay, adorned with many a rickety villa and pleasure-house, from the cracked windows of which may be seen one of the noblest views in the world. One of the villas the guide pointed out with peculiar exultation; it is called by a grand name – Waterloo Park, and has a lodge, and a gate, and a field of a couple of acres, and belongs to a young gentleman, who being able to write Waterloo Park on his card, succeeded in carrying off a young London heiress with a hundred thousand pounds. The young couple had just arrived, and one of them must have been rather astonished, no doubt, at the 'Park.' But what will not love do? With love and a hundred thousand pounds, a cottage may be made to look like a castle, and a park of two acres may be brought to extend for a mile. The night began now to fall, wrapping up in a sober gray livery the bay and mountains, which had just been so gorgeous in sunset; and we turned our backs presently upon the bay, and the villas with the cracked windows, and scaling a road of perpetual ups and downs, went back to Westport. On the way was a pretty cemetery, lying on each side of the road, with a ruined chapel for the ornament of one division, a holy well for the other. In the holy well lives a sacred trout, whom sick people come to consult, and who operates great cures in the neighbourhood. If the patient sees the trout floating on his back, he dies; if on his belly, he lives; or *vice versâ*. The little spot is old, ivy-grown, and picturesque, and I can't fancy a better place for a pilgrim to kneel and say his beads at.

But considering the whole country goes to mass, and that the priests can govern it as they will, teaching what shall be believed and what shall be not credited, would it not be well for their reverences, in the year eighteen hundred and forty-two, to discourage these absurd lies and superstitions, and teach some simple truths to their flock? Leave such figments to magazine-writers and ballad-makers; but, corbleu! it makes one indignant to think that people in the United Kingdom, where a press is at work, and good sense is abroad, and clergymen are eager to educate the people, should countenance such savage superstitions, and silly, grovelling heathenisms.

The chapel is before the inn where I resided, and on Sunday, from a very early hour, the side of the street was thronged with worshippers, who came to attend the various services. Nor are the Catholics the only devout people of this remote district. There is a large Presbyterian church very well attended, as was the Established church service in the pretty church in the park. There was no organ, but the clerk and a choir of children sang hymns sweetly and truly; and a charity sermon being preached for the benefit of the diocesan schools, I saw many pound-notes in the plate, showing that the Protestants here were as ardent as their Roman Catholic brethren. The sermon was extempore, as usual, according to the prevailing taste here. The preacher by putting aside his sermon book may gain in warmth, which we don't want, but lose in reason, which we do. If I were Defender of the Faith, I would issue an order to all priests and deacons to take to the book again; weighing well, before they uttered it, every word they proposed to say upon so great a subject as that of religion; and mistrusting that dangerous facility given by active jaws and a hot imagination. Reverend divines have adopted this habit, and keep us for an hour listening to what might well be told in ten minutes. They are wondrously fluent, considering all things; and though I have heard many a sentence begun whereof the speaker did not evidently know the conclusion; yet, somehow or other, he has always managed to get through the paragraph without any hiatus, except perhaps in the sense. And as far as I can remark, it is not calm, plain, downright preachers who preserve the extemporaneous system for the most part, but pompous orators, indulging in all the cheap graces of rhetoric – exaggerating words and feelings to make effect, and dealing in pious caricature. Church-goers become excited by this loud talk and captivating manner, and can't go back afterwards to a sober discourse read out of a grave old sermon book; appealing to the reason and the gentle feelings, instead of to the passions and the imagination. Beware of too much talk, O parsons! If a man is to give an account of every idle word he utters, for what a number of such loud nothings, windy emphatic tropes and metaphors, spoken not for God's glory but the preacher's, will many a cushion-thumper have to answer! And this rebuke may properly find a place here, because the clergyman by whose discourse it was elicited is not of the eloquent dramatic sort, but a gentleman, it is said, remarkable for old-fashioned learning and quiet habits, that do not seem to be to the taste of the many boisterous young clergy of the present day.

The Catholic chapel was built before their graces the most reverend lord archbishops came into fashion. It is large and gloomy, with one or two attempts at ornament, by way of pictures at the altars, and a good inscription warning the incomer, in a few bold words, of the sacredness of the place he stands in. Bare feet bore away thousands of people who came to pray there; there were numbers of smart equipages for the richer Protestant congregation. Strolling about the town in the balmy summer evening, I heard the sweet tones of a hymn from the people in the Presbyterian praying-house. Indeed, the country is full of piety, and a warm, sincere, undoubting devotion.

On week-days the street before the chapel is scarcely less crowded than on the Sabbath; but it is with women and children merely; for a stream bordered with lime-trees runs pleasantly down the street, and hither come innumerable girls to wash, while the children make dirt-pies and look on. Wilkie was here some years since, and the place affords a great deal of amusement to the painter of character. Sketching, *tant bien que mal*, the bridge and the trees, and some of the nymphs engaged in the stream, the writer became an object of no small attention; and at least a score of dirty brats left their dirt-pies to look on, the bare-legged washing-girls grinning from the water.

One, a regular rustic beauty, whose face and figure would have made the fortune of a frontispiece, seemed particularly

amused and *agaçante*; and I walked round to get a drawing of her fresh jolly face: but directly I came near she pulled her gown over her head, and resolutely turned round her back; and, as that part of her person did not seem to differ in character from the backs of the rest of Europe, there is no need of taking its likeness.

CHAPTER XXI

THE PATTERN AT CROAGH-PATRICK

On the pattern-day, however, the washerwomen and children had all disappeared – nay, the stream, too, seemed to be gone out of town. There was a report current, also, that on the occasion of the pattern, six hundred teetotallers had sworn to revolt; and I fear that it was the hope of witnessing this awful rebellion which induced me to stay a couple of days at Westport. The pattern was commenced on the Sunday, but the priests going up to the mountain took care that there should be no sports nor dancing on that day; but that the people should only content themselves with the performance of what are called religious duties. Religious duties! Heaven help us! If these reverend gentlemen were worshippers of Moloch or Baal, or any deity whose honour demanded bloodshed, and savage rites, and degradation, and torture, one might fancy them encouraging the people to the disgusting penances the poor things here perform. But it's too hard to think that in our days, any priests of any religion should be found superintending such a hideous series of self-sacrifices as are, it appears, performed on this hill.

A friend who ascended the hill brought down the following account of it. The ascent is a very steep and hard one, he says; but it was performed in company of thousands of people who were making their way barefoot to the several 'stations' upon the hill.

'The first station consists of one heap of stones, round which they must walk seven times, casting a stone on the heap each time, and before and after every stone's throw saying a prayer.

'The second station is on the top of the mountain. Here there is a great altar – a shapeless heap of stones. The poor wretches crawl *on their knees* into this place, say fifteen prayers, and after going round the entire top of the mountain fifteen times, say fifteen prayers again.

'The third station is near the bottom of the mountain at the further side from Westport. It consists of three heaps. The penitents must go seven times round these collectively, and seven times afterwards round each individually, saying a prayer before and after each progress.'

My informant describes the people as coming away from this 'frightful exhibition, suffering severe pain, wounded and bleeding in the knees and feet, and some of the women shrieking with the pain of their wounds.' Fancy thousands of these bent upon their work, and priests standing by to encourage them! – for shame, for shame. If all the popes, cardinals, bishops, hermits, priests, and deacons that ever lived, were to come forward and preach this as a truth – that to please God you must macerate your body, that the sight of your agonies is welcome to Him, and that your blood, groans, and degradation find favour in His eyes, I would not believe them. Better have over a company of Fakeers at once, and set the Suttee going.

Of these tortures, however, I had not the fortune to witness a sight; for going towards the mountain for the first four miles, the only conveyance I could find was half the pony of an honest sailor, who said, when applied to, 'I tell you what I do wid you: I give you a spell about;' but as it turned out we were going different ways, this help was but a small one. A car with a spare seat, however, (there were hundreds of others quite full, and scores of rattling country carts covered with people, and thousands of bare legs trudging along the road,) – a car with a spare seat passed by at two miles from the Pattern, and that just time to get comfortably wet through on arriving there. The whole mountain was enveloped in mist; and we could nowhere see thirty yards before us. The women walked forward, with their gowns over their heads; the men sauntered on in the rain, with the utmost indifference to it. The car presently came to a cottage, the court in front of which was black with two hundred horses, and where as many drivers were jangling and bawling; and here we were told to descend. You had to go over a wall and across a brook, and behold the Pattern.

The pleasures of the poor people – for after the business on the mountain came the dancing and love-making at its foot – was woefully spoiled by the rain, which rendered dancing on the grass impossible, nor were the tents big enough for that exercise. Indeed, the whole sight was as dismal and half-savage a one as I have seen. There may have been fifty of these tents squatted round a plain of the most brilliant green grass, behind which the mist curtains seemed to rise immediately; for you could not even see the mountain side beyond them. Here was a great crowd of men and women, all ugly, as the fortune of the day would have it (for the sagacious reader has, no doubt, remarked that there are ugly and pretty days in life). Stalls were spread about, whereof the owners were shrieking out the praises of their wares – great, coarse, damp-looking bannocks of bread for the most part, or, mayhap, a dirty collection of pigs' feet, and such refreshments. Several of the booths professed to belong to 'confectioners' from Westport or Castlebar, the confectionery consisting of huge biscuits and doubtful-looking ginger-beer – ginger-ale, or gingeretta, it is called in this country, by a fanciful people, who love the finest titles. And to these, caldrons containing water for tay, at the door of the booths, other pots full of masses of pale legs of mutton (the owner 'prodding,' every now and then, for a bit, and holding it up and asking the passenger to buy). In the booths, it was impossible to stand upright, or to see much, on account of smoke. Men and women were crowded in these rude tents, huddled together, and disappearing in the darkness. Owners came bustling out to replenish the empty water-jugs, and landladies stood outside in the rain calling strenuously upon all passers by to enter. Here is a design taken from one of the booths, presenting ingeniously an outside and an inside view of the same place – an artifice seldom practised in pictures.

Meanwhile, high up on the invisible mountain, the people were dragging their bleeding knees from altar to altar, flinging stones, and muttering some endless litanies, with the priests standing by. I think I was not sorry that the rain, and the care of my precious health, prevented me from mounting a severe hill, to witness a sight that could only have caused one to be shocked and ashamed that servants of God should encourage

it. The road home was very pleasant, everybody was wet through, but everybody was happy, and by some miracle we were seven on the car. There was the honest Englishman in the military cap, who sung 'The sea, the hopen sea's my ome,' although not any one of the company called upon him for that air. Then the music was taken up by a good-natured lass from Castlebar; then the Englishman again, 'With burnished brand and musketoon;' and there was no end of pushing, pinching, squeezing and laughing. The Englishman, especially, had a favourite yell, with which he saluted and astonished all cottages, passengers, cars, that we met or overtook. Presently came prancing by two dandies, who were especially frightened by the noise. 'Thim's two tailors from Westport,' said the carman, grinning with all his might. 'Come, gat out of the way there, gat along,' piped a small English voice, from above somewhere. I looked up, and saw a little creature, perched on the top of a tandem, which he was driving with the most knowing air – a dreadful young hero, with a white hat, and a white face, and a blue bird's-eye neckcloth. He was five feet high, if an inch, an ensign, and sixteen; and it was a great comfort to think, in case of danger or riot, that one of his years and personal strength was at hand to give help.

'Thim's the afficers,' said the carman, as the tandem

wheeled by, a small groom quivering on behind – and the carman spoke with the greatest respect this time. Two days before, on arriving at Westport, I had seen the same equipage at the door of the inn – where for a moment there happened to be no waiter to receive me. So, shouldering a carpet-bag, I walked into the inn-hall, and asked a gentleman standing there, where was the coffee-room? It was the military tandem-driving youth, who with much grace looked up in my face, and said calmly, '*I dawnt knaw*.' I believe the little creature had just been dining in the very room – and so present my best compliments to him.

The Guide-book will inform the traveller of many a beautiful spot, which lies in the neighbourhood of Westport, and which I had not the time to visit; but I must not take leave of the excellent little inn, without speaking once more of its extreme comfort, nor of the place itself, without another parting word regarding its beauty. It forms an event in one's life to have seen that place, so beautiful is it, and so unlike all other beauties that I know of. Were such beauties lying upon English shores it would be a world's wonder: perhaps, if it were on the Mediterranean or the Baltic English travellers would flock to it by hundreds; why not come and see it in Ireland! Remote as the spot is, Westport is only two days' journey from London now, and lies in a country far more strange to most travellers, than France or Germany can be.

CHAPTER XXII

FROM WESTPORT TO BALLINASLOE

The mail-coach took us next day by Castlebar and Tuam to Ballinasloe, a journey of near eighty miles. The country is interspersed with innumerable seats belonging to the Blakes, the Browns, and the Lynches; and we passed many large domains belonging to bankrupt lords and fugitive squires, with fine lodges, adorned with moss and battered windows, and parks where if the grass was growing on the roads, on the other hand the trees had been weeded out of the grass. About these seats and their owners the guard, an honest shrewd fellow, had all the gossip to tell. This jolly guard himself was a ruin, it turned out; he told me his grandfather was a man of large property; his father, he said, kept a pack of hounds, and had spent everything by the time he, the guard, was sixteen; so the lad made interest to get a mail-car to drive, whence he had been promoted to the guard's seat, and now for forty years had occupied it, travelling eighty miles, and earning seven-and-twopence every day of his life. He had been once ill, he said, for three days; and if a man may be judged by ten hours' talk with him, there are few more shrewd, resolute, simple-minded men to be found on the outside of any coaches or the inside of any houses in Ireland.

During the first five-and-twenty miles of the journey – for the day was very sunny and bright – Croaghpatrick kept us company; and, seated, with your back to the horses, you could see 'on the left that vast aggregation of mountains which stretches southwards to the bay of Galway; on the right, that gigantic assemblage which sweeps in circular outline northward to Killule.' Somewhere amongst those hills the great John Tuam was born, whose mansion and cathedral are to be seen in Tuam town, but whose fame is spread everywhere. To arrive at Castlebar, we go over the undulating valley which

lies between the mountains of Joyce country and Erris; and the
first object which you see on entering the town is a stately
Gothic castle that stands at a short distance from it.

On the gate of the stately Gothic castle was written an
inscription not very hospitable: WITHOUT BEWARE, WITHIN
AMEND; just beneath which is an iron crane of neat construction. The castle is the county gaol, and the iron crane is the
gallows of the district. The town seems neat and lively; there
is a fine church, a grand barracks (celebrated as the residence of
the young fellow with the bird's-eye neckcloth), a club, and a
Whig and Tory newspaper. The road hence to Tuam is very
pretty and lively, from the number of country-seats along the
way, giving comfortable shelter to more Blakes, Browns, and
Lynches.

In the cottages, the inhabitants looked healthy and rosy in
their rags, and the cots themselves in the sunshine almost
comfortable. After a couple of months in the country, the
stranger's eye grows somewhat accustomed to the rags; they
do not frighten him as at first: the people who wear them look
for the most part healthy enough; especially the small children, those who can scarcely totter, and are sitting shading their
eyes at the door, and leaving the unfinished dirtpie to shout as
the coach passes by, are as healthy a looking race as one will
often see. Nor can anyone pass through the land without
being touched by the extreme love of children among the
people; they swarm everywhere, and the whole country rings
with cries of affection towards the children, with the songs of
young ragged nurses dandling babies on their knees, and
warnings of mothers to Patsey to come out of the mud, or
Norey to get off the pig's back.

At Tuam the coach stopped exactly for fourteen minutes
and a half, during which time, those who wished might dine:
but instead, I had the pleasure of inspecting a very mouldy
dirty town, and made my way to the Catholic Cathedral – a
very handsome edifice indeed; handsome without and within,
and of the Gothic sort. Over the door is a huge coat of arms,
surmounted by a Cardinal's hat – the arms of the See, no
doubt, quartered with John Tuam's own patrimonial coat; and
that was a frieze coat, from all accounts, passably ragged at the
elbows. Well, he must be a poor wag who could sneer at an

old coat, because it was old and poor. But if a man changes it for a tawdry gimcrack suit, bedizened with twopenny tinsel, and struts about calling himself his Grace and my Lord, when may we laugh if not then? There is something simple in the way in which these good people belord their clergymen, and respect titles real or sham. Take any Dublin paper – a couple of columns of it are sure to be filled with movements of the small great men of the world. Accounts from Darrynane, state that the Right Honourable the Lord Mayor is in good health – his Lordship went out with his beagles yesterday – or His Grace the Most Reverend the Lord Archbishop of Ballywhack, assisted by the Right Reverend the Lord Bishops of Trincomalee and Hippopotamus, assisted, &c.; or Colonel Tims, of Castle Tims, and lady, have quitted the Shelburne Hotel, with a party for Kilballybathershins, where the *august*★ party propose to enjoy a few days' shrimp-fishing – and so on. Our people are not witty and keen of perceiving the ridiculous, like the Irish; but the bluntness and honesty of the English have well nigh kicked the fashionable humbug down; and except, perhaps, among footmen and about Baker Street, this curiosity about the aristocracy is wearing fast away. Have the Irish so much reason to respect their lords, that they should so chronicle all their movements; and not only admire real lords, but make sham ones of their own to admire *them*?

There is no object of special mark upon the road from Tuam to Ballinasloe, the country being flat for the most part, and the noble Galway and Mayo mountains having disappeared at length, until you came to a glimpse of Old England in the pretty village of Ahascragh. An old oak-tree grows in the neat street, the houses are as trim and white as eye can desire, and about the church and the town are handsome plantations, forming on the whole such a picture of comfort and plenty, as is rarely to be seen in the part of Ireland I have traversed. All these wonders have been wrought by the activity of an excellent resident agent. There was a countryman on the coach deploring that, through family circumstances, this gentleman

---

★ This epithet is applied to the party of a Colonel somebody, in a Dublin paper.

should have been dispossessed of his agency, and declaring that
the village had already begun to deteriorate in consequence. The
marks of such decay were not, however, visible, at least to a new
comer; and, being reminded of it, I indulged in many patriotic
longings for England, as every Englishman does, when he is
travelling out of the country which he is always so willing to
quit.

That a place should instantly begin to deteriorate because a
certain individual was removed from it – that cottagers should
become thriftless, and houses dirty, and house-windows
cracked – all these are points which public economists may
ruminate over, and can't fail to give the carelessest traveller
much matter for painful reflection. How is it that the presence of
one man, more or less, should affect a set of people come to
years of manhood, and knowing that they have their duty to do?
Why should a man at Ahascragh let his home go to ruin, and
stuff his windows with ragged breeches instead of glass, because
Mr Smith is agent in place of Mr Jones? Is he a child, that won't
work unless the schoolmaster be at hand? or are we to suppose,
with the Repealers, that the cause of all this degradation and
misery is the intolerable tyranny of the sister country, and the
pain which poor Ireland has been made to endure? This is very
well at the Corn Exchange, and among patriots after dinner;
but, after all, granting the grievance of the franchise (though it
may not be unfair to presume, that a man who has not strength
of mind enough to mend his own breeches or his own windows,
will always be the tool of one party or another), there is no
Inquisition set up in the country; the law tries to defend the
people as much as they will allow; the odious tithe has even been
whisked off from their shoulders to the landlords; they may live
pretty much as they like. Is it not too monstrous to howl about
English tyranny and suffering Ireland, and call for a Stephen's
Green Parliament, to make the country quiet and the people
industrious? The people are not politically worse treated than
their neighbours in England. The priests and the landlords, if
they chose to co-operate, might do more for the country now
than any kings or laws could. What you want here is not a
Catholic or Protestant party, but an Irish party.

In the midst of these reflections, and by what the reader will
doubtless think a blessed interruption, we came in sight of the

town of Ballinasloe and its 'gash-lamps,' which a fellow-passenger did not fail to point out with admiration. The road-menders, however, did not appear to think that light was by any means necessary; for, having been occupied, in the morning, in digging a fine hole upon the highway, previous to some alterations to be effected there, they had left their work at sun-down, without any lamp to warn coming travellers of the hole, which we only escaped by a wonder. The papers have much such another story. In the Galway and Ballinasloe coach a horse on the road suddenly fell down and died; the coachman drove his coach unicorn-fashion into town; and, as for the dead horse, of course, he left it on the road at the place where it fell, and where another coach coming up was upset over it, bones broken, passengers maimed, coach smashed. By Heavens! the tyranny of England is unendurable: and I have no doubt it had a hand in upsetting that coach.

CHAPTER XXIII

BALLINASLOE TO DUBLIN

During the cattle-fair the celebrated town of Ballinasloe is thronged with farmers from all parts of the kingdom – the cattle being picturesquely exhibited in the park of the noble proprietor of the town, Lord Clancarty. As it was not fair-time, the town did not seem particularly busy, nor was there much to remark in it, except a church, and a magnificent lunatic asylum, that lies outside the town on the Dublin road, and is as handsome and stately as a palace. I think the beggars were more plenteous and more loathsome here than almost anywhere; to one hideous wretch I was obliged to give money to go away, which he did for a moment, only to obtrude his horrible face directly afterwards half eaten away with disease. 'A penny for the sake of poor little Mery,' said another woman, who had a baby sleeping on her withered breast; and how can any one who has a little Mery at home, resist such an appeal? 'Pity the poor blind man!' roared a respectably-dressed grenadier of a fellow. I told him to go to the gentleman with a red neck-cloth and fur cap, (a young buck from Trinity College), to whom the blind man with much simplicity immediately stepped over; and as for the rest of the beggars, what pen or pencil could describe their hideous leering flattery, their cringing swindling humour!

The inn, like the town, being made to accommodate the periodical crowds of visitors who attended the fair, presented in their absence rather a faded and desolate look; and, in spite of the live stock for which the place is famous, the only portion of their produce which I could get to my share, after twelve hours' fasting and an hour's bell-ringing and scolding, was one very lean mutton chop, and one very small damp kidney, brought in by an old tottering waiter to a table spread in a huge black coffee-room, dimly lighted by one little jet of gas.

As this only served very faintly to light up the above banquet, the waiter, upon remonstrance, proceeded to light the other *bec*; but the lamp was sulky, and upon this attempt to force it, as it were, refused to act altogether, and went out. The big room was then accommodated with a couple of yellow mutton-candles. There was a neat, handsome, correct young English officer warming his slippers at the fire, and opposite him sate a worthy gentleman, with a glass of mingled 'materials,' discoursing to him in a very friendly and confidential way.

As I don't know the gentleman's name, and as it is not at all improbable, from the situation in which he was, that he has quite forgotten the night's conversation, I hope there will be no breach of confidence in recalling some part of it. The spreaker was dressed in deep black, worn however with that *dégagé* air peculiar to the votaries of Bacchus, or that nameless god – offspring of Bacchus and Ceres, who may have invented the noble liquor called whiskey. It was fine to see the easy folds in which his neckcloth confined his shirt-collar, moist with the generous drops that trickled from the chin above – its little per centage upon the punch. There was a fine dashing black satin waistcoat that called for its share, and generously disdained to be buttoned. I think this is the only specimen I have seen yet of the personage still so frequently described in the Irish novels – the careless drinking 'squire – the Irish Will Whimble.

'Sir,' says he, 'as I was telling you before this gentleman came in (from Westport, I preshume, sir, by the mail; and "my service to you!"), the butchers in Chume (Tuam) – where I live, and shall be happy to see you and give you a shake-down, a cut of mutton, and the use of as good a brace of pointers as ever you shot over – the butchers say to me, whenever I look in at their shops, and ask for a joint of meat – they say: "Take down that quarther o' mutton, boy, IT'S NO USE WEIGHING IT for Mr Bodkin. He can tell with an eye what's the weight of it to an ounce!" And so, sir, I can; and I'd make a bet to go into any market in Dublin, Tchume, Ballinasloe, where you please, and just by looking at the meat decide its weight.'

At the pause, during which the gentleman, here designated

Bodkin, drank off his materials, the young officer said gravely that this was a very rare and valuable accomplishment, and thanked him for the invitation to Tchume.

The honest gentleman proceeded with his personal memoirs; and (with a charming modesty that authenticated his tale, while it interested his hearers for the teller) he called for a fresh tumbler, and began discoursing about horses. 'Them, I don't know,' says he, confessing the fact at once, 'or, if I do, I've been always so unlucky with them that it's as good as if I didn't.

'To give you an idea of my ill-fortune: Me brother-'n-law Burke once sent me three colts of his to sell at this very fair of Ballinasloe; and, for all I could do, I could only get a bid for one of 'em, and sold her for sixteen pounds. And d'ye know what that mare was, sir?' says Mr Bodkin, giving a thump that made the spoon jump out of the punch glass for fright – 'D'ye know who she was? she was Water-Wagtail, sir – WATER-WAGTAIL! She won fourteen cups and plates in Ireland before she went to Liverpool; and you know what she did *there*?' (We said, 'Oh! of course.') 'Well, sir, the man who bought her from me, sold her for four hunder' guineas; and in England, she fetched eight hunder' pounds.

'Another of them very horses, gentlemen, (Tim, some hot wather – screeching hot, you divil – and a sthroke of the limin) – another of them horses that I was refused fifteen pound for, me brother-in-law sould to Sir Rufford Bufford for a hunder'-and-fifty guineas. Wasn't *that* luck?

'Well, sir, Sir Rufford gives Burke his bill at six months, and don't pay it when it come jue. A pretty pickle Tom Burke was in, as I leave ye to fancy, for he'd paid away the bill, which he thought as good as goold; and sure it ought to be, for Sir Rufford had come of age since the bill was drawn, and before it was due, and, as I needn't tell you, had slipped into a very handsome property.

'On the protest of the bill, Burke goes in a fury to Gresham's in Sackville Street, where the baronet was living, and (would ye believe it?) the latter says he doesn't intend to meet the bill, on the score that he was a minor when he gave it. On which Burke was in such a rage, that he took a horsewhip, and vowed he'd beat the baronet to a jelly and post him in every club in Dublin, and publish every circumstance of the transaction.'

'It *does* seem rather a queer one,' says one of Mr Bodkin's hearers.

'Queer indeed; but that's not it, you see; for Sir Rufford is as honourable a man as ever lived; and after this quarrel he paid Burke his money, and they've been warm friends ever since – but what I want to show ye is our infernal luck. *Three months before, Sir Rufford had sold that very horse for three hunder' guineas.*'

The worthy gentleman had just ordered in a fresh tumbler of his favourite liquor, when we wished him good night; and slept by no means the worse, because the bed-room candle was carried by one of the prettiest young chambermaids possible.

Next morning, surrounded by a crowd of beggars more filthy, hideous, and importunate than any I think in the most favoured towns of the south, we set off, a coach-load, for Dublin. A clergyman, a guard, a Scotch farmer, a butcher, a bookseller's hack, a lad bound for Maynooth, and another for Trinity, made a varied pleasant party enough, where each, according to his lights, had something to say.

I have seldom seen a more dismal and uninteresting road than that which we now took, and which brought us through the 'old, inconvenient, ill-built, and ugly town of Athlone.' The painter would find here, however, some good subjects for his sketch-book, in spite of the commination of the Guide-book: here, too, great improvements are taking place for the Shannon navigation, which will render the town not so inconvenient as at present it is stated to be: and hard by, lies a little village that is known and loved by all the world where English is spoken. It is called Lishoy, but its real name is Auburn, and it gave birth to one Noll Goldsmith, whom Mr Boswell was in the habit of despising very heartily. At the Quaker town of Moate, the butcher and the farmer dropped off, the Clergyman went inside, and their places were filled by four Maynoothians, whose vacation was just at an end. One of them, a freshman, was inside the coach with the clergyman, and told him, with rather a long face, of the dismal discipline of his college. They are not allowed to quit the gates (except on general walks); they are expelled if they read a newspaper; and they begin term with 'a retreat' of a week, which time they are made to devote to silence, and, as it is supposed, to devotion and meditation.

I must say the young fellows drank plenty of whisky on the road, to prepare them for their year's abstinence; and, when at length arrived in the miserable village of Maynooth, determined not to go into college that night, but to devote the evening to 'a lark.' They were simple, kind-hearted young men, sons of farmers or tradesmen seemingly; and, as is always the case here, except among some of the gentry, very gentlemanlike, and pleasing in manners. Their talk was of this companion, and that; how one was in rhetoric, and another in logic, and a third had got his curacy. Wait for a while; and with the happy system pursued within the walls of their college, those smiling good-humoured faces will come out with a scowl, and downcast eyes that seem afraid to look the world in the face. When the time comes for them to take leave of yonder dismal-looking barracks, they will be men no longer, but bound over to the church, body and soul: their free thoughts chained down and kept in darkness, their honest affections mutilated: well, I hope they will be happy to-night at any rate, and talk and laugh to their hearts' content. The poor freshman, whose big chest is carried off by the porter yonder to the inn, has but twelve hours more of hearty, natural, human life. To-morrow, they will begin their work upon him; cramping his mind, and biting his tongue, and firing and cutting at his heart – breaking him to pull the church chariot, Ah! why didn't he stop at home, and dig potatoes and get children.

Part of the drive from Maynooth to Dublin is exceedingly pretty: you are carried through Leixlip, Lucan, Chapelizod, and by scores of parks and villas, until the gas-lamps come in sight. Was there ever a cockney that was not glad to see them; and did not prefer the sight of them, in his heart, to the best lake or mountain ever invented? Pat the waiter comes jumping down to the car, and says, 'Welcome back, sir!' and bustles the trunk into the queer little bed-room, with all the cordial hospitality imaginable.

CHAPTER XXIV

TWO DAYS IN WICKLOW

The little tour we have just been taking has been performed, not only by the myriads of the 'car-drivingest, tay-drinkingest, say-bathingest people in the world,' the inhabitants of the city of Dublin, but also by all the tourists who have come to discover this country for the benefit of the English nation. 'Look here!' says the ragged bearded genius of a guide, at the seven churches; 'this is the spot which Mr Henry Inglis particularly admired, and said it was exactly like Norway. Many's the song I've heard Mr Sam Lover sing here – a pleasant gentleman entirely. Have you seen my picture that's taken off in Mrs Hall's book? all the strangers know me by it, though it makes me much cleverer than I am.' Similar tales has he of Mr Barrow, and the transatlantic Willis, and of Crofton Croker, who has been everywhere.

The guide's remarks concerning the works of these gentlemen inspired me, I must confess, with considerable disgust and jealousy. A plague take them! what remains for me to discover after the gallant adventurers in the service of Paternoster Row have examined every rock, lake, and ruin of the district, exhausted it of all its legends, and 'invented new,' most likely, as their daring genius prompted? Hence it follows, that the description of the two days' jaunt must, of necessity, be short; lest persons who have read former accounts should be led to refer to the same, and make comparisons which might possibly be unfavourable to the present humble pages.

Is there anything new to be said regarding the journey? In the first place, there's the railroad – it's no longer than the railroad to Greenwich, to be sure, and almost as well known; but has it been *done*? that's the question; or has anybody discovered the dandies on the railroad?

250

After wondering at the beggars and carmen of Dublin, the stranger can't help admiring another vast and numerous class of inhabitants of the city – namely, the dandies. Such a number of smartly-dressed young fellows, I don't think any town possesses; no, not Paris, where the young shopmen, with spurs and stays, may be remarked strutting abroad on fête days – nor London, where on Sundays, in the Park, you see thousands of this cheap kind of aristocracy parading – nor Liverpool, famous for the breed of commercial dandies, desk and counter Dorsays, and cotton and sugar-barrel Brummels, and whom one remarks pushing on to business with a brisk determined air – all the above races are only to be encountered on holidays, except by those persons whose affairs take them to shops, docks, or counting-houses, where these fascinating young fellows labour during the week.

But the Dublin breed of dandies is quite distinct from those of the various cities above-named, and altogether superior; for they appear every day, and all day long, not once a week merely, and have an original and splendid character and appearance of their own, very hard to describe, though no doubt every traveller, as well as myself, has admired and observed it. They assume a sort of military and ferocious look, not observable in other cheap dandies, except in Paris perhaps now and then; and are to be remarked, not so much for the splendour of their ornaments, as for the profusion of them. Thus for instance, a hat which is worn straight over the two eyes, costs very likely more than one which hangs upon one ear – a great oily bush of hair to balance the hat (otherwise the head no doubt would fall hopelessly on one side) is even more economical than a crop which requires the barber's scissor's oft-times; – also a tuft on the chin, may be had at a small expense of bear's grease by persons of a proper age; and although big pins are the fashion, I am bound to say, I have never seen so many or so big as here. Large agate marbles or 'taws,' globes terrestrial and celestial, pawnbrokers' balls – I cannot find comparisons large enough for these wonderful ornaments of the person. Canes also should be mentioned, which are sold very splendid, with gold or silver heads, for a shilling on the quays; and the dandy not uncommonly finishes off with a horn quizzing-glass, which being stuck in one eye, contracts the brows and gives a fierce determined look to the whole countenance.

In idleness, at least, these young men can compete with the greatest lords; and the wonder is, how the city can support so many of them, or they themselves; how they manage to spend their time: who gives them money to ride hacks in the 'Phaynix' on field and race days; to have boats at Kingstown during the summer; and to be crowding the railway coaches all the day long. Cars go whirling about all day, bearing squads of them. You see them sauntering at all the railway stations in vast numbers, and jumping out of the carriage as the trains come up, and greeting other dandies with that rich large brogue which some actor ought to make known to the English public: it being the biggest, richest, and coarsest of all the brogues of Ireland.

I think these dandies are the chief objects which arrest the stranger's attention, as he travels on the Kingstown railroad, and I have always been so much occupied in watching and wondering at them, as scarcely to have leisure to look at anything else during the pretty little ride of twenty minutes, so beloved by every Dublin cockney. The waters of the bay wash in many places the piers on which the railway is built, and you see the calm stretch of water beyond, and the big purple hill of Howth, and the light-houses, and the jetties, and the shipping. Yesterday, was a boat-race, (I don't know how many scores of such take place during the season), and you may be sure there were tens of thousands of the dandies to look on. There had been boat-races the two days previous: before that, had been a field day – before that, three days of garrison races – to-day, to-morrow, and the day after, there are races at Howth. There seems some sameness in the sports, but everybody goes; everybody is never tired; and then I suppose comes the punch party and the song in the evening – the same old pleasures, and the same old songs the next day, and so on to the end. As for the boat-race, I saw two little boats in the distance tugging away for the dear life – the beach and piers swarming with spectators, the bay full of small yachts, and innumerable row-boats, and in the midst of the assemblage a convict-ship, lying ready for sail, with a black mass of poor wretches on her deck, who too were eager for pleasure.

Who is not, in this country? Walking away from the pier and King George's column, you arrive upon rows after rows of pleasure-houses, whither all Dublin flocks during the summer time; for every one must have his sea-bathing, and they say that the country houses to the west of the town are to be empty, or had for very small prices; while for those on the coast, especially towards Kingstown, there is the readiest sale at large prices. I have paid frequent visits to one, of which the rent is as great as that of a tolerable London house; and there seems to be others suited to all purses – for instance, there are long lines of two-roomed houses, stretching far back and away from the sea, accommodating, doubtless, small commercial men, or small families, or some of those travelling dandies we have just been talking about, and whose costume is so cheap and so splendid.

A two-horse car, which will accommodate twelve, or will condescend to receive twenty passengers, starts from the railway-station for Bray, running along the coast for the chief part of the journey, though you have but few views of the sea, on account of intervening woods and hills. The whole of this country is covered with handsome villas and their gardens, and pleasure grounds. There are round many of the houses parks of some extent, and always of considerable beauty, among the trees of which the road winds. New churches are likewise to be seen in various places; built like the poor-houses, that are likewise everywhere springing up, pretty much upon one plan – a sort of bastard or Vauxhall Gothic – resembling no architecture of any age, previous to that when Horace Walpole invented the Castle of Otranto, and the other monstrosity upon Strawberry Hill, though it must be confessed that those on the Bray line are by no means so imaginative. Well, what matters, say you, that the churches be ugly, if the truth is preached within? Is it not fair, however, to say that Beauty is the truth too, of its kind? and why should it not be cultivated as well as other truth! Why build these hideous barbaric temples, when at the expense of a little study and taste, beautiful structures might be raised?

After leaving Bray, with its pleasant bay, and pleasant river, and pleasant inn, the little Wicklow tour may be said to commence properly; and, as that romantic and beautiful country has been described many times in familiar terms, our only chance is to speak thereof in romantic and beautiful language, such as no other writer can possibly have employed.

We rang at the gate of the steward's lodge, and said, 'Grant us a pass, we pray, to see the parks of Powerscourt, and to behold the brown deer upon the grass, and the cool shadows under the whispering trees.'

But the steward's son answered, 'You may not see the parks of Powerscourt, for the lord of the castle comes home, and we expect him daily.' So, wondering at this reply, but not understanding the same, we took leave of the son of the steward, and said, 'No doubt Powerscourt is not fit to see. Have we not seen parks in England, my brother, and shall we break our hearts that this Irish one hath its gates closed to us.'

Then the car-boy said, 'My lords, the park is shut, but the waterfall runs for every man; will it please you to see the waterfall?' 'Boy,' we replied, 'we have seen many waterfalls; nevertheless, lead on!' and the boy took his pipe out of his mouth, and belaboured the ribs of his beast.

And the horse made believe, as it were, to trot, and jolted the ardent travellers; and we passed the green trees of Tinnehinch, which the grateful Irish nation bought and consecrated to the race of Grattan; and we said, 'What nation will spend fifty thousand pounds for our benefit?' and we wished we might get it; and we passed on. The birds were, meanwhile, chanting concerts in the woods: and the sun was double-gilding the golden corn.

And we came to a hill, which was steep and long of descent; and the car-boy said, 'My lords, I may never descend this hill with safety to your honours' bones; for my horse is not sure of foot, and loves to kneel in the highway; descend therefore, and I will await your return here on the top of the hill.'

So we descended, and one grumbled greatly; but the other said, 'Sir, be of good heart! the way is pleasant, and the footman will not weary as he travels it,' and we went through the swinging gates of a park, where the harvest-men sate at their potatoes – a mealy meal.

The way was not short, as the companion said, but still it was a pleasant way to walk. Green stretches of grass were there, and a forest nigh at hand. It was but September; yet the autumn had already begun to turn the green ones into red; and the ferns that were waving underneath the trees were reddened and fading too. And as Dr Jones's boys of a Saturday disport in the meadows after school hours; so did the little clouds run races over the waving grass. And as grave ushers who look on smiling at the sports of these little ones; so stood the old trees around the green, whispering and nodding to one another.

Purple mountains rose before us in front, and we began presently to hear a noise and roaring afar off – not a fierce roaring, but one deep and calm, like to the respiration of the great sea, as he lies basking on the sands in the sunshine.

And we came soon to a little hillock of green, which was standing before a huge mountain of purple black, and there were white clouds over the mountains, and some trees waving on the hillock, and between the trunks of them we saw the waters of the waterfall descending; and there was a snob on a rock, who stood and examined the same.

Then we approached the water, passing the clump of oak trees. The waters were white, and the cliffs which they varnished were purple. But those round about were gray, tall, and gray with blue shadows; and ferns, heath, and rusty-coloured funguses sprouting here and there in the same. But in the ravine where the waters fell, roaring, as it were, with the fall, the rocks were dark, and the foam of the cataract was of a yellow colour. And we stood, and were silent, and wondered. And still the trees  continued to wave, and the waters to roar and tumble, and the sun to shine, and the fresh wind to blow.

And we stood and looked: and said in our hearts it was beautiful, and bethought us how shall all this be set down in types and ink? (for our trade is to write books and sell the same – a chapter for a guinea, a line for a penny;) and the waterfall roared in answer, 'For shame, O vain man! think not of thy books and of thy pence now; but look on, and wonder, and be silent. Can types or ink describe my beauty, though aided by thy small wit? I am made for thee to praise and wonder at: be content, and cherish thy wonder. It is enough that thou hast seen a great thing: is it needful that thou shouldst prate of all thou hast seen?'

So we came away silently, and walked through the park without looking back. And there was a man at the gate, who opened it and seemed to say, 'Give me a little sixpence.' But we gave nothing, and walked up the hill, which was sore to climb; and on the summit found the car-boy, who was lolling on his cushions and smoking, as happy as a lord.

Quitting the waterfall at Powerscourt (the grand style in which it has been described, was adopted, in order that the reader, who has probably read other descriptions of the spot, might have at least *something* new in this account of it;) we speedily left behind us the rich and wooded tract of country about Powerscourt, and came to a bleak tract, which perhaps, by way of contrast with so much natural wealth, is not unpleasing, and began ascending what is very properly called the Long Hill. Here you see, in the midst of the loneliness, a grim-looking barrack, that was erected when, after the Rebellion, it was necessary for some time to occupy this most rebellious country; and a church, looking equally dismal, a lean-looking, sham Gothic building, in the midst of this green desert. The road to Luggala, whither we were bound, turns off the Long Hill, up another hill, which seems still longer and steeper, inasmuch as it was ascended perforce on foot, and over lonely, boggy moorlands, enlivened by a huge gray boulder plumped here and there, and come, one wonders how, to the spot. Close to this hill of Slieve-Buck, is marked in the maps a district called 'the uninhabited country,' and these stones probably fell at a period of time, when not only this district, but all the world, was uninhabited – and in some convulsion of the neighbouring mountains, this and other enormous rocks were cast abroad.

From behind one of them, or out of the ground somehow, as we went up the hill, sprang little ragged guides, who are always lurking about in search of stray pence from tourists;

and we had three or four of such at our back by the time we were at the top of the hill. Almost the first sight we saw was a smart coach-and-four, with a loving wedding party within, and a genteel valet and lady's-maid without; I wondered, had they been burying their modest loves in the uninhabited district? – but presently, from the top of the hill, I saw the place on which their honeymoon had been passed; nor could any pair of lovers, nor a pious hermit, bent on retirement from the world, have selected a more sequestered spot.

Standing by a big, shining, granite stone on the hill top, we looked immediately down upon Lough Tay – a little round lake of half a mile in length, which lay beneath us as black as a pool of ink – a high, crumbling, white-sided mountain, falling abruptly into it on the side opposite to us, with a huge ruin of shattered rocks at its base. Northwards, we could see between mountains, a portion of the neighbouring lake of Lough Dan, which, too, was dark, though the Annamoe river, which connects the two lakes, lay coursing through the greenest possible flats, and shining as bright as silver. Brilliant green shores, too, come gently down to the southern side of Lough Tay; through these runs another river, with a small rapid or fall, which makes a music for the lake; and here, amidst beautiful woods, lies a villa, where the four horses, the groom, and valet, the postilions, and the young couple, had, no doubt, been hiding themselves.

Hereabouts, the owner of the villa, Mr Latouche, has a great grazing establishing; and some herd-boys, no doubt seeing strangers on the hill, thought proper that the cattle should stray that way, that they might drive them back again, and parenthetically ask the travellers for money, every body asks travellers for money, as it seems. Next day, admiring in a labourer's arms a little child – his master's son, who could not speak – the labourer, his he-nurse, spoke for him, and demanded a little sixpence to buy the child apples. One grows not a little callous to this sort of beggary; and the only one of our numerous young guides who got a reward, was the raggedest of them. He and his companions had just come from school, he said – not a government school, but a private one, where they paid. I asked how much – 'Was it a penny a week?' 'No; not a penny a week, but so much at the end of the year.'

'Was it a barrel of meal, or a few stone of potatoes, or something of that sort?' 'Yes: something of that sort.'

The something must, however, have been a very small something on the poor lad's part. He was one of four young ones, who lived with their mother, a widow. He had no work; he could get no work; nobody had work. His mother had a cabin, with no land – not a perch of land, no potatoes – nothing but the cabin. How did they live? – the mother knitted stockings. I asked, had she any stockings at home? – the boy said, 'No.' How did he live? – he lived how he could; and we gave him threepence, with which, in delight, he went bounding off to the poor mother. Gracious Heavens! what a history to hear, told by a child looking quite cheerful as he told it, and as if the story was quite a common one. And a common one, too, it is: and God forgive us.

Here is another, and of a similar low kind, but rather pleasanter. We asked the car-boy how much he earned. He said, 'Seven shillings a week, and his chances,' which in the summer season, from the number of tourists who are jolted in his car, must be tolerably good – eight or nine shillings a week more probably. But he said, in winter, his master did not hire him for the car; and he was obliged to look for work elsewhere: as for saving, he never had saved a shilling in his life.

We asked him, was he married? and he said, No, but he was *as good as married*; for he had an old mother and four little brothers to keep, and six mouths to feed, and to dress himself decent to drive the gentlemen. Was not the 'as good as married' a pretty expression? and might not some of what are called their betters learn a little good from these simple poor creatures? There's many a young fellow who sets up in the world, would think it rather hard to have four brothers to support; and I have heard more than one genteel Christian pining over five hundred a year. A few such may read this, perhaps: let them think of the Irish widow, with the four children and *nothing*, and at least be more contented with their port and sherry, and their leg of mutton.

This brings us at once to the subject of dinner; and the little village, Roundwood, which was reached by this time, lying a few miles off from the lakes, and reached by a road not particularly remarkable for any picturesqueness in beauty, though you pass through a simple pleasing landscape, always agreeable as a repose, I think, after viewing a sight so beautiful as those mountain lakes we have just quitted. All the hills up which we had panted had imparted a fierce sensation of hunger; and it was nobly decreed that we should stop in the middle of the street of Roundwood, impartially between the two hotels, and solemnly decide upon a resting-place after having inspected the larders and bedrooms of each.

And here, as an impartial writer, I must say, that the hotel of Mr Wheatly possesses attractions which few men can resist, in the shape of two very handsome young ladies, his daughters, whose faces, were they but painted on his sign-board, instead of the mysterious piece which ornaments it, would infallibly draw tourists into the house, thereby giving the opposition inn of Murphy not the least chance of custom.

A landlord's daughters in England, inhabiting a little country inn, would be apt to lay the cloth for the traveller, and their respected father would bring in the first dish of the dinner; but this arrangement is never known in Ireland: we scarcely ever see the cheering countenance of my landlord. And as for the young ladies of Roundwood, I am bound to say that no young persons in Baker-street could be more genteel; and that our bill, when it was brought the next morning, was written in as pretty and fashionable a lady's hand as ever was formed in the most elegant finishing school at Pimlico.

Of the dozen houses of the little village, the half seem to be houses of entertainment. A green common stretches before these, with its rural accompaniments of geese, pigs, and idlers; a park and plantation at the end of the village, and plenty of trees round about it, give it a happy, comfortable, English look; which is, to my notion, the best compliment that can be paid to a hamlet; for where, after all, are villages so pretty?

Here, rather to one's wonder, for the district was not thickly enough populated to encourage dramatic exhibitions, a sort of theatre was erected on the common; a ragged cloth covering the spectators and the actors, and the former (if there were any) obtaining admittance through two doors on the stage, in front marked PIT & GALERY. Why should the word not be spelt with one L as with two?

The entrance to the pit was stated to be threepence, and to the galery twopence. We heard the drums and pipes of the orchestra, as we sate at dinner; it seemed to be a good opportunity to examine Irish humour of a peculiar sort, and we promised ourselves a pleasant evening in the pit.

But, although the drums began to beat at half-past six, and a crowd of young people formed round the ladder at that hour, to whom the manager of the troop addressed the most vehement invitations to enter, no body seemed to be inclined to mount the steps; for the fact, most likely, was, that not one of the poor fellows possessed the requisite twopence, which would induce the fat old lady who sat by it to fling open the gallery-door. At one time, I thought of offering a half-crown for a purchase of tickets for twenty, and so at once benefiting the management and the crowd of ragged urchins who stood wistfully without his pavilion. But it seemed ostentatious, and we had not the courage to face the tall man in the great-coat, gesticulating and shouting in front of the stage, and make the proposition.

Why not? It would have given the company potatoes, at least, for supper, and made a score of children happy. They would have seen 'the learned pig who spells your name, the feasts of manly activity, the wonderful Italian vaulting;' and they would have heard the comic songs by 'your humble servant.'

'Your humble servant' was the head of the troop: a long man, with a broad accent, a yellow top-coat, and a piteous lean face. What a speculation was this poor fellow's! he must have a company of at least a dozen to keep. There were three girls in trowsers, who danced in front of the stage, in Polish caps, tossing their arms about to the tunes of three musicianers; there was a page, two young tragedy actors, and a clown; there was the fat old woman at the gallery-door, waiting for the twopences; there was the Jack-pudding; and it was evident that there must have been some one within, or else who would take care of the learned pig?

The poor manager stood in front, and shouted to the little Irishry beneath; but no one seemed to move. Then he brought forward Jack Pudding, and had a dialogue with him; the jocularity of which, by Heavens! made the heart ache to hear.

We had determined, at least, to go to the play before that, but the dialogue was too much: we were obliged to walk away, unable to face that dreadful Jack Pudding; and heard the poor manager shouting still, for many hours through the night, and the drums thumping vain invitations to the people. O, unhappy children of the Hibernian Thespis! it is my belief that they must have eaten the learned pig that night for supper.

It was Sunday morning when we left the little inn at Roundwood; the people were flocking in numbers to church, on cars and pillions, neat, comfortable, and well dressed. We saw in this country more health, more beauty, and more shoes than I have remarked in any quarter. That famous resort of sightseers, the Devil's Glen, lies at a few miles distance from the little village; and, having gone on the car as near to the spot as the road permitted, we made across the fields – boggy, stony, ill-tilled fields they were – for about a mile, at the end of which walk, we found ourselves on the brow of the ravine, that has received so ugly a name.

Is there a legend about the place? No doubt, for this, as for almost every other natural curiosity in Ireland, there is some tale of monk, saint, fairy, or devil; but our guide in the present day was a barrister from Dublin, who did not deal in fictions by any means so romantic, and the history, whatever it was, remained untold. Perhaps the little breeches-less cicerone who offered himself, would have given us the story, but we dismissed the urchin with scorn, and had to find our own way through bush and bramble down to the entrance of the gully.

Here we came on a cataract, which looks very big in Messrs Curry's pretty little Guide-book (that every traveller to Wicklow will be sure to have in his pocket), but the waterfall, on this shining Sabbath morning, was disposed to labour as little as possible, and, indeed, is a spirit of a very humble, ordinary sort.

But there is a ravine of a mile and a half, through which a river runs roaring (a lady who keeps the gate, will not object to receive a gratuity), there is a ravine or Devil's glen, which forms a delightful wild walk, and where a Methusaleh of a landscape-painter might find studies for all his life long. All sorts of foliage and colour, all sorts of delightful caprices of light and shadow – the river tumbling and frothing amidst the boulders – raucum per laevia murmur saxa ciens, and a chorus of 150,000 birds (there might be more), hopping, twittering, singing under the clear cloudless Sabbath scene, make this walk one of the most delightful that can be taken; and, indeed, I hope there is no harm in saying, that you may get as much out of an hour's walk there, as out of the best hour's extempore preaching. But this was as a salvo to our conscience for not being at church.

Here, however, was a long aisle, arched gothically over-head, in a much better taste than is seen in some of those dismal new churches; and, by way of painted glass, the sun lighting up multitudes of various-coloured leaves, and the birds for choristers, and the river by way of organ, and in it stones enough to make a whole library of sermons. No man can walk in such a place without feeling grateful, and grave, and humble; and without thanking Heaven for it as he comes away. And, walking and musing in this free happy place, one could not help thinking of a million and a half of brother Cockneys, shut up in their huge prison (the tread-mill for the day being idle), and told by some legislators that relaxation is sinful, that works of art are abominations, except on week-days, and that their proper place of resort is a dingy tabernacle, where a loud-voiced man is howling about hell-fire in bad grammar. Is not this beautiful world too, a part of our religion? Yes, truly, in whatever way my Lord John Russell may vote; and it is to be learned without having recourse to any professor at any Bethesda, Ebenezer, or Jerusalem; there can be no mistake about it; no terror, no bigoted dealing of damnation to one's neighbour – it is taught without false emphasis or vain spouting on the preacher's part – how should there be such with such a preacher?

This wild onslaught upon sermons and preachers needs perhaps an explanation; for which purpose we must whisk back out of the Devil's Glen (improperly so named) to Dublin, and to this day week, when, at this very time, I heard one of the first preachers of the city deliver a sermon that lasted for an hour and twenty minutes – time enough to walk up the Glen and back, and remark a thousand delightful things by the way.

Mr G——'s church (though there would be no harm in mentioning the gentleman's name, for a more conscientious and excellent man, as it is said, cannot be) is close by the Custom-house in Dublin, and crowded morning and evening with his admirers. The service was beautifully read by him, and the audience joined in the responses, and in the psalms and hymns,★ with a fervour which is very unusual in England. Then came the sermon; and what more can be said of it, than that it was extempore, and lasted for an hour and twenty minutes? The orator never failed once for a word, so amazing is his practice; though, as a stranger to this kind of exercise, I could not help trembling for the performer, as one has for Madame Saqui on the slack-rope, in the midst of a blaze of rockets and squibs, expecting every minute she must go over. But the artist was too skilled for that; and, after some tremendous bound of a metaphor, in the midst of which you expect he must tumble neck and heels, and be engulfed in the dark abyss of nonsense, down he was sure to come, in a most graceful attitude too, in the midst of a fluttering 'ah,' from a thousand wondering people.

But I declare solemnly, that when I came to try and recollect of what the exhibition consisted, and give an account of the sermon at dinner that evening, it was quite impossible to remember a word of it; although, to do the orator justice, he repeated many of his opinions a great number of times over. Thus, if he had to discourse of death to us, it was – At the approach of the Dark Angel of the Grave – at the coming of the grim King of Terrors – at the warning of that awful Power to whom all of us must bow down – at the summons of that Pallid Spectre whose equal foot knocks at the monarch's tower or the poor man's cabin – and so forth. There is an examiner of plays, and indeed there ought to be an examiner of sermons,

---

★ Here is an extract from one of the latter:

> 'Hasten to some distant isle,
>   In the bosom of the deep,
> Where the skies for ever smile,
>   *And the blacks forever weep.*

Is it not a shame that such nonsensical false twaddle should be sung in a house of the Church of England, and by people assembled for grave and decent worship?

by which audiences are to be fully as much injured or misguided as by the other named exhibitions. What call have reverend gentlemen to repeat their dicta half-a-dozen times over, like Sir Robert Peel when he says anything that he fancies to be witty? Why are men to be kept for an hour and twenty minutes listening to that which may be more effectually said in twenty?

And it need not be said here, that a church is not a sermon-house – that it is devoted to a purpose much more lofty and sacred, for which has been set apart the noblest service, every single word of which latter has been previously weighed with the most scrupulous and thoughtful reverence. And after this sublime work of genius, learning, and piety is concluded, is it not a shame that a man should mount a desk, who has not taken the trouble to arrange his words beforehand, and speak thence his crude opinions in his doubtful grammar? It will be answered, that the extempore preacher does not deliver crude opinions, but that he arranges his discourse beforehand; to all which it may be answered that Mr—— contradicted himself more than once in the course of the above oration, and repeated himself a half-dozen of times. A man in that place has no right to say a word too much or too little.

And it comes to this – it is the preacher the people follow, not the prayers, or why is this church more frequented than any other? It is that warm emphasis, and word-mouthing, and vulgar imagery, and glib rotundity of phrase, which brings them together and keeps them happy and breathless. Some of this class call the Cathedral Service *Paddy's Opera*; they say it is Popish – downright scarlet – they won't go to it. They will have none but their own hymns – and pretty they are – no ornaments but those of their own minister, his rank incense and tawdry rhetoric. Coming out of the church on the Custom-House steps hard by, there was a fellow with a bald large forehead, a new black coat, a little bible, spouting – spouting 'in omne volubilis aevum' – the very counterpart of the reverend gentleman hard by. It was just the same thing, just as well done, the eloquence quite as easy and round, the amplifications as ready, the big words rolling round the tongue, just as within doors. But we are out of the Devil's

Glen by this time; and perhaps, instead of delivering a sermon there, we had better have been at church hearing one.

The country people, however, are far more pious: and the road along which we went to Glendalough was thronged with happy figures of people plodding to or from mass. A chapel-yard was covered with gray cloaks; and at a little inn hard by, stood numerous carts, cars, shandy-dans, and pillioned horses, awaiting the end of the prayers. The aspect of the country is wild, and beautiful of course; but why try to describe it? I think the Irish scenery just like the Irish melodies – sweet, wild, and sad even in the sunshine. You can neither represent one nor the other by words; but I am sure if one could translate 'The Meeting of the Waters' into form and colours, it would fall into the exact shape of a tender Irish landscape. So, take and play that tune upon your fiddle, and shut your eyes, and muse a little, and you have the whole scene before you.

I don't know if there is any tune about Glendalough; but if there be, it must be the most delicate, fantastic, fairy melody that ever was played. Only fancy can describe the charms of that delightful place. Directly you see it, it smiles at you as innocent and friendly as a little child; and once seen, it becomes your friend for ever, and you are always happy when you think of it. Here is a little lake and little fords across it, surrounded by little mountains, and which lead you now to little islands where there are all sorts of fantastic little old chapels and graveyards; or again into little brakes and shrub-beries where small rivers are crossing over little rocks, plashing and jumping, and singing as loud as ever they can. Thomas Moore has written rather an awful description of it; and it may indeed appear big to *him*, and to the fairies who must have inhabited the place in old days that's clear. For who could be accommodated in it except the little people?

There are seven churches, whereof the clergy must have been the smallest persons, and have had the smallest benefices and the littlest congregations ever known. As for the Cathe-dral, what a bishoplet it must have been that presided there! – the place would hardly hold the Bishop of London, or Mr Sidney Smith – two full sized clergymen of these days – who would be sure to quarrel there for want of room, or for any other reason. There must have been a dean no bigger than Mr Moore before mentioned, and a chapter no bigger than that chapter in Tristram Shandy which does not contain a single word, and mere pop guns of cannons, and a beadle about as tall as Crofton Croker, to whip the little boys who were playing at taw (with peas) in the yard.

They say there was a university, too, in the place, with I don't know how many thousand scholars; but for accounts of this, there is an excellent guide on the spot, who, for a shilling or two, will tell all he knows, and a great deal more too.

There are numerous legends, too, concerning St Kevin, and Fin Mac Coul and the devil, and the deuce knows what. But these stories are, I am bound to say, abominably stupid and stale; and some guide* ought to be seized upon, and choked, and flung into the lake, by way of warning to the others to stop their interminable prate. This is the curse attending curiosity, for visitors to almost all the show-places in the country: you have not only the guide, who himself talks too much, but a string of ragged amateurs starting from bush and briar, ready to carry his honour's umbrella or my lady's cloak, or to help either up a bank or across a stream. And all the while they look wistfully in your face, saying 'Give me sixpence!' as clear as looks can speak. The unconscionable rogues! how dare they, for the sake of a little starvation or so, interrupt gentlefolks in their pleasure.

A long tract of wild country, with a park or two here and there, a police barrack perched on a hill, a half-starved-looking church stretching its long, scraggy steeple over a wide plain, mountains whose base is richly cultivated while their tops are purple and lonely, warm cottages and farms nestling at the foot of the hills, and humble cabins here and there on the wayside, accompany the car that jingles back over fifteen miles of ground through Inniskerry to Bray. You pass by wild gaps and greater and lesser Sugar-Loaves; and about eight

---

* It must be said, for the worthy fellow who accompanied us, and who acted as cicerone previously to the great Willis, the great Hall, the great Barrow, that though he wears a ragged coat his manners are those of a gentleman, and his conversation evinces no small talent, taste, and scholarship.

o'clock, when the sky is quite red with sunset, and the long shadows are of such a purple as (they may say what they like) Claude could no more paint than I can, you catch a glimpse of the sea, beyond Bray, and crying out, 'θαλαττα, θαλαττα!' affect to be wondrously delighted by the sight of that element.

The fact is, however, that at Bray is one of the best inns in Ireland; and there you may be perfectly sure is a good dinner ready, five minutes after the honest car-boy, with innumerable hurroos and smacks of his whip, has brought up his passengers to the door with a gallop.

As for the Vale of Avoca, I have not described that; because (as has been before occasionally remarked) it is vain to attempt to describe natural beauties; and because, secondly (though this is a minor consideration), we did not go thither. But we went on another day to the Dargle, and to Shanganah, and the city of Cabinteely, and to the Scalp – that wild pass: and I have no more to say about them, than about the Vale of Avoca. The Dublin Cockney, who has these places at his door, knows them quite well: and, as for the Londoner, who is meditating a trip to the Rhine for the summer, or to Brittany or Normandy, let us beseech him to see his *own country first* (if Lord Lyndhurst will allow us to call this a part of it), and if, after twenty-four hours of an easy journey from London, the Cockney be not placed in the midst of a country as beautiful, as strange to him, as romantic as the most imaginative man on 'Change can desire – may this work be praised by the critics all around, and never reach a second edition!

CHAPTER XXV

COUNTRY MEETINGS IN KILDARE – MEATH – DROGHEDA

An agricultural show was to be held at the town of Naas, and I was glad, after having seen the grand exhibition at Cork, to be present at a more homely, unpretending country festival, where the eyes of Europe, as the orators say, did not happen to be looking on. Perhaps men are apt, under the idea of this sort of inspection, to assume an air somewhat more pompous and magnificent than that which they wear every day. The Naas meeting was conducted without the slightest attempt at splendour or display – a hearty, modest, matter-of-fact, country meeting.

Market-day was fixed upon of course, and the town, as we drove into it, was thronged with frieze-coats, the market-place bright with a great number of apple-stalls, and the street filled with carts and vans of numerous small tradesmen, vending cheeses, or cheap crockeries, or ready-made clothes, and such goods. A clothier, with a great crowd round him, had arrayed himself in a staring new waistcoat of his stock, and was turning slowly round to exhibit the garment, spout-ing all the while to his audience, and informing them that he could fit out any person in one minute, 'in a complete new shuit from head to fut.' There seemed to be a crowd of gossips at every shop-door, and, of course, a number of gentlemen waiting at the inn-steps, criticising the cars and carriages as they drove up. Only those who live in small towns know what an object of interest the street becomes, and the carriages and horses which pass therein. Most of the gentlemen had sent stock to compete for the prizes. The shepherds were tending the stock. The judges were making their award, and until their sentence was given, no competitors could enter the show-yard. The entrance to that, meanwhile, was thronged by a great posse of people, and as the gate abutted upon an old gray tower, a number of people had scaled that, and were looking at the beasts in the court below. Likewise, there was a tall haystack, which possessed similar advantages of situation, and

was equally thronged with men and boys; the rain had fallen heavily all night, the heavens were still black with it, and the coats of the men and the red feet of many ragged female spectators, were liberally spattered with mud.

The first object of interest we were called upon to see, was a famous stallion; and passing through the little by-streets (dirty and small, but not so small and dirty as other by-streets to be seen in Irish towns), we came to a porte cochère, leading into a yard filled with wet fresh hay, sinking juicily under the feet; and here in a shed was the famous stallion. His sire must have been a French diligence-horse; he was of a roan colour, with a broad chest, and short clean legs. His forehead was ornamented with a blue ribbon, on which his name and prizes were painted, and on his chest hung a couple of medals by a chain – a silver one, awarded to him at Cork, a gold one, carried off by superior merit from other stallions assembled to contend at Dublin. When the points of the animal were sufficiently discussed, a mare, his sister, was produced, and admired still more than himself. Any man who has witnessed the performance of the French horses in the Hâvre diligence, must admire the vast strength and the extraordinary swiftness of the breed; and it was agreed on all hands, that such horses would prove valuable in this country, where it is hard now to get a stout horse for the road, so much has the fashion for blood, and nothing but blood, prevailed of late.

By the time the stallion was seen, the judges had done their arbitration; and we went to the yard, where broad-backed sheep were resting peaceably in their pens; bulls were led about by the nose; enormous turnips, both Swedes and Aberdeens, reposed in the mud; little cribs of geese, hens, and pea-fowl, were come to try for the prize, and pigs might be seen – some encumbered with enormous families, others with fat merely. They poked up one brute to walk for us; he made, after many futile attempts, a desperate rush forward, his leg almost lost in fat, his immense sides quivering and shaking with the exercise; he was then allowed to return to his straw, into which he sunk panting. Let us hope that he went home with a pink ribbon round his tail that night, and got a prize for his obesity.

I think the pink ribbon was, at least to a Cockney, the pleasantest sight of all; for on the evening after the show, we saw many carts going away so adorned, having carried off prizes on the occasion. First came a great bull stepping along, he and his driver having each a bit of pink in their hats; then a cart full of sheep; then a car of good-natured-looking people, having a churn in the midst of them that sported a pink favour. When all the prizes were distributed, a select company sate down to dinner at Macavoy's hotel; and, no doubt, a reporter who was present, has given in the county paper an account of all the good things eaten and said. At our end of the table we had saddle of mutton, and I remarked a boiled leg of the same delicacy, with turnips, at the opposite extremity; before the vice, I observed a large piece of roast beef, which I could not observe at the end of dinner, because it was all swallowed. After the mutton we had cheese, and were just beginning to think that we had dined very sufficiently, when a squadron of apple-pies came smoking in, and convinced us that, in such a glorious cause, Britons are never at fault. We ate up the apple-pies, and then the punch was called for by those who preferred that beverage to wine, and the speeches began.

The chairman gave 'the Queen,' nine times nine and one cheer more; 'Prince Albert and the rest of the Royal Family,' great cheering, 'the Lord Lieutenant;' his Excellency's health was received rather coolly, I thought. And then began the real business of the night – Health of the Naas Society, health of the Agricultural Society, and healths all round; not forgetting the Sallymount Beagles, and the Kildare Foxhounds: which toasts were received with loud cheers and halloos by most of the gentlemen present, and elicited brief speeches from the masters of the respective hounds, promising good sport next season. After the Kildare Foxhounds, an old farmer, in a gray coat, got gravely up, and without being requested to do so in the least, sung a song, stating that——

> 'At seven in the morning by most of the clocks,
> We rode to Kilruddery in search of a fox;'

and at the conclusion of his song, challenged a friend to give another song. Another old farmer, on this rose and sung one of Morris's songs, with a great deal of queer humour: and no doubt, many more songs were sung during the evening, for plenty of hot-water jugs were blocking the door as we went out.

The jolly frieze-coated songster, who celebrated the Kilruddery fox, sung, it must be confessed, most woefully out of tune; but still it was pleasant to hear him, and I think the meeting was the most agreeable one I have seen in Ireland: there was more good humour, more cordial union of classes, more frankness and manliness, than one is accustomed to find in Irish meetings. All the speeches were kind-hearted, straightforward speeches, without a word of politics, or an attempt at oratory: it was impossible to say whether the gentlemen present were Protestant or Catholic – each one had an hearty word of encouragement for his tenant, and a kind welcome for his neighbour. There were forty stout, well-to-do farmers in the room, renters of fifty, seventy, a hundred acres of land. There were no clergymen present, though it would have been pleasant to have seen one of each persuasion, to say grace for the meeting and the meat.

At a similar meeting at Ballytore the next day, I had an opportunity of seeing a still finer collection of stock than had been brought to Naas, and at the same time one of the most beautiful, flourishing villages in Ireland. The road to it from H——town, if not remarkable for its rural beauty, is pleasant to travel, for evidences of neat and prosperous husbandry are around you everywhere – rich crops in the fields, and neat cottages by the roadside, accompanying us as far as Ballytore, a white, straggling village, surrounding green fields, of some five furlongs square, with a river running in the midst of them, and numerous fine cattle in the green. Here is a large windmill, fitted up like a castle, with battlements and towers;

the castellan thereof is a good-natured old Quaker gentleman, and numbers more of his following inhabit the town.

The consequence was, that the shops of the village were the neatest possible, though by no means grand or portentous. Why should Quaker shops be neater than other shops? They suffer to the full as much oppression as the rest of the hereditary bondsmen; and yet, in spite of their tyrants, they prosper.

I must not attempt to pass an opinion upon the stock exhibited at Ballytore; but, in the opinion of some large agricultural proprietors present, it might have figured with advantage in any show in England, and certainly was finer than the exhibition at Naas, which, however, is a very young society. The best part of the show, however, to everybody's thinking, (and it is pleasant to observe the manly fair-play spirit which characterises the society), was, that the prizes of the Irish Agricultural Society were awarded to two men – one a labourer, the other a very small holder, both having reared the best stock exhibited on the occasion. At the dinner, which took place in a barn of the inn, smartly decorated with laurels for the purpose, there was as good and stout a body of yeomen as at Naas the day previous, but only two landlords; and here, too, as at Naas, neither priest nor parson. Cattle-feeding, of course, formed the principal theme of the after-dinner discourse – not, however, altogether to the exclusion of tillage; and there was a good and useful prize for those who could not afford to rear fat oxen – for the best kept cottage and garden, namely, which was won by a poor man, with a large family, and scanty precarious earnings, but who yet found means to make the most of his small means and to keep his little cottage neat and cleanly. The tariff and the plentiful harvest together had helped to bring down prices severely; and we heard from the farmers much desponding talk. I saw hay sold for £2 the ton, and oats for 8s. 3d. the barrel.

In the little village I remarked scarcely a single beggar, and very few bare feet indeed among the crowds who came to see the show. Here the quaker village had the advantage of the town of Naas, in spite of its Poor-house, which was only half-full when we went to see it; but the people prefer beggary and starvation abroad, to comfort and neatness in the Union-house.

A neater establishment cannot be seen than this; and liberty must be very sweet indeed, when people prefer it and starvation, to the certainty of comfort in the Union-house. We went to see it after the show at Naas.

The first persons we saw at the gate of the place were four buxom lasses, in blue jackets and petticoats, who were giggling and laughing as gaily as so many young heiresses of a thousand a year, and who had a colour in their cheeks that any lady of Almack's might envy. They were cleaning pails and carrying in water from a green court or play-ground in front of the house, which some of the able-bodied men of the place were busy in enclosing. Passing through the large entrance of the house, a nondescript Gothic building, we came to a court divided by a road and two low walls: the right enclosure is devoted to the boys of the establishment, of whom there were about fifty at play – boys more healthy or happy it is impossible to see. Separated from them is the nursery; and here were seventy or eighty young children, a shrill clack of happy voices leading the way to the door where they were to be found. Boys and children had a comfortable little uniform, and shoes were furnished for all, though the authorities did not seem particularly severe in enforcing the wearing of the shoes, which most of the young persons left behind them.

In spite of all the *Times's* in the world, the place was a happy one. It is kept with a neatness and comfort to which, until his entrance into the Union-house, the Irish peasant must, per force, have been a stranger. All the rooms and passages are white, well-scoured, and airy; all the windows are glazed; all the beds have a good store of blankets and sheets. In the women's dormitories there lay several infirm persons, not ill enough for the infirmary, and glad of the society of the common room. In one of the men's sleeping-rooms we found a score of old gray-coated men sitting round another who was reading prayers to them; and outside the place we found a woman starving in rags, as she had been ragged and starving for years; her husband was wounded, and lay in his house upon straw; her children were ill with a fever; she had neither meat, nor physic, nor clothing, nor fresh air, nor warmth for them; – and she preferred to starve on rather than enter the house.

The last of our agricultural excursions was to the fair of Castledermot, celebrated for the show of cattle to be seen there, and attended by the farmers and gentry of the neighbouring counties. Long before reaching the place we met troops of cattle coming from it – stock of a beautiful kind, for the most part large, sleek, white, long-backed, most of the larger animals being bound for England. There was very near as fine a show in the pastures along the road, which lies across a light green country, with plenty of trees to ornament the landscape, and some neat cottages along the roadside.

At the turnpike of Castledermot the droves of cattle met us by scores no longer, but by hundreds, and the long street of the place was thronged with oxen, sheep, and horses; and with those who wished to see, to sell, or to buy. The squires were altogether in a cluster at the Police Houses; the owners of the horses rode up and down, showing the best paces of their brutes; among whom you might see Paddy, in his ragged frieze coat, seated on his donkey's bare rump, and proposing him for sale. I think I saw a score of this humble, though useful breed, that were brought for sale to the fair. 'I can sell him,' says one fellow, with a pompous air, 'wid his tackle or widout.' He was looking as grave over the negotiation as if it had been for a thousand pounds. Besides the donkeys, of course, there was plenty of poultry, and there were pigs without number, shrieking and struggling, and pushing hither and thither among the crowd, rebellious to the straw-rope. It was a fine thing to see one huge grunter, and the manner in which he was landed into a cart. The cart was let down on an easy, inclined plane, to tempt him; two men ascending, urged him by the fore legs, other two entreated him by the tail. At length, when more than half of his body had been coaxed upon the cart, it was suddenly whisked up, causing the animal thereby to fall foward: a parting shove sent him altogether into the cart, the two gentlemen inside jump out, and the monster is left to ride home.

The farmers, as usual, were talking of the tariff, predicting ruin to themselves, as farmers will, on account of the decreasing price of stock, and the consequent fall of grain. Perhaps the person most to be pitied is the poor pig-proprietor yonder: it is his rent which he is carrying through the market, squeaking at the end of the straw-rope, and Sir Robert's bill adds insolvency to that poor fellow's misery.

This was the last of the sights which the kind owner of H—— town had invited me into his country to see; and I think they were among the most pleasing I witnessed in Ireland. Rich and poor were working friendlily together; priest and parson were alike interested in these honest, homely, agricultural festivals; not a word was said about hereditary bondage and English tyranny; and one did not much regret the absence of those patriotic topics of conversation. If but for the sake of the change, it was pleasant to pass a few days with people among whom there was no quarrelling; no furious denunciations against Popery on the part of the Protestants, and no tirades against the parsons from their bitter and scornful opponents of the other creed.

Next Sunday, in the County Meath, in a quiet old church, lying amongst meadows and fine old stately avenues of trees, and for the benefit of a congregation of some thirty persons, I heard for the space of an hour and twenty minutes some thorough Protestant doctrine, and the Popish superstitions properly belaboured. Does it strengthen a man in his own creed to hear his neighbour's belief abused? One would imagine so; for though abuse converts nobody, yet many of our pastors think they are not doing their duty by their own fold unless they fling stones at the flock in the next field, and have, for the honour of the service, a match at cudgelling with the shepherd. Our shepherd to-day was of this pugnacious sort.

The Meath landscape, if not varied and picturesque, is extremely rich and pleasant; and we took some drives, along the banks of the Boyne, to the noble park of Slane (still sacred to the memory of George IV, who actually condescended to pass some days there) and to Trim, of which the name occurs so often in Swift's Journals, and where stands an enormous old castle, that was inhabited by Prince John. It was taken from him by an Irish chief, our guide said; and from the Irish chief it was taken by Oliver Cromwell. O'Thuselah was the Irish chief's name, no doubt.

Here, too, stands, in the midst of one of the most wretched towns in Ireland, a pillar erected in honour of the Duke of

Wellington by the gentry of his native county. His birth-place, Dangan, lies not far off; and as we saw the hero's statue, a flight of birds had hovered about it: there was one on each epaulette and two on his marshal's staff; and, besides these wonders, we saw a certain number of beggars, and a madman, who was walking round a mound and preaching a sermon on grace; and a little child's funeral came passing through the dismal town, the only stirring thing in it (the coffin was laid on a one-horse country car – a little deal box, in which the poor child lay – and a great troop of people followed the humble procession); and the inn-keeper, who had caught a few stray gentlefolk in a town where travellers must be rare, and in his inn, which is more gaunt and miserable than the town itself, and which is by no means rendered more cheerful because sundry theological works are left for the rare frequenters in the coffee-room; the inn-keeper brought in a bill which would have been worthy of Long's, and which was paid with much grumbling on both sides.

It would not be a bad rule for the traveller in Ireland to avoid those inns where theological works are left in the coffee-room. He is pretty sure to be made to pay very dearly for these religious privileges.

We waited for the coach at the beautiful lodge and gate of Annsbrook; and one of the sons of the house coming up, invited us to look at the domain, which is as pretty and neatly ordered, as – as any in England. It is hard to use this comparison so often, and must make Irish hearers angry. Can't one see a neat house and grounds, without instantly thinking that they are worthy of the sister country; and implying, in our cool way, its superiority everywhere else? Walking in this gentleman's grounds, I told him, in the simplicity of my heart, that the neighbouring country was like Warwickshire, and the grounds as good as any English park. Is it the fact that English grounds *are* superior, or only that Englishmen are disposed to consider them so?

A pretty little twining river, called the Nanny's Water, runs through the Park: there is a legend about that, as about other places. Once upon a time (ten thousand years go), Saint Patrick being thirsty as he passed by this country, came to the house of an old woman, of whom he asked a drink of milk.

one of them, by a church, is a round tower or fort, with a flag; the church is the successor of one, battered down by Cromwell in 1649, in his frightful siege of the place. The place of one of his batteries is still marked outside the town, and known as 'Cromwell's Mount;' here he 'made the breach assaultable, and, by the help of God, stormed it.' He chose the strongest point of the defence for his attack.

After being twice beaten back, by the divine assistance he was enabled to succeed in a third assault: he 'knocked on the head' all the officers of the garrison; he gave orders that none of the men should be spared. 'I think,' says he, 'that night we put to the sword two thousand men, and one hundred of them, having taken possession of St Peter's steeple and a round tower next the gate, called St Sunday's, I ordered the steeple of St Peter's to be fired, when one in the flames was heard to say, "God confound me, I burn, I burn!"' The Lord General's history of 'this great mercy vouchsafed to us,' concludes with appropriate religious reflections: and prays Mr Speaker of the House of Commons, to remember that 'it is good that God alone have all the glory.' Is not the recollection of this butchery almost enough to make an Irishman turn rebel?

When troops march over the bridge, a young friend of mine, (whom I shrewdly suspected to be an Orangeman in his heart), told me, that their bands played the 'Boyne Water,' – here is another legend of defeat for the Irishman to muse upon; and here it was too, that King Richard II received the homage of four Irish kings, who flung their skenes or daggers at his feet, and knelt to him, and were wonder-stricken by the riches of his tents, and the garments of his knights and ladies. I think it is in Lingard that the story is told; and the antiquarian has no doubt seen that beautiful old manuscript at the British Museum, where these yellow-mantled warriors are seen riding down to the king, splendid in his forked beard, and peaked shoes, and long, dangling, scolloped sleeves, and embroidered gown.

The Boyne winds picturesquely round two sides of the town, and, following it, we came to the Linen Hall – in the days of the linen manufacture a place of note, now the place where Mr O'Connell harangues the people – but all the windows of the house were barricaded when we passed it, and of linen or any other sort of merchandise, there seemed to be none. Three boys were running past it, with a mouse tied to a string, and a dog galloping after: two little children were paddling down the street, one saying to the other, '*Once I had a halfpenny, and bought apples with it.*' The barges were lying lazily on the river, on the opposite side of which was a wood of a gentleman's domain, over which the rooks were cawing, and by the shore were some ruins, 'where Mr Ball once had his kennel of hounds:' – touching reminiscence of former prosperity!

There is a very large and ugly Roman Catholic chapel in the town, and a smaller one of better construction; it was so crowded, however, although on a week day, that we could not pass beyond the chapel-yard; where were great crowds of people, some praying, some talking, some buying and selling. There were two or three stalls in the yard, such as one sees near Continental churches, presided over by old women, with a store of little brass crucifixes, beads, books, and benitiers for the faithful to purchase. The church is large and commodious within, and looks (not like all other churches in Ireland) as if it were frequented. There is a hideous stone monument in the church-yard, representing two corpses half rotted away; – time or neglect had battered away the inscription, nor could we see the dates of some older tomb-stones in the ground, which were mouldering away in the midst of nettles and rank grass on the wall.

By a large public school of some reputation, where a hundred boys were educated – (my young guide, the Orangeman, was one of them: he related with much glee how, on one of the Liberator's visits, a schoolfellow had waved a blue and orange flag from the window, and cried 'King William for ever, and to hell with the Pope!') – there is a fine old gate leading to the river, and in excellent preservation, in spite of time and Oliver Cromwell. It is a good specimen of Irish architecture. By this time, that exceedingly slow coach, the Newry Lark, had arrived at that exceedingly filthy inn where the mail had dropped us an hour before. An enormous Englishman was holding a vain combat of wit with a brawny grinning beggar-woman at the door. 'There's a *clever* gentleman,' says the beggar-woman; 'sure he'll give me something.' 'How much should you like?' says the

Englishman, with playful jocularity. 'Musha,' says she, 'many a *littler* man nor you has given me a shilling.' The coach drives away; the lady had clearly the best of the joking match: but I did not see, for all that, that the Englishman gave her a single farthing.

From Castle Bellingham, as famous for ale as Drogheda, and remarkable likewise for a still better thing than ale, an excellent resident proprietress, whose fine park lies by the road, and by whose care and taste the village has been rendered one of the most neat and elegant I have yet seen in Ireland, the road to Dundalk is exceedingly picturesque, and the traveller has the pleasure of feasting his eye with the noble line of Mourne Mountains, which rise before him while he journeys over a level country for several miles. The Newry Lark, to be sure, disdained to take advantage of the easy roads to accelerate its movements in any way; but the aspect of the country is so pleasant, that one can afford to loiter over it. The fields were yellow with the stubble of the corn, which in this, one of the chief corn counties of Ireland, had just been cut down; and a long straggling line of neat farm-houses and cottages runs almost the whole way from Castle Bellingham to Dundalk. For nearly a couple of miles of the distance, the road runs along the picturesque flat called Lurgan Green; and gentlemen's residences and parks are numerous along the road, and one seems to have come amongst a new race of people, so trim are the cottages, so neat the gates and hedges, in this peaceful smiling district. The people, too, show signs of the general prosperity. A national school has just dismissed its female scholars as we passed through Dunlar; and though the children had most of them bare feet, their clothes were good and clean, their faces rosy and bright, and their long hair as shiny and as nicely combed as young ladies' need to be. Numerous old castles and towers stand on the road here and there; and long before we entered Dundalk we had a sight of a huge factory-chimney in the town, and of the dazzling white walls of the Roman Catholic church lately erected there. The cabin-suburb is not great, and the entrance to the town is much adorned by the Hospital, a handsome Elizabethan building, and a row of houses of a similar architectural style, which lie on the left of the traveller.

CHAPTER XXVI

DUNDALK

The stranger can't fail to be struck with the look of Dundalk, as he has been with the villages and country leading to it, when contrasted with places in the south and west of Ireland. The coach stopped at a cheerful-looking *Place*, of which almost the only dilapidated mansion was the old inn at which it discharged us, and which did not hold out much prospect of comfort. But in justice to the King's Arms it must be said, that good beds and dinners are to be obtained there by voyagers; and if they choose to arrive on days when his Grace the Most Reverend the Lord Archbishop of Armagh, and R.C. Primate of Ireland, is dining with his clergy, the house of course is crowded, and the waiters and the boy who carries in the potatoes, a little hurried and flustered. When their reverences were gone, the laity were served; and I have no doubt, from the leg of a duck which I got, that the breast and wings must have been very tender.

Meanwhile, the walk was pleasant through the bustling little town. A grave old church, with a tall copper spire, defends one end of the main street; and a little way from the inn is the suburb new chapel, which the architect, Mr Duff, has copied from King's College Chapel in Cambridge. The ornamental part of the interior is not yet completed; but the area of the chapel is spacious and noble, and three handsome altars of scagliola (or some composition resembling marble), have been erected of handsome and suitable form. When by the aid of further subscriptions, the church shall be completed, it will be one of the handsomest places of worship the Roman Catholics possess in this country. Opposite the chapel stands a neat low black building – the gaol; in the middle of the building, and over the doorway, is an ominous balcony and window, with an iron beam overhead. Each end of the beam is ornamented with a grinning iron skull! Is this the hanging place? and do these grinning cast-iron skulls facetiously explain the business for which the beam is there? For shame! for shame! Such disgusting emblems ought no longer to disgrace a Christian land. If kill we must, let us do so with as much despatch and decency as possible – not brazen out our misdeeds, and perpetuate them in this frightful satiric way.

A far better cast-iron emblem stands over a handsome shop in the place hard by – a plough namely, which figures over the factory of Mr Shekelton, whose industry and skill seem to have brought the greatest benefit to his fellow-townsmen, of whom he employs numbers in his foundries and workshops. This gentleman was kind enough to show me through his manufactories, where all sorts of iron-works are made, from a steam-engine to a door-key; and I saw everything to admire, and a vast deal more than I could understand, in the busy, cheerful, orderly, bustling, clanging place. Steam-boilers were hammered here; and pins made by a hundred busy hands in a manufactory above. There was the engine-room, where the monster was whirring his ceaseless wheels and directing the whole operations of the factory, fanning the forges, turning the drills, blasting into the pipes of the smelting-houses: he had a house to himself, from which his orders issued to the different establishments round about. One machine was quite awful to me, a gentle Cockney, not used to such things – it was an iron-devourer, a wretch with huge jaws and a narrow mouth, ever opening and shutting, opening and shutting. You put a half-inch iron plate between his jaws, and they shut not a whit slower or quicker than before, and bit through the iron as if it were a sheet of paper. Below the monster's mouth was a punch that performed its duties with similar dreadful calmness, going on its rising and falling.

I was so lucky as to have an introduction to the Vicar of Dundalk, which that gentlemn's kind and generous nature interpreted into a claim for unlimited hospitality; and he was good enough to consider himself bound not only to receive me, but to give up previous engagements abroad in order to do so. I need not say that it afforded me sincere pleasure to witness, for a couple of days, his labours among his people; and indeed it was a delightful occupation to watch both flock and pastor. The world is a wicked, selfish, abominable place, as the parson tells us; but his reverence comes out of his pulpit and gives the flattest contradiction to his doctrine, busying himself with kind actions from morning till night, denying to himself, generous to others, preaching the truth to young and old, clothing the naked, feeding the hungry, consoling the wretched, and giving hope to the sick; – and I do not mean to say that this sort of life is led by the Vicar of Dundalk merely, but do firmly believe that it is the life of the great majority of the Protestant and Roman Catholic clergy of the country. There will be no breach of confidence, I hope, in publishing here the journal of a couple of days spent with one of these reverend gentlemen, and telling some readers, as idle and profitless as the writer, what the clergyman's peaceful labours are.

In the first place, we set out to visit the church – the comfortable, copper-spired old edifice that was noticed two pages back. It stands in a green churchyard of its own, very neat and trimly kept, with an old row of trees that were dropping their red leaves upon a flock of vaults and tombstones below. The building being much injured by flame and time, some hundred years back, was repaired, enlarged, and ornamented – as churches in those days were ornamented – and has consequently lost a good deal of its gothic character. There is a great mixture, therefore, of old style and new style and no style: but, with all this, the church is one of the most commodious and best appointed I have seen in Ireland. The vicar held a council with a builder regarding some ornaments for the roof of the church, which is, as it should be, a great object of his care and architectural taste, and on which he has spent a very large sum of money. To these expenses he is, in a manner bound, for the living is a considerable one, its income being no less than two hundred and fifty pounds a year, out of which he has merely to maintain a couple of curates and a clerk and sexton, to contribute largely towards schools and hospitals, and relieve a few scores of pensioners of his own, who are fitting objects of private bounty.

We went from the church to a school, which has been long a
favourite resort of the good vicar's: indeed, to judge from the
schoolmaster's books, his attendance there is almost daily –
and the number of the scholars some two hundred. The
number was considerably greater until the schools of the
Educational Board were established, when the Roman Catholic clergymen withdrew many of their young people from Mr
Thackeray's establishment.

We found a large room with sixty or seventy boys at work;
in an upper chamber were a considerable number of girls, with
their teachers, two modest and pretty young women; but the
favourite resort of the vicar was evidently the Infant School –
and no wonder; it is impossible to witness a more beautiful or
touching sight.

Eighty of these little people, healthy, clean, and rosy, some
in smart gowns and shoes and stockings, some with patched
pinafores and little bare pink feet, sate upon a half-dozen low
benches, and were singing, at the top of their fourscore fresh
voices, a song when we entered. All the voices were hushed as
the vicar came in, and a great bobbing and curtseying took
place; whilst a hundred and sixty innocent eyes turned
awefully towards the clergyman, who tried to look as uncon-
cerned as possible, and began to make his little ones a speech.
'I have brought,' says he, 'a gentleman from England, who
has heard of my little children and their school, and hopes he
will carry away a good account of it. Now, you know, we
must all do our best to be kind and civil to strangers: what can
we do here for this gentleman that he would like? – do you
think he would like a song?'

(*All the children.*) – 'We'll sing to him!'

Then the schoolmistress, coming forward, sang the first
words of a hymn, which at once eighty little voices took up,
or near eighty – for some of the little things were too young
to sing yet, and all they could do was to beat the measure
with little red hands as the others sang. It was a hymn about
heaven, with a chorus of 'Will not that be joyful, joyful?' and
one of the verses beginning 'Little children, too, are there'.
Some of my fair readers (if I have the honour to find such)
who have been present at similar tender charming concerts,
know the hymn, no doubt. It was the first time I had ever

heard it; and I do not care to own that it brought tears to my eyes, though it is ill to parade such kind of sentiment in print. But I think I will never, while I live, forget that little chorus, nor would any man who has ever loved a child or lost one. God bless you, O little happy singers! What a noble and useful life is his, who, in place of seeking wealth or honour, devotes his life to such a service as this! And all through our country, thank God! in quiet humble corners, that busy citizens and men of the world never hear of, there are thousands of such men employed in such holy pursuits, with no reward beyond that which the fulfilment of duty brings them. Most of these children were Roman Catholics. At this tender age the priests do not care to separate them from their little Protestant brethren: and no wonder. He must be a child-murdering Herod who would find the heart to do so.

After the hymn, the children went through a little scripture catechism, answering very correctly, and all in a breath, as the mistress put the questions. Some of them were, of course, too young to understand the words they uttered; but the answers are so simple that they cannot fail to understand them before long; and they learn in spite of themselves.

The catechism being ended, another song was sung; and now the vicar (who had been humming the chorus along with his young singers, and, in spite of an awful and grave countenance, could not help showing his extreme happiness) made another oration, in which he stated that the gentleman from England was perfectly satisfied; that he would have a good report of the Dundalk children to carry home with him: that the day was very fine, and the schoolmistress would probably like to take a walk, and, finally, would the young people give her a holiday? 'As many,' concluded he, 'as will give the schoolmistress a holiday, hold up their hands!' This question was carried unanimously.

But I am bound to say, when the little people were told that as many as *wouldn't like* a holiday were to hold up *their* hands, all the little hands went up again exactly as before; by which it may be concluded either that the infants did not understand his Reverence's speech, or that they were just as happy to stay at school as to go and play; and the reader may adopt whichever

of the reasons he inclines to. It is probable that both are correct.

The little things are so fond of the school, the vicar told me as we walked away from it, that on returning home they like nothing better than to get a number of their companions who don't go to school, and to play at infant-school.

They may be heard singing their hymns in the narrow alleys and humble houses in which they dwell: and I was told of one dying who sang his song of 'Will not that be joyful, joyful?' to his poor mother weeping at his bedside, and promising her that they should meet where no parting should be.

'There was a child in the school,' said the vicar, 'whose father, a Roman Catholic, was a carpenter by trade, a good workman, and earning a considerable weekly sum, but neglecting his wife and children, and spending his earnings in drink. We have a song against drunkenness that the infants sing; and one evening, going home, the child found her father excited with liquor and ill-treating his wife. The little thing forthwith interposed between them, told her father what she had heard at school regarding the criminality of drunkenness and quarrelling, and finished her little sermon with the hymn. The father was first amused, then touched; and the end of it was, that he kissed his wife and asked her to forgive him, hugged his child, and from that day would always have her in his bed, made her sing to him morning and night, and forsook his old haunts for the sake of his little companion.'

He was quite sober and prosperous for eight months; but the vicar at the end of that time began to remark that the child looked ragged at school, and, passing by her mother's house, saw the poor woman with a black eye. 'If it was anyone but your husband, Mrs C——, who gave you that black eye,' says the vicar, 'tell me; but if he did it, don't say a word.' The woman was silent, and soon after, meeting her husband, the vicar took him to task. 'You were sober for eight months; now tell me fairly, C——,' says he, 'were you happier when you lived at home with your wife and child, or are you more happy now?' The man owned that he was much happier formerly, and the end of the conversation was, that he promised to go home once more, and try the sober life again, and he went home and succeeded.

The vicar continued to hear good accounts of him; but passing one day by his house, he saw the wife there looking very sad. Had her husband relapsed? – No, he was dead, she said – deal of the cholera; but he had been sober ever since his last conversation with the clergyman, and had done his duty to his family up to the time of his death. 'I said to the woman,' said the good old clergyman, in a grave low voice, 'your husband is gone now to the place where, according to his conduct here, his eternal reward will be assigned him; and, let us be thankful to think what a different position he occupies now to that which he must have held, had not his little girl been the means, under God, of converting him.'

Our next walk was to the County Hospital, the handsome edifice which ornaments the Drogheda entrance of the town, and which I had remarked on my arrival. Concerning this hospital, the governors were, when I passed through Dundalk, in a state of no small agitation; for a gentleman by the name of ——, who from being an apothecary's assistant in the place, had gone forth as a sort of amateur-inspector of hospitals, throughout Ireland, had thought fit to censure their extravagance in erecting the new building, stating that the old one was fully sufficient to hold fifty patients, and that the public money might consequently have been spared. Mr——'s plan for the better maintenance of them in general is, that commissioners should be appointed to direct them, and not county gentlemen as heretofore, the discussion of which question does not need to be carried on in this humble work.

My guide, who is one of the governors of the new hospital, conducted me, in the first place, to the old one – a small dirty house, in a damp and low situation; with but three rooms to accommodate patients, and these evidently not fit to hold fifty or even fifteen patients. The new hospital is one of the handsomest buildings of the size and kind in Ireland; an ornament to the town, as the angry commissioner stated, but not after all a building of undue cost, for the expense of its erection was but 3,000*l*., and the sick of the county are far better accommodated in it, than in the damp and unwholesome tenement, regretted by the eccentric commissioner.

An English architect, Mr Smith of Hertford, designed and completed the edifice; strange to say, only exceeding his estimates by the sum of three-and-sixpence, as the worthy governor of the hospital with great triumph told me. The building is certainly a wonder of cheapness, and what is more, so complete for the purpose of which it was intended, and so handsome in appearance, that the architect's name deserves to be published by all who hear it; and if any country newspaper-editors should notice this volume, they are requested to make the fact known. The house is provided with every convenience for men and women, with all the appurtenances of baths, water, gas, airy wards, and a garden for convalescents; and below a dispensary, a handsome board-room, kitchen, and matron's apartments, &c. – indeed, a noble requiring a house for a large establishment need not desire a handsomer one than this, at its moderate price of 3,000*l*. The beauty of this building has, as is almost always the case, created emulation, and a terrace in the same taste has been raised in the neighbourhood of the hospital.

From the hospital we bent our steps to the Institution; of which place I give below the rules, and a copy of the course of study, and the dietary: leaving English parents to consider the fact, that their children can be educated at this place for *thirteen pounds a year*. Nor is there anything in the establishment savouring of the Dotheboys Hall.★ I never saw, in any public school in England, sixty cleaner, smarter, more gentlemanlike boys than were here at work. The upper class had been at work on Euclid as we came in, and were set, by way of amusing the stranger, to perform a sum of compound interest of diabolical complication, which, with its algebraic and arithmetic solution, was handed up to me by three or four of the pupils; and I strove to look as wise as I possibly could. Then they went through questions of mental arithmetic with astonishing correctness and facility; and finding from the master that classics were not taught in the school, I took occasion to lament this circumstance, saying, with a knowing air, that I would like to have examined the lads in a Greek play.

Classics, then, these young fellows do not get. Meat they get but twice a week. Let English parents bear this fact in

---

★ 'Boarders are received from the age of eight to fourteen at 12*l.*, per annum, and 1*l.* for washing, paid quarterly in advance.

'Day Scholars are received from the age of ten to twelve at 2*l.*, paid quarterly in advance.

'The Incorporated Society have abundant cause for believing that the introduction of Boarders into their Establishments has produced far more advantageous results to the public than they could, at so early a period, have anticipated; and that the election of boys to their Foundations *only* after a fair competition with others of a given district, has had the effect of stimulating masters and scholars to exertion and study, and promises to operate most beneficially for the advancement of religious and general knowledge.

'The districts for eligible Candidates are as follows:

'Dundalk Institution embraces the counties of Louth and Down, because the properties which support it lie in this district.

'The Pococke Institution, Kilkenny, embraces the counties of Kilkenny and Waterford, for the same cause.

'The Ranelagh Institution, the towns of Athlone and Roscommon, and three districts in the counties of Galway and Roscommon, which the Incorporated Society hold in fee, or from which they receive impropriate tithes.

(*Signed*) 'CAESAR OTWAY, Secretary.'

mind; but that the lads are healthy and happy, anybody who sees them can have no question; furthermore, they are well instructed in a sound practical education – history, geography,

---

ARRANGEMENT OF SCHOOL BUSINESS IN DUNDALK INSTITUTION

Hours	Monday, Wednesday and Friday	Tuesday and Thursday	Saturday
6 to 7	Rise, wash, &c.	Rise, wash, &c.	Rise, wash, &c.
7 " 7½	Scripture by the Master, and prayer.	Scripture by the Master, and prayer.	Scripture by the Master, and prayer.
7½ " 8½	Reading, History, &c.	Reading, History, &c.	Reading, History, &c.
8½ " 9	Breakfast.	Breakfast.	Breakfast.
9 " 10	Play.	Play.	Play.
10 " 10½	English Grammar.	Geography.	10 to 11, Repetition.
10½ " 11¼	Algebra.	Euclid.	
11¼ " 12	Scripture.	Lecture on principles of Arithmetic.	11 to 12, Use of Globes.
12 " 12¾	Writing.	Writing.	12 to 1, Catechism and Scripture by the Catechist.
12¾ " 2	Arithmetic at Desks, and Book-keeping	Mensuration.	
2 " 2½	Dinner.	Dinner.	Dinner.
2½ " 5	Play.	Play.	The remainder of this
5 " 7½	Spelling, Mental Arithmetic, and Euclid.	Spelling, Mental Arithmetic, and Euclid.	day is devoted to exercise till the hour of Supper, after which
7½ " 8	Supper.	Supper.	the Boys assemble in
8 " 8½	Exercise.	Exercise.	the School-room and
8½ " 9	Scripture by the Master, and prayer in	Scripture by the Master, and prayer	hear a portion of Scripture read and
9	School-room. Retire to bed.	in School-room. Retire to bed.	explained by the Master, as on other days, and conclude with prayer.

The sciences of Navigation and practical Surveying are taught in the Establishment, also a selection of the Pupils, who have a taste for it, are instructed in the art of Drawing.

DIETARY.

Breakfast – Stirabout and Milk, every Morning.

Dinner – On Sunday and Wednesday, Potatoes and Beef; 10 ounces of the latter to each boy. On Monday and Thursday, Bread and Broth; ½lb. of the former to each boy. On Tuesday, Friday, and Saturday, Potatoes and Milk; 2lbs. of the former to each boy.

Supper – ½lb. of Bread with Milk, uniformly, except on Monday and Thursday: on these days, Potatoes and Milk.

mathematics, religion. What a place to know of would this be for many a poor half-pay officer, where he may put his children in all confidence that they will be well cared for and soundly educated! Why have we not State Schools in England, where, for the prime cost – for a sum which never need exceed for a young boy's maintenance 25*l.* a year – our children might be brought up? We are establishing National Schools for the labourer; why not give education to the sons of the poor gentry – the clergyman whose pittance is small, and would still give his son the benefit of a public education – the artist – the officer – the merchant's office-clerk – the literary man? What a benefit might be conferred upon all of us if honest Charter Schools could be established for our children, and where it would be impossible for Squeers to make a profit!*

Our next day's journey led us, by half-past ten o'clock, to the ancient town of Louth, a little poor village now, but a great seat of learning and piety, it is said, formerly, where there stood a university and abbeys, and where Saint Patrick worked wonders. Here my kind friend, the rector, was called upon to marry a smart sergeant of police to a pretty lass, one of the few Protestants who attend his church; and, the ceremony over, we were invited to the house of the bride's father hard by, where the clergyman was bound to cut the cake, and drink a glass of wine to the health of the new-married couple. There was evidently to be a dance and some merriment in the course of the evening; for the good mother of the bride (Oh, blessed is he who has a good mother-in-law!) was busy at a huge fire in the little kitchen, and along the road we met various parties of neatly-dressed people, and several of the sergeant's comrades, who were hastening to the wedding. The mistress of the rector's darling Infant School was one of the bridesmaids, consequently the little ones had a holiday.

---

* The Proprietary Schools of late established have gone far to protect the interests of parents and children; but the masters of these schools take boarders, and of course draw profits from them. Why make the learned man a beef and mutton contractor? It would be easy to arrange the economy of a school so that there should be no possibility of a want of confidence, or of peculation, to the detriment of the pupil.

But he was not to be disappointed of his Infant School in this manner; so, mounting the car again, with a fresh horse, we went a very pretty drive of three miles to the snug lone school-house of Glyde-farm, near a handsome park, I believe of the same name, where the proprietor is building a mansion of the Tudor order.

The pretty scene of Dundalk was here played over again; the children sang their little hymns, the good old clergyman joined delighted in the chorus, the holiday was given, and the little hands held up, and I looked at more clean bright faces, and little rosy feet – the scene need not be repeated in print, but I can understand what pleasure a man must take in the daily witnessing of it, and in the growth of these little plants, which are set and tended by his care. As we returned to Louth, a woman met us with a curtsey, and expressed her sorrow that she had been obliged to withdraw her daughter from one of the rector's schools, which the child was vexed at leaving too. But the orders of the priest were peremptory; and who can say they were unjust? The priest, on his side, was only enforcing the rule which the parson maintains as his: – the latter will not permit his young flock to be educated except upon certain principles and by certain teachers; the former has his own scruples unfortunately also – and so that noble and brotherly scheme of National Education falls to the ground. In Louth, the National School was standing by the side of the priest's chapel – it is so almost everywhere throughout Ireland; the Protestants have rejected, on very good motives doubtless, the chance of union which the Education-board gave them – be it so; if the children of either sect be educated apart, so that they *be* educated, the education scheme will have produced its good, and the union will come afterwards.

The church at Louth stands boldly upon a hill looking down on the village, and has nothing remarkable in it but neatness, except the monument of a former rector, Dr Little, which attracts the spectator's attention from the extreme inappropriateness of the motto on the coat of arms of the reverend defunct. It looks rather unorthodox to read in a Christian temple, where a man's bones have the honour to lie, and where, if anywhere, humility is requisite – that there is *multum in parvo,* 'a great deal in Little'. O Little, in life you were not much, and lo! you are less now; why should filial piety engrave that pert pun upon your monument, to cause people to laugh in a place where they ought to be grave? The defunct doctor built a very handsome rectory-house, with a set of stables that would be useful to a nobleman, but are rather too commodious for a peaceful rector who does not ride to hounds; and it was in Little's time, I believe, that the church was removed from the old abbey, where it formerly stood, to its present proud position on the hill.

The abbey is a fine ruin, the windows of a good style, the tracings of carvings on many of them; but a great number of stones and ornaments were removed formerly to build farm-buildings withal, and the place is now as rank and ruinous as the generality of Irish burying-places seem to be. Skulls lie in clusters amongst nettle-beds by the abbey-walls; graves are only partially covered with rude stones; a fresh coffin was lying, broken in pieces, within the abbey; and the surgeon of the dispensary hard by might procure subjects here, almost without grave breaking. Hard by the abbey is a building, of which I beg to leave to offer the following interesting sketch.

The legend in the country goes, that the place was built for the accommodation of Saint 'Murtogh,' who lying down to sleep here in the open fields, not having any place to house under, found to his surprise, on waking in the morning, the above edifice, which the angels had built. The angelic architecture, it will be seen, is of rather a rude kind: and the village antiquary, who takes a pride in showing the place, says that the building was erected *two thousand years ago.* In the handsome grounds of the rectory is another spot visited by popular tradition – a fairy's ring; a regular mound of some thirty feet in height, flat and even on the top, and provided with a winding path for the foot-passengers to ascend. Some trees grew on the mound, one of which was removed in order to make the walk. But the country-people cried out loudly at this desecration, and vowed that the 'little people' had quitted the country side for ever in consequence.

While walking in the town, a woman meets the Rector, with a number of curtsies and compliments, and vows that 'tis your reverence is the friend of the poor, and may the Lord preserve you to us, and lady; and having poured out blessings innumerable, concludes by producing a paper for her son that's in trouble in England. The paper ran to the effect, that, 'We, the undersigned, inhabitants of the parish of Louth, have known Daniel Horgan ever since his youth, and can speak confidently as to his integrity, piety, and good conduct.' In fact, the paper stated that Daniel Horgan was an honour to his country, and consequently quite incapable of the crime of sack-stealing, I think, with which at present he was charged, and lay in prison in Durham Castle. The paper had, I should think, come down to the poor mother from Durham, with a direction ready written to despatch it back again when signed, and was evidently the work of one of those benevolent individuals in assize-towns, who, following the profession of the law, delight to extricate unhappy young men of whose innocence (from various six-and-eightpenny motives) they feel convinced. There stood the poor mother, as the rector examined the document, with a huge wafer in her hand, ready to forward it so soon as it was signed; for the truth is, that 'We, the undersigned,' were as yet merely imaginary.

'You don't come to church,' says the Rector. 'I know nothing of you or your son: why don't you go to the priest?'

'O your Reverence, my son's to be tried next Tuesday,' whimpered the woman; and then said the Priest was not in the way, but as we had seen him a few minutes before, recalled the assertion, and she confessed that she *had* been to the Priest, and that he would not sign, – and fell to prayers, tears, and unbounded supplications to induce the Rector to give his signature. But that hard-hearted divine, stating that he had *not* known Daniel Horgan from his youth upwards, that he could not certify as to his honesty or dishonesty, enjoined the woman to make an attempt upon the R.C. Curate, to whose hand-writing he would certify if need were.

The upshot of the matter was, that the woman returned with a certificate from the R.C. Curate, as to her son's good behaviour while in the village, and the Rector certified that the hand-writing was that of the R.C. clergyman in question, and the woman popped her big red wafer into the letter, and went her way.

Tuesday is passed long ere this: Mr Horgan's guilt or innocence is long since clearly proved, and he celebrates the latter in freedom, or expiates the former at the mill. Indeed, I don't know that there was any call to introduce his adventures to the public, except, perhaps it may be good to see how in this little distant Irish village the blood of life is running. Here goes a happy party to a marriage, and the parson prays a 'God bless you!' upon them, and the world begins for them. Yonder lies a stall-fed rector in his tomb, flaunting over his nothingness, his pompous heraldic motto: and yonder lie the fresh fragments of a nameless deal coffin, which any foot may kick over. Presently you hear the clear voices of little children praising God: and here comes a mother wringing her hands and asking for succour for her lad, who was a child but the other day. Such motus animorum atque haec certamina tanta, are going on in an hour of an October day in a little pinch of clay in the county Louth.

Perhaps – being in the moralizing strain – the honest surgeon at the dispensary might come in as an illustration. He inhabits a neat humble house, a story higher than his neighbours', but with a thatched roof. He relieves a thousand patients yearly at the dispensary, he visits seven hundred in the parish – he supplies the medicines gratis; and receiving for these services the sum of about one hundred pounds yearly, some county economists and calculators are loud against the extravagance of his salary, and threaten his removal. All these individuals and their histories we presently turn our backs upon, for, after all, dinner is at five o'clock, and we have to see the new road to Dundalk, which the county has lately been making.

Of this undertaking, which shows some skilful engineering

– some gallant cutting of rocks and hills, and filling of valleys, with a tall and handsome stone bridge thrown across the river, and connecting the high embankments on which the new road at that place is formed – I can say little, except that it is a vast convenience to the county, and a great credit to the surveyor and contractor too; for the latter though a poor man, and losing heavily by his bargain, has yet refused to mulct his labourers of their wages; and, as cheerfully as he can, still pays them their shilling a day.

CHAPTER XXVII

NEWRY, ARMAGH, BELFAST – FROM DUNDALK TO NEWRY

My kind host gave orders to the small ragged boy that drove the car, to take 'particular care of the little gentleman;' and the car-boy, grinning in appreciation of the joke, drove off at his best pace, and landed his cargo at Newry, after a pleasant two hours' drive. The country for the most part is wild, but not gloomy – the mountains round about are adorned with woods and gentlemen's seats; and the car-boy pointed out one hill – that of Slievegullion, which kept us company all the way – as the highest hill in Ireland. Ignorant or deceiving car-boy! I have seen a dozen hills, each the highest in Ireland, in my way through the country, of which the inexorable Guide-book gives the measurement and destroys the claim. Well, it was the tallest hill, in the estimation of the car-boy; and in this respect the world is full of car-boys. Has not every mother of a family a Slievegullion of a son, who, according to her measurement, towers above all other sons? Is not the patriot, who believes himself equal to three Frenchmen, a car-boy in heart? There was a kind young creature, with a child in her lap, that evidently held this notion. She paid the child a series of compliments, which would have led one to fancy he was an angel from heaven at the least; and her husband sate gravely by, very silent, with his arms round a barometer.

Beyond these there were no incidents or characters of note, except an old hostler that they said was ninety years old, and watered the horse at a lone inn on the road. 'Stop!' cries this wonder of years and rags, as the car, after considerable parley, got under weigh. The car-boy pulled up, thinking a fresh passenger was coming out of the inn.

'*Stop, till one of the gentlemen gives me something,*' says the old man, coming slowly up with us; which speech created a laugh, and got him a penny: he received it without the least thankfulness, and went away grumbling to his pail.

Newry is remarkable as being the only town I have seen which had no cabin suburb; strange to say, the houses begin all at once, handsomely coated and hatted with stone and slate; and if Dundalk was prosperous, Newry is better still. Such a sight of neatness and comfort is exceedingly welcome to an English traveller, who, moreover, finds himself, after driving through a plain bustling clean street, landed at a large plain comfortable inn, where business seems to be done, where there are smart waiters to receive him, and a comfortable warm coffee-room that bears no traces of dilapidation.

What the merits of the *cuisine* may be I can't say for the information of travellers; a gentleman to whom I had brought a letter from Dundalk taking care to provide me at his own table, accompanying me previously to visit the lions of the town. A river divides it, and the counties of Armagh and Down – the river runs into the sea at Carlingford Bay, and is connected by a canal with Lough Neagh, and thus with the North of Ireland. Steamers to Liverpool and Glasgow sail continually. There are mills, foundries, and manufactories, of which the Guide-book will give particulars; and the town, of 13,000 inhabitants, is the busiest and most thriving that I have yet seen in Ireland.

Our first walk was to the church; a large and handsome building, although built in the unlucky period when the Gothic style was coming into vogue. Hence one must question the propriety of many of the ornaments, though the whole is massive, well-finished, and stately. Near the church stands the Roman Catholic chapel, a very fine building, the work of the same architect, Mr Duff, who erected the chapel at Dundalk; but, like almost all other edifices of the kind in Ireland that I have seen, the interior is quite unfinished, and already so dirty and ruinous, that one would think a sort of genius for dilapidation must have been exercised in order to bring it to its present condition. There are tattered green baize doors to enter at, a dirty clay floor, and cracked plaster walls, with an injunction to the public not to spit on the floor. Maynooth itself is scarcely more dreary. The architect's work, however, does him the highest credit; the interior of the church is noble and simple in style: and one can't but grieve to see a fine work of art, that might have done good to the country, so defaced and ruined as this is.

The Newry poor-house is as neatly ordered and comfortable as any house, public or private, in Ireland: the same look of health which was so pleasant to see among the Naas children of the union house, was to be remarked here: the same care and comfort for the old people. Of able-bodied there were but few in the house: it is in winter that there are most applicants for this kind of relief; the sunshine attracts the women out of the place, and the harvest relieves it of the men. Cleanliness, the matron said, is more intolerable to most of the inmates, than any other regulation of the house; and instantly on quitting the house they relapse into their darling dirt, and of course at their periodical return are subject to the unavoidable initiatory lustration.

Newry has many comfortable and handsome public buildings; the streets have a business-like look, the shops and people are not too poor, and the southern grandiloquence is not shown here in the shape of fine words for small wares. Even the beggars are not so numerous I fancy, or so coaxing and wheedling in their talk. Perhaps, too, among the gentry, the same moral change may be remarked, and they seem more downright and plain in their manner; but one must not pretend to speak of national characteristics, from such a small experience as a couple of evenings' intercourse may give.

Although not equal in natural beauty to a hundred other routes which the traveller takes in the south, the ride from Newry to Armagh is an extremely pleasant one, on account of the undeniable increase of prosperity which is visible through the country. Well-tilled fields, neat farm-houses, well-dressed people, meet one everywhere, and people and landscape alike have a plain, hearty, flourishing look.

The greater part of Armagh has the aspect of a good stout old English town, although round about the steep on which the cathedral stands (the Roman Catholics have taken possession of another hill, and are building an opposition cathedral on this eminence), there are some decidedly Irish streets, and that dismal combination of house and pig-sty which is so common in Munster and Connaught.

But the main streets, though not fine, are bustling, substantial, and prosperous; and a fine green has some old trees and some good houses, and even handsome stately public buildings, round about it, that remind one of a comfortable cathedral city across the water.

The cathedral service is more completely performed here than in any English town, I think. The church is small, but extremely neat, fresh, and handsome – almost too handsome; covered with spic-and-span gilding, and carved work in the style of the thirteenth century: every pew as smart and well-cushioned as my lord's own seat in the country church; and for the clergy and their chief, stalls and thrones quite curious for their ornament and splendour. The Primate with his blue riband and badge (to whom the two clergymen bow reverently as, passing between them, he enters at the gate of the altar rail), looks like a noble Prince of the Church; and I had heard enough of his magnificent charity and kindness to look with reverence at his lofty handsome features.

Will it be believed that the sermon lasted only for twenty minutes? Can this be Ireland? I think this wonderful circumstance impressed me more than any other with the difference between north and south, and, having the Primate's own countenance for the opinion, may confess a great admiration for orthodoxy in this particular.

A beautiful monument to Archbishop Stuart, by Chantrey; a magnificent stained window, containing the arms of the clergy of the diocese (in the very midst of which I was glad to recognise the sober old family coat of the kind and venerable rector of Louth), and numberless carvings and decorations, will please the lover of church architecture here. I must confess, however, that in my idea, the cathedral is quite too complete. It is of the twelfth century, but not the least venerable. It is as neat and trim as a lady's drawing-room. It wants a hundred years at least to cool the raw colours of the stones, and to dull the brightness of the gilding; all which benefits, no doubt, time will bring to pass, and future cockneys setting off from London-bridge after breakfast in an aerial machine, may come to hear the morning-service here, and not remark the faults which have struck a too susceptible tourist of the nineteenth century.

Strolling round the town after service, I saw more decided signs that Protestantism was there in the ascendant. I saw no less than three different ladies on the prowl, dropping religious tracts at various doors; and felt not a little ashamed to be seen by one of them getting into a car with bag and baggage, being bound for Belfast.

The ride of ten miles from Armagh to Portadown was not the prettiest, but one of the pleasantest, drives I have had in Ireland, for the country is well cultivated along the whole of the road, the trees in plenty, and villages and neat houses always in sight. The little farms, with their orchards and comfortable buildings, were as clean and trim as could be wished; they are mostly of one story, with long thatched roofs and shining windows, such as those that may be seen in Normandy and Picardy. As it was Sunday evening, all the people seemed to be abroad, some sauntering quietly down the roads – a pair of girls here and there pacing leisurely in a field – a little group seated under the trees of an orchard, which pretty adjunct to the farm is very common in this district; and the crop of apples seemed this year to be extremely plenty. The physiognomy of the people too has quite changed: the girls have their hair neatly braided up, not loose over their faces as in the south; and not only are bare feet very rare, and stockings extremely neat and white, but I am sure I saw at least a dozen good silk gowns upon the women along the road, and scarcely one which was not clean and in good order. The men for the most part figured in jackets, caps, and trowsers, eschewing the old well of a hat which covers the popular head at the other end of the island, the breeches, and the long ill-made tail-coat. The people's faces are sharp and neat, not broad, lazy, knowing-looking, like that of many a shambling Diogenes who may be seen lounging before his cabin in Cork or Kerry. As for the cabins, they have disappeared; and the houses of the people may rank decidedly as cottages. The accent, too, is quite different; but this is hard to describe in print. The people speak with a Scotch twang, and, as I fancied, much more simply and to the point. A man gives you a downright answer, without any grin or joke, or attempt at flattery. To be sure, these are rather early days to begin to judge of national characteristics; and very likely the above distinctions have been drawn after profoundly studying a Northern and a Southern waiter at the inn at Armagh.

At any rate, it is clear that the towns are vastly improved, the cottages and villages no less so; the people look active and well-dressed; a sort of weight seems all at once to be taken from the Englishman's mind on entering the province, when he finds himself once more looking upon comfort and activity, and resolution. What is the cause of this improvement? *Protestantism* is, more than one Church-of-England man said to me; but, for Protestantism, would it not be as well to read Scotchism? – meaning thrift, prudence, perseverance, boldness, and common sense, with which qualities any body of men, of any Christian denomination, would no doubt prosper.

The little brisk town of Portadown, with its comfortable unpretending houses, its squares and market-place, its pretty quay, with craft along the river, – a steamer building on the dock, close to mills and warehouses that look in a full state of prosperity, – was a pleasant conclusion to this ten miles' drive, that ended at the newly opened railway-station. The distance hence to Belfast is twenty-five miles; Lough Neah may be seen at one point of the line, and the Guide-book says, that the station-towns of Lurgan and Lisburn are extremely picturesque; but it was night when I passed by them, and after a journey of an hour and a-quarter reached Belfast.

That city has been discovered by another eminent Cockney traveller (for though born in America, the dear old Bow-bell blood must run in the veins of Mr N.P. Willis), and I have met, in the periodical works of the country, with repeated angry allusions to his description of Belfast, the pink-heels of the chambermaid who conducted him to bed (what business had he to be looking at the young woman's legs at all?) and his wrath at the beggary of the town and the laziness of the inhabitants, as marked by a line of dirt running along the walls, and showing where they were in the habit of lolling.

These observations struck me as rather hard when applied to Belfast, though possibly pink-heels and beggary might be remarked in other cities of the kingdom; but the town of

Belfast seemed to me really to be as neat, prosperous, and handsome a city as need be seen; and, with respect to the inn, that in which I stayed (Kearn's) was as comfortable and well-ordered an establishment as the most fastidious Cockney can desire: and with an advantage which some people, perhaps, do not care for, that the dinners which cost seven shillings at London taverns, are here served for half-a-crown, but, I must repeat here, in justice to the public, what I stated to Mr William the waiter: viz, that half-a-pint of port wine *does* contain more than two glasses – at least it does in happy, happy England. . . . Only to be sure, here the wine is good, whereas the port wine in England is not port, but, for the most part, an abominable drink of which it would be a mercy only to give us two glasses; which, however, is clearly wandering from the subject in hand.

They call Belfast the Irish Liverpool; if people are for calling names, it would be better to call it the Irish London at once – the chief city of the kingdom, at any rate. It looks hearty, thriving, and prosperous, as if it had money in its pockets, and roast-beef for dinner: it has no pretentions to fashion, but looks mayhap better in its honest broad-cloth than *some people* in their shabby brocade. The houses are as handsome as at Dublin, with this advantage, that the people seem to live in them. They have no attempt at ornament, for the most part, but are grave, stout, red-brick edifices, laid out at four angles in orderly streets and squares.

The stranger cannot fail to be struck (and haply a little frightened) by the great number of meeting-houses that decorate the town, and give evidence of great sermonising on Sundays. These buildings do not affect the Gothic, like many of the meagre edifices of the Established and the Roman Catholic churches, but have a physiognomy of their own – a thick-set citizen look. Porticos have they, to be sure, and ornaments Doric, Ionic, and what not; but the meeting-house peeps through all these classical friezes and entablatures; and though one reads of 'Imitations of the Ionic Temple of Ilissus, near Athens,' the classic temple is made to assume a bluff, downright, Presbyterian air, which would astonish the original builder, doubtless. The churches of the Establishment are handsome and stately; – the Catholics are building a brick cathedral, no doubt of the Tudor style. The present chapel, flanked by the National Schools, is an exceedingly unprepossessing building of the Strawberry-Hill or Castle-of-Otranto Gothic; the keys and mitre figuring in the centre – 'The cross-keys and night-cap,' as a hard-hearted Presbyterian called them to me, with his blunt humour.

The three churches are here pretty equally balanced – Presbyterians 25,000, Catholics 20,000, Episcopalians 17,000: each party has two or more newspaper organs, and the wars between them are dire and unceasing, as the reader may imagine. For whereas, in other parts of Ireland where Catholic and Episcopalians prevail, and the Presbyterian body is too small, each party has but one opponent to belabour; here, the Ulster politician, whatever may be his way of thinking, has the great advantage of possessing two enemies on whom he may exercise his eloquence: and in this triangular duel all do their duty nobly. Then there are subdivisions of hostility. For the Church there is a High-church and a Low-church journal; for the Liberals, there is a Repeal journal and a No-repeal journal. For the Presbyterians, there are yet more varieties of journalist opinion, of which it does not become a stranger to pass a judgment. If the 'Northern Whig' says that the 'Banner of Ulster' 'is a polluted rag, which has hoisted the red banner of falsehood' (which elegant words may be found in the first-named journal of the 13th October), let us be sure the 'Banner' has a compliment for the 'Northern Whig' in return: if the Repeal 'Vindicator' and the priests attack the Presbyterian journals and the Home Missions, the reverend gentlemen of Geneva are quite as ready with the pen as their brethren of Rome, and not much more scrupulous in their language than the laity. When I was in Belfast, violent disputes were raging between Presbyterian and Episcopalian Conservatives with regard to the Marriage Bill; between Presbyterians and Catholics on the subject of the Home Missions; between the Liberals and Conservatives, of course. 'Thank God,' for instance, writes a Repeal journal, 'that the honour and power *of Ireland* are not involved in the disgraceful Afghan war!' – a sentiment insinuating Repeal and something more; disowning, not merely this or that ministry, but the sovereign and her jurisdiction altogether. But details of these quarrels, religious or political, can tend to edify but few readers out of the country. Even in it, as there are some nine shades of politico-religious differences, an observer pretending to impartiality must necessarily displease eight parties, and almost certainly the whole nine; and the reader who desires to judge the politics of Belfast must study for himself. Nine journals, publishing four hundred numbers in a year, each number containing about as much as an octavo volume: these and the back numbers of former years, sedulously read, will give the student a notion of the subject in question. And then, after having read the statements on either side, he must ascertain the truth of them, by which time more labour of the same kind will have grown upon him, and he will have attained a good old age.

Amongst the poor, the Catholics and Presbyterians are said to go in a pretty friendly manner to the National Schools; but among the Presbyterians themselves it appears there are great differences and quarrels, by which a fine institution, the Belfast Academy, seems to have suffered considerably. It is almost the only building in this large and substantial place that bears, to the stranger's eye, an unprosperous air. A vast building, standing fairly in the midst of a handsome green and place, and with snug, comfortable red-brick streets stretching away at neat right-angles all around – the Presbyterian College looks handsome enough at a short distance, but on a nearer view it is found in a woful state of dilapidation. It does not possess the supreme dirt and filth of Maynooth – *that* can but belong to one place, even in Ireland; – but the building is in a dismal state of unrepair, steps and windows broken, doors and stairs battered. Of scholars I saw but a few, and these were in the drawing academy. The fine arts do not appear as yet to flourish in Belfast. The models from which the lads were copying were not good: one was copying a bad copy of a drawing by Prout; one was colouring a print. The ragged children in a German National School have better models before them, and are made acquainted with truer principles of art and beauty.

Hard by is the Belfast Museum, where an exhibition of pictures was in preparation, under the patronage of the Belfast Art-Union. Artists in all parts of the kingdom had been invited to send their works, of which the Union pays the carriage; and the porters and secretary were busy unpacking cases, in which I recognized some of the works which had before figured on the walls of the London exhibition-rooms.

The book-shops which I saw in this thriving town said much for the religious disposition of the Belfast public; there were numerous portraits of reverend gentlemen, and their works of every variety: – 'The Sinners' Friend,' 'The Watchman on the Tower,' 'The Peep of Day,' 'Sermons delivered at Bethesda Chapel,' by so-and-so; with hundreds of the neat little gilt books with bad prints, scriptural titles, and gilt edges, that come from one or two serious publishing houses in London, and in considerable numbers from the neighbouring Scotch shores. As for the Theatre, with such a public the drama can be expected to find but little favour; and the gentleman who accompanied me in my walk, and to whom I am indebted for many kindnesses during my stay, said not only that he had never been in the play-house, but that he never heard of any one going thither. I found out the place where the poor neglected dramatic Muse of Ulster hid herself, and was of a party of six in the boxes, the benches of the pit being dotted over with about a score more. Well, it was a comfort to see that the gallery was quite full, and exceedingly happy and noisy; they stamped, and stormed, and shouted, and clapped in a way that was pleasant to hear. One young god, between the acts, favoured the public with a song – extremely ill sung, certainly, but the intention was everything; and his brethren above stamped in chorus with roars of delight.

As for the piece performed, it was a good old melodrama of the British sort, inculcating a thorough detestation of vice, and a warm sympathy with suffering virtue. The serious are surely too hard upon poor play-goers. We never for a moment allow rascality to triumph beyond a certain part of the third act: we sympathise with the woes of young lovers – her in ringlets and a Polish cap, him in tights and a Vandyke collar; we abhor avarice or tyranny in the person of 'the first old man,' with the white wig and red stockings; or of the villain with the roaring voice and black whiskers; we applaud the honest wag (he is a good fellow in spite of his cowardice) in his hearty jests at the tyrant before mentioned; and feel a kindly sympathy with all mankind as the curtain falls over all the characters in a group, of which successful love is the happy centre. Reverend gentlemen in meeting-house and church, who shout against the immoralities of this poor stage, and threaten all play-goers with the fate which is awarded to unsuccessful plays, should try and bear less hardly upon us.

An artist, who in spite of the Art-Union, can scarcely, I should think, flourish in a place that seems devoted to preaching, politics, and trade, has somehow found its way to this humble little theatre, and decorated it with some exceedingly pretty scenery – almost the only indication of a taste for the fine arts which I have found as yet in the country.

A fine night-exhibition in the town is that of the huge spinning-mills which surround it, and of which the thousand windows are lighted up at night-fall, and may be seen from almost all quarters of the city.

A gentleman to whom I had brought an introduction, good-naturedly left his work to walk with me to one of these mills, and stated by whom he had been introduced to me to the mill-proprietor, Mr Mulholland. 'That recommendation,' said Mr Mulholland gallantly, 'is welcome anywhere.' It was from my kind friend Mr Lever. What a privilege some men have, who can sit quietly in their studies, and make friends all the world over!

Here is the figure of a girl sketched in the place; there are nearly five hundred girls employed in it. They work in huge long chambers, lighted by numbers of windows, hot with steam, buzzing and humming with hundreds of thousands of whirling wheels that all take their motion from a steam-engine which lives apart in a hot cast-iron temple of its own, from which it communicates with the innumerable machines that the five hundred girls preside over. They have seemingly but to take away the work when done – the enormous monster in the cast-iron room does it all. He cards the flax, and combs it, and spins it, and beats it, and twists it; the five hundred girls stand by to feed him, or take the material from him, when he has had will of it. There is something frightful in the vastness as in the minuteness of this power. Every thread writhes and twirls as the steam-fate orders it, – every thread, of which would take a hundred to make the thickness of a hair.

I have seldom, I think, seen more good looks than amongst the young women employed in this place. They work for twelve hours daily, in rooms of which the heat is intolerable to a stranger; but in spite of it they looked gay, stout, and healthy; nor were their forms much concealed by the very simple clothes they wear while in the mill.

The stranger will be struck by the good looks not only of these spinsters, but of almost all the young women in the streets. I never saw a town where so many women are to be met – so many and so pretty: with and without bonnets, with good figures, in neat homely shawls and dresses; the grisettes of Belfast are among the handsomest ornaments of it, and as good, no doubt, and irreproachable in morals as their sisters in the rest of Ireland.

Many of the merchants' counting-houses are crowded in little old-fashioned 'entries,' or courts, such as one sees about the Bank in London. In and about these, and in the principal streets in the day-time, is a great activity, and homely unpretending bustle. The men have a business look, too, and one sees very few flaunting dandies, as in Dublin. The shopkeepers do not brag upon their signboards, or keep 'emporiums,' as elsewhere – their places of business being for the most part homely; though one may see some splendid shops, which are not to be surpassed by London. The docks and quays are busy with their craft and shipping, upon the beautiful borders of the Lough; – the large red warehouses

stretching along the shores, with ships loading, or unloading, or building, hammers clanging, pitch-pots flaming and boiling, seamen cheering in the ships, or lolling lazily on the shore. The life and movement of a port here give the stranger plenty to admire and observe. And nature has likewise done everything for the place – surrounding it with picturesque hills and water; – for which latter I must confess I was not very sorry to leave the town behind me, and its mills, and its meeting-houses, and its commerce, and its theologians, and its politicians.

CHAPTER XXVIII

BELFAST TO THE CAUSEWAY

The Lough of Belfast has a reputation for beauty, almost as great as that of the Bay of Dublin; but though, on the day I left Belfast for Larne, the morning was fine, and the sky clear and blue above, a envious mist lay on the water, which hid all its beauties from the dozen of passengers on the Larne coach. All we could see were ghostly-looking *silhouettes* of ships gliding here and there through the clouds; and I am sure the coachman's remark was quite correct, that it was a pity the day was so misty. I found myself, before I was aware, entrapped into a theological controversy with two grave gentlemen outside the coach – another fog, which did not subside much before we reached Carrickfergus. The road from the Ulster capital to that little town seemed meanwhile to be extremely lively; cars and omnibuses passed thickly peopled. For some miles along the road is a string of hand-some country-houses, belonging to the rich citizens of the town; and we passed by neat-looking churches and chapels, factories and rows of cottages clustered round them, like villages of old at the foot of feudal castles. Furthermore, it was hard to see, for the mist which lay on the water had enveloped the mountains too, and we only had a glimpse or two of smiling comfortable fields and gardens.

Carrickfergus rejoices in a real romantic-looking castle, jutting bravely into the sea, and famous as a back-ground for a picture. It is of use for little else now, luckily, nor has it been put to any real warlike purposes since the day when honest Thurot stormed, took, and evacuated it. Let any romancer who is in want of a hero, peruse the second volume, or it may be the third, of the 'Annual Register,' where the adventures of that gallant fellow are related. He was a gentleman, a genius, and, to crown all, a smuggler. He lived for some time in

311

Ireland, and in England, in disguise; he had love passages and
romantic adventures; he landed a body of his countrymen on
these shores, and died in the third volume, after a battle
gallantly fought on both sides, but in which victory rested
with the British arms. What can a novelist want more? Willam
III also landed here; and as for the rest – 'M'Skimin, the
accurate and laborious historian of the town informs us that
the founding of the castle is lost in the depths of antiquity:' – it
is pleasant to give a little historic glance at a place, as one
passes through. The above facts may be relied on as coming
from Messrs Curry's excellent new Guide-book, with the
exception of the history of Mons. Thurot, which is 'private
information,' drawn years ago from the scarce work previously mentioned. By the way, another excellent companion
to the traveller in Ireland is the collection of the 'Irish Penny
Magazine,' which may be purchased for a guinea, and contains
a mass of information regarding the customs and places of the
country. Willis's work is amusing, as everything is, written by
that lively author, and the engravings accompanying it as
unfaithful as any ever made.

Meanwhile, asking pardon for this double digression,
which has been made while the guard-coachman is delivering
his mail-bags – while the landlady stands looking on in the
sun, her hands folded a little below the waist – while a
company of tall burly troops from the castle has passed by,
'surrounded' by a very mean, mealy-faced, uneasy-looking
little subaltern – while the poor, epileptic idiot of the town,
wallowing and grinning in the road, and snorting out supplications for a halfpenny, has tottered away in possession of the
coin: – meanwhile, fresh horses are brought out, and the small
boy who acts behind the coach, makes an unequal and
disagreeable tootooing on a horn kept to warn sleepy carmen,
and celebrate triumphal entries into and exits from cities. As
the mist clears up, the country shows round about wild but
friendly; at one place we passed a village, where a crowd of
well-dressed people were collected at an auction of farm-
furniture, and many more figures might be seen coming over
the fields and issuing from the mist: the owner of the carts and
machines is going to emigrate to America. Presently we come
to the demesne of Red Hall, 'through which is a pretty drive of

upwards of a mile in length: it contains a rocky glen, the bed
of a mountain stream – which is perfectly dry, except in
winter – and the woods about it are picturesque, and it is
occasionally the resort of summer-parties of pleasure.'
Nothing can be more just than the first part of the description,
and there is very little doubt that the latter paragraph is equally
faithful; – with which we come to Larne, a 'most thriving
town,' the same authority says, but a most dirty and narrow-
streeted and ill-built one. Some of the houses reminded one of
the south, as thus:-

A benevolent fellow-passenger said
that the window was 'a convanience;'
and here, after a drive of nineteen miles
upon a comfortable coach, we were
transferred with the mail-bags to a comfortable car, that makes the journey to
Ballycastle. There is no harm in saying
that there was a very pretty smiling
buxom young lass for a travelling companion; and somehow, to a lonely person, the landscape always looks prettier
in such society. The 'Antrim coast
road,' which we now, after a few miles, begin to follow,
besides being one of the most noble and gallant works of art
that is to be seen in any country, is likewise a route highly
picturesque and romantic; the sea spreading wide before the
spectator's eyes upon one side of the route, the tall cliffs of
limestone rising abruptly above him on the other. There are in
the map of Curry's Guide-book, points indicating castles and
abbey ruins in the vicinity of Glenarm; and the little place
looked so comfortable, as we abruptly came upon it, round a
rock, that I was glad to have a excuse for staying, and felt an
extreme curiosity with regard to the abbey and the castle.

The abbey only exists in the unromantic shape of a wall; the
castle, however, far from being a ruin, is an antique in the
most complete order – an old castle repaired so as to look like
new, and increased by modern wings, towers, gables, and
terraces, so extremely old that the whole forms a grand and
imposing-looking baronial edifice, towering above the little
town which it seems to protect, and with which it is connected

by a bridge and a severe-looking armed tower and gate. In the town is a town-house, with a campanile in the Italian taste, and a school or chapel opposite, in the early English; so that the inhabitants can enjoy a considerable architectural variety. A grave-looking church, with a beautiful steeple, stands amid some trees, hard by a second handsome bridge and the little quay; and here, too, was perched a poor little wandering theatre (gallery 1*d.*, pit 2*d.*), and proposing that night to play 'Bombastes Furioso, and the Comic Bally of Glenarm in an Uproar.' I heard the thumping of the drum in the evening, but, as at Roundwood, nobody patronized the poor players: at nine o'clock there was not a single taper lighted under their awning, and my heart, (perhaps it is too susceptible) bled for Fusbos.

The severe gate of the castle was opened by a kind, good natured old porteress, instead of a rough gallowglass with a battle-axe and yellow shirt (more fitting guardian of so stern a postern), and the old dame insisted upon my making an application to see the grounds of the castle, which request was very kindly granted, and afforded a delightful half-hour's walk. The grounds are beautiful, and excellently kept; the trees in their autumn livery of red, yellow, and brown, except some stout ones, that keep to their green summer clothes, and the laurels and their like, who wear pretty much the same dress all the year round. The birds were singing with the most astonishing vehemence in the dark glistening shrubberies; but the only sound in the walks was that of the rakes pulling together the falling leaves. There was of these walks one especially, flanked towards the river by a turreted wall covered with ivy, and having on the one side a row of lime trees that had turned quite yellow, while opposite them was a green slope, and a quaint terrace-stair, and a long range of fantastic gables, towers, and chimneys; – there was, I say, one of these walks which Mr Cattermole would hit off with a few strokes of his gallant pencil, and which I could fancy to be frequented by some of those long-trained, tender, gentle-looking, young beauties, whom Mr Stone loves to design. – Here they come, talking of love in a tone that is between a sigh and a whisper, and gliding in rustling shot silks over the fallen leaves.

There seemed to be a good deal of stir in the little port, where, says the Guide-book, a couple of hundred vessels take in cargoes annually of the produce of the district. Stone and lime are the chief articles exported, of which the cliffs for miles give an unfailing supply; and, as one travels the mountains at night, the kilns may be seen lighted up in the lonely places, and flaring red in the darkness.

If the road from Larne to Glenarm is beautiful, the coast route from the latter place to Cushendall is still more so; and, except peerless Westport, I have seen nothing in Ireland so picturesque as this noble line of coast-scenery. The new road, luckily, is not yet completed, and the lover of natural beauties had better hasten to the spot in time, ere, by flattening and improving the road, and leading it along the sea-shore, half the magnificent prospects are shut out, now visible from along the mountainous old road, which, according to the good old fashion, gallantly takes all the hills in its course, disdaining to turn them. At three miles' distance, near the village of Cairlough, Glenarm looks more beautiful than when you are close upon it; and, as the car travels on to the stupendous Garron Head, the traveller, looking back, has a view of the whole line of coast southward as far as Isle Magee, with its bays and white villages, and tall precipitous cliffs, green, white, and gray. Eyes left, you may look with wonder at the mountains rising above, or presently at the pretty park and grounds of Drumnasole. Here, near the woods of Nappan, which are dressed in ten thousand colours – ash leaves turned yellow, nut trees red, birch leaves brown, lime leaves speckled over with black spots (marks of a disease which they will never get over), stands a school-house that looks like a French château, having probably been a villa in former days, and discharges as we pass a cluster of fair-haired children, that begin running madly down the hill, their fair hair streaming behind them. Down the hill goes the car, madly too, and you wonder and bless your stars that the horse does not fall, or crush the children that are running before, or you that are sitting behind. Every now and then, at a trip of the horse, a disguised lady's maid, with a canary bird in her lap, and a vast anxiety about her best bonnet in the band-box, begins to scream; at which the car-boy grins, and rattles down the hill only the quicker. The road, which almost always skirts the hill side, has been torn sheer through the rock here and there; and immense work of levelling, shovelling, picking, blasting, filling, is going on along the whole line. As I was looking up a vast cliff, decorated with patches of green here and there at its summit, and at its base, where the sea had beaten until now, with long, thin, waving grass, that I told a grocer, my neighbour, was like mermaids' hair (though he did not in the least coincide in the simile) – as I was looking up the hill, admiring two goats that were browsing on a little patch of green, and two sheep perched yet higher (I had never seen such agility in mutton) – as, I say once more, I was looking at these phenomena, the grocer nudges me, and says, '*Look on to this side – that's Scotland, yon.*' If ever this book reaches a second edition, a sonnet shall be inserted in this place, describing the author's feelings on HIS FIRST VIEW OF SCOTLAND. Meanwhile, Scotch mountains remain undisturbed, looking blue and solemn, far away in the placid sea.

Rounding Garron Head, we come upon the inlet which is called Red Bay, the shores and sides of which are of red clay, that has taken the place of limestone, and towards which, between two noble ranges of mountains, stretches a long green plain, forming, together with the hills that protect it, and the sea that washes it, one of the most beautiful landscapes of this most beautiful country. A fair writer, whom the Guide-book quotes, breaks out into strains of admiration, in speaking of this district, calls it 'Switzerland in miniature,' celebrates its mountains of Glenariff and Lurgethan, and lauds, in terms of equal admiration, the rivers, waterfalls, and other natural beauties that lie within the glen.

The writer's enthusiasm regarding this tract of country is quite warranted, nor can any praise in admiration of it be too high; but, alas! in calling a place 'Switzerland in miniature,' do we describe it? In joining together cataracts, valleys, rushing streams, and blue mountains, with all the emphasis and picturesqueness of which type is capable, we cannot get near to a copy of Nature's sublime countenance; and the writer can't hope to describe such grand sights so as to make them visible to the fireside reader, but can only, to the best of his taste and experience, warn the future traveller where he may look out for objects to admire. I think this sentiment has been repeated a score of times in this journal; but it comes upon one at every new display of beauty and magnificence, such as here the Almighty in his bounty has set before us; and every such scene seems to warn one, that it is not made to talk about too much, but to think of and love, and be grateful for.

Rounding this beautiful bay and valley, we passed by some caves that penetrate deep into the red rock, and are inhabited – one by a blacksmith, whose forge was blazing in the dark; one by cattle; and one by an old woman that has sold whiskey here for time out of mind. The road then passes under an arch cut in the rock by the same spirited individual who has cleared away many of the difficulties in the route to Glenarm, and beside a conical hill, where for some time previous have been visible the ruins of the 'ancient ould castle' of Red Bay. At a distance, it looks very grand upon its height; but on coming close it has dwindled down to a mere wall, and not a high one. Hence, quickly we reach Cushendall, where the grocer's family are on the look out for him; the driver begins to blow his little bugle, and the disguised lady's maid begins to smooth her bonnet and hair.

At this place a good dinner of fresh whiting, broiled bacon, and small beer, was served up to me for the sum of eightpence while the lady's maid in question took her tea. 'This town is full of Papists,' said her ladyship, with an extremely genteel air; and, either in consequence of this, or because she ate up one of the fish, which she had clearly no right to, a disagreement arose between us, and we did not exchange another word for the rest of the journey. The road led us for fourteen miles by wild mountains, and across a fine aqueduct to Ballycastle; but it was dark as we left Cushendall, and it was difficult to see more in the gray evening but that the country was savage and lonely, except where the kilns were lighted up here and there in the hills, and a shining river might be seen winding in the dark ravines. Not far from Ballycastle lies a little old ruin, called the Abbey of Bonamargy; by it the Margy river runs into the sea, upon which you come suddenly; and on the shore are some tall buildings and factories, that looked as well in the moonlight as if they had not been in ruins: and hence, a fine avenue of limes leads to Ballycastle. They must have been planted at the time recorded in the Guide-book, when a mine was discovered near the town, and the works and warehouses on the quay erected. At present, the place has little trade, and half-a-dozen carts with apples, potatoes, dried fish, and turf, seem to contain the commerce of the market.

The picturesque sort of vehicle which is here designed, is said to be going much out of fashion in the country, the solid wheels giving place to those common to the rest of Europe. A fine and edifying conversation took place between the designer and the owner of the vehicle. 'Stand still for a minute, you and the car, and I will give you twopence!' 'What do you want to do with it?' says the latter. 'To draw it.' 'To *draw* it?' says he, with a wild look of surprise, 'and as it is you'll draw it?' 'I mean, I want to take a picture of it; you know what a picture is!' 'No, I don't,' 'Here's one,' says I, showing him a book. 'O faith, sir,' says the carman, drawing back rather alarmed, 'I'm no scholar!' and he concluded by saying, '*Will you buy the turf, or will you not?*' by which straight-forward question he showed himself to be a real practical man of sense; and, as he got an unsatisfactory reply to this query, he forthwith gave a lash to his pony, and declined to wait a minute longer. As for the twopence, he certainly accepted that handsome sum, and put it into his pocket, but with an air of extreme wonder at the transaction, and of contempt for the giver, which very likely was perfectly justifiable. I have seen men despised in genteel companies with not half so good a cause.

In respect to the fine arts, I am bound to say, that the people in the South and West showed much more curiosity and interest with regard to a sketch and its progress, than has been shown by the *badauds* of the North; the former looking on by dozens, and exclaiming 'That's Frank Mahony's house!' or, 'Look at Biddy Mullins and the child!' or, 'He's taking off the chimney now!' as the case may be; whereas, sketching in the North, I have collected no such spectators, the people not taking the slightest notice of the transaction.

The little town of Ballycastle does not contain much to occupy the traveller: behind the church stands a ruined old mansion with round turrets, that must have been a stately tower in former days. The town is more modern, but almost as dismal as the tower. A little street behind it slides off into a potato field – the peaceful barrier of the place; and hence I could see the tall rock of Bengore, with the sea beyond it, and a pleasing landscape stretching towards it.

Dr Hamilton's elegant and learned book has an awful picture of yonder head of Bengore; and hard by it the Guide-book says is a coal-mine, where Mr Barrow found a globular stone hammer, which he infers was used in the coal-mine before weapons of iron were invented. The former writer insinuates that the mine must have been worked more than a thousand years ago, 'before the turbulent chaos of events that succeeded the eighty century.' Shall I go and see a coal-mine that may have been worked a thousand years since? Why go see it? says idleness: to be able to say that I have seen it. Sheridan's advice to his son here came into my mind;* and I shall reserve a description of the mine, and an antiquarian dissertation regarding it, for publication elsewhere.

Ballycastle must not be left without recording the fact, that one of the snuggest inns in the country is kept by the post-master there; who has also a stable full of good horses for travellers who take his little inn on the way to the Giant's Causeway.

The road to the Causeway is bleak, wild, and hilly. The

---

* 'I want to go into a coal-mine,' says Tom Sheridan, 'in order to say I have been there.' 'Well, then, say so,' replied the admirable father.

cabins along the road are scarcely better than those of Kerry,
the inmates as ragged, and more fierce and dark-looking. I
never was so pestered by juvenile beggars, as in the dismal
village of Ballintoy. A crowd of them rushed after the car,
calling for money in a fierce manner, as if it was their right:
dogs as fierce as the children came yelling after the vehicle; and
the faces which scowled out of the black cabins were not a
whit more good-humoured. We passed by one or two more
clumps of cabins, with their turf and corn-stacks lying
together at the foot of the hills; placed there for the convenience of the children, doubtless, who can thus accompany the
car either way, and shriek out their 'Bonny gantleman, gie us a
hap'ny.' A couple of churches, one with a pair of its pinnacles
blown off, stood in the dismal open country; and a
gentleman's house here and there: there were no trees about
them, but a brown grass round about – hills rising and falling
in front, and the sea beyond. The occasional view of the coast
was noble, wild Bengore towering eastwards as we went
along; Raghery Island before us, in the steep rocks and caves
of which Bruce took shelter when driven from yonder
Scottish coast, that one sees stretching blue in the north-east.

I think this wild gloomy tract through which one passes, is a
good prelude for what is to be the great sight of the day; and
got my mind to a proper state of awe by the time we were near
the journey's end; and turning away shorewards by the fine
house of Sir Francis Macnaghten, went towards a lone handsome inn, that stands close to the Causeway. The landlord at
Ballycastle had lent me Hamilton's book, to read on the road;
but I had not time then to read more than half a dozen pages of
it. They described how the author, a clergyman distinguished
as a man of science, had been thrust out of a friend's house by
the frightened servants one wild night, and butchered by some
White Boys, who were waiting outside, and called for his
blood. I had been told at Belfast, that there was a corpse in the
inn; was it there now? It had driven off, the car-boy said, 'in a
handsome hearse and four to Dublin the whole way.' It was
gone, but I thought the house looked as if the ghost were there.
See, yonder are the black rocks stretching to Portrush; how
leaden and gray the sea looks! how gray and leaden the sky!
You hear the waters roaring evermore, as they have done since

the beginning of the world. The car drives up with a dismal grinding noise of the wheels to the big lone house; there's no smoke in the chimeys; the doors are locked; three savage-looking men rush after the car: are they the men who took out Mr Hamilton – took him out and butchered him in the moonlight? Is everybody, I wonder, dead in that big house? Will they let us in before those men are up? Out comes a pretty smiling girl, with a curtsey, just as the savages are at the car, and you are ushered into a very comfortable room; and the men turn out to be guides. Well, thank Heaven it's no worse! I had fifteen pounds still left; and, when desperate, have no doubt should fight like a lion.

CHAPTER XXIX

THE GIANT'S CAUSEWAY – COLERAINE – PORTRUSH

The traveller no sooner issues from the inn, by a back door, which he is informed will lead him straight to the Causeway, than the guides pounce upon him, with a dozen rough boatmen, who are likewise lying in wait; and a crew of shrill beggar-boys, with boxes of spars, ready to tear him and each other to pieces seemingly, yell and bawl incessantly round him. 'I'm the guide Miss Henry recommends,' shouts one; 'I'm Mr Macdonald's guide,' pushes in another; 'This way,' roars a third, and drags his prey down a precipice; the rest of them clambering and quarreling after. I had no friends, I was perfectly helpless, I wanted to walk down to the shore by myself, but they would not let me, and I had nothing for it but to yield myself into the hands of the guide who had seized me, who hurried me down the steep to a little wild bay, flanked on each side by rugged cliffs and rocks, against which the waters came tumbling, frothing, and roaring furiously. Upon some of these black rocks two or three boats were lying; four men seized a boat, pushed it shouting into the water, and ravished me into it. We had slid between two rocks, where the channel came gurgling in; we were up one swelling wave that came in a huge advancing body ten feet above us, and were plunging madly down another, (the descent causes a sensation in the lower regions of the stomach, which it is not at all necessary here to describe), before I had leisure to ask myself why the deuce I was in that boat, with four rowers hurrooing and bounding madly from one huge liquid mountain to another – four rowers whom I was bound to pay. I saw, the query came qualmishly across me, why the devil I was there, and why not walking calmly on the shore.

The guide began pouring his professional jargon into my

ears. – 'Every one of them bays,' says he, 'has a name (take my place, and the spray won't come over you); that is Port Noffer, and the next, Port na Gange; them rocks is the Stookawns (for every rock has its name as well as every bay): and yonder – give way my boys, – hurray, we're over it now, has it wet you much, sir? – that's the little cave; it goes five hundred feet under ground, and the boats goes into it easy of a calm day.'

'Is it a fine day or a rough one, now?' said I; the internal disturbance going on with more severity than ever.

'It's betwixt and between; or, I may say, neither one nor the other. Sit up, sir; look at the entrance of the cave: don't be afraid, sir; never has an accident happened in any one of these boats, and the most delicate ladies has rode in them on rougher days than this. Now, boys, pull to the big cave; that, sir, is six hundred and sixty yards in length, though some say it goes for miles inland, where the people sleeping in their houses hears the waters roaring under them.'

The water was tossing and tumbling into the mouth of the little cave. I looked, – for the guide would not let me alone till I did, – and saw what might be expected; – a black hole of some forty feet high, into which it was no more possible to see than into a mill-stone. 'For Heaven's sake, sir,' says I, 'if you've no particular wish to see the mouth of the big cave, put about and let us see the Causeway and get ashore.' This was done, the guide meanwhile telling some story of a ship of the Spanish Armada having fired her guns at two peaks of rock, then visible, which the crew mistook for chimney-pots – what benighted fools these Spanish Armadilloes must have been – it is easier to see a rock than a chimney-pot; it is easy to know that chimney-pots do not grow on rocks: – but where, if you please is the Causeway?

'That's the Causeway before you,' says the guide.

'Which?'

'That pier which you see jutting out into the bay, right a-head.'

'Mon Dieu! and have I travelled a hundred and fifty miles to see *that*?'

I declare, upon my conscience, the barge moored at Hungerford market is a more majestic object, and seems to occupy as much space. As for telling a man that the Causeway is merely part of the sight; that he is there for the purpose of examining the surrounding scenery; that if he looks to the westward he will see Portrush and Donegal-head before him; that the cliffs immediately in his front are green in some places, black in others, interspersed with blotches of brown and streaks of verdure; – what is all this to a lonely individual lying sick in a boat, between two immense waves that only give him momentary glimpses of the land in question, to show that it is frightfully near, and yet you are an hour from it? They won't let you go away – that cursed guide *will* tell out his stock of legends and stories. The boatmen insist upon your looking at boxes of 'specimens,' which you must buy of them; they laugh as you grow paler and paler; they offer you more and more 'specimens;' even the dirty lad who pulls number three, and is not allowed by his comrades to speak, puts in *his* oar, and hands you over a piece of Irish diamond (it looks like half sucked alicompayne), and scorns you. 'Hurray, lads, now for it, give way!' how the oars do hurtle in the rullocks, as the boat goes up an aqueous mountain, and then down into one of those cursed maritime valleys where there is no rest as on shore!

At last, after they had pulled me enough about, and sold me all the boxes of specimens, I was permitted to land at the spot whence we set out, and whence, though we had been rowing for an hour, we had never been above five hundred yards distant. Let al! Cockneys take warning from this; let the solitary one caught issuing from the back door of the hotel, shout at once to the boatmen to be gone – that he will have none of them. Let him, at any rate, go first down to the water to determine whether it be smooth enough to allow him to take any decent pleasure by riding on its surface. For after all, it must be remembered that it *is* pleasure we come for – that we are not *obliged* to take those boats. – Well, well! I paid ten shillings for mine, and ten minutes before would cheerfully have paid five pounds to be allowed to quit it: it was no hard bargain after all. As for the boxes of spar and specimens, I at once, being on terra firma, broke my promise, and said I would see them all – first. It is wrong to swear, I know; but sometimes it relieves one *so* much!

The first act on shore was to make a sacrifice to Sanctissima Tellus; offering up to her a neat and becoming Taglioni coat, bought for a guinea in Covent Garden only three months back. I sprawled on my back on the smoothest of rocks that is, and tore the elbows to pieces: the guide picked me up; the boatmen did not stir, for they had had their will of me; the guide alone picked me up, I say, and bade me follow him. We went across a boggy ground in one of the little bays, round which rise the green walls of the cliff, terminated on either side by a black crag, and the line of the shore washed by the poluphlosboiotic, nay, the poluphlosboiotatotic sea. Two beggars stepped over the bog after us howling for money, and each holding up a cursed box of specimens. No oaths, threats, entreaties, would drive these vermin away; for some time the whole scene had been spoilt by the incessant and abominable jargon of them, the boatmen, and the guides. I was obliged to give them money to be left in quiet, and if, as no doubt will be the case, the Giant's Causeway shall be a still greater resort of travellers than ever, the county must put policemen on the rocks to keep the beggars away, or fling them in the water when they appear.

And now, by force of money, having got rid of the sea and land beggars, you are liberty to examine at your leisure the wonders of the place. There is not the least need for a guide to attend the stranger, unless the latter have a mind to listen to a parcel of legends, which may be well from the mouth of a wild simple peasant who believes in his tales; but are odious from a dullard who narrates them at the rate of sixpence a lie. Fee him and the other beggars, and at last you are left tranquil to look at the strange scene with your own eyes, and enjoy your own thoughts at leisure.

That is if the thoughts awakened by such a scene may be called enjoyment; but for me, I confess, they are too near akin to fear to be pleasant; and I don't know that I would desire to change that sensation of awe and terror which the hour's walk occasioned, for a greater familiarity with this wild, sad, lonely place. The solitude is awful. I can't understand how those chattering guides dare to lift up their voices here, and cry for money.

It looks like the beginning of the world, somehow: the sea looks older than in other places, the hills and rocks strange, and formed differently from other rocks and hills – as those vast dubious monsters were formed who possessed the earth before man. The hill-tops are shattered into a thousand cragged fantastical shapes; the water comes swelling into scores of little strange creeks, or goes off with a leap, roaring into those mysterious caves yonder, which penetrates who knows how far into our common world? The savage rock-sides are painted of a hundred colours. Does the sun ever shine here? When the world was moulded and fashioned out of formless chaos, this must have been the *bit over* – a remnant of chaos! Think of that! – it is a tailor's simile. Well, I am a Cockney: I wish I were in Pall Mall! Yonder is a kelp-burner: a lurid smoke from his burning kelp rises up to the leaden sky, and he looks as naked and fierce as Cain. Bubbling up out of the rocks at the very brim of the sea rises a little crystal spring: how comes it there? and there is an old gray hag beside, who has been there for hundreds and hundreds of years, and there sits and sells whiskey at the extremity of creation! How do you dare to sell whiskey there, old woman? Did you serve old Saturn with a glass when he lay along the causeway here? In reply, she says, she has no change for a shilling: she never has; but her whiskey is good.

This is not a description of the Giant's Causeway (as some clever critic will remark), but of a Londoner there, who is by no means so interesting an object as the natural curiosity in question. That single hint is sufficient; I have not a word more to say. 'If,' says he, 'you cannot describe the scene lying before us – if you cannot state from your personal observation that the number of basaltic pillars composing the Causeway has been computed at about forty thousand, which vary in diameter, their surface presenting the appearance of a tesselated pavement of polygonal stones – that each pillar is formed of several distinct joints, the convex end of the one being accurately fitted in the concave of the next, and the length of the joints varying from five feet to four inches – that although the pillars are polygonal, there is but one of three sides in the whole forty thousand (think of that!), but three of nine sides, and that it may be safely computed that ninety-nine out of one hundred pillars have either five, six, or seven sides; – if you canot state something useful, you had much better, sir, retire and get your dinner.'

Never was summons more gladly obeyed. The dinner must be ready by this time; so, remain you, and look on at the awful scene, and copy it down in words if you can. If at the end of the trial you are dissatisfied with your skill as a painter, and find that the biggest of your words cannot render the hues and vastness of that tremendous swelling sea – of those lean solitary crags standing rigid along the shore, where they have been watching the ocean ever since it was made – of those gray towers of Dunluce standing upon a leaden rock, and looking as if some old, old princess, of old, old fairy times, were dragon-guarded within – of yon flat stretches of sand where the Scotch and Irish mermaids hold conference – come away too, and prate no more about the scene? There is that in nature, dear Jenkins, which passes even our powers. We can feel the beauty of a magnificent landscape, perhaps: but we can describe a leg of mutton and turnips better. Come, then, this scene is for our betters to depict. If Mr Tennyson were to come hither for a month, and brood over the place, he might, in some of those lofty heroic lines which the Author of the 'Morte d'Arthur' knows how to pile up, convey to the reader a sense of this gigantic desolate scene. What ! you, too, are a poet? Well, then Jenkins, stay! but believe me, you had best take my advice, and come off.

The worthy landlady made her appearance with the politest of bows and an apology, – for what does the reader think a lady should apologize in the most lonely rude spot in the world? – because a plain servant-woman was about to bring in the dinner, the waiter being absent on leave at Coleraine! O heaven and earth! what will the genteel end? I replied philo-sophically, that I did not care twopence for the plainness or beauty of the waiter, but that it was the dinner I looked to, the frying whereof made a great noise in the huge lonely house; and it must be said, that though the lady *was* plain, the repast was exceedingly good. 'I have expended my little all,' says the landlady, stepping in with a speech after dinner, 'in the building of this establishment; and though to a man its profits may appear small, to such a *being* as I am it will bring, I trust, a sufficient return;' and on my asking her why she took the place, she replied that she had always, from her earliest youth, a fancy to dwell in that spot, and had accordingly realized her wish by building this hotel – this mausoleum. In spite of the bright fire, and the good dinner, and the good wine, it was impossible to feel comfortable in the place; and when the car wheels were heard, I jumped up with joy to take my departure and forget the awful lonely shore, that wild, dismal, genteel inn. A ride over a wide gusty country, in a gray, misty, half-moonlight, the loss of a wheel at Bushmills, and the escape from a tumble, were the delightful varieties after the late awful occurrences. 'Such a being' as I am, would die of loneliness in that hotel; and so let all brother Cockneys be warned.

Some time before we came to it, we saw the long line of mist that lay above the Bann, and coming through a dirty suburb of low cottages, passed down a broad street with gas and lamps in it (thank heaven, there are people once more!), and at length drove up in state, across a gas-pipe, in a market-place, before an hotel in the town of Coleraine, famous for linen and for Beautiful Kitty, who must be old and ugly now, for it's a good five-and-thirty years since she broke her pitcher, according to Mr Moore's account of her. The scene as we entered the Diamond was rather a lively one – a score of little stalls were brilliant with lights; the people were thronging in the place, making their Saturday bargains; the town clock began to toll nine; and hark! faithful to a minute, the horn of the Derry mail was heard tootooing, and four commercial gentlemen, with Scotch accents, rushed into the hotel at the same time with myself.

Among the beauties of Coleraine may be mentioned the price of beef, which a gentleman told me may be had for fourpence a pound; and I saw him purchase an excellent codfish for a shilling. I am bound, too, to state for the benefit of aspiring radicals, what two conservative citizens of the place stated to me, viz.: – that though there were two conservative candidates then canvassing the town, on account of a vacancy in the representation, the voters were so truly liberal that they would elect any person of any other political creed, who would simply bring money enough to purchase their votes. There are 220 voters, it appears; of whom it is not, however, necessary to 'argue' with more than fifty, who alone are open to conviction; but as parties are pretty equally balanced, the votes of the quinquagint, of course, carry an immense weight with them. Well, this is all discussed calmly standing on an inn-steps, with a jolly landlord and a professional man of the town, to give the information. So, Heaven bless us, the ways of London are beginning to be known even here. Gentility has already taken up her seat in the Giant's Causeway, where she apologises for the plainness of her look:

and, lo! here is bribery as bold as in the most civilized places –
hundreds and hundreds of miles away from St Stephen's and
Pall Mall. I wonder, in that little island of Raghery, so wild
and lonely, whether civilization is beginning to draw upon
them? – whether they bribe and are genteel? But for the rough
sea of yesterday, I think I would have fled thither to make the
trial.

The town of Coleraine, with a number of cabin suburbs
belonging to it, lies picturesquely grouped on the Bann river:
and the whole of the little city was echoing with psalms as I
walked through it on the Sunday morning. The piety of the
people seems remarkable; some of the inns even will not
receive travellers on Sunday; and this is written in an hotel, of
which every room is provided with a testament, containing an
injunction on the part of the landlord to consider this world
itself as only a passing abode. Is it well that Boniface should
furnish his guest with Bibles as well as bills, and sometimes
shut his door on a traveller who has no other choice but to
read it on a Sunday? I heard of a gentleman arriving from
shipboard at Kilrush on a Sunday, when the pious hotel-
keeper refused him admittance; and some more tales, which to
go into would require the introduction of private names and
circumstances, but would tend to show that the Protestant of
the north is as much priest-ridden as the Catholic of the
south;—— priest and old woman-ridden, for there are certain
expounders of doctrine in our church, who are not, I believe,
to be found in the church of Rome; and woe betide the
stranger who comes to settle in these parts, if his 'seriousness'
be not satisfactory to the heads (with false fronts to most of
them) of the congregations.

Look at that little snug harbour of Portrush; a hideous new
castle standing on a rock protects it on one side, a snug row of
gentlemen's cottages curves round the shore facing northwards, a bath-house, an hotel, more smart houses, face the
beach westward, defended by another mound of rocks. In the
centre of the little town stands a new-built church; and the
whole place has an air of comfort and neatness which is
seldom seen in Ireland. One would fancy that all the tenants of
these pretty snug habitations, sheltered in this nook far away
from the world, have nothing to do but to be happy, and

spend their little comfortable means in snug little hospitalities among one another, and kind little charities among the poor. What does a man in active life ask for more than to retire to such a competence, to such a snug nook of the world; and there repose with a stock of healthy children round the fireside, a friend within call, and the means of decent hospitality wherewith to treat him?

Let anyone meditating this pleasant sort of retreat, and charmed with the look of this or that place as peculiarly suited to his purpose, take a special care to understand his neighbourhood first, before he commit himself, by lease-signing or house-buying. It is not sufficient that you should be honest, kind-hearted, hospitable, of good family – what are your opinions upon religious subjects? Are they such as agree with the notions of old Lady This, or Mrs That, who are the patronesses of the village? If not, woe betide you! you will be shunned by the rest of the society, thwarted in your attempts to do good, whispered against over evangelical bohea and serious muffins. Lady This will inform every new arrival that you are a reprobate, and lost, and Mrs That will consign you and your daughters, and your wife (a worthy woman, but, alas! united to that sad worldly man!) to damnation. The clergyman who partakes of the muffins and bohea before mentioned, will very possibly preach sermons against you from the pulpit: this was not done at Portstewart to my knowledge, but I have had the pleasure of sitting under a minister in Ireland who insulted the very patron who gave him his living, discoursing upon the sinfulness of partridge-shooting, and threatening hell-fire as the last 'meet' for fox-hunters; until the squire, one of the best and most charitable resident landlords in Ireland, was absolutely driven out of the church where his fathers had worshipped for hundreds of years, by the insults of this howling evangelical inquisitor.

So much as this I did not hear at Portstewart; but I was told that at yonder neat looking bath-house *a dying woman* was denied a bath on a Sunday. By a clause of the lease by which the bath owner rents his establishment, he is forbidden to give baths to any one on the Sunday. The landlord of the inn, forsooth, shuts his gates on the same day, and his conscience on week days will not allow him to supply his guests with whiskey or ardent spirits. I was told by my friend, that because he refused to subscribe for some fancy charity, he received a letter to state that 'he spent more in one dinner than in charity in the course of the year.' My worthy friend did not care to contradict the statement, as why should a man deign to meddle with such a lie? But think how all the fishes, and all the pieces of meat, and all the people who went in and out of his snug cottage by the sea-side must have been watched by the serious round about! The sea is not more constant roaring there, than scandal is whispering. How happy I felt, while hearing these histories (demure heads in crimped caps peeping over the blinds at us as we walked on the beach), to think I am a Cockney, and don't know the name of the man who lives next door to me!

I have heard various stories, of course from persons of various ways of thinking, charging their opponents with hypocrisy, and proving the charge by statements clearly showing that the priests, the preachers, or the professing religionists in question, belied their professions woefully by their practice. But in matters of religion, hypocrisy is so awful a charge to make against a man, that I think it is almost unfair to mention even the cases in which it is proven, and which, – as, pray God, they are but exceptional, – a person should be very careful of mentioning, lest they be considered to apply generally. *Tartuffe* has been always a disgusting play to me to see, in spite of its sense and its wit; and so, instead of printing, here or elsewhere, a few stories of the Tartuffe kind which I have heard in Ireland, the best way will be to try and forget them. It is an awful thing to say of any man walking under God's sun by the side of us, 'You are a hypocrite, lying as you use the Most Sacred Name, knowing that you lie while you use it.' Let it be the privilege of any sect that is so minded, to imagine that there is perdition in store for all the rest of God's creatures who do not think with them: but the easy countercharge of hypocrisy, which the world has been in the habit of making in its turn, is surely just as fatal and bigoted an accusation, as any that the sects make against the world.

What has this disquisition to do apropos of a walk on the beach at Portstewart? Why, it may be made here as well as in other parts of Ireland, or elsewhere as well, perhaps, as here. It is the most priest-ridden of coutries; Catholic clergymen lord it over their ragged flocks, as Protestant preachers, lay and clerical, over their more genteel co-religionists. Bound to inculcate peace and good-will, their whole life is one of enmity and distrust.

Walking away from the little bay and the disquisition which has somehow been raging there, we went across some wild dreary highlands to the neighbouring little town of Portrush, where is a neat town and houses, and a harbour, and a new church too, so like the last-named place that I thought for a moment we had only made a round, and were back again at Portstewart. Some gentlemen of the place, and my guide, who had a neighbourly liking for it, showed me the new church, and seemed to be well pleased with the edifice, which is indeed a neat and convenient one, of a rather irregular Gothic. The best thing about the church, I think, was the history of it. The old church had lain some miles off, in the most inconvenient part of the parish, whereupon the clergy-man and some of the gentry had raised a subscription in order to build the present church. The expenses had exceeded the estimates, or the subscriptions had fallen short of the sums necessary; and the church, in consequence, was opened with debt on it which the rector and two more of the gentry had taken on their shoulders. The living is a small one, the other two gentlemen going bail for the edifice not so rich as to think light of the payment of a couple of hundred pounds beyond their previous subscriptions – the lists are therefore still open; and the clergyman expressed himself perfectly satisfied either that he would be reimbursed one day or other, or that he would be able to make out the payment of the money for which he stood engaged. Most of the Roman Catholic churches that I have seen through the country have been built in this way, – begun when money enough was levied for constructing the foundation, elevated by degrees as fresh subscriptions came in, and finished – by the way, I don't think I *have* seen one finished; – but there is something noble in the spirit (however certain economists may cavil at it) that leads people to commence these pious undertakings with the firm trust that 'Heaven will provide.'

Eastwards from Portrush, we came upon a beautiful level sand which leads to the White Rocks, a famous place of resort for the frequenters of the neighbouring watering-places. Here are caves, and for a considerable distance a view of the wild and gloomy Antrim coast as far as Bengore. Midway, jutting into the sea, (and I was glad it was so far off), was the Causeway; and nearer, the gray towers of Dunluce.

Looking north, were the blue Scotch hills and the neighbouring Raghery Island. Nearer Portrush are two rocky islands, called the Skerries, of which a sportsman of our party vaunted the capabilities, regretting that my stay was not longer, so that I might land and shoot a few ducks there. This unlucky lateness of the season struck me also as a most afflicting circumstance. He said also that fish were caught off

the island – not fish good to eat, but very strong at pulling, eager of biting, and affording a great deal of sport. And so we turned our backs once more upon the Giant's Causeway, and the grim coast on which it lies; and as my taste in life leads me to prefer looking at the smiling fresh face of a young cheerful beauty, rather than at the fierce countenance and high features of a fierce dishevelled Meg Merrilies, I must say again that I was glad to turn my back on that severe part of the Antrim coast, and my steps towards Derry.

CHAPTER XXX

PEG OF LIMAVADDY

Between Coleraine and Derry there is a daily car (besides one or two occasional queer-looking coaches), and I had this vehicle, with an intelligent driver, and a horse with a hideous raw on his shoulder, entirely to myself for the five-and-twenty miles of our journey. The cabins of Coleraine are not parted with in a hurry, and we crossed the bridge, and went up and down the hills of one of the suburban streets, the Ban flowing picturesquely to our left; a large Catholic chapel, the before-mentioned cabins, and farther on, some neat-looking houses and plantations, to our right. Then we began ascending wide lonely hills, pools of bog shining here and there amongst them, with birds, both black and white, both geese and crows, on the hunt. Some of the stubble was already ploughed up, but by the side of most cottages you saw a black potato field that it was time to dig now, for the weather was changing and the winds beginning to roar. Woods, whenever we passed them, were flinging round eddies of mustard-coloured leaves; the white trunks of lime and ash trees beginning to look very bare.

Then we stopped to give the raw-backed horse water; then we trotted down a hill with a noble bleak prospect of Lough Foyle and the surrounding mountains before us, until we reached the town of Newtown Limavaddy, where the raw-backed horse was exchanged for another not much more agreeable in his appearance, though, like his comrade, not slow on the road.

Newtown Limavaddy is the third town in the county of Londonderry. It comprises three well-built streets, the others are inferior; it is, however, respectably inhabited; all this may be true, as the well-informed Guide-book avers, but I am bound to say that I was thinking of something else as we drove through the town, having fallen eternally in love during the ten minutes of our stay.

335

Yes, Peggy of Limavaddy, if Barrow and Inglis have gone to Connemara to fall in love with the Misses Flynn, let us be allowed to come to Ulster and offer a tribute of praise at your feet – at your stockingless feet, O Margaret! Do you remember the October day ('twas the first day of the hard weather), when the way-worn traveller entered your inn? But the circumstances of this passion had better be chronicled in deathless verse.

PEG OF LIMAVADDY

Riding from Coleraine
  (Famed for lovely Kitty),
Came a Cockney bound
  Unto Derry city,
Weary was his soul,
  Shivering and sad he
Bumped along the road
  Leads to Limavaddy.

Mountains stretch'd around,
  Gloomy was their tinting,
And the horse's hoofs
  Made a dismal clinting;
Wind upon the heath
  Howling was and piping,
On the heath and bog,
  Black with many a snipe in;
'Mid the bogs of black,
  Silver pools were flashing,
Crows upon their sides
  Picking were and splashing,
Cockney on the car
  Closer folds his plaidy,
Grumbling at the road
  Leads to Limavaddy.

Through the crashing woods
  Autumn brawl'd and bluster'd,
Tossing round about
  Leaves the hue of mustard;

Yonder lay Lough Foyle,
   Which a storm was whipping,
Covering with mist
   Lake, and shores, and shipping.
Up and down the hill
   (Nothing could be bolder),
Horse went with a raw,
   Bleeding on his shoulder.
'Where are horses changed?'
   Said I to the laddy
Driving on the box:
   'Sir, at Limavaddy.'

Limavaddy inn's
   But a humble baithouse,
Where you may procure
   Whiskey and potatoes;
Landlord at the door
   Gives a smiling welcome
To the shivering wights
   Who to his hotel come.
Landlady within
   Sits and knits a stocking,
With a wary foot
   Baby's cradle rocking.

To the chimney nook,
   Having found admittance,
There I watch a pup
   Playing with two kittens;
(Playing round the fire,
   Which of blazing turf is,
Roaring to the pot
   Which bubbles with the mur-
And the cradled babe   [phies);
   Fond the mother nursed it!
Singing it a song
   As she twists the worsted!

Up and down the stair
   Two more young ones patter

(Twins were never seen
   Dirtier nor fatter);
Both have mottled legs,
   Both have snubby noses,
Both have – Here the Host
   Kindly interposes;
'Sure you must be froze
   With the sleet and hail, sir,
So will you have some punch,
   Or will you have some ale, sir?'

Presently a maid
   Enters with the liquor,
(Half a pint of ale
   Frothing in a beaker).
Gods! I didn't Know
   What my beating heart meant,
Hebe's self I thought
   Enter'd the apartment.
As she came she smiled,
   And the smile bewitching,
On my word and honour,
   Lighted all the kitchen!

With a curtsey neat
   Greeting the new comer,
Lovely, smiling Peg
   Offers me the rummer;
But my trembling hand
   Up the beaker tilted,
And the glass of ale
   Every drop I spilt it:
Spilt it every drop
   (Dames, who read my volumes,
Pardon such a word,)
   On my whatd'ycall'ems!

Witnessing the sight
   Of that dire disaster,
Out began to laugh
   Missis, maid, and master;

Such a merry peal,
  'Specially Miss Peg's was,
(As the glass of ale
  Trickling down my legs was),
That the joyful sound
  Of that ringing laughter
Echoed in my ears
  Many a long day after.

Such a silver peal!
  In the meadows listening,
You who've heard the bells
  Ringing to a christening;
You who ever heard
  Caradori pretty,

Smiling like an angel
    Singing 'Giovinetti,'
Fancy Peggy's laugh,
    Sweet, and clear, and cheerful,
At my pantaloons
    With half a pint of beer full!

When the laugh was done,
    Peg, the pretty hussy,
Moved about the room
    Wonderfully busy;
Now she looks to see
    If the kettle keep hot,
Now she rubs the spoons,
    Now she cleans the teapot;
Now she sets the cups
    Trimly and secure,
Now she scours a pot
    And so it was I drew her.

Thus it was I drew her
    Scouring of a kettle,★
(Faith! her blushing cheeks
    Redden'd on the metal!)
Ah! but 'tis in vain
    That I try to sketch it;
The pot perhaps is like,
    But Peggy's face is wretched.
No: the best of lead,
    And of Indian-rubber,
Never could depict
    That sweet kettle-scrubber!

★ The late Mr Pope represents Camilla as '*scouring the plain*,' an absurd and useless task. Peggy's occupation with the kettle is much more simple and noble. The second line of this poem (whereof the author scorns to deny an obligation), is from the celebrated Frithiof of Esaias Tigner. A maiden is serving warriors to drink, and is standing by a shield – 'Und die Runde des Schildes ward wie das Mägdelein roth,' – perhaps the above is the best thing in both poems.

See her as she moves!
    Scarce the ground she touches,
Airy as a fay,
    Graceful as a duchess;
Bare her rounded arm,
    Bare her little leg is,
Vestris never show'd
    Ankles like to Peggy's:
Braided is her hair,
    Soft her look and modest,
Slim her little waist
    Comfortably boddiced.

This I do declare,
    Happy is the laddy
Who the heart can share
    Of Peg of Limavaddy;
Married if she were,
    Blest would be the daddy
Of the children fair
    Of Peg of Limavaddy;
Beauty is not rare
    In the land of Paddy,
Fair beyond compare
    Is Peg of Limavaddy.

Citizen or squire,
    Tory, Whig, or Radi-
cal would all desire
    Peg of Limavaddy.
Had I Homer's fire,
    Or that of Sergeant Taddy,
Meetly I'd admire
    Peg of Limavaddy.
And till I expire,
    Or till I grow mad, I
Will sing unto my lyre
    Peg of Limavaddy!

CHAPTER XXXI

TEMPLEMOYLE – DERRY

From Newtown Limavaddy to Derry the traveller has many
wild and noble prospects of Lough Foyle and the plains and
mountains round it, and of scenes which may possibly in this
country be still more agreeable to him – of smiling cultivation,
and comfortable well-built villages, such as are only too rare
in Ireland. Of a great part of this district the London Companies are landlords – the best of landlords, too, according to
the report I could gather; and their good stewardship shows
itself especially in the neat villages of Muff and Ballikelly,
through both of which I passed. In Ballikelly, besides numerous simple, stout, brick-built dwellings for the peasantry,
with their shining windows and trim garden-plots, is a
Presbyterian meeting-house, so well-built, substantial, and
handsome, so different from the lean, pretentious, sham-
Gothic ecclesiastical edifices which have been erected of late
years in Ireland, that it can't fail to strike the tourist who has
made architecture his study or his pleasure. The gentleman's
seats in the district are numerous and handsome; and the
whole movement along the road betokened cheerfulness and
prosperous activity.

As the carman had no other passengers but myself, he made
no objection to carry me a couple of miles out of his way,
through the village of Muff, belonging to the Grocers of
London (and so handsomely and comfortably built by them as
to cause all Cockneys to exclaim, 'Well done our side!') and
thence to a very interesting institution, which was established
some fifteen years since in the neighbourhood – the Agricultural Seminary of Templemoyle. It lies on a hill in a pretty
wooded country, and is most curiously secluded from the
world by the tortuousness of the road which approaches it.

Of course it is not my business to report upon the agricultural system practised there, or to discourse on the state of the land or the crops; the best testimony on this subject is the fact, that the Institution hired, at a small rental, a tract of land, which was reclaimed and farmed, and that of this farm the landlord has now taken possession, leaving the young farmers to labour on a new tract of land for which they pay five times as much rent as for their former holding. But though a person versed in agriculture could give a far more satisfactory account of the place than one to whom such pursuits are quite unfamiliar, there is a great deal about the establishment which any citizen can remark on; and he must be a very difficult Cockney indeed who won't be pleased here.

After winding in and out, and up and down, and round about the eminence on which the house stands, we at last found an entrance to it, by a court-yard, neat, well-built, and spacious, where are the stables and numerous offices of the farm. The scholars were at dinner off a comfortable meal of boiled beef, potatoes, and cabbages, when I arrived; a master was reading a book of history to them; and silence, it appears, is preserved during the dinner. Seventy scholars were here assembled, some young, and some expanded into six feet and whiskers – all, however, are made to maintain exactly the same discipline, whether whiskered or not.

The 'head farmer' of the school, Mr Campbell, a very intelligent Scotch gentleman, was good enough to conduct me over the place and the farm, and to give a history of the establishment and the course pursued there. The Seminary was founded in 1827, by the North-west of Ireland Society, by members of which and others about three thousand pounds were subscribed, and the buildings of the school erected. These are spacious, simple, and comfortable; there is a good stone house, with airy dormitories, school-rooms, &c., and large and convenient offices. The establishment had, at first, some difficulties to contend with, and for some time did not number more than thirty pupils. At present, there are seventy scholars, paying *ten pounds* a year, with which sum, and the labour of the pupils on the farm, and the produce of it, the school is entirely supported. The reader will, perhaps, like to see an extract from the Report of the school, which contains more details regarding it.

TEMPLEMOYLE WORK AND SCHOOL TABLE
From 20th March to 23rd September.
Boys divided into two classes, A and B.

Hours.		At work.	At school.
5½	All rise.		
6–8	. . . .	A	B
8–9	Breakfast.		
9–1	. . . .	A	B
1–2	Dinner and recreation.		
2–6	. . . .	B	A
6–7	Recreation.		
7–9	Prepare lessons for next day.		
9	To bed.		

On Tuesday B commences work in the morning and A at school, and so on alternate days.

Each class is again subdivided into three divisions, over each of which is placed a monitor, selected from the steadiest and best informed boys; he receives the Head Farmer's directions as to the work to be done, and super-intends his party while performing it.

In winter the time of labour is shortened according to the length of the day, and the hours at school increased.

In wet days, when the boys cannot work out, all are required to attend school.

DIETARY

BREAKFAST. – Eleven ounces of oatmeal made in stirabout, one pint of sweet milk.

DINNER. – Sunday – Three quarters of a pound of beef stewed with pepper and onions, or one half-pound of corned beef with cabbage, and three and a-half pounds of potatoes.

Monday – One half-pound of pickled beef, three and a half pounds of potatoes, one pint of buttermilk.

Tuesday – Broth made of one half-pound of beef, with leeks, cabbage, and parsley, and three and a half pounds of potatoes.

Wednesday – Two ounces of butter, eight ounces of oatmeal made into bread, three and a half pounds of potatoes, and one pint of sweet milk.

Thursday – Half a pound of pickled pork, with cabbage or turnips, and three and a half pounds of potatoes.

Friday – Two ounces of butter, eight ounces wheat meal made into bread, one pint of sweet milk or fresh buttermilk, three and a half pounds of potatoes.

Saturday – Two ounces of butter, one pound of potatoes mashed, eight ounces of wheat meal made into bread, two and a half pounds of potatoes, one pint of buttermilk.

SUPPER. – In summer, flummery made of one pound of oatmeal seeds, and one pint of sweet milk. In winter, three and a half pounds of potatoes, and one pint of buttermilk or sweet milk.

RULES FOR THE TEMPLEMOYLE SCHOOL

1. The pupils are required to say their prayers in the morning, before leaving the dormitory, and at night, before retiring to rest, each separately, and after the manner to which he has been habituated.

2. The pupils are requested to wash their hands and faces before the commencement of business in the morning, on returning from agricultural labour, and after dinner.

3. The pupils are required to pay the strictest attention to their instructors, both during the hours of agricultural and literary occupation.

4. Strife, disobedience, inattention, or any description of riotous or disorderly conduct, is punishable by extra labour or confinement, as directed by the Committee, according to circumstances.

5. Diligent and respectful behaviour, continued for a considerable time, will be rewarded by occasional permission for the pupil so distinguished to visit his home.

6. No pupil, on obtaining leave of absence, shall presume to continue it for a longer period than that prescribed to him on leaving the Seminary.

7. During their rural labour, the pupils are to consider themselves amenable to the authority of their Agricultural Instructor alone, and during their attendance in the school-room, to that of their Literary Instructor alone.

8. Non-attendance during any part of the time allotted either for literary or agricultural employment, will be punished as a serious offence.

9. During the hours of recreation the pupils are to be under the superintendence of their Instructors, and not suffered to pass beyond the limits of the farm, except under their guidance, or with a written permission from one of them.

10. The pupils are required to make up their beds, and keep those clothes not in immediate use neatly folded up in their trunks, and to be particular in never suffering any garment, book, implement, or other article belonging to or used by them, to lie about in a slovenly or disorderly manner.

11. Respect to superiors, and gentleness of demeanour, both among the pupils themselves and towards the servants and labourers of the establishment, are particularly insisted upon, and will be considered a prominent ground of approbation and reward.

12. On Sundays the pupils are required to attend their respective places of worship, accompanied by their Instructors or Monitors; and it is earnestly recommended to them to employ a part of the remainder of the day in sincerely reading the Word of God, and in such other devotional exercises as their respective ministers may point out.

At certain points of the year, when all hands are required, such as harvest, &c., the literary labours of the scholars are stopped, and they are all in the field. On the present occasion we followed them into a potato field, where an army of them were employed digging out the potatoes; while another regiment were trenching-in elsewhere for the winter: the boys were leading the carts to and fro. To reach the potatoes we had to pass a field, part of which was newly ploughed: the ploughing was the work of the boys, too; one of them being left with an experienced ploughman for a fortnight at a time, in which space the lad can acquire some practice in the art. Amongst the potatoes and the boys digging them, I observed a number of girls, taking them up as dug and removing the soil from the roots. Such a society for seventy young men would, in any other country in the world, be not a little dangerous; but Mr Campbell said that no instance of harm had ever occurred in consequence, and I believe his statement may be fully relied on: the whole country bears testimony to this noble purity of morals. Is there any other in Europe which in this point can compare with it?

In winter the farm works do not occupy the pupils so much, and they give more time to their literary studies. They get a good English education; they are grounded in arithmetic and mathematics; and I saw a good map of an adjacent farm, made from actual survey by one of the pupils. Some of them are good draughtsmen likewise, but of their performances I could see no specimen, the artists being abroad, occupied wisely in digging the potatoes.

And here, apropos, not of the school but of potatoes, let me tell a potato story, which is, I think, to the purpose, wherever it is told. In the county of Mayo a gentleman by the name of Crofton is a landed proprietor, in whose neighbourhood great distress prevailed among the peasantry during the spring and summer, when the potatoes of the last year were consumed, and before those of the present season were up. Mr Crofton, by liberal donations on his own part, and by a subscription which was set on foot among his friends in England as well as in Ireland, was enabled to collect a sum of money sufficient to purchase meal for the people, which was given to them, or sold at very low prices, until the pressure of want was withdrawn, and the blessed potato crop came in. Some time in October, a smart night's frost made Mr Crofton think that it was time to take in and pit his own potatoes, and he told his stewards to get labourers accordingly.

Next day, on going to the potato-grounds, he found the whole fields swarming with people; the whole crop was out of the ground, and again under it, pitted and covered, and the people gone, in a few hours. It was as if the fairies that we read of in the Irish legends, as coming to the aid of good people and helping them in their labours, had taken a liking to this good landlord, and taken in his harvest for him. Mr Crofton, who knew who his helpers had been, sent the steward to pay them their day's wages, and to thank them at the same time for having come to help him at a time when their labour was so useful to him. One and all refused a penny; and their spokesman said, 'They wished they could do more for the likes of him or his family.' I have heard of many conspiracies in this country; is not this one as worthy to be told as any of them?

Round the house of Templemoyle is a pretty garden, which the pupils take pleasure in cultivating, filled not with fruit (for this, though there are seventy gardeners, the superintendent said somehow seldom reached a ripe state) but with kitchen herbs, and a few beds of pretty flowers, such as are best suited to cottage horticulture. Such simple carpenters' and masons' work as the young men can do is likewise confided to them; and though the dietary may appear to the Englishman as rather a scanty one, and though the English lads certainly make at first very wry faces at the stirabout porridge (as they naturally will when first put in the presence of that abominable mixture), yet after a time, strange to say, they begin to find it actually palatable; and the best proof of the excellence of the diet is, that nobody is ever ill in the institution; colds and fevers and the ailments of lazy, gluttonous gentility, are unknown; and the doctor's bill for the last year, for seventy pupils, amounted to thirty-five shillings. *O beati agricoliculae!* You do not know what it is to feel a little uneasy after half-a-crown's worth of raspberry-tarts, as lads do at the best public schools; you don't know in what majestic polished hexameters the Roman poet has described your pursuits; you are not fagged and flogged into Latin and Greek at the cost of two hundred pounds a-year. Let these be the privileges of your youthful betters; meanwhile content yourselves with thinking that you *are* preparing for a profession, while they are *not*; that you are learning something useful, while they, for the most part, are not; for after all, as a man grows old in the world, old and fat, cricket is discovered not to be any longer very advantageous to him – even to have pulled in the Trinity boat does not in old age amount to a substantial advantage; and though to read a Greek play be an immense pleasure, yet it must be confessed few enjoy it. In the first place, of the race of Etonians, and Harrovians, and Carthusians that one meets in the world, very few *can* read the Greek; of those few – there are not, as I believe, any considerable majority of poets. Stout men in the bow-windows of clubs (for such young Etonians by time become) are not generally remarkable for a taste for Æschylus.* You do not hear much poetry in Westminster Hall, or I believe at the bar-tables afterwards; and if occasionally, in the House of Commons, Sir Robert Peel lets off a quotation – a pocket-pistol wadded with a leaf torn out of Horace – depend on it it is only to astonish the country gentlemen who don't understand him: and it is my firm conviction that Sir Robert no more cares for poetry than you or I do.

Such thoughts will suggest themselves to a man who has had the benefit of what is called an education at a public school in England, when he sees seventy lads from all parts of the empire learning what his Latin poets and philosophers have informed him is the best of all pursuits, – finds them educated at one-twentieth part of the cost which has been bestowed on his own precious person; orderly without the necessity of submitting to degrading personal punishment; young, and full of health and blood, though vice is unknown among them; and brought up decently and honestly to know the things which it is good for them in their profession to know. So it is, however: all the world is improving except the gentlemen. There are at this present writing five hundred boys at Eton, kicked, and licked, and bullied, by another hundred – scrubbing shoes, running errands, making false concords, and (as if that were a natural consequence!) putting their posteriors on a block for Dr Hawtrey to lash at; and still calling it education. They are proud of it – good heavens! – absolutely vain of it; as what dull barbarians are not proud of their dulness and barbarism? They call it the good old English system: nothing like classics, says Sir John, to give a boy a taste, you know, and a habit of reading – (Sir John, who reads the Racing Calendar, and belongs to a race of men of all the world the least given to reading,) – it's the good old English system; every boy fights for himself – hardens 'em, eh, Jack? Jack grins, and helps himself to another glass of claret, and presently tells you how Tibbs and Miller fought for an hour

---

* And then, how much Latin and Greek does the public school-boy know? Also, does he know anything else, and what? Is it history, or geography, or mathematics, or divinity?

and twenty minutes 'like good uns.' . . . Let us come to an end, however, of this moralising; the car-driver has brought the old raw-shouldered horse out of the stable, and says it is time to be off again.

Before quitting Templemoyle, one thing more may be said in its favour. It is one of the very few public establishments in Ireland where pupils of the two religious denominations are received, and where no religious disputes have taken place. The pupils are called upon, morning and evening, to say their prayers privately. On Sunday, each division, Presbyterian, Roman Catholic, and Episcopalian, is marched to its proper place of worship. The pastors of each sect may visit their young flock when so inclined; and the lads devote the Sabbath evening to reading the books pointed out to them by their clergymen.

Would not the Agricultural Society of Ireland, the success of whose peaceful labours for the national prosperity every Irish newspaper I read brings some new indication, do well to show some mark of its sympathy for this excellent institution of Templemoyle? A silver medal given by the Society to the most deserving pupil of the year, would be a great object of emulation amongst the young men educated at the place, and would be almost a certain passport for the winner in seeking for a situation in after life. I do not know if similar seminaries exist in England. Other seminaries of a like nature have been tried in this country, and have failed: but English country gentlemen cannot, I should think, find a better object of their attention than this school; and our farmers would surely find such establishments of great benefit to them: where their children might procure a sound literary education at a small charge, and at the same time be made acquainted with the latest improvements in their profession. I can't help saying here, once more, what I have said *apropos* of the excellent school at Dundalk, and begging the English middle classes to think of the subject. If government will not act (upon what never can be effectual, perhaps, until it become a national measure), let small communities act for themselves, and tradesmen and the middle classes set up CHEAP PROPRIETARY SCHOOLS. Will country newspaper editors, into whose hands this book may fall, be kind enough to speak upon this hint, and extract the tables of the Templemoyle and Dundalk establishments, to show how, and with what small means, boys may be well, soundly, and humanely educated – not brutally, as some of us have been, under the bitter fagging and the shameful rod. It is no plea for the barbarity that use has made us accustomed to it; and in seeing these institutions for humble lads, where the system taught is at once useful, manly, and kindly, and thought of what I had undergone in my own youth, – of the frivolous monkish trifling in which it was wasted, of the brutal tyranny to which it was subjected, – I could not look at the lads but with a sort of envy: please God, their lot will be shared by thousands of their equals and their betters before long!

It was a proud day for Dundalk, Mr Thackeray well said, when, at the end of one of the vacations there, fourteen English boys, and an Englishman with his little son in his hand, landed from the Liverpool packet, and, walking through the streets of the town, went into the school-house quite happy. That *was* a proud day in truth for a distant Irish town, and I can't help saying that I grudge them the cause of their pride somewhat. Why should there not be schools in England as good, and as cheap, and as happy?

With this, shaking Mr Campbell gratefully by the hand, and begging all English tourists to go and visit his establishment, we trotted off for Londonderry, leaving at about a mile's distance from the town, and at the pretty lodge of Saint Columb's a letter, which was the cause of much delightful hospitality.

Saint Columb's Chapel, the walls of which still stands picturesquely in Sir George Hill's park, and from which that gentleman's seat takes its name, was here since the sixth century. It is but fair to give precedence to the mention of the old abbey, which was the father, as it would seem, of the town. The approach to the latter from three quarters, certainly, by which various avenues I had occasion to see it, is always noble. We had seen the spire of the cathedral peering over the hills for four miles on our way; it stands, a stalwart and handsome building upon an eminence, round which the old-fashioned stout red houses of the town cluster, girt in with the ramparts and walls that kept out James's soldiers of old.

Quays, factories, huge red warehouses, have grown round this famous old barrier, and now stretch along the river. A couple of large steamers and other craft, lay within the bridge; and, as we passed over that stout wooden edifice, stretching eleven hundred feet across the noble expanse of the Foyle, we heard along the quays a great thundering and clattering of iron-work in an enormous steam frigate which has been built in Derry, and seems to lie alongside a whole street of houses. The suburb, too, through which we passed was bustling and comfortable; and the view was not only pleasing from its natural beauties, but has a manly, thriving, honest air of prosperity, which is no bad feature, surely, for a landscape.

Nor does the town itself, as one enters it, belie, as many other Irish towns do, its first flourishing look. It is not splendid, but comfortable; a brisk movement in the streets: good downright shops, without particularly grand titles; few beggars. Nor have the common people, as they address you, that eager smile, – that manner of compound fawning and swaggering, which an Englishman finds in the town's-people of the West and South. As in the North of England, too, when compared with other districts, the people are greatly more familiar, though by no means disrespectful to the stranger.

On the other hand, after such a commerce as a traveller has with the race of waiters, postboys, porters, and the like (and it may be that the vast race of postboys, &c., whom I did not see in the North, are quite unlike those unlucky specimens with whom I come in contact), I was struck by their excessive greediness after the traveller's gratuities, and their fierce dissatisfaction if not sufficiently rewarded. To the gentleman who brushed my clothes at the comfortable hotel at Belfast, and carried my bags to the coach, I tendered the sum of two shillings, which seemed to me quite a sufficient reward for his services; he battled and bawled with me for more, and got it too; for a street-dispute with a porter calls together a number of delighted bystanders, whose remarks and company are by no means agreeable to a solitary gentleman. Then, again, was the famous case of Boots of Ballycastle, which, being upon the subject, I may as well mention here: Boots of Ballycastle, that romantic little village near the Giant's Causeway, had cleaned a pair of shoes for me certainly, but declined either to brush

my clothes, or to carry down my two carpet bags to the car,
leaving me to perform those offices for myself, which I did,
and indeed they were not very difficult. But immediately I was
seated on the car, Mr Boots stepped forward and wrapped a
mackintosh very considerately round me, and begged me at the
same time to 'remember him.'

There was an old beggar-woman standing by, to whom I
had a desire to present a penny; and having no coin of that
value, I begged Mr Boots, out of a sixpence which I tendered to
him, to subtract a penny, and present it to the old lady in
question. Mr Boots took the money, looked at me, and his
countenance, not naturally good-humoured, assumed an
expression of the most indignant contempt and hatred as he
said, 'I'm thinking I've no call to give my money away.
Sixpence is my right for what I've done.'

'Sir,' says I, 'you must remember that you did but black one
pair of shoes, and that you blacked them very badly too.'

'Sixpence is my right,' says Boots, 'a *gentleman* would give
me sixpence!' and though I represented to him that a pair of
shoes might be blacked in a minute – that fivepence a minute
was not usual wages in the country – that many gentlemen,
half-pay officers, briefless barristers, unfortunate literary
gentlemen, would gladly black twelve pairs of shoes per diem
if rewarded with five shillings for so doing, there was no means
of convincing Mr Boots. I then demanded back the sixpence,
which proposal, however, he declined, saying, after a struggle,
he would give the money, but a gentleman would have given
sixpence; and so left me with furious rage and contempt.

As for the city of Derry, a carman who drove me one mile
out to dinner at a gentleman's house, where he himself was
provided with a comfortable meal, was dissatisfied with
eighteen-pence, vowing that a 'dinner job' was always paid
half-a-crown, and not only asserted this, but continued to
assert it for a quarter of an hour with the most noble though
unsuccessful perseverance. A second car-boy, to whom I gave
a shilling for a drive of two miles altogether, attacked me
because I gave the other boy eighteen-pence; and the porter
who brought my bags fifty yards from the coach, entertained
me with a dialogue that lasted at least a couple of minutes, and
said, 'I should have had sixpence for carrying one of 'em.'

For the car which carried me two miles the landlord of the inn made me pay the sum of five shillings. He is a godly landlord, has Bibles in the coffee-room, the drawing-room, and every bed-room in the house, with this inscription–

UT MIGRATURUS HABITA.
THE TRAVELLER'S TRUE REFUGE.
Jones's Hotel, Londonderry.

This pious double or triple entendre, the reader will, no doubt, admire – the first simile establishing the resemblance between this life and an inn; the second allegory showing that the inn and the Bible are both the traveller's refuge.

In life we are in death – the hotel in question is about as gay as a family vault: a severe figure of a landlord, in seedy black, is occasionally seen in the dark passages or on the creaking old stairs of the black inn. He does not bow to you – very few landlords in Ireland condescend to acknowledge their guests – he only warns you, – a silent solemn gentleman who looks to be something between a clergyman and a sexton – 'ut migraturus habita!' – the 'migraturus' was a vast comfort in the clause.

It must, however, be said, for the consolation of future travellers, that when at evening, in the old lonely parlour of the inn, the great gaunt fireplace is filled with coals, two dreary funereal candles and sticks glimmering upon the old-fashioned round table, the rain pattering fiercely without, the wind roaring and thumping in the streets, this worthy gentleman can produce a pint of port wine for the use of his migratory guest, which causes the latter to be almost reconciled to the cemetery in which he is resting himself, and he finds himself, to his surprise, almost cheerful. There is a mouldy-looking old kitchen, too, which, strange to say, sends out an excellent comfortable dinner, so that the sensation of fear gradually wears off.

As in Chester, the ramparts of the town form a pleasant promenade; and the batteries, with a few of the cannon, are preserved, with which the stout 'prentice boys of Derry beat off King James in '88. The guns bear the names of the London Companies – venerable Cockney titles! It is pleasant for a

Londoner to read them, and see how, at a pinch, the sturdy citizens can do their work.

The public buildings of Derry are, I think, among the best I have seen in Ireland; and the Lunatic Asylum, especially, is to be pointed out as a model of neatness and comfort. When will the middle classes be allowed to send their own afflicted relatives to public institutions of this excellent kind, where violence is never practised – where it is never to the interest of the keeper of the asylum to exaggerate his patient's malady, or to retain him in durance, for the sake of the enormous sums which the sufferer's relatives are made to pay? The gentry of three counties which contribute to the Asylum have no such resource for members of their own body, should any be so afflicted – the condition of entering this admirable asylum is, that the patient must be a pauper, and on this account he is supplied with every comfort and the best curative means, and his relations are in perfect security. Are the rich in any way so lucky? – and if not, why not?

The rest of the occurrences at Derry belong, unhappily, to the domain of private life, and though very pleasant to recall, are not honestly to be printed. Otherwise, what popular descriptions might be written of the hospitalities of St Columb's, of the jovialities of the mess of the –th Regiment, of the speeches made and the songs sung, and the devilled turkey at twelve o'clock, and the head-ache afterwards; all which events could be described in an exceedingly facetious manner. But these amusements are to be met with in every other part of her Majesty's dominions; and the only point which may be mentioned here as peculiar to this part of Ireland, is the difference of the manner of the gentry to that in the South. The Northern manner is far more *English* than that of the other provinces of Ireland – whether it is *better* for being English is a question of taste, of which an Englishman can scarcely be a fair judge.

CHAPTER XXXII

DUBLIN AT LAST

A wedding party that went across Derry Bridge to the sound of bell and cannon, had to flounder through a thick coat of frozen snow, that covered the slippery planks, and the hills round about were whitened over by the same inclement material. Nor was the weather, implacable towards young lovers and unhappy buckskin postilions, shivering in white favours, at all more polite towards the passengers of her Majesty's mail that runs from Derry to Ballyshannon.

Hence the aspect of the country between those two places can only be described at the rate of nine miles an hour, and from such points of observation as may be had through a coach window, starred with ice and mud. While horses were changed we saw a very dirty town, called Strabane; and had to visit the old house of the O'Donnels in Donegal during a quarter-of-an-hour's pause that the coach made there – and with an umbrella over-head. The pursuit of the picturesque under umbrellas let us leave to more venturesome souls: the fine weather of the finest season known for many long years in Ireland was over, and I thought with a great deal of yearning of Pat the waiter, at the Shelbourne Hotel, Stephen's Green, Dublin, and the gas lamps, and the covered cars, and the good dinners to which they take you.

Farewell, then, O wild Donegal! and ye stern passes through which the astonished traveller windeth! Farewell Ballyshannon, and thy salmon-leap, and thy bar of sand, over which the white head of the troubled Atlantic was peeping! Likewise, adieu to Lough Erne, and its numberless green islands, and winding river-lake, and wavy fir-clad hills! Good-by, moreover, neat Enniskillen, over the bridge and churches whereof the sun peepeth as the coach starteth from the inn! See, how he shines now on Lord Belmore's stately palace and park, with gleaming porticoes and brilliant grassy chases: now, behold he is yet higher in the heavens, as the twanging horn proclaims the approach to beggarly Cavan, where a beggarly breakfast awaits the hungry voyager.

Snatching up a roll wherewith to satisfy the pangs of hunger, sharpened by the mockery of breakfast, the tourist now hastens in his arduous course, through Virginia, Kells, Navan, by Tara's threadbare mountain, and Skreen's green hill; day darkens, and a hundred thousand lamps twinkle in the gray horizon – see above the darkling trees a stumpy column rise, see on its base the name of Wellington (though this, because 'tis night thou canst not see), and cry, 'It is the *Phaynix!*' – On and on, across the iron bridge, and through the streets, (dear streets, though dirty, to the citizen's heart how dear you be!) and lo, now, with a bump, the dirty coach stops at the seedy inn, six ragged porters battle for the bags, six wheedling carmen recommend their cars, and (giving first the coachman eighteenpence) the Cockney says, 'Drive, car-boy, to the Shelbourne.'

And so having reached Dublin – and seeing the ominous 400 which figures upon the last page, it becomes necessary to curtail the observations which were to be made upon that city: which surely ought to have a volume to itself – the humours of Dublin at least require so much space. For instance, there was the dinner at the Kildare-street Club, or the Hotel opposite, – the dinner in Trinity College Hall, – that at Mr——, the publisher's, where a dozen of the literary men of Ireland were assembled, – and those (say fifty) with Harry Lorrequer himself, at his mansion of Templeogue. What a favourable opportunity to discourse upon the peculiarities of Irish character! to describe men of letters, of fashion, and university dons!

Sketches of these personages may be prepared, and sent over, perhaps, in confidence to Mrs Sigourney in America – (who will of course not print them) – but the English habit does not allow of these happy communications between writers and the public; and the author who wishes to dine again at his friend's cost, must needs have a care how he puts him in print.

Suffice it to say, that at Kildare-street we had white neck-cloths, black waiters, wax candles, and some of the best wine in Europe; at Mr——, the publisher's, wax-candles, and some of the best wine in Europe; at Mr Lever's, wax-candles, and some of the best wine in Europe; at Trinity College – but there is no need to mention what took place at Trinity College; for on returning to London, and recounting the circumstances of the repast, my friend B——, a Master of Arts of that university, solemnly declared the thing was impossible: – no stranger *could* dine at Trinity college; it was too great a privilege – in a word, he would not believe the story, nor will he to this day; and why, therefore, tell it in vain?

I am sure if the Fellows of Colleges in Oxford and Cambridge were told that the Fellows of T.C.D. only drink beer at dinner, they would not believe *that*. Such, however, was the fact, or may be it was a dream, which was followed by another dream of about four-and-twenty gentlemen seated round a common room table after dinner; and, by a subsequent vision, of a tray of oysters in the apartments of a tutor of the university, sometime before midnight. Did we swallow them or not? – the oysters are an open question.

Of the Catholic College of Maynooth, I must likewise speak briefly, for the reason that an accurate description of that establishment would be of necessity so disagreeable, that it is best to pass it over in a few words. An Irish union-house is a palace to it. Ruin so needless, filth so disgusting, such a look of lazy squalor, no Englishman who has not seen can conceive. Lecture-room and dining-hall, kitchen and students'-room, were all the same. I shall never forget the sight of scores of shoulders of mutton lying on the filthy floor in the former, or the view of a bed and dressing-table that I saw in the other. Let the next Maynooth grant include a few shillings'-worth of whitewash and a few hundredweights of soap; and if to this be added a half-score of drill-sergeants, to see that the students appear clean at lecture, and to teach them to keep their heads up and to look people in the face, Parliament will introduce some cheap reforms into the seminary, which were never needed more than here. Why should the place be so shamefully ruinous and foully dirty? Lime is cheap, and water plenty at the canal hard by. Why should a stranger, after a week's stay in the country, be able to discover a priest by the scowl on his face, and his doubtful, downcast manner? Is it a point of discipline that his reverence should be made to look as ill-humoured as possible? And I hope these words will not be taken hostilely. It would have been quite as easy, and more pleasant, to say the contrary, had the contrary seemed to me to have been the fact; and to have declared that the priests were remarkable for their expression of candour, and their college for its extreme neatness and cleanliness.

This complaint of neglect applies to other public institutions besides Maynooth. The Mansion-house, when I saw it, was a very dingy abode for the Right Honourable Lord Mayor, and that Lord Mayor Mr O'Connell. I saw him in full council, in a brilliant robe of crimson velvet, ornamented with white satin bows, and sable collar, in an enormous cocked-hat, like a slice of an eclipsed moon – in the following costume, in fact–

The Aldermen and Common Council, in a black oak parlour, and at a dingy green table, were assembled around him, and a debate of thrilling interest to the town ensued. It related, I think, to water-pipes; the great man did not speak publicly, but was occupied chiefly at the end of the table, giving audiences to at least a score of clients and petitioners.

The next day I saw him in the famous Corn Exchange. The building without has a substantial look, but the hall within is rude, dirty, and ill-kept. Hundreds of persons were assembled in the black, steaming place; no inconsiderable share of frieze-coats were among them; and many small repealers, who could but lately have assumed their breeches, ragged as they were. These kept up a great chorus of shouting, and 'hear, hear!' at every pause in the great repealer's address. Mr O'Connell was reading a report from his repeal-wardens; which proved that when repeal took place, commerce and prosperity would instantly flow into the country; its innumerable harbours would be filled with countless ships, its immense water-power would be directed to the turning of myriads of mills; its vast energies and resources brought into full action. At the end of the report, three cheers were given for repeal, and in the midst of a great shouting Mr O'Connell leaves the room.

'Mr Quiglan, Mr Quiglan!' roars an active aide-de-camp to the door-keeper, 'a covered kyar for the Lard Mayre.' The covered car came; I saw his lordship get into it. Next day he was Lord Mayor no longer; but Alderman O'Connell in his state-coach, with the handsome grays whose manes were tied up with green ribbon, following the new Lord Mayor to the right honourable inauguration. Javelin men, city marshals (looking like military undertakers), private carriages, glass coaches, cars, covered and uncovered, and thousands of yelling ragamuffins, formed the civic procession of that faded, worn out, insolvent, old Dublin Corporation.

The walls of this city had been placarded with huge notices to the public, that O'Connell's rent-day was at hand; and I went round to all the chapels in the town on that Sunday (not a little to the scandal of some Protestant friends), to see the popular behaviour. Every door was barred, of course, with plate-holders; and heaps of pence at the humble entrances, and bank-notes at the front gates, told the willingness of the people to reward their champion. The car-boy who drove me had paid his little tribute of fourpence at morning mass; the waiter who brings my breakfast had added to the national subscription with his humble shilling; and the Catholic gentleman with whom I dined, and between whom and Mr O'Connell there is no great love lost, pays his annual donation, out of gratitude for old services, and to the man who won Catholic Emancipation for Ireland. The piety of the people at the chapels is a sight, too, always well worthy to behold. Nor indeed is this religious fervour less in the Protestant places of worship: the warmth and attention of the congregation, the enthusiasm with which hymns are sung and responses uttered, contrasts curiously with the cool formality of worshippers at home.

The service at St Patrick's is finely sung; and the shameless English custom of retreating after the anthem, is properly prevented by locking the gates, and having the music after the sermon. The interior of the cathedral itself, however, to an Englishman who has seen the neat and beautiful edifices of his own country, will be anything but an object of admiration. The greater part of the huge old building is suffered to remain in gaunt decay, and with its stalls of sham Gothic, and the tawdry old rags and gimcracks of the 'most illustrious order of Saint Patrick,' (whose pasteboard helmets, and calico banners, and lath swords, well characterise the humbug of chivalry which they are made to represent,) looks like a theatre behind the scenes. 'Paddy's Opera,' however, is a noble performance; and the Englishman may here listen to a half-hour sermon, and in the anthem to a bass singer whose voice is one of the finest ever heard.

The Drama does not flourish much more in Dublin than in any other part of the country. Operatic stars make their appearance occasionally, and managers lose money. I was at a fine concert, at which Lablache and others performed, where there were not a hundred people in the pit of the pretty theatre, and where the only encore given was to a young woman in ringlets and yellow satin, who stepped forward and sung 'Coming through the rye,' or some other scientific composition, in an exceedingly small voice. On the nights when the regular drama was enacted, the audience was still smaller. The theatre of Fishamble-street was given up to the performances of the Rev Mr Gregg and his Protestant company, whose soirées I did not attend; and, at the Abbey-street Theatre, whither I went in order to see, if possible, some specimens of the national humour, I found a company of English people ranting through a melodrama, the tragedy whereof was the only laughable thing to be witnessed.

Humbler popular recreations may be seen by the curious. One night I paid twopence to see a puppet-show – such an entertainment as may have been popular a hundred and thirty years ago, and is described in the Spectator. But the company here assembled were not, it scarcely need be said, of the genteel sort. There were a score of boys, however, and a dozen of labouring men, who were quite happy and contented with the piece performed, and loudly applauded. Then in passing homewards of a night, you hear, at the humble public-houses, the sound of many a fiddle, and the stamp of feet dancing the good old jig, which is still maintaining a struggle with Teetotalism, and, though vanquished now, may rally some day and overcome the enemy. At Kingstown, especially, the old 'fire-worshippers' yet seem to muster pretty strongly; loud is the music to be heard in the taverns there, and the cries of encouragement to the dancers.

Of the numberless amusements that take place in the *Phaynix*, it is not very necessary to speak. Here you may behold garrison races, and reviews; lord-lieutenants in brown great coats; aides-de-camp scampering about like mad in blue; fat colonels roaring 'charge' to immense heavy dragoons; dark riflemen lining woods and firing; galloping cannoneers banging and blazing right and left. Here comes his Excellency the Commander-in-chief, with his huge feathers, and white hair, and hooked nose; and yonder sits his Excellency the Ambassador from the republic of Topinambo in a glass coach, smoking a cigar. The honest Dublinites make a great deal of such small dignitaries as his excellency of the glass coach; you hear everybody talking of him, and asking which is he; and when presently one of Sir Robert Peel's sons makes his appearance on the course, the public rush delighted to look at him.

They love great folks, those honest Emerald islanders, more intensely than any people I ever heard of, except the Americans. They still cherish the memory of the sacred George IV. They chronicle genteel small beer with never-failing assiduity. They go in long trains to a sham court – simpering in tights and bags, with swords between their legs. Oh, heaven and earth what joy! Why are the Irish noblemen absentees? If their lordships like respect, where would they get it so well as in their own country?

The Irish noblemen are very likely going through the same delightful routine of duty before their real sovereign – in *real* tights and bag-wigs, as it were, performing their graceful and lofty duties, and celebrating the august service of the throne. These, of course, the truly loyal heart can only respect: and I think a drawing-room at St James's the grandest spectacle that ever feasted the eye or exercised the intellect. The crown, surrounded by its knights and nobles, its priests, its sages, and their respective ladies; illustrious foreigners, men learned in the law, heroes of land and sea, beef-eaters, gold sticks, gentlemen at arms, rallying round the throne and defending it with those swords which ever knew defeat (and would surely, if tried, secure victory): these are sights and characters which every man must look upon with a thrill of respectful awe, and count amongst the glories of his country. What lady that sees this will not confess that she reads every one of the drawing-room costumes, from Majesty down to Miss Ann Maria Smith; and all the names of the presentations from Prince Baccabocksky (by the Russian ambassador) to Ensign Stubbs on his appointment?

We are bound to read these accounts. It is our pride, our duty as Britons. But though one may honour the respect of the aristocracy of the land for the sovereign, yet there is no reason why those who are not of the aristocracy should be aping their betters: and the Dublin Castle business has, I cannot but think, a very high-life below stairs look. There is no aristocracy in Dublin. Its magnates are tradesmen – Sir Fiat Haustus, Sir Blacker Dosy, Mr Serjeant Bluebag, or Mr Counsellor O'Fee. Brass plates are their titles of honour, and they live by their boluses or their briefs. What call have these worthy people to be dangling and grinning at lord-lieutenants' levees, and playing sham aristocracy before a sham sovereign? Oh, that old humbug of a castle! It is the greatest sham of all the shams in Ireland.

Although the season may be said to have begun, for the Courts are opened, and the noblesse de la robe have assembled, I do not think the genteel quarters of the town look much more cheerful. They still, for the most part, wear their faded appearance, and lean half-pay look. There is the beggar still dawdling here and there. Sound of carriages or footmen do not deaden the clink of the burly policeman's boot heels. You may see possibly, a smutty-faced nursemaid leading out her little charges to walk; or the observer may catch a glimpse of Mick the footman lolling at the door, and grinning as he talks to some dubious tradesman. MICK and JOHN are very different characters externally and inwardly; – profound essays (involving the histories of the two countries for a thousand years) might be written regarding Mick and John, and the moral and political influences which have developed the flunkeys of the two nations. The friend, too, with whom Mick talks at the door is a puzzle to a Londoner. I have hardly ever entered a Dublin house without meeting with some such character on my way in or out. He looks too shabby for a dun, and not exactly ragged enough for a beggar – a doubtful, lazy, dirty family vassal – a guerilla footman. I think it is he who makes a great noise, and whispering, and clattering, handing in the dishes to Mick from outside of the dining-room door. When an Irishman comes to London, he brings Erin with him; and ten to one you will find one of these queer retainers about his place.

London one can only take leave of by degrees: the great town melts away into suburbs, which soften, as it were, the parting between the Cockney and his darling birth-place. But you pass from some of the stately fine Dublin streets straight into the country. After No. 46, Eccles Street, for instance, potatoes begin at once. You are on a wide green plain, diversified by occasional cabbage plots, by drying grounds white with chemises, in the midst of which the chartered wind is revelling; and though in the map some fanciful engineer has laid down streets and squares, they exist but on paper; nor, indeed, can there be any need of them at present, in a quarter where houses are not wanted so much as people to dwell in the same.

If the genteel portions of the town look to the full as melancholy as they did, the downright poverty ceases, I fear, to make so strong an impression as it made four months ago. Going over the same ground again, places appear to have quite a different aspect; and, with their strangeness, poverty and misery have lost much of their terror. The people, though dirtier and more ragged seem certainly happier than those in London.

Near to the King's Court, for instance (a noble building, as are almost all the public edifices of the city), is a straggling green suburb, containing numberless little shabby, patched, broken-windowed huts, with rickety gardens dotted with rags that have been washed, and children that have not; and thronged with all sorts of ragged inhabitants. Near to the suburb in the town, is a dingy, old, mysterious district, called Stoney-batter, where some houses have been allowed to reach an old age, extraordinary in this country of premature ruin, and look as if they had been built some sixscore years since. In these and the neighbouring tenements, not so old, but equally ruinous and mouldy, there is a sort of vermin swarm of humanity; dirty faces at all the dirty windows; children on all the broken steps; smutty slip-shod women clacking and bustling about, and old men dawdling. Well, only paint and prop the tumbling gates and huts in the suburb, and fancy the Stoney-batterites clean, and you would have rather a gay and agreeable picture of human life – of work-people and their families reposing after their labours. They are all happy, and sober, and kindhearted, – they seem kind, and playing with the children – the young women having a gay good-natured joke for the passer-by; the old seemingly contented, and buzzing to one another. It is only the costume, as it were, that has frightened the stranger, and made him fancy that people so ragged must be unhappy. Observation grows used to the rags as much as the people do, and my impression of the walk through this district, on a sunshiny, clear, autumn evening, is that of a fête. I am almost ashamed it should be so.

Near to Stoney-batter lies a group of huge gloomy edifices – an hospital, a penitentiary, a madhouse, and a poor-house. I visited the latter of these, the North Dublin Union-house, an enormous establishment, which accommodates two thousand beggars. Like all the public institutions of the country, it seems to be well-conducted, and is a vast orderly and cleanly place, wherein the prisoners are better clothed, better fed, and better housed than they can hope to be when at liberty. We were taken into all the wards in due order – the schools and nursery for the children; the dining-rooms, day-rooms, &c., of the men and women. Each division is so accommodated, as also with a large court or ground to walk and exercise in.

Among the men, there are very few able-bodied, the most of them, the keeper said, having gone out for the harvest time, or as soon as the potatoes came in. If they go out, they cannot return before the expiration of a month: the guardians have been obliged to establish this prohibition, lest the persons requiring relief should go in and out too frequently. The old men were assembled in considerable numbers in a long day-room that is comfortable and warm. Some of them were picking oakum by way of employment; but most of them were past work, all such inmates of the houses as are able-bodied, being occupied upon the premises. Their hall was airy and as clean as brush and water could make it: the men equally clean, and their gray jackets and Scotch caps stout and warm. Thence we were led, with a sort of satisfaction, by the guardian, to the kitchen – a large room, at the end of which might be seen certain coppers, emitting, it must be owned, a very faint inhospitable smell. It was Friday, and rice-milk is the food on that day, each man being served with a pint-canful, of which cans a greater number stood smoking upon stretchers – the platters were laid, each with its portion of salt, in the large clean dining-room hard by. 'Look at that rice,' said the keeper, taking up a bit, 'try, it sir, it's delicious.' I'm sure I hope it is.

The old women's room was crowded with, I should think, at least four hundred old ladies – neat and nice, in white clothes and caps – sitting demurely on benches, doing nothing for the most part; but some employed, like the old men, in fiddling with the oakum. 'There's tobacco here,' says the guardian, in a loud voice, 'who's smoking tobacco?' 'Fait, and I wish dere *was* some tabaccy here,' says one old lady, 'and my service to you, Mr Leary, and I hope one of the gentlemen has a snuff-box, and a pinch for a poor old woman.' But we had no boxes; and if any person who reads this visit, goes to a poor-house or lunatic asylum, let him carry a box, if for that day only – a pinch is like Dives's drop of water to those poor limboed souls. Some of the poor old creatures began to stand up as we came in – I can't say how painful such an honour seemed to me.

There was a separate room for the able-bodied females; and the place and courts were full of stout, red-cheeked, bouncing women. If the old ladies looked respectable, I cannot say the young ones were particularly good-looking; there were some Hogarthian faces amongst them – sly, leering, and hideous. I fancied I could see only too well what these girls had been. Is it charitable or not to hope that such bad faces could only belong to bad women?

'Here, sir, is the nursery,' said the guide, flinging open the door of a long room. There may have been eighty babies in it, with as many nurses and mothers. Close to the door sat one with as beautiful a face as I almost ever saw: she had at her breast a very sickly and puny child, and looked up, as we entered, with a pair of angelical eyes, and a face that Mr Eastlake could paint – a face that *had* been angelical that is, for there was the snow still, as it were, but with the footmark on it. I asked her how old she was – she did not know. She could not have been more than fifteen years, the poor child. She said she had been a servant – and there was no need of asking anything more about her story. I saw her grinning at one of her comrades as we went out of the room; her face did not look angelical then. Ah, young master or old, young or old villain, who did this! – have you not enough wickedness of your own to answer for, that you must take another's sins upon your shoulders; and be this wretched child's sponsor in crime? . . .

But this chapter must be made as short as possible; and so I will not say how much prouder Mr Leary, the keeper, was of his fat pigs than of his paupers – how he pointed us out the burial-ground of the family of the poor – their coffins were quite visible through the niggardly mould; and the children might peep at their fathers over the burial-ground-play-ground-wall – nor, how we went to see the Linen Hall of Dubin – that huge, useless, lonely, decayed place, in the vast windy solitudes of which stands the simpering statue of George IV, pointing to some bales of shirting, over which he is supposed to extend his august protection.

The cheers of the rabble hailing the new Lord Mayor were the last sounds that I heard in Dublin: and I quitted the kind friends I had made there with the sincerest regret. As for forming 'an opinion of Ireland,' such as is occasionally asked from a traveller on his return – that is as difficult an opinion to form as to express; and the puzzle which has perplexed the gravest and wisest, may be confessed by a humble writer of light literature, whose aim it only was to look at the manners and the scenery of the country, and who does not venture to meddle with questions of more serious import.

To have 'an opinion about Ireland,' one must begin by getting the truth; and where is it to be had in the country? Or rather, there are two truths, the Catholic truth and the Protestant truth. The two parties do not see things with the same eyes. I recollect, for instance, a Catholic gentleman telling me that the Primate had forty-three thousand *five hundred* a year; a Protestant clergyman gave me, chapter and verse, the history of a shameful perjury and malversation of money on the part of a Catholic priest; nor was one tale more true than the other. But belief is made a party business; and the receiving of the archbishop's income would probably not convince the Catholic, any more than the clearest evidence to the contrary altered the Protestant's opinion. Ask about an estate, you may be sure almost that people will make mis-state-ments, or volunteer them if not asked. Ask a cottager about his rent, or his landlord; you cannot trust him. I shall never forget the glee with which a gentleman in Munster told me how he had sent off MM. Tocqueville and Beaumont 'with *such* a set of stories.' Inglis was seized, as I am told, and mystified in the same way. In the midst of all these truths, attested with 'I give ye my sacred honour and word,' which is the stranger to select? And how are we to trust philosophers who make theories upon such data?

Meanwhile it is satisfactory to know, upon testimony so general as to be equivalent almost to fact, that, wretched as it is, the country is steadily advancing, nor nearly so wretched now as it was a score of years since, and let us hope that the *middle class*, which this increase of prosperity must generate (and of which our laws have hitherto forbidden the existence in Ireland, making there a population of Protestant aristocracy and Catholic peasantry), will exercise the greatest and most beneficial influence over the country. Too independent to be bullied by priest or squire – having their interest in quiet, and alike indisposed to servility or to rebellion; may not as much be hoped from the gradual formation of such a class, as from any legislative meddling? It is the want of the middle class that has rendered the squire so arrogant, and the clerical or political demagogue so powerful; and I think Mr O'Connell himself would say that the existence of such a body would do more for the steady acquirement of orderly freedom, than the occasional outbreak of any crowd, influenced by any eloquence from altar or tribune.

J. SHERIDAN LE FANU

IN A GLASS DARKLY

With Dr Martin Hesselius, five of whose 'cases' are brought together in this superb collection, Sheridan Le Fanu contributed a major figure to the ranks of those occult doctors, forensic experts, and special investigators who enthralled the Victorian reading public.

Each case presents its own peculiar revelation. In 'Green Tea' a quiet English clergyman is haunted by a spectral monkey. Captain Barton of Dublin is scared literally to death by the appearance *in miniature* of a man whom he knows to have died in Naples; this is his 'Familiar'. The young narrator of 'The Room in the Dragon Volant' is more or less buried alive in a French roadside inn. The hanging judge, Mr Justice Harbottle, in the story of that name, is condemned to hang himself. 'Carmilla' links sexual perversion and vampirism in the woods of lower Austria.

George Moore

THE UNTILLED FIELD

Acclaimed by Frank O'Connor as a 'masterpiece', this collection of George Moore's stories of rural Ireland at the turn of the century has proved to be instrumental in establishing the tradition of the modern Irish short story.

Influenced by the continental innovations in narrative technique he had learnt during his life in Paris, Moore returned to Ireland 'to paint the portrait of my country'. Against a backdrop of Gaelic revivalism and American emigration, he depicts an Ireland where there are miracles for some – the visions of the 'saintly' Biddy McHale of 'The Window' and the fond remembrances of Granny Kirwin in 'The Wedding Gown'; and frustrations and disappointments for others – the fatal infatuation of Edward Dempsey in 'The Clerk's Quest' and the idealistic ambition of Father James in 'A Play-House in the Waste'; while over everywhere, it seems, lies 'Julia Cahill's Curse', and the fields of Ireland are left untilled.

MARIA EDGEWORTH

ORMOND

It is a sharp knock at the window which alerts Lady O'Shane to the pale, bloodstained figure of Harry Ormond standing outside. During a drunken brawl he has shot his provoker, Moriarty Carroll. Though Carroll survives, this is not enough to prevent Ormond's scheming guardian, Sir Ulick O'Shane, from banishing his ward from Castle Hermitage.

Thus Ormond starts out on his adventures, travelling to the isolated Black Islands, home of the benevolent King Corny, back to Castle Hermitage and the passionately anti-Papist Mrs McCrule, then on to Paris, with its vibrant literary scene, and the regal splendours of the Court of Versailles.

Penetrating characterization, a lively plot and vivid description combine in this exciting story of underhand dealings and the search for love in eighteenth-century Ireland.